Passchendaele

Also by Nick Lloyd

Hundred Days: The End of the Great War
The Amritsar Massacre: The Untold Story of One Fateful Day
Loos 1915

PASSCHENDAELE

The Lost Victory
of World War I

Nick Lloyd

BASIC BOOKS
New York

Published by Basic Books,
an imprint of Perseus Books, LLC,
a subsidiary of Hachette Book Group, Inc.

First published in 2017 by Penguin Random House UK.

Typeset by Jouve (UK), Milton Keynes

Library of Congress Control Number: 2017933594
ISBN: 978-0-465-09477-6 (hardcover)
ISBN: 978-0-465-09478-3 (e-book)

10 9 8 7 6 5 4 3 2 1

For Eleanor, Isabel and Louise

The moment I saw the name on the trench-map,
intuitively I knew what was going to happen.

Wyndham Lewis

Contents

List of Illustrations

NPG = National Portrait Gallery; IWM = Imperial War Museum; AWM = Australian War Memorial; CWM = Canadian War Museum; BayHStA = Bayerisches Hauptstaatsarchiv.

1. The British Prime Minister, David Lloyd George (*NPG: x12475*).
2. Field Marshal Sir Douglas Haig, Commander-in-Chief of the BEF (*NPG: x84291*).
3. General Sir William Robertson, Chief of the Imperial General Staff (*NPG: x84583*).
4. Kaiser Wilhelm II studying maps at the German High Command (*IWM: Q23746*).
5. Crown Prince Rupprecht of Bavaria (*IWM: Q45320*).
6. General Sir Hubert Gough, commander of the British Fifth Army (*IWM: Q35825B*).
7. British stretcher-bearers in the ruins of Pilckem, 31 July 1917 (*IWM: Q2630*).
8. Men of a pioneer battalion getting out of light railway trucks, 31 July 1917 (*IWM: Q5713*).
9. Pack mules loaded up with shells move forward to the front somewhere near Ypres, 1 August 1917 (*IWM: Q5940*).
10. British troops moving forward over shell-torn ground near Pilckem, 16 August 1917 (*IWM: Q2708*).
11. Crown Prince Rupprecht distributing medals in Flanders (*IWM: Q52820*).
12. Kaiser Wilhelm II pays a visit to Flanders, August 1917 (*IWM: Q023728*).
13. Wounded German soldiers at the command post of 19 Infantry Regiment, somewhere near Ypres, August 1917 (*BayHStA: Bs-III-k-9-d-49-g*).

List of Maps

Glossary

5.9: 15cm German field howitzer

Army: Collection of corps (usually between two and seven) commanded by a General

Army Group: Collection of armies (usually consisting of two or three)

Battalion: Unit of infantry (nominally up to 1,000 strong) commanded by a Lieutenant-Colonel

Battery: Organization of artillery pieces (usually containing between four and six guns)

'Bite and hold': Operational method that prioritized limited attacks against local points of tactical importance aimed at provoking wasteful counter-attacks

Boche or Bosche: Slang term for Germans

Brigade: Major tactical formation commanded by a Brigadier-General. Three brigades made up a British division (each brigade containing four battalions). French and German brigades operated on a different system, each with two regiments

Corduroy road: Makeshift wooden road covered with sand, often used in swampy conditions

Corps: Group of divisions (usually between two and five) commanded by a Lieutenant-General

Creeping barrage: Moving wall of shellfire that swept across the battlefield at a predetermined pace. Designed to keep defenders' heads down and escort infantry on to their objectives

Digger: Term for Australian troops

Division: Basic tactical unit on the battlefield employing between 10,000 and 15,000 men, with supporting medical, engineering and artillery arms, commanded by a Major-General. By 1917 most divisions were not up to this strength, with many German divisions containing only around 8,000 infantry

Eingreif Division: Literally 'intervention division'. Specially trained reserve unit kept out of range of enemy artillery and brought forward to seal off enemy penetrations and counter-attack whenever possible. A key element of German defensive tactics in 1917

Flanders Lines (*Flandern Stellungen*)**:** A series of three heavily defended Flanders Lines ran from Lille to the Belgian coast

Group: German corps assigned to a permanent sector of the front

Hindenburg Line: Major German defensive system constructed during 1916–17

Jagdgeschwader: German Air Service fighter wing (containing four *Jagdstaffel*)

Jagdstaffel ('*Jasta*')**:** German Air Service fighter squadron (usually containing between nine and twelve aircraft)

Jäger: Elite German light infantry

Landsturm: German militia units comprising inferior troops used for local defence

Lewis gun: American-designed light machine-gun first introduced in 1915 and widely used in the BEF

Materialschlacht: Literally 'material battle'. German term for the kind of industrialized, mass warfare that emerged on the Western Front in 1916

Minenwerfer: German heavy trench mortar

Pillbox: Reinforced concrete blockhouse

Poilus: Literally 'hairy ones'. Slang for French soldiers

Regiment: Organization of infantry battalions. French and German divisions contained four regiments (each of three battalions). The British regimental system differed from continental use and regarded the regiment as a permanent organizational unit for its battalions

Zero Hour: Time at which an attack would commence

Abbreviations

AIF: Australian Imperial Force
ANZAC: Australian and New Zealand Army Corps
AWM: Australian War Memorial, Canberra
BA-MA: Bundesarchiv-Militärarchiv, Freiburg
BEF: British Expeditionary Force
CAB: Cabinet Office files
CIGS: Chief of the Imperial General Staff
C-in-C: Commander-in-Chief
CLIP: Canadian Letters and Images Project
CMR: Canadian Mounted Rifles
CWM: Canadian War Museum, Ottawa
DTA: Deutsches Tagebucharchiv, Emmendingen
GHQ: General Headquarters (British Expeditionary Force)
GOC: General Officer Commanding
GQG: *Grand Quartier Général* (French High Command)
IWM: Imperial War Museum, London
KA: Bayerisches Hauptstaatsarchiv, Abteilung IV: Kriegsarchiv, Munich
LAC: Library and Archives Canada, Ottawa
LHCMA: Liddell Hart Centre for Military Archives, King's College London
MG: Machine-gun
NCO: Non-Commissioned Officer
OHL: *Obersteheeresleitung* (German Supreme Command)
PPCLI: Princess Patricia's Canadian Light Infantry
RFA: Royal Field Artillery
RFC: Royal Flying Corps
TNA: The National Archives, Kew
WO: War Office files

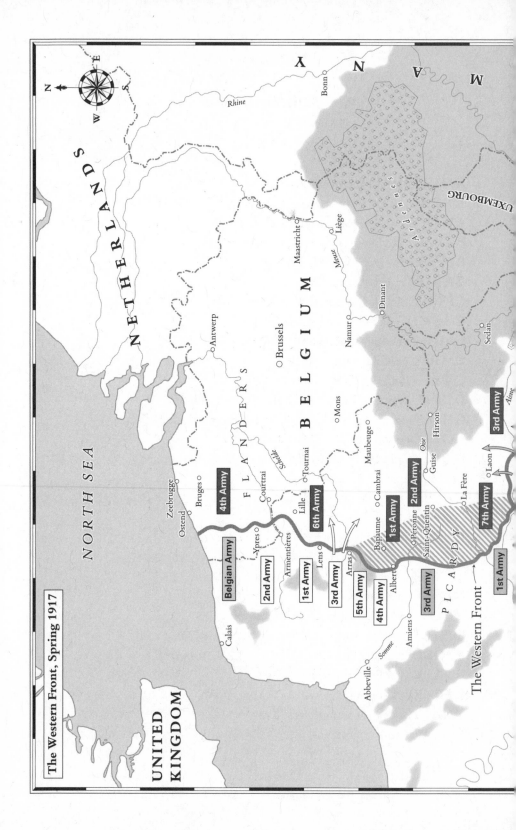

The Western Front, Spring 1917

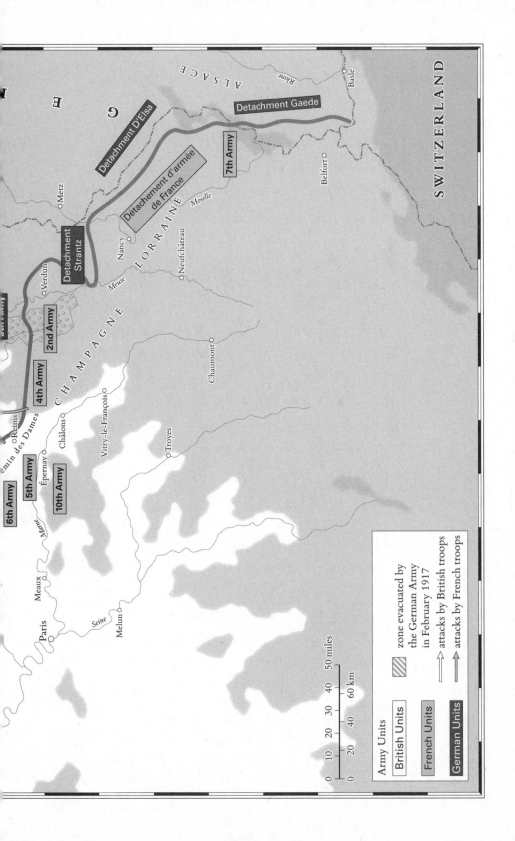

SWITZERLAND

ALSACE

Rhine

Basle

E

G

Detachment Gaede

Detachment D'Elsa

Metz

7th Army

Belfort

Détachement d'armée
de France

Moselle

Detachment
Strantz

LORRAINE

Nancy

Neufchâteau

Verdun

Meuse

2nd Army

CHAMPAGNE

Chaumont

4th Army

Reims

Chemin des Dames

6th Army

5th Army

Épernay

Châlons

Vitry-le-François

10th Army

Marne

Troyes

Meaux

Paris

Seine

Melun

Army Units

| British Units |
| French Units |
| German Units |

▨ zone evacuated by
the German Army
in February 1917

⟶ attacks by British troops

⟶ attacks by French troops

0   10   20   30   40   50 miles

0   20   40   60 km

Introduction

'*Good God, did we really send men to fight in that?*'

The words of Sir Launcelot Kiggell, a senior staff officer at British GHQ, upon visiting the Passchendaele battlefield, are some of the most notorious in the history of warfare. Sharp, to the point, shot through with horror and shock, they seem to encapsulate perfectly the appalling way in which battles were conducted between 1914 and 1918; by almost criminally negligent 'chateau generals' with no idea of the conditions on the front, who sent a generation of young men to squalid, terrifying deaths. The story first appeared in Basil Liddell Hart's *The Real War*, which was published in 1930, and was an explosive *exposé* of the Great War written by one of Britain's foremost military thinkers. Kiggell himself was not named (something Liddell Hart would only reveal after Kiggell's death in 1954),[1] with Liddell Hart referring instead to a 'highly-placed officer from General Headquarters who was on his first visit to the battle front':

> Growing increasingly uneasy as the car approached the swamp-like edges of the battle area, he eventually burst into tears, crying, 'Good God, did we really send men to fight in that?' To which his companion replied that the ground was far worse ahead. If the exclamation was a credit to his heart, it revealed on what a foundation of delusion and inexcusable ignorance his indomitable 'offensiveness' had been based.[2]

For Liddell Hart, the Flanders campaign of 1917 was the perfect illustration of the myopia that British High Command suffered from and its terrible consequences. Passchendaele has become, he wrote, 'like Walcheren a century before, a synonym for military failure – a name black-bordered in the records of the British Army'.[3]

Whether Kiggell ever made these remarks has been regularly disputed, with a number of historians casting doubt on the veracity of the incident and questioning whether Liddell Hart – a notorious gossip – could really be trusted on such an issue.[4] Others have argued that there was simply no way that British commanders could have been as ignorant of front-line conditions as Liddell Hart claimed.[5] The story originally seems to have come from Sir James Edmonds, who was then working on the multi-volume official history of the war. Liddell Hart regularly corresponded with Edmonds, sending him drafts of his books, and the two would often meet up over lunch and discuss old times. Contained in Liddell Hart's papers is the note he made after a talk with Edmonds in October 1927, which sketched out the incident, albeit with a slightly different quotation ('Did we really order men to advance over such ground?'). It must have resonated with Liddell Hart because he included it in *The Real War*, after of course conveniently redrafting Kiggell's words to enhance their dramatic effect. *Thus a legend was born.*[6]

The story of the 'weeping staff officer' has become firmly established within the popular memory of the war. Kiggell's words have found their way into collections of military quotations and psychology textbooks, and are a ready-made soundbite for commentators eager to spark an emotional response.[7] Indeed, to some, even if not strictly accurate, Kiggell's story reveals a larger truth. When the literary scholar Paul Fussell examined the quotation, he felt that it sounded 'too literary to be quite true, as if originally either conceived or noted down by someone who knew his Greek tragedy and perhaps Shakespeare's history plays', but it was nonetheless 'true in spirit'.[8] This book is, in a sense, an investigation into Kiggell's haunting words; an attempt to unearth the reality of one of the most infamous battles of the twentieth century. Why was it fought? How was it even possible? How could men fight and die in such awful surroundings and for what seemed like such pitiful gains? The questions over Passchendaele, why and how it was fought and what it meant, remain to be answered, or at least considered afresh, one hundred years on.

The battle took place between 31 July and 10 November 1917, a few miles east of the town of Ypres – the place where the great German advance of 1914 had come to a halt – and left a legacy of carnage and bitterness that was still palpable decades later. In four months of intensive fighting, upwards of 500,000 men were killed or wounded, maimed, gassed, drowned or buried here in this small corner of Belgium. As the poignant Memorial to the Missing at the Menin Gate in Ypres reminds us, many of the bodies were never found; they just disappeared into the thick, glutinous Flanders mud. Indeed, in a war that came to symbolize futility, Passchendaele stood out as the ultimate expression of meaningless, industrialized slaughter. According to the historian Dan Todman, the battle has become 'a cultural reference point that sums up everything bad about war – what it does or does not mean, how it is fought, and above all the risk of a disconnection between ends and means'.[9]

The British would officially call it the Third Battle of Ypres. For the Germans it was the *Flandernschlacht* (the Battle of Flanders). Yet it has become more commonly known as Passchendaele, named after the small hamlet that marked the apex of the British advance that year. This village, pulverized by shellfire into a muddy smear, came to symbolize the lost hopes and pitiful achievements of an offensive that the British Commander-in-Chief, Field Marshal Sir Douglas Haig, hoped would have a decisive effect on the war. Originally conceived as a mass offensive that would break through the German line, liberate much of Belgium and seize the enemy's submarine bases along the coast, by the time operations came to a halt in November 1917, the British had advanced just five miles. If the Somme of 1916, particularly its ghastly first day, has become a metaphor for a kind of innocence lost, when a generation of Britons faced the awful reality of total warfare, then Third Ypres is a slough of despond; a descent into the perils of Dante's *Inferno* with no possibility of redemption. As the historian A. J. P. Taylor once wrote: 'Third Ypres was the blindest slaughter of a blind war.'[10]

With hindsight it would seem almost prophetic that the war poet Siegfried Sassoon's 'open letter', in which he spoke out against the war, appeared in *The Times* on the day the offensive began. Sassoon's 'wilful defiance of military authority' called into question whether the war had become one of conquest and was being 'deliberately prolonged by those who had the power to end it'.[11] Sassoon never fought at Ypres, but he would pen one of the most moving poems about the battle – 'Memorial Tablet' – with its barren description of death in the Salient:

> Squire nagged and bullied till I went to fight
> (Under Lord Derby's Scheme). I died in Hell –
> (They called it Passchendaele); my wound was slight,
> And I was hobbling back, and then a shell
> Burst slick upon the duckboards; so I fell
> Into the bottomless mud, and lost the light.[12]

It was little wonder that the battle has become defined by mud. Britain's wartime Prime Minister, David Lloyd George, would call it 'the campaign of the mud' in the second volume of his *War Memoirs*, which was published in 1936. Lloyd George excoriated what he saw as Haig's myriad blunders in the battle ('one of the greatest disasters of the war'), and accused both him and the Chief of the Imperial General Staff, Sir William Robertson, of misleading the War Cabinet on several vital issues, including the condition of the French Army, the (apparently) inferior numbers of the enemy, and the state of the ground. 'Victories were much overstated. Virtual defeats were represented as victories, however limited their scope. Our casualties were understated. Enemy losses became pyramidal . . . All disconcerting and discouraging facts were suppressed', while 'every bright feather of success was waved and flourished in our faces'. Haig had 'completely lost his balance' and 'persevered stubbornly with his attacks' rather than admit his failure. Third Ypres was a 'senseless campaign' that 'imperilled the chances of final victory'.[13]

Lloyd George's wholly negative account of the battle was heavily influenced by Liddell Hart (who had been employed as an adviser on *War Memoirs*) and directed squarely at his enemies in the General Staff. Yet he did not have it all his own way and there were always those – including senior commanders and military historians – who argued that the campaign was both worthwhile and necessary. One of those was the Conservative MP Duff Cooper (author of a biography of Haig in 1936), who tried to push back against this tide of 'mud and blood', emphasizing both the logic and rationale behind fighting in Flanders – undoubtedly Britain's most vital sector of the Western

Front – and the need to take pressure off the French Army. For Cooper, the battle was certainly fearful, but by the time it ended the British had improved their positions around Ypres, their French Allies had recovered, and the German Army had 'been given no respite in which to heal their wounds or to produce new plans'.[14]

It was not until after the Second World War that the official account of Third Ypres was published, by which time the battle lines were already deeply entrenched. Of all the volumes of the British Official History, none were more troublesome than or went through such a tortuous birth as *Military Operations 1917: Volume II*. Work began in September 1939, but it proceeded at a slow pace, suffering from frequent rewrites and disagreements over content.[15] It was eventually published in 1948 – the last of the British official histories to be completed. Its author, Sir James Edmonds, tried his best to dispel some of the myths that had grown up around the battle, particularly 'the mud legend', which had been peddled by what he called 'eminent civilian critics with the ear of the public' – an unmistakeable shot at Lloyd George and Liddell Hart. Although Edmonds did not shy away from criticizing the Commander-in-Chief – particularly over the choice of General Sir Hubert Gough (GOC Fifth Army) to command the main assault – he was broadly supportive of Haig's conduct of the campaign, including the choice of battlefield and its objectives. In the conclusion he returned to one of the major themes of his work: the lack of preparation for a major continental war before 1914 and its inevitable, baneful results in wartime. 'A nation cannot expect great and immediate victories', Edmonds warned, 'unless it supplies the means, the men and the material.'[16]

As was perhaps to be expected, *Military Operations 1917: Volume II* was never to find universal acceptance. When it appeared, it provoked flurries of correspondence, with Frances Lloyd George (née Stevenson) accusing Edmonds of 'whitewashing' the Passchendaele campaign.[17] The former Chief of the Air Staff, Lord Trenchard, disagreed, calling it 'exhaustive and accurate',[18] and Sir John Davidson (who had worked at GHQ) said that it was 'fair and reasonable' and allowed readers 'to place Lord Haig's responsibilities and decisions in a proper perspective'.[19] As for Liddell Hart, he was convinced that

Edmonds had deliberately presented a more moderate and pro-Haig interpretation of the battle than the evidence warranted, apparently because his official position and his close military friendships meant it was impossible for him to 'put the hard truth' into print (which was perhaps why he had been so keen to share his anecdote about the 'weeping staff officer').[20] Whether this was true or not, Edmonds's attempt to tell Haig's side of the story, or at least to banish some of the more outlandish criticisms of the offensive, were destined to fail. *Military Operations 1917: Volume II* would never be able to shift the dominant perception of Passchendaele that Lloyd George and Liddell Hart had fostered; that high ground had already been taken.[21]

Even as memories of the battle began to fade, the arguments continued. In the late 1950s the historian John Terraine began what would become a lifelong attempt to rehabilitate the reputation of Sir Douglas Haig, who was by now condemned as the chief 'donkey'. For Terraine, Lloyd George and Liddell Hart had been responsible for 'a distortion of history' and a 'deep injustice' to those who had planned and fought the battle.[22] Objecting to an overly emotional reading of what happened (he would never use the term 'Passchendaele', preferring instead the more sober 'Third Ypres'), Terraine continued along the path Edmonds had sketched out: emphasizing the strategic importance of the Belgian coast, the urgent need to keep the pressure off the French Army, and the terrible effect that fighting in Flanders had on the defenders. The battle may have failed in its grandiose objectives, but it marked the moment when German morale on the Western Front began to collapse. It also, moreover, contributed to the developments in British tactical skill and weaponry that would culminate later in the war, particularly at the Battle of Amiens in August 1918, and which, for Terraine, allowed Ypres to be understood in its proper context as an important milestone on the road to victory.[23]

Liddell Hart and Terraine argued with each other for years; disputing everything from the reliability of Haig's diaries to British and German casualty statistics; a debate that was continued by subsequent writers, albeit frequently generating much heat but little light.[24] Leon Wolff, a US Air Force officer, wrote one of the most widely read accounts of the battle, *In Flanders Fields* (1958), which was very much in the mould of Liddell Hart, portraying Passchendaele as a meaningless slaughter conducted by commanders without understanding or imagination. Although Wolff claimed that he had originally intended to write his account with what he called 'inhuman neutrality', he admitted that 'I could not believe what I was writing.'[25] Little had changed by the time Lyn Macdonald's *They Called It Passchendaele* was published in 1978. Based upon over 600 eyewitness accounts, Macdonald's book brought the story of those 'Tommies and Anzacs and Canucks' who served at Ypres to a whole new generation. Although she generally avoided outright condemnation of either Lloyd George or Haig, she noted that, in places, her book read more like a novel or a horror story than a sober work of military history, and its great popularity helped to solidify further the popular understanding of Passchendaele as being a 'blood-bath . . . beyond imagining'.[26]

By the 1990s, increasing numbers of scholars, from both Britain and the Commonwealth, were beginning to re-examine the performance of British arms on the Western Front and spread the idea of a more positive 'learning curve'. Yet Passchendaele remained immune from this tide of revisionism. In 1996, the Australian historians Robin Prior and Trevor Wilson published *Passchendaele. The Untold Story*, but far from rehabilitating the battle, they described an even darker story. While the defenders of Lloyd George and Haig had slugged it out for years, shifting blame and trading blows over responsibility for the battle, Prior and Wilson emphasized *both* the 'delusions of the military command' *and* the 'waywardness of the political leadership'. The British Prime Minister was portrayed as a curious amalgam of energy and lethargy, determination and disinterest; a man who grudgingly supported the Flanders campaign, yet who declined to take responsibility for it or grasp the nettle and suspend it as he undoubtedly should have done. Meanwhile Haig was criticized for consistently failing to learn the lessons of previous battles and for an almost pathological over-optimism in the face of stubborn enemy resistance. It was, as the authors concluded, 'in no sense a pinnacle of the military art'.[27]

So why a new book on Passchendaele? Despite its iconic status,

Third Ypres remains – by the standards of some other Great War battles – relatively underwritten. When researching their own book in the 1990s, Prior and Wilson found historical research on the battle to be 'astonishingly thin' – and only limited amounts of work have been done to rectify this in the intervening years.[28] Most of the recent focus has been on the imperial aspect of the battle and Australian, New Zealand and Canadian historians have added much to our understanding of how far and wide the impact of Passchendaele would spread.[29] Nevertheless, important elements of Third Ypres remain to be explored. The German story is the largest omission, with most accounts spending little or no time on how the German Army fought the battle and, in particular, how it adapted to the changing tactical and operational demands that fighting in Flanders presented.[30]

Passchendaele: The Lost Victory of World War I attempts to retell the story of this infamous battle, considering it afresh with the accumulated knowledge of a century of scholarship. It is based upon a greater array of source material than any previous history, including personal accounts, letters, memoirs, official reports and war diaries from both sides. It aims to present a new account of the battle, what it was like to experience, and what it meant for the overall war efforts of both the Allies and the Central Powers. It provides a fresh discussion of the battle at strategic, operational and tactical levels, and spends considerable time examining the 'other side of the hill'. About a third of the book deals with the soldiers of the German Army and how they defended their positions in the Ypres Salient. Their story is a remarkable one of courage and ingenuity in the face of almost unimaginable horrors. Indeed, it is only by combining the British and German experiences that we can reassess the battle in new ways and appreciate how near Haig's forces came to decisive success in September and October 1917. It could even be said that Third Ypres was, in some respects, one of the 'lost victories' of the war.

The idea of 'decisive success' or a 'lost victory' at Passchendaele seems, at first glance, to be bizarre and counter-intuitive. Yet, looking again at the battle, it is striking how close the British came to forcing the German Army to make a major retreat in Belgium in

October 1917. By raising the tempo of operations and inflicting an increasingly unacceptable casualty rate on the German Army, British forces opened up a window of opportunity for significant political and strategic results – maybe even some kind of compromise peace. This story has, in the opinion of this author, never been told fully before and stands in sharp contrast to the dominant perception of the battle as being totally futile and devoid of meaning or purpose. On the contrary, major success was within Britain's grasp in the summer and autumn of 1917, and had the battle been managed slightly differently, it is not too difficult to imagine that the course of the war could have been transformed dramatically.

Passchendaele has a complex and lengthy history. It took months to emerge and develop; frequently intertwining with other battles and running in parallel with them, before finally becoming the focal point of the war in the late summer and autumn of 1917. Its story begins in the winter of 1916–17 when new Allied leadership, both political and military, tried to salvage a war effort that seemed to be drifting along dangerous lines. The enormous battles of 1916, at Verdun and the Somme, had not produced decisive results, only added hundreds of thousands of names to French, British and German casualty lists. With the war in France and Belgium frozen into what seemed like a permanent stalemate, major decisions had to be made about how the war was going to be won and what, if any, support would be given to other fronts. In the east, the Russian Army was approaching the limit of its endurance and increasingly unable to hold off the Central Powers, while the Italian war effort was already proving too much for the country to sustain. Out of this tortuous situation would emerge what is, at once, the most frightening, yet most fascinating, battle fought on the Western Front. One hundred years on, the Third Battle of Ypres is still deserving of our attention.

Prologue:
The Nivelle Offensive

We now have the formula.

Robert Nivelle[1]

16 April 1917

Victory was certain. The new Commander-in-Chief, General Robert Georges Nivelle, had promised as much. Appointed to command France's northern armies in December 1916, replacing the tired figure of Joseph Joffre (who had held the burden since 1911), Nivelle wanted a more vigorous and active prosecution of the war. For a nation that was urgently seeking a way out of an agonizing attritional struggle, Nivelle seemed the perfect candidate. As an army commander at Verdun in 1916, he had overseen the recapture of Fort Douaumont utilizing the latest artillery techniques – including the much-heralded 'creeping barrage' – that enabled his infantry to break into enemy positions which had hitherto been regarded as invulnerable. With a new method of coordinating infantry and artillery proving a tactical success, Nivelle believed that he had found the solution to the riddle of trench warfare. He now planned to apply it on a much larger scale. There could be no doubt, he said, confidently and assuredly, this time the Allies would achieve decisive victory.

Nivelle proposed that the massive Allied offensive, now scheduled for April 1917, would usher in a shattering defeat of German forces on the Western Front. After British and French troops had conducted preliminary attacks around Arras on 9 April, his Reserve Army Group, comprising nearly forty divisions, would strike the decisive blow along the River Aisne a week later. Once they had cleared the enemy defences along the Chemin des Dames, French troops would manoeuvre the remaining German units into the open and then, in Nivelle's defiant phrase, 'destroy the principal mass of the enemy's forces on the Western Front'. If everything went to plan, he reckoned this decisive phase would occur within 24–48 hours of the beginning of the attack. It was nothing short of breathtaking.[2]

A wave of optimism swept through the country. 'Never had the Army been in more magnificent shape', reports noted. 'The closer the launching of the offensive became, the greater hopes were raised. People talked about French troops going on to Laon and Mézières. They dreamed of the march of the Allies, victorious on the Meuse.'[3] Yet whatever qualities Nivelle may have possessed, he was unfortunate that the one element Napoleon had prized above all others – *luck* – deserted him. A month before his offensive was to go in, the German Army began a pre-planned withdrawal from its over-extended positions between Arras and Soissons, occupying a specially constructed rear line known as the Hindenburg Line. The redeployment began on 16 March and, over the next three days, four armies pulled back on a front of over 100 miles, leaving a torn and ravaged wilderness in their wake. The aim was to deprive the enemy of anything that might be of use in the evacuated zone – railways, roads, bridges, and houses to billet troops – and the German Army went about its task with ruthless application. It was, as one senior officer noted grimly, 'an orgy of dynamite'.[4] By occupying the Hindenburg Line before Nivelle could strike, the defenders pulled off an immense strategic coup. Their front had been shortened by nearly fifty kilometres, freeing up thirteen divisions and fifty heavy batteries, thus providing the German High Command with a readily available strategic reserve.[5]

The changed situation did not, however, prompt any modification in Nivelle's plans. Conscious that so much seemed to be riding on his offensive, the French commander decided to persist with his existing strategy, convinced that the attack must go ahead, and unwilling to admit that his guns had already been spiked. Even worse, his plans were now known to the German High Command, who had managed to get their hands on copies of corps and army orders weeks before the attack (Nivelle's headquarters being notoriously relaxed about secrecy). In contrast to Nivelle's frozen optimism, growing numbers of field commanders, both British and French, began to suspect that something was terribly wrong. In March the French Premier, Alexandre Ribot, interviewed three of his Army Group commanders, who all expressed reservations about whether they would be able to achieve Nivelle's grandiose objectives.[6] Yet their warnings went unheeded; Nivelle was allowed to go ahead and march the French Army to its destiny on the Chemin des Dames on the morning of 16 April 1917.

When the attack finally went ahead, the result was a disaster; a shambles of flesh against steel as French infantry, heavily encumbered with food and supplies, found their dreams of reaching open ground dying in front of their eyes. The appalling experience of 10th Colonial Infantry Division in the Sixth Army was typical of what French, and frequently Senegalese, infantry faced on that cold, deadly morning. The ground was the first obstacle. There had been 'an almost complete absence' of proper observation over the German lines prior to the attack. Most of the defenders had access to underground shelters (known as *creutes*) that were impossible to pinpoint, while the French artillery had only limited room to deploy. The weather did not help. Out of a total of nine days' preliminary bombardment, only twenty-one hours of uninterrupted fire had been possible because of the low cloud and rain. 'Their artillery', on the contrary, 'fired back infrequently but with deadly accuracy on the French batteries literally piled up in the ravines . . .'[7]

The awful weather seemed to get even worse in the hours before the attack, with wind, rain and snow battering against the huddled lines of infantry waiting to go over. The colonial soldiers from Africa had never experienced such conditions and were, in places, up to their waists in water. When the order to attack was given, 10th Division was almost immediately stopped in its tracks. The men were supposed to advance at a rate of 100 metres every three minutes – the speed of Nivelle's famous 'creeping barrage' – but this was much too quick. When units came up against obstacles and their pace slowed, they lost their artillery support. Disaster was now inevitable:

The enemy, allowing them to pass, came out of their underground tunnels and killed the infantry at their leisure without suffering any losses themselves ... Heavily laden with three days' supplies, in expectation of a 'certain' advance, [and carrying] only two or three grenades, the men took only a few minutes to get rid of their rations and the grenades that were exploding in their haversacks. Jammed, clogged machine-guns proved useless and were thrown away. The Senegalese lost their officers, clustered together and were decimated.[8]

A report on the action concluded that beforehand the morale of the men had been higher than ever. 'Right through the ranks there was an absolute certainty of success. Higher up, there was a certain unease but they still had faith. They thought that the High Command's assessment was such that the operation was necessary and certain to succeed.'[9]

Sadly, the tragic story of 10th Division was not unique on that fatal 16 April. The French divisions battered themselves in vain attempts to get forward; columns of frightened *poilus*, sheltering from the rain under their dull *horizon-bleu* coats, were bowed as if walking through a hailstorm, as German shelling and dug-in machine-guns tore bloodied holes in their ranks. Whole battalions were wiped out in the storm of shellfire, while the few French tanks that had been able to reach the starting line soon became magnets for enemy gunfire. A British liaison officer, Major Edward Spears, tried to get to the front to see what was happening, only to be met by columns of wounded coming back and hundreds of men on stretchers, all 'covered with mud and blood'. One man, thoroughly broken in spirit, muttered to him:

'It's all up, we can't do it, we shall never do it. *C'est impossible.*'

That night the rain, which had fallen all day, turned to sleet and then froze, covering the battlefield, the huddled corpses and the dead horses in a silvery cloak of white snow. 'On the German side', Spears noted, 'great bouquets of blood-red flowers grew and fell slowly with exasperating regularity.' At one point, he stumbled across a campfire, around which a few *poilus* sat smoking. The men 'had the blank faces and staring eyes of extreme fatigue' and the scene struck him as being one of the most dejected and disillusioned sights he witnessed during the whole war. He continued on his lonely journey, trying to return to the rear lines, every so often glancing back over his shoulder at the smouldering front to the north.

> Presently we were held up by one of the eternal traffic blocks. Looking back towards the Aisne, I could see sudden flares of light and hear the sound of distant explosions which seemed to indicate a recrudescence of fighting. Guns would suddenly rumble as if endeavouring to fill the depressing immensity of what seemed stillness after the din of the day. Now and then a machine-gun rat-tatted and was answered by others; the sound of rifle shots in the distance pin-pricked the silence irregularly, sounding more violent and angry than the implacable machine-guns. It was easy to conjure up a picture of what was going on over there in the night full of living shadows each one separated from the world of shadows only by a sharp pang of pain from a bullet in head or heart, or by the few minutes' or hours' agony of a fatal wound.[10]

These sounds were the death rattle of Nivelle's grand battle of decision. The 'last Napoleonic offensive in French history' had failed.[11]

Photographs of General Nivelle taken after the battle show a distracted figure, with a haunted look in his eyes, as if he had seen things that he could never forget. Because all his charm and affability – so celebrated when he had replaced his predecessor – counted for nothing as the grim casualty returns came into GQG and the realization sank in that the offensive was going nowhere. A staff officer, Jean de Pierrefeu, took a *communiqué* to Nivelle that evening and found him 'anxious' with none of his legendary charm or cheerfulness. 'His height seemed to grow less, and swellings marred the strong lines of his face', he wrote. 'He was wearing heavy artillery boots which rendered his step heavier as though dejected. His eyes were rarely lighted up, and his always grave expression had taken on a look of sadness.' Nivelle read the *communiqué* slowly and deliberately. 10,000 prisoners had been taken, but not many villages or towns of note had fallen and few German guns were in French hands. The general, in silence, added a few words to the end of the paper (abridging a passage relating to the strength of the enemy), before initialling it and dismissing Pierrefeu. Nivelle's spell – one he had cast so successfully since the winter – had been broken.[12]

Fighting on the Aisne and in Champagne continued, on and off, until 9 May when the Nivelle Offensive was finally cancelled. Although it was true there were gains – some important tactical ground and the capture of 20,000 enemy soldiers – these spoils felt meagre and disappointing when compared to the enormous damage that France had sustained. After ten days of fighting, the French Army had suffered over 95,000 casualties, including 15,000 killed in action.[13] So much hope had been invested in Nivelle's promise of victory that the let-down was shattering. Nivelle was sacked a week later and shunted off to command France's troops in North Africa. Yet the implications of the battle were far more significant than the humiliation of one general, however senior. The shock of 16 April came like a heart attack to the French war effort. Within days, troop morale, right across the front, began to crumble. While significant sections of the French Army remained steady, an alarming number of divisions began to mutiny, refusing to go into the line and indulging in what the French Official History called 'collective acts of indiscipline'. For the French nation, this would be the most perilous stage of the war.

The mutinies that rippled through the French Army in the spring and summer of 1917 were the result of many things, not least the appalling cost of trying to defeat an enemy that was in a position of immense strategic strength, and doing so with inadequate resources. The official account blamed it, 'without a shadow of a doubt', on the length of hostilities.[14] Hailing the Russian Revolution, which had broken out in March, and asking for peace, more leave, and better conditions and food, thousands of *poilus* from fifty-four divisions decided to oppose their officers. They would defend their lines, if they had to, but they would not attack again; not until their grievances were addressed. The first units began to fail in late April – most coming from the Sixth Army, which had been heavily engaged on the Aisne – and during the following month serious indiscipline threw France's Army into turmoil, paralysing any possibility of new offensives.

Red flags appeared at railway carriage doors, revolutionary cries could be heard in the stations the trains passed through, windows were broken, locomotives uncoupled, water tanks drained, non-combat soldiers, station police – and occasionally police superintendents – were insulted and struck and shots were fired.[15]

Had the enemy guessed what was happening, the whole French sector of the Western Front could have collapsed.

Nivelle's successor was the Army Group commander General Henri Philippe Pétain. He was charged with restoring the health of the Army and doing what he could to maintain France's dwindling military strength. He may have possessed little of his predecessor's flair or charm, but Pétain was an exceptional soldier, known throughout France as a man who cared for his troops. Immediately he sprang into action, travelling along the front and visiting up to ninety divisions within a single month. He would spend hours talking to the *poilus*, speaking to their officers and NCOs, listening to their grievances, before telling them – his eyes blue and ice-cold – that mutiny in the presence of the enemy was 'a monstrous crime'. He would be merciless towards those who had endangered France's safety, but would also do what he could to see that the men received better care and attention. Jean de Pierrefeu was an immediate supporter of the new Commander-in-Chief, and lauded Pétain's 'prestige, his authority, his masterful attitude', which rallied the flagging morale of his army. 'He spoke as a man to men, dominating them with his prestige, without trying to put himself on a lower level . . . The General derived all his strength, in fact, from his humanity. He loathed sentimentality, but he was never able to meet an ambulance without emotion.' As Pierrefeu later noted, within a matter of weeks 'all traces of mutiny were wiped out'.[16]

Pétain dealt speedily and carefully with his army's battered morale, but the disasters of the spring had underscored how fragile France's continued participation in the war had become. There would be more fighting to follow, but from now on the French would require help. As Pétain put it: there would be no more offensives. *They would wait for the tanks and for the Americans.* The only problem was time. Tank production remained behind schedule and mired in technical and industrial problems, while the Americans, although newly joined in the war, would require months – maybe years – of planning and organizing before they could put an army into the field. For the moment the Allied war effort in the west came to a shuddering halt. There could be no denying it: 1917 was the darkest year of the war.

I.

Manoeuvres of War

The period we were about to enter was full of contradictions,
cross-currents, hesitations and doubts.

Edward Spears[1]

5 December 1916–6 May 1917

Four months before General Nivelle's ill-fated offensive would flounder on the bloodied slopes of the Chemin des Dames, David Lloyd
George became British Prime Minister, promising to deliver a 'knock
out blow' against Germany. On 8 December 1916, *The Times* proclaimed him to be 'the man of the moment'.[2] 'All notion of "crisis" had
disappeared from London yesterday long before the official intimation
was made that Mr Lloyd George had been received by the King and
had kissed hands on his appointment as Prime Minister', it read.
Andrew Bonar Law's Unionist Party – then the largest party in the
House of Commons – pledged its support, while many Liberals now
'flocked to Lloyd George's standard'. The widespread impression was
that the Government would be a strong one ('possibly unusual in type',
noted the editorial), 'but well fitted for the immediate work before it'.[3]

The accession of Lloyd George to the premier position in British
political life was a remarkable achievement. A radical and energetic
politician who prided himself on his unconventional approach to
life, Lloyd George had long been characterized as wily and untrust-
worthy. Many in his own Liberal Party had never warmed to him;
for the Tories, his opposition to the war in South Africa (1899–1902)
had put a black mark against his name that took years to wipe clean.
Yet for all his foibles, there was still *something* about Lloyd George

that made a deep impression on all those who came into his orbit. Sir Maurice Hankey, the Secretary of the War Cabinet, described the Prime Minister as emanating 'an extraordinary sense of power and strength, such as I have never encountered in any other'. He was 'rather small, but he possessed the stocky solid frame of many of his fellow-countrymen, and his healthy complexion gave evidence of a sound constitution. His head was square and large, with a wealth of black hair gradually turned grey by the cares of office. The dominating feature of his face was his eyes, ever changing, now tender with emotion, now sparkling with fun, now flashing with anger; eyes astute, unfathomable.'[4]

While other leading figures found their reputations sinking during the war – Herbert Asquith, Winston Churchill and Edward Grey to name a few – Lloyd George enjoyed an enviable rise. By the time he entered 10 Downing Street, he had carved out a formidable reputation as a man of drive, invention and – as Minister of Munitions – 'push and go'. Although he was born in the smoky suburbs of Manchester, his Welsh background (his father was the Baptist pastor of Llanystumdwy in Caernarvonshire) always made him an uneasy fit in the corridors of power and he constantly railed against the drift and muddle that he swore bedevilled Britain's war effort. He acted almost immediately, forming a new War Cabinet with just five members, including himself and his chief ally, Bonar Law.[5] This was supposed to inject a much-needed dose of his legendary action and dynamism into a Westminster that had, for too long, been run on the lines of 'business as usual'.

There was no doubt that such urgent leadership was required. After two and a half years of war, the Allied war effort seemed to be drifting, steadily and inexorably, towards defeat. The German invasion of France and Belgium in 1914 may have been halted, but repeated Allied offensives throughout the following two years had failed to drive the enemy out of more than a handful of villages and towns, while producing appalling losses. By the end of 1916 the French Army had suffered almost 1.2 million dead or missing in action.[6] The British had not suffered anything like French casualties, but found their hopes of a major decision on the Somme being torn to pieces by

machine-gun fire and shellfire (at the cost of over 400,000 dead, missing or wounded).[7] Elsewhere the Allies had met with what seemed
like nothing but disaster. The intervention in Gallipoli, intended to
knock Ottoman Turkey out of the war, had been a bloody fiasco,
while a joint Anglo-French landing in the Balkans – a gallant if
belated attempt to help the Serbs – found itself cooped up in Salonika
in an expedition that soon became a byword for strategic incoher-
ency and waste.

Initially, Lloyd George had been deeply sceptical of Nivelle's plans
for a grand attack in the west in the spring of 1917. He doubted
whether Germany's vast and powerful Army could ever be destroyed,
and instinctively looked elsewhere. The answer was not to fight on
the Western Front, but to defeat Germany's allies in turn and then,
once she was alone and weakened, Britain would wield a great Euro-
pean alliance to vanquish the Kaiser. He had been a staunch advocate
of the Salonika expedition and, despite its disappointments, maintained that if the Allies massed sufficient combat power they could
knock Bulgaria out of the war. Failing that, it would make sense to
send as many men and guns as possible to the Italians, then struggling
against the Austro-Hungarians. What was essential, he said repeatedly, was that the Allies must win *something*, somewhere soon, or else
their peoples would not be able to keep going.[8] But however elo-
quently or passionately Lloyd George urged the War Cabinet to alter
British strategy and to look elsewhere than France, he constantly
came up against the roadblock that was the professional head of the
British Army, the Chief of the Imperial General Staff, Sir William
Robertson.

Robertson was a rock of a man. A contemporary described him as
being 'solidly built' and of 'striking appearance'. 'He appears to eman-
ate strength; you instinctively feel you are in the presence of a man
of iron will and constitution. His sturdy, compact frame gives an
impression of tremendous energy.'[9] The only man ever to rise through
every rank of the British Army – from private to field marshal –
Robertson was the son of a Lincolnshire postmaster, and possessed of
a mind that was logical, thorough and supremely competent. For
Robertson, the war could only be won in France. As he had written

in November 1915, victory could only be attained 'by the defeat or exhaustion of the predominant partner in the Central Alliance', namely Germany. 'Every plan of operation must therefore be examined from the point of view of its bearing on this result' – the decisive defeat of the German Armies on the Western Front. Anything that did not contribute to this aim should be discarded.[10]

Much of what Robertson said was correct, but Lloyd George could never accept it. For him, the CIGS was symptomatic of a military caste that was unimaginative, stupid and incapable of prosecuting the war with any sense of vigour or intelligence. Accusing Robertson of being 'cowed' and 'bullied' by the commander in France, Field Marshal Sir Douglas Haig (who was, in any case, his senior in the Army List), Lloyd George considered that he had been 'completely failed' by the CIGS, who was unable to rise to the 'full significance and responsibility' of his great position. Robertson was possessed of qualities, he wrote, 'which made for speedy promotion in the Army'. He was 'cautious' and 'discreet'; 'non-committal' and 'sternly orthodox'; 'sound' but 'commonplace'. 'Such mistakes therefore as he committed were all of the negative kind, and as these were always in accordance with Army regulations and traditions they counted in his favour and helped his promotion.' 'Such men always get on in any vocation', added Lloyd George sardonically.[11]

The problem was that the Prime Minister found it impossible to get rid of his enemies, either Robertson or Haig. In order to ensure backing from senior Unionists, Lloyd George had agreed to retain Haig as Commander-in-Chief in France. Moreover, because Lord Derby (known as 'the soldiers' friend') was Secretary of State for War, it meant that Lloyd George found himself boxed in on more than one occasion by advisers who did not share his strategic outlook.[12] It was, therefore, extremely difficult to approach strategic questions with the kind of 'blank sheet' that Lloyd George evidently demanded. When he became Prime Minister he found that the game was already in play, moves had been made and strategies adopted, and he could not simply reset the board to his liking.

The Prime Minister remained deeply sceptical of the prospects for any offensive on the Western Front in 1917, but, in spite of himself, found his doubts massaged away by the big, reassuring presence of General Nivelle.[13] The French commander's promise of a 'smashing victory' within 24–48 hours may not have been exactly what Lloyd George wanted to hear, but at least the French would shoulder the burden of the offensive. The only problem was making sure that Britain's armies played their part and, here, Lloyd George was determined to assert his authority. When, in January 1917, Haig expressed concerns over the state of the French railway system, which was under severe strain, and how this might delay taking over much of the French line as had already been agreed with Nivelle, Lloyd George decided to act. Lacking the nerve to take on GHQ directly, he plotted with the French Government to make Haig a subordinate of the French Commander-in-Chief, whereby his independence would be blunted. Lloyd George felt that only by acting as a single, unified army could the Allies operate effectively on the Western Front. Now this reasoning was perfectly sound – a year later Ferdinand Foch would become Allied *Generalissimo* with some success – but the way he tried to bring this about was symptomatic of a political animal who preferred to operate in the shadows.

Lloyd George's scheme – to make Haig no more than an Army Group commander under Nivelle – had been unveiled to the British military delegation, including Robertson, at a joint Allied conference in Calais on 26 February (which had ostensibly been called to discuss the railway issue that Haig had raised). At an appropriate moment (and carefully prompted by Lloyd George), Nivelle proposed that from 1 March the French Commander-in-Chief (himself) should exercise full authority over the BEF, particularly in how it conducted operations in the field. To ensure this worked smoothly, a senior British staff officer would be sent to GQG to act as a link between both armies and ensure that French directives were followed.[14] That such an incredible proposal could have been entertained was down to Lloyd George, who had made clear to his French counterpart, Aristide Briand, that the British Government wanted such an arrangement. For the French delegation this was excellent news. Now they would be able to control and direct their greatest ally; one, moreover, that had shown itself, from their perspective, to be dangerously and habitually independent. Finally, after two and a half years, the British would have to conform to *their* plans.

For Robertson and Haig – who had been totally unaware of what Lloyd George was planning – there was exasperated surprise, choked by growing anger. Robertson was amazed that the Prime Minister was seriously considering handing over their armies, 'within forty-eight hours and for an indefinite period, to a foreign General having no experience in the duties of High Command, and whose optimistic views of the coming campaign were shared by no responsible soldier in the British Army and by few or none in the French'.[15] It was fortunate that Britain's delegation contained staff officers of the highest calibre, including Robertson's Director of Military Operations, Sir Frederick Maurice, and the ever-present Maurice Hankey; men who had acquired the poise and political antennae of palace courtiers and who went to work, quietly and efficiently, at 'redrafting' Nivelle's note. Throughout the night they clattered away on typewriters in their rooms and mulled over a face-saving compromise that could command general agreement. Eventually, after a herculean effort, a proposal was hammered out that put Haig under Nivelle's orders, but *only* for the duration of the forthcoming operation – Nivelle's push on the Aisne and Haig's preliminary attack around Arras – and, crucially, included an escape clause allowing Haig to appeal to his own government if he felt the orders of the French Commander-in-Chief 'endangered the safety' of his army.[16]

The only thing that could have justified Lloyd George's actions at Calais would have been the complete and runaway success of Nivelle's main attack. Its lamentable failure, however, left him exposed and weakened, and both Robertson and Haig never forgot Lloyd George's perfidy. 'Sir Douglas Haig had come out on top in this fight between the two chiefs', wrote the Prime Minister's secretary, Frances Stevenson, 'and I fear David will have to be very careful in future as to his backings of the French against the English.'[17] Even more galling for the Prime Minister were the plaudits that Haig was now receiving for his supporting operation at Arras, which had begun in spectacular fashion on 9 April. That morning the Canadian Corps stormed Vimy Ridge, pushing through sleet and hail to capture one of the toughest defensive positions on the Western Front. Elsewhere, General Sir Edmund Allenby's Third Army had also succeeded in driving the enemy from its positions east of Arras, delivering a smashing blow to the German Sixth Army and causing a mini-crisis at the German High Command.

Arras may have been a promising beginning, but the collapse of General Nivelle's main offensive left the Allies at a strategic dead-end, full of gloom; and only partially lightened by the US declaration of war on Germany on 6 April. If anything the situation seemed bleaker than it had been in the winter; at least then Allied hearts had been warmed by the flickering hope that Nivelle had something magical up his sleeve. Now, with the French commander exposed as a charlatan, a growing sense of war-weariness and despair began to take hold in the Allied capitals. In London, Lloyd George sensed a turning point had arrived. Since August 1914, Britain's strategy to defeat the Central Powers had been based upon four pillars: the strength of the Russian Army; the effectiveness of the French Army; British naval superiority; and her position as a financial powerhouse. By the spring of 1917, one by one, these pillars were crumbling. Russia's armed forces had been crippled by horrific casualties, high rates of desertion, and endemic indiscipline for months, while unrest in St Petersburg had finally forced the abdication of the Tsar, Emperor Nicholas II, on 8 March.[18] Although it was hoped that the new provisional government would rule more effectively, it only marked another stage in the progressive decline of Russia's war effort. Elsewhere, Britain's credit was running out and, most worrying of all, the Royal Navy was struggling to contain a new offensive by Germany's U-boats that threatened to cut her shipping lifelines.[19]

On 1 May, Lloyd George chaired a meeting of the Imperial War Cabinet and the Minister for Defence, the former Boer commander, General Jan Smuts, delivered a report on 'the general and military situation'. While having 'no confidence' that a breakthrough on the Western Front could be achieved 'on any large scale' in the near future, Smuts nevertheless felt that something must be done. If the French adopted Pétain's policy of 'active defence', then Britain's forces should be concentrated in the north for a thrust towards Zeebrugge and Ostend. 'I see more advantages in an offensive intended to recover the Belgian coast and deprive the enemy of two advanced submarine bases, than in the present offensive', he noted. Although this would undoubtedly present a number of difficulties, it was preferable to operations designed simply to liberate more French territory. Whatever decision was taken, Smuts noted, the time had surely come for a thorough review of Britain's strategic situation, military and naval, in order to give her commanders the best chance of achieving victory.[20]

Robertson also circulated his own document at the meeting, which commented upon some of the points Smuts had raised. The CIGS was convinced there was only one course to follow: 'continuing the battle we and the French have started'. He recognized that their allies might be unwilling to pursue heavy attacks for the time being, but warned the Cabinet of the dangers of inaction: namely that there was a possibility Germany would use any breathing space to crush either Russia or Italy. In any case, was it certain 'that our own shipping will hold out for another year, and that the French and British peoples will stand the strain of a year of inactivity while they have to endure continually increasing privations?' Robertson's opinion was that doing nothing was too risky. Therefore, they must bring as much pressure as possible to bear on the French to keep going, but, if not, they should insist on them taking over more of the front and then dusting off preparations for an attack in Belgium. To go on to the defensive would, in Robertson's cold words, 'look very much like our defeat'.[21]

Lloyd George took up his customary position and argued against any more offensives on the Western Front for the time being. He felt that Pétain's outlook – of a strategic defensive and biding their time until the Americans arrived – should not be dismissed out of hand. Furthermore, if the British attacked alone, they would be faced with the 'great bulk' of the German reserves and might exhaust their own manpower without achieving anything substantial. In any case, the problems with shipping, and the urgent need to float more tonnage, meant that the Prime Minister was seriously considering withdrawing men from the Army to support the shipbuilding industry, which was 'our weakest flank'. Yet, much to Lloyd George's frustration, the Cabinet agreed with their military advisers that inactivity was unacceptable. Should the French authorities not be moved by their appeal to continue the offensive, then the British 'should insist on our entire freedom of action and on the French Army reoccupying the trenches recently taken over by the British forces'. What would happen after that remained unclear. The BEF would attack, but where and how remained an open question.[22]

When Lloyd George travelled to Paris for a meeting of alliance leaders three days later, he ran into the same strategic impasse. Robertson pressed for a continuation of the offensive on the Western Front, albeit aimed at 'wearing down and exhausting the enemy's resistance' rather than trying to break through the line. The French Premier, Alexandre Ribot, concurred with Robertson's views and stated that the French Army would maintain its offensive with its full power. Nevertheless, these operations would not be undertaken as part of a 'strategy of the rupture', but would be 'limited' and intended to produce 'the minimum of loss', while conserving her resources.[23] Nivelle did attend the conference, but he was overshadowed by the presence of Pétain, whose strategic realism would now come to define the French war effort. The breakthrough, if it was ever possible, had now been confined to history.

In Lloyd George's mind then, the situation was wholly unsatisfactory. His legendary persuasive skills, his much-touted Welsh charm, no longer seemed to work. Steering his commanders and Cabinet colleagues away from France had proved far more difficult than he had anticipated and, once again, they had shown themselves irresistibly drawn to the Western Front. Much to his chagrin, his 'Italian venture' never got off the ground; even the Italians were lukewarm towards Lloyd George's overtures. They feared attacking on their own – and hence attracting German reserves – and knew that any loan of heavy guns (which were regularly offered) would only be a temporary measure.[24] At Paris, therefore, Lloyd George had little choice but to execute a tactical retreat. It was agreed to continue attacking 'relentlessly' on the Western Front, but with 'limited objectives, while making the fullest use of our artillery'. The 'time and

place' for these operations 'must be left to the responsible Generals' –
a resolution that the Prime Minister would later come to regret.
Haig, for his part, was delighted. 'Mr Lloyd George made two excellent speeches in which he stated that he had no pretensions to be a
strategist, that he left that to his military advisers, that I as C-in-C of
the British Forces in France, had full power to attack where and when
I thought best.'[25] For now it seemed undeniable: the Welsh 'wizard'
had run out of spells.

Three days before Lloyd George had become Prime Minister, the
Romanian capital of Bucharest fell to troops of the German Ninth
Army. At the Supreme Command in Pless in Silesia, the Chief of the
General Staff, Paul von Hindenburg, heard the news with undis-
guised delight. That evening he finished his report on the military
situation with the words, 'A splendid day.' He stepped outside into
the winter snow to hear church bells pealing out news of the great
victory. 'For a long time I had been thinking of nothing else but the
wonderful achievements of our brave army and hoping that these
feats would bring us nearer to the conclusion of the terrible struggle
and its great sacrifices', he wrote. In less than four months, Romania,
which had declared war on Germany and her allies in August 1916,
had been overrun. When an aide informed him that the remnants of
the Romanian Army were now fleeing northwards towards Russia,
an old rhyme came to mind: '*If anyone wants a disastrous war, then let him
pick a quarrel with the Germans.*'[26]

Hindenburg could be forgiven for his hubris on that winter night,
as news came in of yet another triumph for the Central Powers.
Everywhere their arms were undefeated. The invasion of northern
France may not have reached Paris, but everywhere else, in the east
and in the Balkans, Germany's military might had delivered successive blows against their enemies: Russia, Romania, Serbia and Italy;
carving out a vast new empire in the process. The following evening
OHL hosted a victory celebration in honour of Field Marshal August
von Mackensen, the Army Group commander who had led the campaign. Kaiser Wilhelm II drank his health and toasted the victorious
Army in Romania, whispering to an aide that 'since Mackensen

already possessed every honour a military man could be awarded, the next battle cruiser should be named after him'.[27] That night, after all that had passed, it seemed possible to think that victory was only months away.

Field Marshal Paul von Hindenburg, the 69-year-old Chief of the General Staff of the German Field Army, had been appointed after the downfall of his predecessor, Erich von Falkenhayn, in August 1916. He was assisted by his close friend and ally, Erich Ludendorff, who took the title of First Quartermaster-General (although he was in reality more a Chief of Staff). The relationship between Hindenburg and his chief lieutenant was a kind of 'military marriage', with both men bringing separate, but essential, qualities to their roles. As the Kaiser's son, Crown Prince Wilhelm, once remarked, 'Never have I seen any other two men of such different character furnish the exact complement of one another so as to form one single entity as did these two.' Hindenburg was the unflappable military giant, while Ludendorff was his younger foil, a uniquely gifted and energetic soldier who, it was said, had been Alfred von Schlieffen's favourite pupil at the Berlin *Kriegsakademie* before the war. For the Crown Prince, Ludendorff was the personification 'of steely energy and keenly sharpened intellect . . . a Prussian leader of the traditional glorious type in the best sense of the term'.[28] It was up to these men to ensure that Germany was able, not just to continue the war, but to win it.

Despite the euphoria that swept the German High Command in the aftermath of the fall of Romania, this latest battlefield triumph could not mask the growing strain the war was placing on Germany and her allies, particularly the Dual Monarchy of Austria–Hungary, whose quarrel with Serbia had plunged Europe into war in 1914. War-weariness and growing sectarian antagonism were now threatening the survival of the empire. The Emperor Franz Joseph – the man who had led his country to war – passed away on 21 November 1916, bringing his grandnephew, the 29-year-old Karl, to the throne. Karl had seen for himself Austria's declining military power and lacked the fight of the old emperor. He was convinced that if the war continued it would mean the final and irrevocable destruction of the House of Hapsburg. He tried his best to detach the empire from the suffocating German embrace, sending intermediaries to President Poincaré of France in the spring of 1917, but this only made the German grip tighter than ever.[29] Increasingly Austria–Hungary would find itself, not an equal and valued ally of Imperial Germany, but a vassal state with a gun pointed straight at its head.

The alliance's centre of gravity remained the German Army. It was the powerhouse of the Central Powers; the ultimate guarantor of victory and of Austria–Hungary's continuance in the war. Yet the field army, which had fought so tenaciously throughout the brutal summer of 1916, at Verdun and the Somme, was exhausted. According to the German Official History, there were 'clear signs of reduced resistance' on the Western Front in the closing months of the year. 'The deterioration of the Army – that the enemy was clearly aiming at – had reached a not unperilous degree', which it blamed on the 'quite extraordinarily increased force' of the Allies, particularly the impact of their artillery.[30] Heavy losses had bitten deep into the strength of many divisions, and morale had been battered by the effect of ceaseless, draining combat in the west. The Somme alone had cost the Army up to 500,000 casualties.[31] At the end of September 1916, Army Group Crown Prince Rupprecht issued a situation report warning of the deterioration that 'Somme fighting' was having on the Army. 'It cannot be denied that our infantry is not the same as earlier', it reported. 'After heavy losses, the fought-out divisions are barely refreshed. They are forced to redeploy to another sector immediately without a day of rest.'[32]

In spite of their best instincts, by the winter of 1916–17 both Hindenburg and Ludendorff recognized that during the coming year the German Army in France, the *Westheer*, would be obliged to stand on the defensive. Such a decision was not taken lightly – Hindenburg called it a 'dreadful disappointment' – but nevertheless both commanders felt it was absolutely necessary to adopt a kind of 'strategic stand-to' on the Western Front, while rebuilding their reserves and stockpiling shells and guns through an intensified programme of industrial rearmament.[33] Yet withdrawing from exposed positions and 'combing out' more men from industry could only ever be a temporary solution. While the German Army in the west would stand on the defensive in 1917, it had not given up hope of final victory. At a Crown Council meeting at OHL on 9 January 1917, the German Naval Staff declared that if Germany were to adopt unrestricted submarine warfare, then England could be defeated within 4–6 months. When the Kaiser received a telegram from his attaché in Washington, warning that America would declare war on Germany if she persisted in the sinkings, he was unimpressed, scrawling, 'I do not care!' in the margins.[34]

The decision to go for broke at sea had not been an easy one. Indeed, nothing seemed to divide the Kaiser's military and civilian advisers more than the submarine question. The Imperial Chancellor, Theobald von Bethmann Hollweg, remained the main sceptic of unrestricted sinkings, arguing consistently that such a policy was too risky and was '*the last card*' Germany could play.[35] The Kaiser, as befitted his notoriously fragile personality, was torn: fearful of the ignominy that would fall on his house should his navy sink dozens of passenger liners, yet aware that he must be seen to do whatever was necessary to win the war. When, in the glowing aftermath of the fall of Bucharest, Hindenburg demanded that the question of unrestricted submarine warfare be reopened, the Kaiser agreed. To mollify Bethmann Hollweg, he sanctioned one more effort to make peace (or at least to present Germany's case to the world) and on 12 December the Chancellor issued a note to 'all hostile powers' calling upon them to enter peace negotiations. Recent events have given proof, it stated, of the 'indestructible strength' of Germany and her allies, which also demonstrated 'that a continuation of the war can not break their resisting power'. They did not seek to 'crush or annihilate their enemies', but 'conscious of their military and economic strength' and desirous 'to stem the flood of blood and to bring the horrors of war to an end', the four powers – Germany, Austria–Hungary, Bulgaria and Turkey – now wanted negotiations.[36]

The Allied reaction to these developments was, as might have been expected, resolutely unimpressed. The French President, Aristide Briand, poured cold water on the German note in a speech to the Chamber of Deputies on 13 December. 'It is after proclaiming her victory on every front that Germany, feeling that she can not win, throws out to us certain phrases about which I can not refrain from making a few remarks.' No proposals had yet been made, and while he could not give an official response until her allies had been fully consulted, he wished to warn the chamber 'against this possible poisoning of our country'.[37] While the Allies were careful not to reject Bethmann Hollweg's note out of hand – particularly after President Woodrow Wilson had called on all sides to make their peace terms public – their response (issued on 29 December) was dismissive of the German note. It 'appears less as an offer of peace than as a manoeuvre of war' and there could be no peace until 'the reparation of violated rights and liberties, the acknowledgement of the principle of nationalities and of the free existence of small States' was assured. With that the German note fizzled out.[38]

The failure of the Chancellor's efforts left the way clear for the renewed U-boat campaign, which began on 1 February. Hopes were high that it would fulfil the extravagant aims of the German High Command and coerce Britain into ending the war. Over 570,000 tons of British, Allied and neutral shipping were sunk in March, leaving the Admiralty in London to issue a stark warning that things would probably get worse, particularly as intelligence predicted '*the certainty of an increase, month by month, in the number of hostile submarines*'.[39] The mood at OHL briefly soared at the apparent triumph of the U-boats. Ludendorff was convinced that they only had to keep up the pressure to yield potentially decisive results. Coming at a time when the Central Powers were virtually unopposed in the east, as Russia began her descent into revolution and, eventually, Bolshevism, the spring of 1917 seemed ripe with possibilities. When the Kaiser visited General Headquarters on 30 April, he was, according to an aide, in 'a jubilant mood'. 'He insists that if the English now came forward with peace proposals he would reject them out of hand. They must be made to grovel.'[40]

Yet for all the Kaiser's bluster, final victory would remain elusive. Although Russia would go out of the war later in the year, the U-boat campaign would prove to be an expensive and ineffective mistake. Not only did it finally provoke full-scale US retaliation, but it also failed to smash the British blockade. When Germany announced unrestricted submarine warfare, Admiral Henning von Holtzendorff at the Naval Staff estimated that if they could sink 600,000 tons of shipping every month for five months, then they would 'succeed in breaking England's backbone'.[41] Yet Holtzendorff's memorandum contained 'considerable wishful thinking' that significantly underestimated the robustness of the British economy or the degree to which she could conserve food supplies.[42] In any case, the German U-boat fleet did not have the capability to inflict such a catastrophic defeat upon Britain. Losses peaked at over 540,000 tons of British shipping in April 1917 – with 155 ships sunk – but Germany could never repeat this figure. In the months afterwards the number of sinkings gradually settled down and by July only 240,000 tons of shipping were lost – just seventy ships. While this was still undoubtedly painful, it was nowhere near enough to cripple Britain's ability to continue the war.[43]

Meanwhile, the Western Front remained. During the battles of the spring the German line in France had bent, but not broken. Nevertheless, the strain on the Army had been severe. In just three months, between April and June, it sustained 384,000 casualties, including over 120,000 dead or missing.[44] Although the Allied offensive had largely failed, the effectiveness of the British attack at Arras on 9 April – Ludendorff's birthday – came as a rude shock to the German High Command. Watching events from OHL (now based at Kreuznach in the Rhineland), Hindenburg noted that his reports revealed 'a dark picture. Many shadows – little light.' So shaken was Ludendorff at the loss of Vimy Ridge that Hindenburg had to try and bolster his confidence, slapping his friend on the back and exclaiming:

'We have lived through more critical times than to-day together.'[45]

Ludendorff shrugged. 'A day like April 9 threw all calculations to the winds', he replied.[46]

The Allies may have been repulsed, but heavy fighting throughout April and May only heightened these concerns. Although the German Army was actually bigger than it had been in the autumn of 1916 (by over 600,000 men), the average strength of German battalions on the Western Front had fallen to 713 men (as opposed to 750 prior to the offensives) and there seemed little hope that this would improve drastically in the near future.[47] Worryingly, there were growing concerns that replacements making their way to France were of decreasing quality. Army investigations concluded that the average eighteen-year-old was 'not yet sufficiently developed' to cope with life at the front. Concerns were also being expressed that those recruits from the corners of the empire, from Alsace–Lorraine and the Polish-speaking districts, were unreliable and lacking in 'discipline and soldierly attitude'. Poor food (the bread ration was reduced in April) combined with very limited allowances of leave, and the consequent grumbles about long separation from home and family, prompted OHL to introduce so-called 'patriotic education' in the field. This measure controlled reading material and tried to counteract the decline in the Army's fighting spirit that it feared had been gnawed away by social democratic 'subversion' and the duration and intensity of the war.[48]

The question that Hindenburg and Ludendorff now faced was how could the Army hold its ground against the seemingly inexorable material and economic superiority of Germany's enemies? It was true that the British and French had never really achieved a seismic breakthrough on the Western Front, but the experience of these 'battles of materiel' (what the Germans called the *Materialschlacht*) proved hugely trying. As Allied tactics became more sophisticated, and as the Allies brought greater and greater amounts of artillery on to the battlefield, German losses in her front-line garrisons rose exponentially. Yet it was essential that German troops maintain their positions, to give time for the U-boat campaign to work and for Russia to be finished off. OHL did its best to bolster its divisions, ordering greater quantities of light machine-guns, field guns and howitzers, but it would take months before the whole Army was re-equipped.[49] In the meantime it became evident that tactical changes were required to economize on manpower and counteract the increasingly disadvantageous situation facing the Army.

On 1 December 1916, a new defensive doctrine, 'Conduct of the Defensive Battle', was issued to all German divisions on the Western Front.[50] This document outlined a new approach to defensive fighting that was intended to nullify the advantages in firepower that the Allies now possessed. Ever since the early months of 1915, German troops had become accustomed to holding their front line and immediately counter-attacking whenever a position was lost, but this had proved increasingly costly on the Somme, and the new doctrine confirmed that its purpose was 'to exhaust and drain the attackers while conserving one's own strength'. The defence should be conducted 'mainly through the use of machinery (artillery, mortars, machine-guns etc.)' and higher command should 'not rigidly cling on to territory'. On the contrary, commanders 'should conduct the defensive battle in such a manner that our own troops get the favourable, and attackers the unfavourable, ground'.[51] What this meant in practice was that German troops would not now be tied down to the unconditional holding of front-line positions – and thus waiting to be pummelled by an 'iron rain' of shellfire – but would be deployed much deeper behind the front and occupy mutually supporting positions (rather than trenches), with tactics focusing on the counter-attack.

On 21 January 1917, German units on the Western Front were issued with further instructions on how to counter-attack 'in depth'. Orders advocated the deployment of strong reserves of infantry, usually a collection of battalions, somewhere between three and five miles from the front line, supported by a mobile reserve of artillery. These local reserves – known as *Eingreif* divisions – would be thrown into battle as soon as an enemy attack penetrated the front-line trench system, hoping to capitalize upon the exhaustion and dislocation of any attacking forces. The 'principal difficulty' was launching the counter-attack at the right moment and carefully preparing it so that those units knew exactly what they were doing. The order noted that 'the farther the enemy penetrates into our position, the more favourable becomes the situation for the counter-attack, as the enemy has not had time to consolidate that position and to arrange for and receive ammunition and other supplies'. If the counter-attack was conducted at just the right moment, it could, in theory, dislocate the entire enemy assault.[52] As far as battlefield tactics went, it was nothing short of revolutionary. If and how the Allies could counter this development remained the great tactical conundrum of 1917 – a tussle that would reach its zenith on the Flanders battlefield later that year.

2.

Haig and the 'Northern Operation'

In my opinion the war can only be won here in Flanders.

Sir Douglas Haig[1]

7–31 May 1917

The British had first passed through Flanders, a low-lying, agricultural area of western Belgium, in the autumn of 1914. After the so-called 'Race to the Sea', when the opposing forces had worked northwards after the Battle of the Marne, the British found themselves holding the line at the Flemish town of Ypres. Famous for its wool trade with England, and noticeable for miles around by its thirteenth-century Cloth Hall, Ypres would become an enduring symbol of Allied defiance. By the end of 1914, after furious attacks by the German Fourth and Sixth Armies failed to break through, the British still held the town, although by now it was pockmarked by shellfire and ringed with trenches. In a war when up to a quarter of British dead would have no known grave, around Ypres this figure climbed to a third; an appalling indication of how treacherous, yet vital, this ground was.[2]

The intensity of the fighting around Ypres in 1914 was testament to its strategic importance. The German gas attack of April 1915 (known as the Second Battle of Ypres), which caused panic and blew a hole in the Allied line, only underscored why Britain could not lose this position. It was here where British strategic interests pressed most clearly on the battlefield – she had, after all, gone to war to uphold Belgian independence. Flanders was uncomfortably close to the Channel ports where the bulk of the BEF's supplies were landed and through which their communications to England ran. If the British were ever to be forced from their trenches, then there was very little depth to their position. From the ramparts of Ypres, it was barely sixty miles to Boulogne and even closer to Calais and Dunkirk. A strong German attack might cause the catastrophic collapse of their line, hence the British Government's chronic insecurity about the situation in Flanders. The grim naval situation only added more weight to these considerations. On 23 November 1916 – in the final days of Asquith's premiership – the War Committee of the British Cabinet had stated that there was 'no measure' to which it 'attached greater importance than the expulsion of the enemy from the Belgian coast', primarily because of the submarine bases at Ostend and Zeebrugge.[3] These bases were a permanent menace to the movement of supplies and men across the Channel, and the Admiralty had long been concerned about the sowing of mines across the straits of Dover. The declaration of unrestricted warfare only heightened these concerns.[4]

For Germany, too, Belgium was a key war aim. The Reich had long imagined knitting the Low Countries together into some kind of economic union with the Fatherland and giving up most or all of Belgium was anathema to the German Government. In September 1914, Bethmann Hollweg announced that even if Belgium were allowed to continue to exist, it would be reduced to a 'vassal state' within the German Empire, occupied by German troops and becoming 'economically' a German province. Luxembourg and Holland would also be brought 'into closer relationship' with Berlin.[5] In military terms, it was essential that Germany maintain control of the key rail junction at Roulers and the important U-boat bases along the coast. While there were places on the Western Front the German Army could give up, this was not the case with Belgium. Here the Germans would stand and here they would fight.

There may have been compelling strategic reasons why the British should attack in Flanders, but as a battlefield it could hardly have been less suitable for major offensive operations. 'Water is unquestionably the predominant landscape feature', wrote the historian Peter Barton, 'for after rain it is everywhere held in place on or close to the surface by the geological sub-stratum, a bed of largely impervious clay up to 100 metres in thickness.'[6] Drainage in this area was always difficult and slow, and the landscape was criss-crossed with narrow ditches – known as *bekes* – which were intended to carry the water away, but after heavy rain became, in places, impassable small rivers. The high water table, barely a metre under the surface, also meant that on much of this sector it was impossible to build trenches of the depth and complexity seen on other parts of the line, so recourse had to be made to the construction of breastworks above the surface. While these certainly helped to keep troops out of the water, they were never as sturdy or as protective as deep trenches, and casualties were, on average, always higher in the Flanders sector than they were on other parts of the line.

It was not just the problem of water that helped Ypres to acquire notoriety unlike any other place on the Western Front. Essentially, Ypres was faced with a low range of wooded hills to the south and east, which formed a kind of natural amphitheatre ('like the rim of a saucer', as one veteran put it).[7] This high ground ran from Messines, south of Ypres, and continued up to the northeast around the village of Passchendaele. From this main spur sprang a series of lesser ridges – 'really no more than rises' wrote the official historian – named after the villages that crested them – Bellewaarde and Gheluvelt; Pilckem and Frezenberg; Zonnebeke and Gravenstafel – right up to the Passchendaele Ridge. To the casual observer these heights may not have seemed particularly imposing. They were barely fifty metres above sea level (although parts of the Gheluvelt Plateau reached a dizzying 55–60 metres), but they gave the occupier a definite advantage in a war of position.[8] German troops overran this ground in 1914 and had held it ever since, enjoying the unrestricted view it gave them over the town. This meant that the battered defenders soon found themselves in a salient – a bulge in the line that was overlooked by the enemy on three sides. An unhealthier spot of the Western Front would have been hard to find.

One man who had never forgotten the importance of Flanders was Field Marshal Sir Douglas Haig, the Commander-in-Chief of the BEF. It was Haig's corps, their ranks thinned by heavy casualties, who had halted the Prussian Guard just in front of Ypres in November 1914, Haig himself rallying troops along the shell-swept Menin Road. In just two weeks of bitter fighting, Haig's I Corps had been reduced from 18,000 men to barely 3,000 effectives.[9] And so, three years later, Haig found himself commanding the most powerful army Britain would ever field, nursing a sense of unfinished business. When he had agreed to operate under Nivelle, Haig had arranged with the French commander that should the offensive on the Chemin des Dames fail, then he would 'prepare to launch attacks near Ypres to clear the Belgian coast'; a plan that was approved by the War Cabinet on 14 March.[10] Now that Nivelle had been replaced, Haig was released from his orders to subordinate the BEF to French command and, finally, he was free to dust off plans that had already been maturing some months; his so-called 'northern operation'.

Proposals for some kind of Belgian campaign had been circulating at GHQ since the winter, but no firm agreement had been reached. In November 1916, as the Battle of the Somme was ending, Haig asked General Sir Herbert Plumer, commander of the British Second Army, to look into the matter. Plumer, an old warrior who sported a bushy white moustache, had been in the Salient since the early months of 1915 and had garnered a reputation for the care and attention with which he planned operations.[11] He took about a month to respond and argued that any offensive should comprise three simultaneous assaults: against Hill 29 on the rising ground at Pilckem (north of Ypres); against Hill 60 and Mount Sorrell (on the heights southeast of Ypres); and then against the Messines–Wytschaete Ridge (to the south). Possession of these heights would 'not only improve our position enormously but their capture is an essential prelude to an advance either eastwards or north-eastwards, which will be of great strategic importance'. Nothing more was added and Plumer made no mention of any subsequent operations that would presumably have to take place before a grand offensive along the Belgian coast could be mounted.[12]

Plumer's plans brought him little favour with GHQ. In line with the aggressive direction that General Nivelle wanted to take in the spring, Haig felt that Second Army had not got into the spirit of things and that, typically, Plumer was being too cautious. He tasked his Chief of Staff, Sir Launcelot Kiggell, with writing to Plumer on 6 January to bring his attention to the way in which the Field Marshal wanted things to proceed. Because the French and British attacks (under Nivelle) would have already taken place (and 'the enemy will have been severely handled'), it was to be assumed that most of the German reserves would have been engaged. Therefore, under such circumstances, 'it is essential that the plan should be based on rapid action and entail the breaking through of the enemy's defences on a wide front without delay'. Because Plumer's plans seemed to be based upon 'a sustained and deliberate offensive', GHQ wanted him to resubmit his recommendations for 'inflicting a decisive defeat on the enemy' and freeing the Belgian coast by the end of the month.[13]

At the same time as urging on Plumer, Haig also set up a sub-section of the General Staff at Montreuil (under Lieutenant-Colonel C. N. MacMullen) to work out their own plan of operations. They were reminded that Plumer's proposals for 'a steady, deliberate advance' had already been rejected and that the 'whole essence is to attack with rapidity and push through quickly'.[14] Not content with two plans being drawn up, Haig also approached one of his other army commanders, General Sir Henry Rawlinson, and asked him to look again at the Ypres problem, on the assumption that he would command some element of it – possibly an amphibious landing from the coast that would link up with the main assault. When Rawlinson – who had little familiarity with Flanders – went to Ypres he was unable to agree on army boundaries with Plumer and so was not able to produce a plan, leaving Haig wondering what on earth was going on.

At the end of January, Plumer sent off his amended proposals to GHQ. Although he had been told to push for 'rapid action', Plumer could not be moved from his natural caution about advancing too far. The Messines–Wytschaete Ridge should be taken in three stages, before the 'northern operation' secured the crest of Pilckem Ridge along a six-mile front. Presumably – although this was not made explicit – a series of further advances would then be mounted towards Passchendaele and on to the Belgian coast. While this was fine in itself, Plumer claimed that for this operation he would need over forty divisions and about 5,000 guns – resources that were simply not available. By this time Rawlinson had been able to consider the operation and argued that the attacks on the ridges should not be simultaneous. In other words, given the constraints on the number of guns, they should attack Messines first, and then – within two or three days – mount a further push towards

Pilckem and Gheluvelt. This would allow just enough time to redeploy their artillery to support the attacks on the other ridges.[15]

The problem, as Haig saw it, was that neither Plumer nor Rawlinson seemed able to give him what he wanted. They were too cautious; obsessed with securing the high ground and not placing enough emphasis on rushing forward in a dramatic manoeuvre that would break the line. Belying his reputation as a methodical, somewhat plodding staff officer, Haig was always drawn to decisive offensives and, in this respect, shared much with the ill-fated General Nivelle. In part this was because of what he had learnt at the Staff College at Camberley back in 1896. Battle was, he was told, composed of four distinct elements: manoeuvre, the preparatory or wearing-out stage, the decisive engagement, and then the pursuit – presumably with cavalry.[16] For Haig this process from manoeuvre to pursuit became an article of faith. It was how he planned his battles and how he fought his war: frequently believing that the moment for decisive action had arrived and that he must rise to it.[17] This had been one of the main problems behind the Somme offensive of 1916, when Haig had disregarded the concerns of his army commander (Rawlinson), and urged him to adopt a highly ambitious and, as it proved, disastrous 'all out' attack. Whereas Rawlinson wanted to conduct a more limited operation that would gradually blast its way through the German defences, one trench at a time, Haig overruled him.[18] For Haig the powerful, almost Napoleonic, thrust through an enemy's defences would be the central point of any offensive, and as long as it was pressed with determination and high morale then, surely, his troops would not fail. It was these principles that he took with him on to the battlefields of 1917.

On 7 May, just three days after the Paris conference, Haig held a meeting with his army commanders at Doullens and briefed them on how he saw the campaign proceeding. Now that Nivelle's offensive had been terminated, it was essential to consider what other operations should be conducted for the rest of the year. Haig made it clear that he was now absolutely focused on operations in the north to free the Belgian coast. He had decided that the attack in Flanders would be split into two phases. The first would be the capture of the Messines Ridge on or around 7 June, which would secure the southern flank for any subsequent offensive. Once this had been completed, a second and decisive main attack would go in. This 'northern operation' would attack the high ground east of Ypres, shatter the German defensive position in Flanders, and allow for a major advance, which would take place 'some weeks later'. Meanwhile, operations at Arras would be brought to a halt, while guns and men were gradually sent north, in preparation for what Haig hoped would be the decisive blow.[19]

But who would command the assault? Haig decided to leave Plumer in charge of the preliminary operation at Messines. Second Army knew the ground, and ever since the trenches had solidified in 1915, work had begun on a series of huge mines about 80–120 feet under the German lines. Over the next two years, twenty-five mines were planted, laboriously and at great risk, through a deep layer of blue clay, right under the noses of the German defenders. These would be essential in any assault on such a commanding position, and Plumer was hopeful that they would be highly effective if properly coordinated with artillery and infantry.[20] This was exactly the kind of operation that Plumer excelled at and Haig was happy to let him get on with it. As for Rawlinson, doubts about his competency, his failure to secure a clean breakthrough on the Somme the previous summer, and his penchant for preferring limited attacks to more decisive operations meant that Haig was never entirely convinced of his suitability for the main attack. There was, as he saw it, only one commander left who could possibly mount the kind of breakthrough he desired: Hubert de la Poer Gough, commander of the British Fifth Army, and a man very much in Haig's mould. A week before Haig briefed his army commanders at Doullens, he informed Gough that, following Plumer's attack at Messines, he would command the main 'northern operation' in Flanders. Surely if anyone could break out of the Ypres Salient, it would be Gough.

For Haig, the decisive moment had now arrived. For the first time, the British Army had a chance to seize the initiative and escape from the shadow of her allies, and he was determined to take it. But the idea of mounting such an ambitious series of operations did not meet with universal acceptance. Although Smuts had raised the possibility of an attack in Flanders on 1 May, other senior British politicians looked upon it with considerable unease. Lloyd George later claimed that the

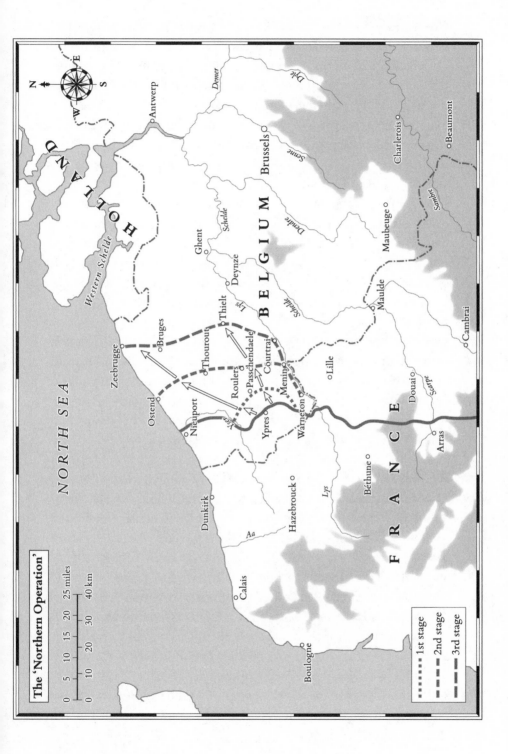

Government could in no way be blamed for what subsequently happened. He had not seen detailed plans until the attack on Messines had already taken place, and, in any case, there was no formal agreement that a major effort should even be made in Flanders. His understanding was that the conference in Paris had merely committed them to maintaining pressure on the Western Front, while reserving the right, at some future point, to reconsider other operations. Therefore Haig's eagerness to get started in Flanders was of his own making and directly against the guidance he received from London.[21]

In truth, the subject of a Belgian offensive had been widely mooted in Whitehall since the close of 1916 and had periodically resurfaced in conversations with GHQ ever since. Work to improve the transportation links between the northern ports and Flanders had even been ordered in December 1916, presumably to support any future offensive in the region. But Lloyd George preferred to look the other way, interpreting the meeting in Paris as being in line with his strategic vision, and assuming that he would always be able to control his generals. The problem was that Haig did not see it this way. From his perspective, the Prime Minister had authorized his commanders to get on with things as they saw fit, and this was exactly what they were doing. Because Haig was not someone who would dawdle or play for time; he was, on the contrary, a man in a hurry.[22]

Lloyd George's interpretation of events may have been questionable, but Haig had an equally tough job persuading his chief allies that his plan was sensible. It had been assumed throughout that the French would play some part in the attack, even if just mounting operations to draw off German reserves (as had been agreed at Paris several days earlier). Yet over the coming weeks this assumption gradually fell away. As outbreaks of mutinies and indiscipline began to spread, rumours reached GHQ that something was very wrong in the French Army. When Haig met Pétain on 18 May, he asked him bluntly:

'Did the French intend to play their full part as promised at the Paris Conference? Could I rely on his whole-hearted co-operation?'

Nodding slowly, the French Commander-in-Chief gave Haig his full assurances that the French would continue to attack. He was planning, he said, four minor operations, including one scheduled to take place at La Malmaison, on the Chemin des Dames, on 10 June. He had also agreed to send six divisions, under General Paul Anthoine, to Flanders to cooperate on the left of Haig's forces.[23]

Pétain did, however, express a murmur of concern. He was afraid that Haig would repeat the mistakes of General Nivelle. The objectives for the 'northern offensive' were too deep, too far into the German line, too ambitious. He suggested that they should be shorter and more limited, although, of course, that was up to the British Commander-in-Chief to decide.[24] It was a warning though: a clear call to rethink some aspects of Haig's plan; to look again at the viability of a major breakthrough and to learn lessons from Nivelle's failure. It was a warning that Haig would have been well advised to heed. But, fossilized in his own certainties, he took no notice of it. He had confidence in his own army, because, after all, his men were improving their effectiveness all the time, as shown in their recent operations at Arras, where British and Dominion forces had supported Nivelle's main thrust with a series of powerful preliminary attacks. Moreover, their morale remained high and they were showing little or no signs of the indiscipline that was eating away at the French. For Haig, Pétain was a pessimist, and pessimists never won wars.

Much of Haig's confidence about what could be achieved for the remainder of the year stemmed from his profound faith in the ability of the men he commanded. By May 1917 the BEF was approaching its peak; it was split into five armies, which held the front from Boesinghe, in Flanders, down to the city of Saint-Quentin, in the rolling hills of Picardy. With over 1.8 million men under arms and supported by an impressive array of weaponry and equipment, it was, by some considerable margin, the most powerful army Britain had ever raised.[25] The original expeditionary force had been manned by long-service regulars – the legendary 'old contemptibles' – who could fire twenty-five aimed rounds per minute and put the fear of God into the German Army at Mons in 1914. Yet three years later, most of them had gone: either killed or invalided home; their ranks thinned on the murderous fields of Ypres and Aubers Ridge, Loos and the Somme.

The loss of most of Britain's regular soldiers meant that the Army of

1917 would be a radically different organization. The ranks of the BEF had initially been bolstered by a combination of territorials and reservists, before the legions of Kitchener's volunteers – those who had joined the colours after the outbreak of war – began deploying to France from the summer of 1915. However, the continuing expansion of the Army, combined with heavy losses at the front, meant that the British Government had to resort to more direct methods to keep up the strength of Britain's forces. On 27 January 1916 the Military Service Act became law. This ordered the conscription of single men between eighteen and forty-one (exempting conscientious objectors or those unfit) and was followed four months later by the second Military Service Act, which extended its provisions to include all men, married or single. Thus, the Army that fought at Third Ypres was closer to being a 'nation in arms' than at almost any point in Britain's history.[26]

Haig's army reflected the nature of the society it came from: solid, dependable, patriotic, but also light-hearted with a self-deprecating sense of humour. Perhaps it was not as effective or as glamorous as other armies, it had a certain stuffiness to it that contemporaries noted, and many of its key positions were still held by old regulars who had never been entirely happy with the rapid expansion of the Army in 1914 and 1915. Yet it was difficult to beat, tenacious and determined in defence, and increasingly effective in attack – and it brought with it the tremendous industrial and economic power of the British Empire, which was then reaching its zenith. Hundreds of thousands of men from the great Dominions of the empire would come to the Western Front during the war: Canadians, Australians, New Zealanders and South Africans; and all would find themselves drawn to the Flanders battlefield in that fateful summer of 1917.

Fighting at Arras continued, fitfully and in gradually worsening conditions, until 17 May, when operations were finally brought to a halt. The battle may have opened with great success on 9 April, but the last operations had a familiar, Somme-like quality with poor ground conditions and murderous trench warfare that consumed divisions at an alarming rate. At Bullecourt, a nondescript and by now ruined village southeast of Arras, two brutal battles were fought as British and Australian troops tried to push forward against sections of the heavily defended Hindenburg Line. In charge of the operation was General Sir Hubert Gough – the man who would make the main assault at Ypres – and Bullecourt would offer his critics further proof, if any were needed, of his aggression and stubbornness. After two weeks of heavy fighting, the village of Bullecourt was evacuated by the enemy, but it hardly felt like a victory. In this one sector alone, the BEF had sustained 14,000 casualties, with the dead lying in clumps on the battlefield.[27]

Gradually, as operations at Arras were shut down, British battalions began their move to Ypres. In the warm spring air, units marched, or were bussed, to their new billets, swapping the undulating uplands of the Somme or the coke-smeared industrial zone of Lens, for the flat, ominous landscape of Flanders. Undoubtedly the Somme could be beautiful at times, particularly in the summer when the air buzzed with skylarks, but Flanders – the 'wet Flanders plain', as the novelist Henry Williamson put it – was always a dreary, shell-plastered wasteland and Ypres, its capital, was always a city of the dead.[28] By 1917 'Wipers', as the British called it (being chronically unable to get the Belgian pronunciation correct), had become a byword for the perils of trench warfare. On other sectors Tommies could look forward to months of 'live and let live', enjoying regular periods of peace and quiet, and perhaps organizing a series of mutually beneficial 'arrangements' with the enemy, but this was never the case at Ypres. Troops coming into the line knew they were entering a perilous place where shelling and sniping were constant dangers – made even worse by the grandstand view the enemy had of all your movements. *'Here "Fritz" was right on top of you.'*[29]

Few soldiers looked forward to going there. Lance Corporal H. S. Taylor, an NCO with the Liverpool Scottish (1/10th King's Liverpool Regiment), remembered coming into Ypres that spring, travelling from Poperinge in a small passenger train that was shunted up in the darkness. The mood among the men was phlegmatic and depressed at the prospect of going into the Salient, knowledge that was evidently too much for one of his platoon – a young private who 'shattered the index finger of his right hand with a bullet from his own rifle' during the journey. From the station they took what would become a familiar rite of passage: marching through the ruins of Ypres before taking their positions at the front. The worst part, according to Taylor, was traversing the large expanse of the Grande Place, feeling 'very exposed' as they sidled past what remained of the Cloth Hall. It was 'an eerie experience for me, and I have no doubt many others', he wrote, 'as it was frequently shelled at night with shrapnel and high explosive. One felt an irresistible urge to hurry into the nearest side street where there might be a little shelter. Shell-holes were endlessly being filled in . . . for the benefit of the night transport.'[30]

While Ypres would remain the focus for the remaining months of the summer and autumn, for the time being the Messines Ridge took centre stage. Plumer's attack would illustrate many of the developments that were transforming the BEF's way of war. As had been seen on 9 April, the British were rapidly evolving a tactical system that could break into almost any position on the Western Front, and do so at an acceptable cost. The problem was that infantry on their own could not cross no-man's-land – that blasted wasteland between the opposing sides – without exposing themselves to heavy gunfire, from rifles and machine-guns, that could shatter the cohesion of the attacking waves. They were also extremely vulnerable to pre-planned enemy barrages that were zeroed in on no-man's-land and came down within minutes of an assault, thus preventing any supports or reserves from coming up. Even if they were able to close with the enemy trenches, the attacking waves would then run into rows of barbed wire that funnelled them into killing zones or stopped their progress dead. The battles of 1915–16, the barren years of suffering and trial and error, were littered with episodes that made survivors shudder: of rows of corpses in no-man's-land; of entire companies 'hanging on the barbed wire'; of great hopes lying shattered in the mud.

Artillery fire seemed to offer the obvious solution to the dilemma of trench warfare. If enough shellfire was concentrated on the right target, then it could cut barbed wire, neutralize the defending garrison (at least temporarily), and destroy enemy batteries. The problem, however, lay in the detail: in getting the artillery to hit the correct target at the right time (and with a suitable weight of shellfire). In earlier years, British guns had simply not been up to the job. They were frequently inaccurate. Their shells were often unstable, meaning that a considerable proportion failed to explode (perhaps as many as a third on the Somme).[31] Even the type of shell mattered as tests showed that shrapnel – the most widely available munition – was frequently ineffective against thick wire entanglements, with many units preferring high explosive (which was only available in limited quantities). In addition, it was always difficult to locate enemy gun batteries. They moved regularly and were usually hidden behind ridges or woods and, in any case, offered only a very small target.

The solution to all of this took years to develop and perfect. After the 'shells scandal' of 1915 – when shortages of vital munitions had caused a grave political crisis – a Ministry of Munitions had been formed that was instrumental in energizing British industrial production. Although it took some time for new factories to be built and become operational, by 1917 the effects of this revolution were being felt. The BEF now had access to many more guns (including the vital 'heavies') and shells were being produced in almost unlimited quantities (and were generally much more reliable). Pioneering efforts were also being made to locate enemy batteries through the techniques of 'sound ranging' and 'flash spotting'. Essentially, this entailed recording the sound waves of passing shells through a series of microphones, and then working out where they came from. Observers were also tasked with watching out for the muzzle flash of enemy guns and locating their position through a process of triangulation.[32] Moreover, by the time the British fought at Arras, there had been a 'huge increase' in the technical skills of the Royal Artillery. Gunnery officers were now making much more effort to fire accurately, by taking measurements of the wind and air pressure, and the effects of shell weight and propellant, and then adjusting the range and bearing accordingly. This was a long way from the approach of 1914, which had been based on guesswork: open fire, see where the shell landed, and then adjust.[33]

Yet being able to deluge targets with sustained and accurate shell-fire was only one element of the Army's increasingly combined approach. The Royal Flying Corps took on a growing role in artillery spotting and 'contact patrols' throughout the war. Aircraft ranged over the lines photographing or bombing targets and attacking enemy aircraft. But this was never easy. In the spring of 1917 the

RFC had faced its toughest test in the skies above Arras. In what become known as 'Bloody April', the British struggled to deal with superior German aircraft (such as the Albatros D.I, D.II and D.III) that were faster and able to outclimb their machines. Organized into *Jastas*, and led by elite pilots such as Baron Manfred von Richthofen, the German air force enjoyed a period of remarkable success.[34] In April alone, 275 British aircraft were shot down, causing the death of over 200 pilots and observers. It was even estimated that many of those who died had barely 100 hours' flying time before they came under the guns of Germany's elite fighter squadrons.[35]

The answer to the 'Red Baron' and his ilk was, as with the artillery, partly technological, partly tactical. The RFC had to get on with the job of supporting the ground forces as best it could while waiting, impatiently, for a new generation of aircraft to roll out of the factories. By early summer, however, things were beginning to turn in their favour. New aircraft, including the SE5 and Sopwith Camel, were arriving in France in significant numbers and helped the British re-establish their edge in the air. The SE5 was first introduced to the elite 56 Squadron in April 1917 and, although initially experiencing some teething problems, it went on to become one of the most famous aircraft of the war: fast, able to climb quickly and safely, and a match for all German fighters. Captain James McCudden, a pilot with 56 Squadron, called the SE5 'a most efficient fighting machine, far and away superior to the enemy machines of the period', which was also 'almost warm, comfortable [and] an easy machine to fly'.[36] Together with the Sopwith Camel, which would become the most successful Allied fighter of the war, the British had the aircraft to secure control of the air above the Western Front by the summer of 1917.[37]

Artillery and aircraft were not the only weapons transforming the nature of war. Eight months earlier, in the charnel house of the Somme, Britain had pioneered the use of armoured vehicles, known as tanks. By the time of Messines, the original Mark I had undergone considerable modification, and the latest variant, the Mark IV, was now arriving in France. It was a considerable improvement on its predecessor, with thicker armour (to protect against German armour-piercing bullets) and better internal mechanics (an armoured petrol tank and a more reliable fuel delivery system) that resulted in improved performance on the battlefield and prompted, in the German Army, a growing scramble for adequate counter-measures. Although the tank clearly remained a weapon of the future, and mechanical reliability was always an enduring challenge, it was another indication of just how hard the British were working to break the trench deadlock.[38]

In all this, the infantry – the lone man among the chaos – was not forgotten. Platoons were now being equipped with a variety of weapons that would enable them to fight their own way forward if necessary. As well as the rifle and bayonet, British soldiers now had access to the Mills bomb (a reliable time-fused grenade); rifle grenades (which attached to a special cup fitted to the muzzle of a rifle); the Lewis gun (a semi-portable light machine-gun); and, from March 1917, the 3-inch Stokes mortar (which provided a short-range deluge of fire, either high-explosive or smoke). With these weapons it was now much easier for British infantry to take on German strongpoints or deal with counter-attacks. When combined with new tactics that emphasized 'fire and movement', with flank attacks and infiltration being employed to help them get across that 'fire swept' zone, British infantry now had a much better chance of surviving on the battlefield than they had the previous year.[39]

Despite the tactical and technological sophistication with which the BEF now approached battle, considerable hurdles still remained to be cleared. Breaking into an enemy position could be achieved with a degree of certainty (particularly when compared with a year earlier), but serious questions were being asked about how far troops should go, and whether any large-scale breakthrough could ever be achieved. With the failure of Nivelle's offensive, Pétain realigned the French Army towards the worship of heavy shellfire and slow, sure advances (so-called 'Pétain tactics'), but the British never came to such a clear epiphany. Haig, for one, was never entirely happy with the French Commander-in-Chief and was always convinced that a breakthrough could be achieved, even if growing numbers of his subordinates, including numerous senior corps and army commanders, were much less sanguine about the prospects for such a climactic attack. This friction between limited and unlimited attacks would run through the entire history of the BEF on the Western Front.[40]

Sir Henry Rawlinson, Fourth Army commander (and the man whom Haig had put in charge of a possible amphibious landing), was the leading advocate of so-called 'bite-and-hold' attacks. Echoing Pétain's conclusions about renouncing large-scale offensives aiming to drive deep into the German line, Rawlinson felt the Army should fight in an avowedly attritional manner. Utilizing as much firepower as possible, they should conduct limited, 'step-by-step' operations to seize local points of tactical importance, ideally on high ground. Once these had been 'bitten off', the enemy would be compelled to counter-attack at a disadvantage, allowing the British to bring their artillery to bear and cause the enemy heavy losses. As early as 8 February 1915, Rawlinson had written that 'If the Germans are to be defeated they must be beaten by a process of slow attrition, by a slow and gradual advance on our part, each step being prepared by a predominant artillery fire and great expenditure of ammunition.'[41] Although at that time the amount of firepower required was simply not available, as an operational concept it was a revelation. The only problem was that Haig remained unconvinced. For him, 'bite and hold' could be no more than a temporary, limited response to conditions in the field. The breakthrough and the decisive offensive would always remain an article of faith and the essence of campaigning.

Notwithstanding Haig's natural aversion to 'bite and hold', the opening of the Arras offensive began with a series of well-planned, limited attacks. Because of the nature of the ground, and the absolute necessity of securing the Messines Ridge, Plumer would be allowed to do the same: to concentrate his combat power on a clear, definitive objective without going for an 'all-out' success.[42] At Messines, the infantry and artillery would be coordinated into a set-piece attack that was timed to perfection. Firstly, Plumer's mines would be blown, hopefully fatally weakening the German defence and allowing the infantry to seize their objectives. In the weeks preceding the attack, they were specially trained for the assault. Plumer wanted every man to know as much about his objectives as possible, so large-scale models and training grounds were constructed that allowed the troops of each battalion to familiarize themselves with their objectives and conduct exercises over them. Even if their officers became casualties, through the smoke and fire, the British soldier should still know what to do.[43]

The attacking infantry would be supported by one of the most elaborate displays of firepower in the history of war. An eleven-day bombardment would soften up the defences along 17,000 yards of front, with Plumer's guns eventually hurling a total of 3.5 million shells into the German positions. Following the explosion of the mines, all of Second Army's artillery – over 2,000 barrels – would open fire simultaneously at Zero Hour, forming three lines of barrage fire that would obliterate what was left of the German front line. At the same time, heavier batteries would deluge all known enemy gun positions with concentrated shellfire, aiming to prevent any possible retaliation. As if that were not enough, Plumer also managed to get his hands on seventy-two Mark IV tanks, which would be parcelled out across the front and used against specially selected strongpoints, where their thick armour and 6-pounder guns would prove very useful should the advance be held up. As far as preparations went, it was remarkably impressive. Plumer – more than any other British commander on the Western Front – vowed to leave nothing to chance.[44]

Time was now of the utmost importance. Nivelle's operation had backfired spectacularly, but there were still enough months in the remainder of the campaigning season for one more major effort. Morale in Second Army headquarters at Cassel was excellent. Haig visited Plumer on 22 May and found him 'in very good spirits now that his Second Army occupies the first place in our thoughts!'[45] According to Plumer's Chief of Staff, Tim Harington, when they received the go-ahead from GHQ, they became 'full of hope'. 'The Second Army had its chance at last. We were going to be tried out. It was a wonderful month. Everything we wanted we were given.'[46] As they were speaking, the final elements of Plumer's plan were clicking into place: the artillery bombardment had already begun softening up the enemy defences, while the assault troops were going over their final deployment orders. In the half-light of dawn on 7 June, the attack on Messines Ridge began. It would be the first part of Haig's long-awaited Flanders campaign.

3.

'A Great Sea of Flames'

A simple calculation of blood, iron and square kilometres.

Werner Beumelburg[1]

1–20 June 1917

Shortly before three o'clock on the morning of 7 June, General Sir Herbert Plumer knelt by his bedside to pray. His staff had marched up to Cassel Hill, a short walk from their headquarters, to watch the mines being blown, but Plumer – a portly gentleman who had spent a lifetime soldiering – could not bring himself to join them. At that moment his thoughts were with his men in their trenches as they waited silently and anxiously for the moment to go. He was confident that the attack had been prepared as well as possible, but still needed some time for silent reflection. As Tim Harington later noted, Plumer was 'a wonderful study in human nature. He treated the whole Army as a family', putting all his success down to three fundamentals: trust, training and thoroughness. By the time it got light it was evident that the battle had gone well. News arrived that the first and second objectives had been captured.[2]

Zero Hour was timed for 3.10 a.m. Captain Robert Cuthbert Grieve, commanding 'A' Company of 37/Battalion (3rd Australian Division), would never forget the exhilarating, yet deeply frightening moment when the mines were blown, as if some unholy, primeval force had been unleashed from deep within the planet:

Then the whole earth was shaken by the effect of the mines. The trenches rocked and trembled and I fully expected that they would cave in – the whole surroundings right along the battle front were weirdly lit up by the flash from them. The largest mine on the front was close to us – containing 20 tons of gun cotton – so I will endeavour to describe the effect of this one. All were on the tip-toe of expectation for this one to be sprung. Our first warning that she was fired was by sounds like distant rumblings of thunder – then gradually getting closer – then directly to our front the earth was seen to be rising like a huge mushroom – suddenly to be flung into space with an awe-inspiring roar and the earth trembled – to me it appeared as if with mingled fear and relief – fear of the dread power she had stored in her bowels – relief because it had vented its fury and although she was sadly torn, its menace gone.[3]

The mine blew a crater 300 feet wide and almost 100 feet deep, and as debris rained down, Grieve's company went forward 'like ants as they swarmed up the face of the hill'.

In total, 80,000 men from three corps would make the assault: X Corps striking southeast against the northern shoulder of the ridge; IX Corps due east towards the village of Wytschaete; and II ANZAC Corps towards Messines on the southern edge. In the opening phases enemy resistance was light. A few scattered machine-guns rang out, but most of the enemy garrison had been either killed or stunned into submission by the violence of the onslaught. Although in places smoke, mist and clouds of gas reduced visibility and caused some dislocation, the attackers were able to seize the German front and support trenches without heavy loss. As the war diary of II ANZAC Corps noted: 'The attack up to this point has proceeded with machine like precision. The creeping barrage of the artillery was preceded by a similar machine-gun barrage from 144 machine-guns . . . The combination of the two swept away the majority of the enemy opposition and enabled the infantry to capture their successive objectives at the time laid down.' Enemy artillery fire was, on the contrary, 'ragged and ill-directed'.[4]

The battle may have seemed to run like clockwork to signallers and commanders in the rear, but at the front the experience of taking the ridge could be wildly disorientating. 'Our trench rocked like a ship in a strong sea and it seemed as if the very earth had been rent asunder', remembered Albert Johnson of 11/Royal West Kents (41st Division). 'What passed in that journey across "no mans land" was only a passing vision of moving figures intent on gaining their object-ive, pausing only for a breather in a shell hole for the vicinity was as if an earthquake had passed over it so great had been the havoc wrought by our splendid artillery.'[5] When Walter Guinness, Brigade Major of 74 Brigade (25th Division), went forward to try and find out where the attacking battalions were, he was forced to rely on a com-pass bearing because 'the whole ground was changed'. 'Trees and hedges, reduced to poles and sticks before, had now nearly dis-appeared, and the ground was like giant pumice stone, huge pits and craters up to ten feet deep. Streams of wounded walking back and a certain number of bewildered men wandering about not knowing where they were.'[6]

Despite the ruin of the German defences on the ridge, the day was not without its disappointments. Because British and Dominion casualties had been much lighter than expected in the initial assault, by mid-morning large numbers of troops began to mass on the ridge-line, offering tempting targets for enemy observers watching from their rear positions. Soon hostile artillery fire, as well as long-range machine-guns, began to play on the newly won positions, forcing the British and Anzac troops to take cover wherever they could.[7] While this was unfortunate, the German Army showed little appetite to retake the ridge. German defensive doctrine, which emphasized a series of swift and decisive counter-attacks, should have been applied vigorously before the British could consolidate their gains. However, because of tactical confusion and unrealistic assumptions about how long the German defences could be expected to hold in any attack, the *Eingreif* divisions were deployed too far back to make a decisive impact. When a few battalions did begin to approach the ridge later that day, heavy machine-guns and shellfire swiftly repulsed them.[8]

By the evening of 7 June, Plumer's corps had a firm hold on the Messines Ridge. Although fighting would continue for another week, and crowding on the crest meant that casualties had risen more than they otherwise would have done, the capture of Messines Ridge was a remarkable achievement – perhaps the finest example of a 'bite-and-hold' operation ever conducted – proving that, under the right conditions, the BEF could secure even the most heavily defended locations. A Second Army Intelligence Summary proclaimed that the ridge gave the German defenders 'complete observation' over the Ypres Salient from where they could overlook all the preparations for the attack. 'The battle, therefore, was a gauge of the ability of German troops to stop our advance under conditions as favourable to them as an army can ever hope for, with every advantage of ground and preparation.' Yet the ridge had fallen, and with it over 7,000 prisoners and 200 machine-guns.[9] The anchor of the German defence in Flanders was now in their hands.

The full horror of what happened to the German Army on 7 June 1917 has often not been fully realized. The few surviving accounts convey only a hazy impression of the murderous events that followed the explosion of Plumer's mines. At Zero Hour, Lieutenant Eugen Reitinger of 17 Bavarian Infantry Regiment was in a concrete block-house just north of Messines when he heard 'an almighty roar' go up from the front line. Swiftly evacuating his position, he struggled outside to see a vision of Hell. The ridge was 'enveloped in a great sea of flames' with 'fiery volcanoes and masses of earth' erupting vertically into the sky 'colouring it a blood red'. As tons of earth and rubble began to rain down, Reitinger came under heavy artillery bombardment, which scattered his unit. Shortly afterwards a runner, ragged and out of breath, came in from the front lines. He reported that III Battalion had been 'blown sky high'. The defenders on this part of the front had largely ceased to exist.[10]

The explosion of nineteen enormous mines – some containing up to 95,000 pounds of ammonal – under the Messines Ridge shocked even hardened observers.[11] 'The moral effect of the explosions was simply staggering', wrote Ludendorff, 'at several points our troops fell back before the onslaught of the enemy infantry. Powerful artillery fire penetrating the Wytschaete Salient hindered effective intervention by our reserves and the recovery of the position.'[12] Years later veterans would still recall the shock of the mines going off in a flaming arc of destruction that crowned the ridge in plumes of choking smoke and dust. When the German Army Group commander Crown Prince Rupprecht saw the battlefield he was appalled by what faced him: 'All around Messines', he noted sadly, 'the ground was said to have been covered by the bodies of Bavarian soldiers.'[13] German casualties were over 23,000, most being sustained in the initial explosive earthquake that blew their positions sky high.[14]

For German commanders in Flanders, there was a palpable sense of shock. Although their men – those who had not been vaporized in the explosions – fought with determination, they could not prevent the ridge from falling within five hours and giving General Plumer a signal victory. Albrecht von Thaer, Chief of Staff to XIX Saxon Corps, heard the mines go off while at Douai and thought it must have been an accident, perhaps a munitions depot catching fire. When he was told the news, he was appalled:

> Nineteen craters are said to have appeared within a second, right next to one another that were so big and deep that a five-storey block of flats would have fitted inside each one. Whatever living things had been alive there were dead in the moment of this terrible explosion. The English rushed straight ahead after this to the offensive and made a good deal of ground because the defenders had, of course, been wiped out.

When Thaer was summoned to Fourth Army headquarters at Courtrai four days later, he found an atmosphere bordering on panic. Major Stapff, Chief of Staff at Sixth Army, usually 'a reliable and intelligent man', was now 'quite agitated and nervous, and also uncertain about what he should do towards OHL concerning requirements for new troops and new material which, as is well known, one never gets by oneself but always needs to fight for'.[15]

Fortunately for the German Army, the BEF was not in any position to follow up the Messines operation with another major attack. By 14 June Plumer's forces had consolidated their positions and chased off the evacuating German divisions, but had gone little further. Haig's decision to opt for a new commander to lead the second stage of the operation meant that there would be no rapid breakout. For the dazed German commanders, the failure of the British to properly exploit the shock of Messines was curious. At his headquarters in Courtrai, Crown Prince Rupprecht fully expected the operations on 7 June to mark the start of a major British push around Ypres, particularly against the Tower Hamlets Ridge, one mile to the west of the village of Gheluvelt. Had this high ground been attacked, the British would have had excellent observation over the entire sector north of the Menin Road, which would have made German movements increasingly difficult.[16] On 12 June, he confided to his diary that a further British offensive was 'certain': it would be aimed at freeing the Belgian coast, probably with a landing from the sea. But, much to Rupprecht's relief, nothing happened, which gave the Germans a priceless opportunity to bring reinforcements into the line.[17]

Despite the carnage at Messines, the Ypres Salient had not yet acquired a particularly dark reputation among German soldiers (unlike their wearied enemy). On the contrary, many of those who travelled to Flanders did so with a sense of relief, at least when compared to the other destinations they could have been deployed to: Verdun, the Somme or Artois. Johann Schärdel travelled with his unit (6th Bavarian Reserve Division) to Becelaere, southeast of Zonnebeke, and was favourably impressed with their new surroundings:

We came from the fighting of the Battle of Arras, which was already drawing to a close when we were deployed but whose final attacks we yet had to await and survive. Now we were lying a long way behind the front line as an army reserve in the beautiful, green Flanders, in this beautiful country with its clean towns and friendly people, its countless shady copses, its pleasant landscape of alternating fields and meadows, its scattered farms, its wide and cobbled roads that ran straight with endless avenues of cottonwood poplars through the countryside, all the way to the horizon. Such a peaceful picture, the tranquillity of which was heightened further by the still waters of the canals and the peaceful turning of the sails of the wind mills, so that one could have nearly forgotten the enormity of war, if one didn't have to practise 'warcraft' every day, and if the thunder and roar of the front wasn't booming across the distance, always warning and threatening.[18]

Schärdel's men enjoyed themselves in a landscape they felt was much friendlier than their previous tour in French Artois. Flowers bloomed in the windows; the Flemish language sounded happily familiar to German; and trips to Ghent allowed his men to drink beer in the *estaminets* and pick up 'loose women' in the side streets.

Others were equally pleased at being sent to this corner of the Western Front. 'From our observation point, we see the old town of Ypres directly ahead', wrote Reinhard Lewald, whose battery was deployed northeast of Gheluvelt. 'We find a nice dry meadow and pitch our tents. With the beautiful weather, life is glorious', he recorded. 'The constant fighting is very lively here. The English have taken our front positions after extensive blasting.' Lewald's main task was to disrupt or destroy the enemy gun batteries that were beginning to crowd into the Salient. Every day they would fire around 100 shells, assisted by aircraft observation and balloon reports, and had 'good success' with the regular blowing-up of the ammunition dumps that dotted the landscape. Everyone expected a major attack to come soon.[19]

By June 1917 the balance of forces on the Western Front was delicately poised, without significant advantage to either side. Combined, the British and French Armies could muster 175 divisions (including small Belgian and Portuguese contingents), while the German Army in the west totalled 156 divisions (with another eighty in the east). In reality, the numerical advantage possessed by the Allies was probably greater than a mere nineteen divisions on paper. British divisions (sixty-two in total) were considerably stronger than their German equivalents (by around a third), and could count on an almost unlimited amount of ammunition, more machine-guns and significantly better food. In artillery the Allies possessed still further superiority, with over 7,300 guns opposed to 4,800.[20] Nevertheless, whatever advantages the Allies possessed in men and guns was more than countered by the inherent professionalism and coherency of the German Army, and the natural strength of its defensive position across the Western Front.

In Flanders, the Germans could boast a formidable series of defensive lines that ruled out any prospect of a swift Allied breakthrough.

As the northern extension of the famed Hindenburg Line, three so-called 'Flanders Lines' had been constructed in the winter of 1916–17. Beginning at the outskirts of Lille and continuing through Flanders up to the coast between Ostend and Middelkerke, the Flanders Lines provided a firm foundation for any defensive campaign in this sector. Although they had not been fully completed – the rearmost line, Flanders III, had only just been surveyed – the Germans judged (correctly) that should the Allies attack, they would have enough time to strengthen it before it was breached. Nevertheless, the German High Command realized that if their armies were to retreat even a relatively short distance on this sector, it would be much more difficult, if not impossible, to hold on to the Belgian ports and the key railway junction at Roulers. Therefore, following the strike at Messines, the German defences needed to be bolstered at all costs.

By June, the ground between Flanders I (which ran from the high ground in front of Passchendaele, along to Broodseinde and down to Gheluvelt) and the British front line was rapidly being converted into a further series of defensive zones, thickly forested with concrete gun emplacements and battery positions. As well as the main defences opposite the British trenches, a second line had been dug (the Albrecht Line), and a third went from Zandvoorde up to Zonnebeke and beyond (the Wilhelm position). Each one was a fortified zone between 2,000 and 3,000 yards deep, with the front line being held by relatively few troops, and reserves echeloned in depth and out of range of most British guns.[21] One witness noted how they were 'in some places concreted trenches, elsewhere strongly revetted with high hurdlework held in position by strong timbers or stakes firmly driven into the ground'. The machine-gun emplacements were all made of reinforced concrete shaped into pillboxes. In places small tramways had been built right up to the front line, which offered an invaluable method of bringing up supplies.[22]

The plan, as it had been drawn up by OHL, was to conduct the defensive battle according to the principles that had been proven during the spring. 'An opponent who has advanced over the weakly occupied front line should use up his strength on the opposition which gets stronger after the front-line trenches have been taken, and is then thrown back again by troops who have been held ready behind it.' Furthermore:

> With the enemy's great superiority in numbers, particularly in artillery, you have to expect loss of ground. To restrict it to a minimum, however, was especially necessary as the distance to the Belgian ports was only slight. There was, therefore, diligent work carried out on the extension of rear emplacements, as well as on the construction of defensive walls between the emplacements, even if with limited manpower, in order to prevent the lateral exploitation of any breakthroughs. A new operational emplacement system was explored to the rear of the fortified zones, which were already in existence or under construction.[23]

At OHL, Ludendorff knew they needed more than new defences; they needed someone who could pull it all together. He ordered Colonel Friedrich Karl 'Fritz' von Lossberg (then serving with the Sixth Army) to report immediately to General Sixt von Armin's Fourth Army, which held the front in Flanders. Lossberg had long been known as a tactical expert in defensive warfare in the German Army and was often sent, like a travelling salesman, to units which the High Command felt would benefit from his advice.[24] On the morning of 13 June, Lossberg drove to Fourth Army Headquarters and met his new commanding officer. As a corps commander on the Somme, Armin had 'acquitted himself splendidly as a superior leader', and he immediately welcomed Lossberg to his headquarters. He was convinced that the British and French were both preparing 'a mighty full-scale attack' against his army and there was much to do.[25]

Fourth Army was split into five groups (essentially equivalent to a British corps), which were named after their respective sectors: Lille; Wytschaete; Ypres; Dixmude; and Nord.[26] The most important zones were in the central section of the line around the Salient: Groups Wytschaete and Ypres. Here von Armin could rely on seasoned troops and experienced subordinates. Commanded by Major-General Karl Dieffenbach – a long-serving Rhinelander who had spent most of the war on the Eastern Front – Group Wytschaete held the front from Warneton to Bellewaarde Lake and was built around IX Reserve Corps, with five divisions in the front line. To the north was Group Ypres, commanded by Major-General Freiherr von Stein, a gifted artillery officer who had entered the Bavarian Army in 1879. His three front-line divisions were part of III Bavarian Corps and were dug in all the way to the village of Langemarck. Behind them lay five counter-attacking divisions – essential if the defence-in-depth plan was to work.[27]

After a long talk with von Armin, Lossberg (who was now acting as his Chief of Staff) contacted OHL and requested a reinforcement of operational staff, who were in short supply. These men would be needed to manage the coming battle – a request that Ludendorff soon granted. Lossberg then drove out to the front and met a number of senior officers in the line, including most of the divisional commanders in Fourth Army. He had last been to Flanders in the autumn of 1914 and immediately began reacquainting himself with this sector. Kneeling down by the side of the road, he examined the soil, the mixture of sand and clay breaking apart in his hands. Lossberg knew how important the ground would be in the coming battle:

> The Flemish soil consists of a very soft and fertile humus layer, which reaches as far as 1 to 3 metres below the earth's surface. Under the deep layer of soil lies an impermeable layer of clay of around a metre thick. If this is broken up by the effect of the artillery, then the groundwater wells up and fills the shell holes up to the top with water. Almost all the emplacements that have been built here had to be mounted on the humus layer, and thus were easily recognizable for the enemy. With continuing dry weather, the topsoil becomes very hard. Then the attacker finds favourable conditions. In heavy rain, which often occurs in Flanders, the humus layer changes into a swamp-like pulp. Then the defender has the advantage.[28]

Lossberg spent most of the night working out the number of divisions and guns he would need to hold the front, requests that OHL was able to grant without difficulty. Despite the urgent requirements that needed to be taken in hand, he was confident the German position would hold.

There is little doubt that Lossberg's arrival galvanized the German defence in Flanders. Albrecht von Thaer, for one, was delighted. He was absolutely certain that a 'decisive battle' was now imminent in Flanders and that something needed to be done to reorganize the German defence. Despite 'never-ending work', he was pleased that Lossberg was now in place. 'The fact that Lossberg is our chief really is a blessing for the situation as I see it', he felt. 'He really is a devil of a brave man, a first-class worker. Everyone trusts him. He impresses the commanding generals and from the Supreme Command he gets what is required in terms of troops, artillery and munitions.'[29] Thaer found himself being transferred from the Saxon Corps to IX Reserve Corps, which held the front southeast of Ypres. In any coming offensive, this ground would be of the greatest importance.

At his headquarters in Courtrai, Lossberg lost no time in getting ready. He demanded an improvement in his communications network and made sure that all his artillery brigades and aerodromes were linked up to the higher command posts and plugged into his small office. 'This network covered thousands of kilometres', he boasted. 'Its existence had truly proved its worth in the Battle of Flanders. From my desk, I could speak to all field commanders, divisions, artillery brigades and aerodromes at the same time by plugging the lines together. The individual departments of the army staff were always connected in such conversations, listening in, and then acting according to my orders, which I had discussed in advance with the Supreme Commander of the Army.' With every day that passed, Lossberg – a man who buzzed with urgency and energy – was given more time to complete his arrangements: like a chess player lining up his pieces for the perfect defence.

General Sir Hubert Gough's headquarters moved up to the front on 1 June. He occupied the chateau at La Lovie, a few miles north of Poperinge, where he would remain for the duration of the battle. Neither Gough nor his staff were particularly fond of their new home. It was 'an ugly red building' only redeemed by the large gardens where a forest of tents and Nissen huts were erected for the growing Fifth Army staff. Unfortunately, there was a large pond in the grounds, which would have been a perfect aiming point for

German bombers had the chateau been targeted with any determination.[30] Soon after their arrival, rumours began circulating that the residents (a Belgian count and his family) were secretly in touch with the enemy, which explained why the house was never hit (in a landscape almost entirely flattened by shellfire). According to Gough, 'I do not believe there was a word of truth in these stories, though it remained a mystery to me why and how the chateau escaped destruction.'[31]

Sir Hubert Gough was a 46-year-old cavalryman whose family had one of the most illustrious pedigrees in the British Army: his father, uncle and brother had all won the Victoria Cross.[32] Gough was, by some considerable margin, the youngest army commander in the BEF, and had enjoyed an impressive rise since the outbreak of war. A deeply self-confident man who could, in turns, be witty and charming or petty and vindictive, Gough was, sadly, a limited soldier. He had suffered the curse of over-promotion and by the summer of 1917 Fifth Army had acquired an unhealthy – if not entirely undeserved – reputation for the carelessness with which it prepared attacks, which was often contrasted with the detailed care and attention that Plumer's Second Army took with its operations. Nevertheless, Gough's instinctive aggression and his reputation as a 'thruster' meant that Haig looked kindly upon him.

The decision to give command of the main attack to Gough has long been regarded as one of Haig's cardinal mistakes.[33] It was not that Gough was an incompetent officer; he was, on the contrary, a hard-fighting soldier who had earned plaudits for his handling of the attack on the Ancre in November 1916. The problem was that Gough lacked the in-depth knowledge of the ground (as compared to Plumer) and never convinced subordinates that he had the necessary touch to command such a large operation. Moreover, Gough suffered from 'an incomplete grasp of the realities of battle' and cultivated a 'climate of fear' among his subordinates.[34] His performance at Bullecourt had further heightened concerns that he was not up to the job. Australian troops, who had been thrown into the battle and suffered severely, always regarded Gough with suspicion afterwards. Charles Bean, the Australian official historian, criticized the Fifth Army commander for his 'almost boyish eagerness to deliver a death blow' to the German Army at Bullecourt. 'He attempted a deep penetration on a narrow front', thus breaking 'at every stage through [*sic*] rules recognised even by platoon commanders'.[35] It would have to be seen how Gough would approach the much more formidable task in front of him at Ypres.

Gough did his best. He was out every day, usually spending up to twelve hours away from La Lovie roaming the lines. On horseback he would visit the units that comprised Fifth Army: engineers or gunners, infantry or signallers, and impress upon the officers the importance of working together. 'If you do that, you'll learn how to help one another when the battle begins' was a remark he often repeated.[36] Gough was usually accompanied by his Chief of Staff, Neill Malcolm, and together they angled for a better view of the battlefield. Unfortunately, most of the German positions lay on the reverse slope of the ridgelines, meaning that they were invisible from the British sector. Binoculars in hand they trotted up and down the front working out how they could seize the high ground, while feeding in the intelligence reports they received every day. Fifth Army's orders were to secure the Passchendaele Ridge and the crucial Roulers–Torhout railway line, thus facilitating an amphibious assault at Ostend, which would allow for the 'possession of the Belgian coast'.[37] But how was this to be achieved? For Haig the attack would be a decisive one: a smashing blow that would unhinge the German right flank, secure the coast, and perhaps even prompt a general advance all across the line. While Gough understood this, he recognized that such an objective could only be achieved in a number of bounds, and although he was certainly more sanguine about his prospects than either Plumer or Rawlinson had been, his plans were still more methodical than Haig would have liked. The stage was thus set for an attack plan riven with contradictions, overseen by a commander unsure of his goal.[38]

Meanwhile, British strategy remained as torn as ever. Five days after the stunning blow at Messines, Haig prepared a memorandum on his future plans for the War Cabinet in London – the first time Lloyd George and his colleagues had been given a detailed insight into the projected Flanders operation. Good progress was being achieved, Haig stressed, and should he receive the numbers of drafts and guns he had requested, then success at Ypres would be more likely. He considered that any operation intended to improve the line would probably counterbalance the natural wastage that a sector like Ypres tended to produce. Therefore, plans for his so-called 'northern operation' were being pushed ahead with all possible speed, although these would naturally take some time to mature. At this point he reminded the War Cabinet of how the 'endurance of the German nation is being tested so severely that discontent there has already assumed formidable proportions'. According to his sources, the German Army was already showing 'unmistakeable signs of deterioration'. If Britain were to relax its pressure now, then 'waning hope' in Germany would be revived, with a correspondingly depressing effect on the morale of France. However, if they were to concentrate their resources, 'great results' could be obtained that summer – 'results which make final victory more assured and which may even bring it within reach this year'.[39]

Haig's optimism, his dogged and continuing belief that victory was just around the corner, was always one of his chief flaws as a commander. While an unquenchable belief in victory is essential to any soldier, with Haig this tended to overwhelm a more objective and reasoned appreciation of what could be achieved in any given situation.[40] Some of the blame for this has landed on the shoulders of his Head of Intelligence, John Charteris (pronounced 'Charters'), who, it was alleged, was a spineless 'yes man', feeding his boss with endless fantastic accounts of how close the Allies were to victory. Lieutenant-Colonel J. F. C. Fuller, a staff officer at the Tank Corps, called Charteris 'a hale and hearty back-slapping fellow, as optimistic as Candide, who conjured forth resounding victories . . . like rabbits from a hat'.[41] The reality, however, was more prosaic. While Charteris's reports certainly emphasized evidence of German decline, Haig was his own man; and his notorious over-confidence – reinforced by a powerful sense of religious destiny – was embedded deep within his soul. As he continued to monitor the preparations for his 'northern offensive', Haig became convinced that the climactic moment in the war had arrived and that he would be able to deliver the *coup de grâce*.[42]

Yet few shared Haig's optimism. On 2 June Major Neville Lytton, Press Liaison Officer at GHQ, briefed Haig on the attitude of French newspaper correspondents towards the war and made it clear how deep a 'feeling of despondency' had taken root. Further bad news arrived later that evening when Major-General Eugène Debeney (Pétain's Chief of Staff) visited Haig's chateau at Beaurepaire. He had brought with him a letter from Pétain, saying that he had been entrusted to put the 'whole situation' of the French Army before Haig. According to Debeney, French soldiers were dissatisfied and unhappy at their lot, meaning that many had to be sent on leave immediately. Unfortunately, this would prevent Pétain from making his attack on 10 June, which could not be conducted for another month. Although the word 'mutiny' was never used, the grim look on Debeney's face told its own story, leaving Haig to draw his own conclusions about how much French support he could really count on.[43]

Both Lytton and Debeney may have brought bad news, but Haig did not see any reason to reconsider his plans for the remainder of 1917. Indeed, if anything it simply confirmed to him that it was essential to win a major victory to revive flagging morale. A day before Haig had sent off his memorandum on future plans, Charteris had written an appreciation of the situation that buttressed his chief's arguments in detail. German casualties were enormous, he reported, not less than 250,000 per month, and the morale of her troops was 'very markedly' worse than it had been in 1916. Germany was, he prophesied, within 4–6 months of being unable to maintain her present strength in the field, and should fighting continue at its present intensity, 'then Germany may well be forced to conclude a peace on our terms before the end of the year'.[44] Such was the buoyant frame of mind that Haig took with him when he travelled to London to attend a meeting of the War Cabinet on 19 June.

Haig's rosy appreciation of the situation contrasted sharply to the growing scepticism, even depression, spreading through Whitehall. The morale of the British Army remained good, but all was not well at home and war-weariness was more evident with every month that passed. Between 30 April and 12 May industrial unrest swept the country as over 200,000 workers went on strike over fears of further so-called 'dilution' of private work.[45] The mood was worsened by the intensification of aerial warfare against Britain's capital. Between 25 May and 1 October, London and the southeast of England were subjected to a renewed German bombing campaign. The great dirigibles, the 'Zeppelins', had been the primary aerial threat to England since 1914, but the decision by the German Air Service to place its faith in large, twin-engined bombers known as 'Gothas', marked a new stage in the air war. On 13 June the most lethal air raid on London since the beginning of the war took place – with eighteen Gothas crossing the English Channel and scattering bombs across a wide area. In all, the raid caused over £125,000 worth of damage, killed 162 and wounded over 400 Londoners, including scores of children at a school in Poplar where a 50kg bomb exploded in a classroom.[46] The shock across London was palpable. When the War Cabinet met on the afternoon of the raid, it was agreed to increase the number of RFC squadrons and pour more resources into home defence.[47]

Despite the darkening scene, Haig's undiminished enthusiasm was on display when he arrived in London. Beforehand, Robertson had warned him to be careful and not to promise more than he could deliver. Lloyd George, said Robertson, was convinced that the war could be won from Italy and wanted twelve divisions and 300 heavy guns sent immediately. However, Robertson assured Haig that as long as he was CIGS, this would never happen. Furthermore:

> What I do wish to impress on you is this: Don't argue that you can finish the war this year, or that the German is already beaten. Argue that your plan is the best plan – as it is – that no other would even be *safe* let alone decisive, and then leave them to reject your advice and mine. They dare not do that.[48]

This was typical of Robertson. He may have been a staunch 'westerner' who believed that victory could only be achieved in France, but he was never an uncritical devotee of Haig. Like a number of other senior British commanders, he always favoured the 'bite-and-hold' approach to operations and naturally veered away from the full-blooded optimism that frequently swept through Haig's GHQ like a summer fever. Nevertheless, his instinctive aversion to politicians and civilians, particularly intriguers like Lloyd George, meant that he tried to present a unified front, feeling that he had little choice but to support Haig and his plans, even if, now and again, he sent guarded hints to GHQ about not trying to go for ambitious breakthroughs.

What Haig thought of Robertson's periodic interventions remains unclear. He had a habit of dismissing uncomfortable information and would have probably chalked it up, not as a piece of sage and prudent advice, but as a further indication of Robertson's unsoundness of mind. Indeed, it might have reinforced Haig's growing belief that the CIGS needed to go. While he was in London he even met with Lloyd George to discuss the possibility of moving Robertson to the Admiralty.[49] Thus Robertson found himself in a dangerous no-man's-land: between a Prime Minister who made no secret of his frustrations with the CIGS and a Commander-in-Chief who was equally sensitive to anything he perceived as not being total, unqualified support. Robertson, as he had always done, simply got on with it as best he could, ploughing his lone furrow in Westminster; a warrior without an army.

In London the scene was now set for what Hankey called 'a regular battle royal'.[50] Haig opened proceedings and explained how his forces were going to clear the Belgian coast. Now that the Messines Ridge had been secured, Gough's Fifth Army, assisted by French and Belgian forces (as well as Plumer's Second Army), was to push on to the Passchendaele–Staden Ridge. This would be the first step in a progressive offensive and might, as Haig admitted, 'entail very hard fighting perhaps lasting for weeks'. Nevertheless, once this had been achieved, Gough would attack northeastwards towards Thourout, while a further operation would drive the enemy from Nieuport on the coast (in combination with naval and amphibious forces). The offensive would then be directed towards Ostend and Bruges, with the possibility that an opportunity for the use of *'cavalry in masses'* might appear. Haig was confident that the *'general situation'* was such that the results of any offensive might exceed expectations and result in *'great developments'* in the war.[51] Moreover, the Field Marshal stressed that *'now* was the favourable moment' and that all efforts must be made to defeat the German Army. Flourishing Charteris's report, Haig claimed that 'Germany was within 6 months of the total exhaustion of her available manpower, *if the fighting continues at its present intensity*.'[52]

For Lloyd George, fidgeting in his chair, this was exactly what he did not want to hear. Admittedly, he had been impressed with Messines, but felt that the idea of a major offensive in Flanders needed very careful consideration. He never forgave Haig for demonstrating his plans on a relief map of the Western Front, with his hands sketching out how far his forces would advance: 'first the right hand brushing along the surface irresistibly, and then came the left, his outer finger ultimately touching the German frontier with the nail across'.[53] At a War Policy Committee meeting on 21 June, the Prime Minister outlined his objections to the scheme, including the low chances of success given the slender superiority of Allied to German manpower (barely 15 per cent), the equality in numbers of guns, and the unlikelihood of significant French support. Failure would 'be a very serious business', he grumbled. If they were unable to clear the Belgian coast, perhaps making an advance of 'only' seven or eight miles (while suffering heavy casualties), then 'the effect would be very bad throughout the world'. In his opinion, success would require 'overwhelming' force, a strong diversionary operation and a significant collapse in the enemy's morale; conditions that he believed were nowhere close to being fulfilled. Furthermore, what possible reason, he asked, was there for believing they could achieve more than they had on the Somme, when it had taken five months to gain five or six miles? 'Yet, our military advisers were just as sanguine then as they were now.'[54]

There was no doubt that clearing the Belgian coast would be a strategic prize of the highest order. The First Sea Lord, Admiral Jellicoe, pressed for some kind of ground operation, telling the War Cabinet that there was no use making plans for 1918 because 'we cannot go on'. Although few shared the Admiral's pessimism about the U-boat campaign, it added further weight to Haig's contention that his was the best plan to adopt.[55] The question was whether, as Lord Milner conceded, 'it was worth the risk involved, and the losses which would be incurred'.[56] In the end, Lloyd George blinked first. He had no wish 'to take the strategy of the War out of the hands

of their military advisers'. If, after having taken into consideration
the views of the Cabinet, the generals still 'adhered to their previous
opinion, then the responsibility for their advice must rest with them'.
Robertson and Haig were left to mull over Lloyd George's appeal,
while considering three points: whether 'more active cooperation'
could be gained from the French; the feasibility of an attack on the
Italian Front; and the 'possibility and desirability of asking the French
to send guns to Italy'.[57]

When the War Policy Committee reconvened on 25 June, little
had changed. Lloyd George tried to open up fissures between Robertson and Haig, asking pointedly whether the CIGS shared Haig's
views on the likelihood of the 'northern operation' being a success.
Robertson seemed to blanch at this, but eventually held firm. Results
would depend on circumstances out of his control, and although he
admitted to using 'deliberately guarded language', he believed Haig's
plan was 'the best course to adopt' – thus staying loyal to his entreaty
to Haig that they must remain united. Lloyd George tried again, asking whether Robertson's views in Paris the previous month (that
unless the French 'put in the whole of their strength' the British
should not act alone) were now inconsistent with his current position,
but Robertson refused to bite. In Paris they had committed to continue the offensive on the Western Front with the 'whole of the forces'
available. 'Without fighting', Robertson added wearily, 'we would
never win the war.' At this point Lloyd George relented. Haig was
permitted to continue his preparations for the time being, while
renewed pressure was to be placed on the French Government to do
all it could to cooperate with Haig's plans.[58] It was an unsatisfactory
situation from all sides: Haig returned from London feeling somewhat battered; while Lloyd George squirmed frantically as the
strategic straitjacket closed around him – one moreover that he lacked
the strength of will to break out of.

4.

'Have We Time to Accomplish?'

Never has an army been so ready to fight a defensive battle. The troops and divisional commanders face it full of confidence.

Fritz von Lossberg[1]

21 June–15 July 1917

'The longest day of the year, and we have not yet even begun the really big effort', lamented John Charteris at GHQ. It was 21 June 1917; almost three years to the day since Gavrilo Princip, a Serbian terrorist, had assassinated the Archduke Franz Ferdinand, heir to the Austro-Hungarian throne, in the backstreets of Sarajevo. Every evening Charteris would stand outside his office and smoke, listening to the wind in the trees and the frequent birdsong, which was accompanied, as always, by the eternal rumbling of artillery fire at the front. Now, sadly, the endless summery nights began to draw in as the year turned and thoughts fell on the prospect of another winter at war; another winter in the damp, open trenches at the front. It was a sober and unwelcome reminder of the misfortune that had hampered the Allied war effort and of their hopes for victory that seemed to flicker and threaten to die out; a guttering candle surrounded only by darkness.

'Six months ago I thought by this time we should have been near peace', Charteris wrote. He was depressed at the prospects of the war not ending any time soon:

> Now it looks as if nothing can prevent another full year of war. In six weeks the 'three years' that seemed the extreme possible limit will be passed. Except that America is now with us we are not much better

off than, if as well as, we were this time last year. Then, as now, we were getting ready for a big attack, but then, Russia was still hopeful and France was fighting well. Now Russia is out of the picture, and so, for the time being, is France. We cannot hope for much from Italy. The Dardanelles venture is dead. Salonika is useless, worse than useless indeed. Mesopotamia does not matter either way. We fight alone here, the only army active.

Despite the all-encompassing gloom, Charteris remained confident in the fighting ability of Britain's forces. 'We shall do well, of that there is no reasonable doubt.' Yet one thing nagged away at him. 'Have we time to accomplish?'[2]

It had been two weeks since Plumer's stunning strike at Messines; two weeks since Crown Prince Rupprecht had lamented the horrifying sight of Bavarian soldiers lying scattered around the battlefield, killed by the explosion of a million pounds of high explosive. Yet there was still no Flanders offensive, and in the hot June weather some could be forgiven for thinking there was no war on. One of Fifth Army's liaison officers was the artist Paul Maze, who spent his days studying the ground and sketching the positions they were to attack. Every day he would lie 'hidden among the poppies' and stare out across the Flanders landscape: from the Passchendaele Ridge on the right, to the 'heroic remnants' of Ypres, behind him, with its medieval Cloth Hall (which looked 'like a birthday cake after the guests have had their share'). Despite the great damage Ypres had sustained from earlier fighting – as well as being a perfect aiming point for German gunners – Maze thought the town 'impressively strong and undaunted'. 'Its aspect constantly changed with the varying light. Sometimes it would be a grey mass of walls, like a huge crypt; at other times every house took on a prominence and came out with a distinctness that threw the surrounding landscape into secondary place.'[3]

In view of how bad the weather would be in late July and August the delay between the attack at Messines and the beginning of the main offensive would have significant repercussions. Henry Rawlinson had originally recommended a pause of only two or three days between the two phases, just enough time to move the guns and register new targets, but in total it would be nearly eight weeks. It took time for Gough to organize his forces and plan his attack, and the addition of Anthoine's French troops on the left delayed things even further. At La Lovie, Gough watched, with growing unease, the increase in German strength opposite him. Not only were more German air squadrons being encountered by the RFC, but the number of enemy divisions his intelligence was spotting also began to grow disconcertingly. Gough could do little else but emphasize the importance of camouflage and deception to his subordinates, while comforting himself that the German reinforcement was 'in accordance with Haig's strategical idea of compelling the Germans to concentrate' against them rather than the French.[4]

Gradually the offensive began to take shape. By late June Gough had devised a plan that, he hoped, would allow for a swift and decisive push out of the Ypres Salient. The file he received from GHQ envisaged an advance, during the first day, of about a mile. This would be just enough to capture the German second line, before a further advance – perhaps one or two days later – was made on to the Gheluvelt Plateau on the right. Once this had been secured, operations would then resume in the centre, pushing further eastwards past the Steenbeek and on to the Passchendaele Ridge. After being briefed by Haig (who was very clear about the need to break out of the Salient), Gough redrew these plans to take account of this more ambitious approach. Another objective was added – out to the German third line – and, should that be achieved, his troops would then march on to a fourth objective, another mile eastwards towards the main ridge at Broodseinde. After a pause for several days, the offensive would be renewed towards the apex of the Salient, and then out on to the coast.[5]

In order to achieve this, Gough put all four of his corps into the line, from left to right along an eight-mile section of front, hoping to spread German defences and guns across his whole sector. He was concerned that if he concentrated his men and guns for a push towards Gheluvelt, this would make it easier for the enemy to contain his advance. At a series of conferences on 26 June, Gough went over many

of the key aspects of the operation, including the sequence of objectives and the all-important artillery support. There would be three
stages to the attack. The first (the Blue Line) was about 1,000 yards into
the German position and included the villages of Hooge and Verlorenhoek. The second (the Black Line) was another 1,000 yards in and
ran up to Westhoek, Frezenberg and Pilckem. The final objective (the
Green Line) lay about 1,500 yards further on, out towards Polygon
Wood and Saint-Julien. Should this ground be taken, Gough then recommended a further advance up to Broodseinde (the Red Line). This
took the total advance, should everything go well, up to 5,000 yards –
nearly three miles into the German position.[6]

Just as Gough was finalizing his plans, there was a murmur of concern from GHQ. On 26 June, Brigadier-General John Davidson,
Haig's Head of Operations, sent a memorandum to La Lovie warning
of the dangers of pushing the infantry as far as was proposed.
Although Haig certainly wanted a major advance, he was happy
enough to let Davidson raise the issue. 'Experience shows that such
action may, and often does, obtain spectacular results for the actual
day of operations, but these results are obtained at the expense of such
disorganization of the forces employed as to render the resumption of
the battle under advantageous circumstances at an early date highly
improbable.' Instead of Gough's ambitious plans, Davidson proposed
a 'deliberate and sustained advance' at two- or three-day intervals,
with units pushing forward between 1,500 and 3,000 yards each time
(not the 5,000-yard leap Gough was proposing). Furthermore:

> It has been proved beyond doubt that with sufficient and efficient
> artillery preparation we can push our infantry through to a depth of
> a mile without undue losses or disorganization, and I recommend
> strongly that the operations for the capture of the Passchendaele–
> Staden Ridge should be conducted on the principle of a series of such
> operations, following one another at short intervals, in such a manner
> as to avoid at a particular period wholesale reliefs, wholesale displace-
> ment of artillery, and the wholesale hurrying forward of guns,
> troops, ammunition, and supplies over ground which is practically
> devoid of communications.

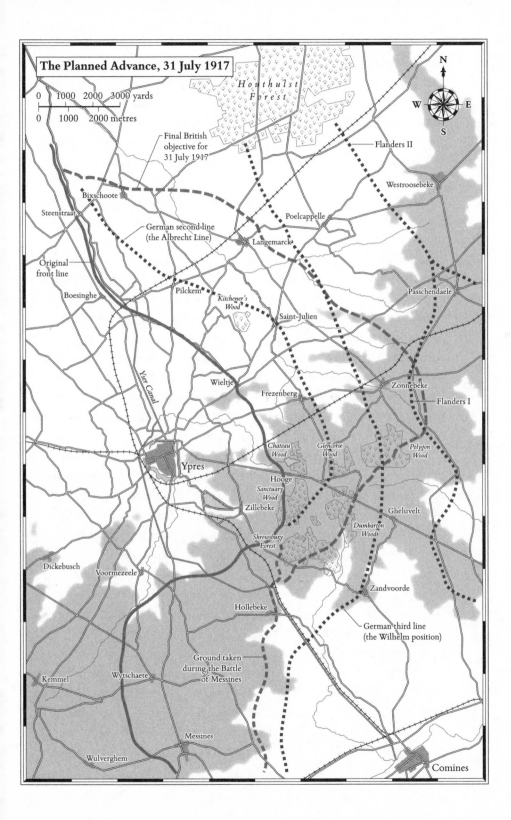

The Planned Advance, 31 July 1917

0   1000   2000   3000 yards

0   1000   2000 metres

Houthulst Forest

N
W   E
S

Flanders II

Final British
objective for
31 July 1917

Westroosebeke

Bixschoote

Steenstraat

Poelcappelle

German second line
(the Albrecht Line)

Langemarck

Original
front line

Boesinghe

Pilckem

Kitchener's Wood

Saint-Julien

Passchendaele

Yser Canal

Wieltje

Frezenberg

Zonnebeke

Flanders I

Chateau Wood

Glencorse Wood

Polygon Wood

Ypres

Hooge

Sanctuary Wood

Zillebeke

Dumbarton Wood

Gheluvelt

Shrewsbury Forest

Dickebusch

Voormezeele

Zandvoorde

Hollebeke

German third line
(the Wilhelm position)

Kemmel

Wytschaete

Ground taken
during the Battle
of Messines

Messines

Wulverghem

Comines

For Davidson, the Germans would bring forward reserves to contain their advance, so it was better to accept battle when they were organized and well-supported, rather than being tired and stretched far from their communications. Like Plumer and Rawlinson, he saw 'bite and hold' as the only way to fight on the Western Front.[7]

Gough was unmoved by Davidson's intervention. 'Is not this written by a somewhat pedantic, if you like methodical, mind?' he asked Sir James Edmonds after the war.[8] In his reply (which he wrote two days later) Gough was more diplomatic. 'In its broad principles', he noted, 'I am in agreement with this paper, in so far as it advocates a continuous succession of organized attacks.' The point for discussion, Gough felt, was whether they should try to go as far as they could on the first day – perhaps up to the Red Line – and take advantage of the weeks of preparation they had already made. It would be wasteful not to 'reap all the advantages' of battle on the first day, and push their men and guns as far forward as possible, rather than making a series of time-consuming lurches forward, which would be just as tiresome as one deeper advance. Nevertheless, Gough saw his battle as being 'a succession of organized attacks' at short intervals – say one major push forward every ten days.[9]

What Davidson's memorandum highlighted was a fundamental difference of opinion within British High Command about how operations should be conducted. According to Gough, the main matter of difference was whether there should be a limited and defined objective or an undefined one. 'GHQ favoured the former, I the latter.' The principal reason for his view, argued Gough, was the 'examples of many operations which had achieved much less than they might have done, owing to excessive caution'. He cited the actions at Loos in September 1915, the night attack on the Somme in July 1916, and the capture of Vimy and Messines Ridges earlier that year as evidence that halting victorious troops on prearranged lines 'at the moment when the enemy was completely disorganised' often resulted in the failure to capture ground 'which lay completely open to us and could have been seized without almost any opposition'.[10] With all the preparation and planning that had gone on, Gough reasoned – no doubt with some justification – that it was best to go as far as they could on the first day, rather than hold the men back on some arbitrary line.

For John Davidson, his intervention was aimed at forcing a debate within GHQ about what exactly the attack should look like and whether the attack was too ambitious. A conference of army commanders was arranged for 28 June to try and settle the matter. After some discussion, it was agreed that Fifth Army's scheme would remain unaltered, although Haig did mention to Gough how important his right flank, on the Gheluvelt Plateau, would be. He stressed making sure this was secured before taking the Broodseinde and Passchendaele Ridges; otherwise his corps would be pushing further into another salient, exposed to artillery fire on three sides.[11] Yet, in what would be one of the fatal moments prior to the attack – one of those 'terrible ifs' – Gough took little or no notice of Haig's suggestions and kept his plans unaltered, with his four corps in line, next to one another, all going for that big leap on the first day.

Historians have generally regarded Gough's plan as mistaken: overambitious and faulty, and riven with contradiction. Indeed, it satisfied no one. The infantry were deployed across a wide stretch of front and were being ordered to advance much further than they had gone at Messines (where the maximum push had been no more than 2,000 yards). There was also no specific concentration of troops on the right, as Haig seemed to want, where the Gheluvelt Plateau formed a formidable obstacle. Gough believed that he had to take the opportunity of going as far as he could on the first day, hopefully sweeping everything before him, so went for a wide and deep push and hoped for the best. Indeed, Fifth Army's plans were always going to have something reckless about them, particularly when compared to Plumer's more modest proposals. The problem with all this was that Gough's attack required British guns to subdue or destroy the enemy's fortifications across a wide belt of front, something that was highly unlikely, but Gough – as was his nature – seemed not too concerned. He was confident his troops would deliver him victory.[12]

The employment of tanks also brought up the question of whether Gough's scheme had really been thought through. Fifth Army's battle plan was based upon the coordination of artillery and infantry, but it would also be able to call upon three brigades of tanks (216 machines in total), which had been brought up to assist in clearing the German second line and supporting the advance to the third.[13] Whether tanks could make a meaningful contribution to the breakout in Flanders was a point of some conjecture. Brigadier-General Hugh Elles (GOC Tank Corps) warned GHQ before the battle that tanks could only function if the ground was *not* heavily shelled and that any extensive bombardment would reduce their chances considerably. His Chief Intelligence Officer, Captain Frederick Hotblack, even distributed regular 'swamp maps', which detailed the effects of the preliminary bombardment and showed how the destruction of drainage ditches had turned the Steenbeek (a stream that ran parallel to the front line) into 'a wide moat of liquid mud'. Yet these concerns seem to have been dismissed – GHQ abruptly instructing the Tank Corps to stop sending them.[14]

Whether tanks should have ever been deployed to Flanders remains a moot point, but there was an argument that, however difficult the conditions became, every possible effort, and every possible weapon, should be used for such an important offensive and Gough evidently shared this view.[15] Yet one could feel sympathy for the tank commanders who watched helplessly as the lengthy preliminary bombardment, and extensive counter-battery struggle, began to pulverize the battlefield and progressively turn it into a porridge-like sludge. Over heavily shelled ground, it was unlikely that tanks could cover more than 10–20 yards a minute at best; on very wet ground this rate would be much slower; and in areas covered with tree stumps and woodland debris tanks would be unable to manoeuvre at all – leaving them sitting ducks for German field guns.[16] As one tank commander, W. H. L. Watson, later wrote, 'The thought of tanks in the Salient made those of us shiver a little who knew the country.'[17]

Much now devolved on Gough's corps commanders; the men who would make the assault on the German line. They were all tough soldiers; men who had seen enough of the Western Front to know what was at stake and how much relied on their decisions. Fifth Army deployed four corps in line from Boesinghe (where it joined the French) to Zillebeke (south of Ypres): Lord Cavan's XIV Corps; Sir

Ivor Maxse's XVIII Corps; Herbert Watts's XIX Corps; and Sir Claud Jacob's II Corps. None of the attacks would be easy, but it was generally agreed that Jacob had the least favourable part of the line, with his men facing the rise of the Gheluvelt Plateau and the dark shadows of a series of shattered woodlands – Shrewsbury Forest, Sanctuary Wood, Chateau Wood and Inverness Copse. This was the area that Haig had flagged up to Gough on 28 June, stating – correctly as it turned out – that unless this right flank was secure, it would be impossible to push further eastwards without being exposed to heavy enfilade fire. As the countdown to the attack got underway, it quickly became apparent that much of the success or failure of the offensive would depend on Jacob. Whatever else happened, the Gheluvelt Plateau had to be cleared of German guns.

As Gough's commanders worked out their plans, much needed to be done. Thousands of tons of supplies had to be moved up; communication and support trenches dug; and batteries assembled into position. Yet there were never enough men for these purposes and soon the French commander, Anthoine, was complaining about not being able to dig sufficient gun pits and ammunition stores for his artillery. He visited Haig on 2 July and warned him that it was essential for the French Army that the Flanders offensive was an 'absolute success' with infantry only being sent 'over the top' after 'methodical and comprehensive preparation' had been completed.[18] Haig sent him over 7,000 men to help, but on 7 July Gough was forced to come back to GHQ, cap in hand, and beg for a postponement of the offensive. The date of attack was originally scheduled for 25 July (the date when Gough's corps commanders felt they would be ready), but after a further conference with Haig it was finally agreed to mount the offensive three days later, on 28 July.[19]

Below the corps commanders lay the hundreds of subordinate officers that made up Fifth Army: divisional and brigade commanders; lieutenant-colonels or majors in charge of battalions or batteries; captains with their companies; and second lieutenants with their platoons. They had to familiarize themselves with their sectors and work out how they were going to achieve their objectives. Across the front, in dugouts and trenches, shell-pitted villages and tented fields, often by candlelight, the details of the coming battle came together. Movement orders were issued; stores were stockpiled; tactics were honed. In XIV Corps, divisional instructions dealt with intelligence briefings; trench models; the use of the rifle; flanking parties; liaison with the French; lessons from Canadian operations at Vimy Ridge; contact aeroplanes (which would follow the progress of the attack); the consolidation of captured trenches; and the importance of officers being 'cheerful' in front of their men.[20] By now the BEF was a functioning machine that knew its business. The eager, if somewhat amateurish, Army that had made its debut on the Somme the previous summer was no more. Now there could be no denying the seriousness of the situation or the professionalism it demanded. War had been a hard taskmaster, but now, in 1917, there was a sense that, at long last, the British were getting the hang of it. While victory might not have been a foregone conclusion, they would at least make a formidable effort this time.

By late June, following the lull in the fighting on the Western Front, the German Supreme Command could survey the situation calmly. In a report written on 25 June, General Ludendorff found things to be not too unfavourable. A recent attack by the Italians had been contained by the Austro-Hungarian Army without the need for German reinforcements (the Tenth Battle of the Isonzo); the situation in the Balkans and on the Turkish front was no cause for immediate concern; and hopes were still high for a separate peace with Russia. On the Western Front it seemed clear that the French Army's power of attack was waning and it had been exhausted, at least temporarily, on the Aisne. The British attack at Arras had been contained, although the success at Messines had created the conditions for future offensives in Flanders. While this was all well and good, Ludendorff overestimated wildly the effect that unrestricted submarine warfare was having on the Allied war effort. 'England needs quick results', he wrote, 'because of the effects of the U-boat war on her maritime economy.' Furthermore:

> Wood shortages prevail in England, coal shortages in Italy and France. Quite obviously our opponents do not have the same

quantities of munitions as on the Somme. A fall in the production of
ammunition and in the supply of munitions to the Western Front can
be perceived. France is determined to make new blood sacrifices as
well, despite the bad mood which prevails, due to the spring failures
with their tremendous losses, and which finds expression in the
change of High Command. We have clear evidence, which has not
yet been published, that indiscipline in the French Army is growing
ever more out of control. In Russia, the decomposition proceeds.

For Ludendorff the longer Germany kept up her maritime pressure,
the better. He even predicted that the arrival of the Americans would
not fundamentally alter this (which would be another major miscal-
culation). He was absolutely certain that 'the prerequisite for victory
is merely that we remain united and keep our nerve'.[21]

Nevertheless, the Supreme Command were not entirely happy. In
particular, they were concerned about the state of morale at home
and here they sensed trouble – what Ludendorff called 'manifest-
ations of weakness'.[22] For some time they had felt little confidence that
the Imperial Chancellor, Bethmann Hollweg, had the necessary
stomach for the fight. For the generals, any expression of weakness
within Germany, any official acceptance of anything less than total,
unconstrained victory, would hearten their enemies and prolong the
war; hence their suspicion of a man who had long been in favour of a
negotiated peace. The tipping point came on 19 June when Hindenburg wrote to the Chancellor informing him that he must prepare
the nation to face a fourth year of war. The Chief of the General Staff
admitted that the submarine campaign had not achieved as much as
they had hoped, but there was no doubt that it needed to be continued 'with ruthless energy and for a sufficient length of time' to
compel their enemies to make peace. In the meantime, it would be
necessary to strengthen public morale at home and make it clear that
Germany would never consent to 'a premature surrender'.[23]

Bethmann Hollweg's response was one of disbelief followed by
gathering gloom. 'This would be a tremendous disappointment since
it was rumoured in Berlin that it would be over by the autumn', he
told a colleague, who described him as being 'very pessimistic' and

'very angry with the High Command'.[24] The Chancellor eventually replied on 25 June, offering a 'word of caution' on the possibility that the U-boat campaign would eventually succeed. 'The assumptions based on statistics have proved themselves too unreliable to be repeated with the force of conviction.' Furthermore, the idea of a peace dictated only by Germany was illusory. He urged Hindenburg not to cast aside the prospect of a 'peace of understanding'. Austria–Hungary would find it difficult to continue the war through the winter – by which time there was little chance that England would have capitulated. What they had to do, he urged the High Command, was to weaken their enemies, particularly England, as much as possible, but without imperilling the chance of them coming to terms.[25]

Bethmann Hollweg had hardly made any radical, defeatist statements – he was, after all, only proposing that a compromise peace should not be dismissed out of hand – but even this was too much for the Supreme Command, who expected nothing less than supine loyalty from their politicians. Ludendorff offered his resignation on 12 July, stating that he had no confidence in the Chancellor and sparking off a full-blown political crisis.[26] While the conservative and nationalistic wing of German political life – the Army, OHL, industrialists and advocates of pan-German expansion – had long been anxious to remove the Chancellor, the more moderate elements within the Reichstag were also tiring of him. On 27 June the Majority Social Democrats, the largest party in parliament, visited Bethmann Hollweg and demanded that not only did they require a clear statement that Germany was in favour of a negotiated peace without annexations, but also that there needed to be more internal reform, primarily the introduction of an equal franchise in Prussia. Should this be rejected, they threatened to veto the next round of war credits, which had to be voted through within days. This was followed by Matthias Erzberger's speech to the Reichstag on 6 July in which he announced the need for an immediate peace.[27]

The two poles of German political life were now squaring up to one another. It would be a fight between those who wanted a ruthless prosecution of the war until Germany could dictate terms to her enemies, and those, primarily the leftist deputies in parliament, who wanted less formidable war aims. For Bethmann Hollweg, Erzberger's declaration on 6 July meant that his position was becoming untenable. He eventually resigned on 13 July, to be replaced by Dr Georg Michaelis, Under-Secretary in the Prussian Ministry of Finance, a relative unknown who immediately made it clear that he would act 'in constant agreement' with the High Command. He was what officials described as a 'good administrative man'; someone the generals could rely on to hold the line at home.[28] The Kaiser – moping about the Bellevue Palace in Berlin – was aware of how weak he was being made to look. On 16 July he told Admiral von Müller (Chief of the Naval Cabinet) how Ludendorff had blackmailed him over the issue. Yet the Kaiser still tried to maintain the illusion that he was somehow still master of the situation. 'He had played a little trick on Hindenburg and Ludendorff because he had accepted the Chancellor's resignation before they arrived at Berlin and received them with the words: "What do you want then? The Chancellor has gone a long time ago."'[29] So had the primacy of politics in German life. Backed up by Hindenburg, Ludendorff's word was now 'an immutable law of nature'. Whether she knew it or not, Germany had taken another step towards military dictatorship.[30]

In Flanders, preparations for what seemed like an inevitable Allied offensive continued apace. 'Never before had we seen such masses of aircraft and air combat as at the front above Ypres', wrote the German soldier Johann Schärdel, who gazed at the aerial duels that took place every day; ending – as they always did – with pilots falling from burning aircraft with no parachutes to save them. He was tasked with helping to maintain the telephone lines that ran between brigade and regimental headquarters, which was not easy given the intensity of the shelling. It was a dangerous game: dodging between the glare of white and red alarm flares; trying to find the ends of severed wires amid the wreckage of shell craters, often under violent shelling. He was not alone in noticing that the military cemeteries behind the line were getting bigger. His men watched militia troops laying out corpses in mass graves, wearing gas masks to protect themselves from the 'obnoxious odour of decay'. Every day the tension seemed to increase. 'A feverish restlessness lay on everything . . .'[31]

At his headquarters in Courtrai, Crown Prince Rupprecht, the commander of Germany's northern Army Group, was convinced an enemy attack was coming – *the tell-tale signs were all there* – and awaited events with a sense of resignation born of long experience. The son of Ludwig III, the last King of Bavaria, Rupprecht was a calm and competent soldier, seeming to have inherited little, if any, of his family's legendary eccentricity.[32] As a member of the Bavarian Royal Family, Rupprecht would inevitably be given a key role in the war and he did not disappoint. He had been involved in some of the heaviest fighting of 1914 as commander of Sixth Army and had been on the Western Front ever since. Apart from the great invasion of France, most of Rupprecht's time had been spent on the defensive, shuffling his divisions around to hold off the increasing Allied attacks. He may have wanted to go on to the offensive, but the larger strategic situation ruled this out. His task was simple: to hold on, whatever the cost.

Rupprecht was promoted to Field Marshal in August 1916 (when he assumed command of his Army Group). He was now responsible for the Western Front between the North Sea and the Oise River – perhaps the most critical part of the line. His Army Group consisted of sixty-five infantry divisions and a cavalry division, which were divided into three armies. While on paper this seemed equal in strength to the Allied forces opposite him – the Belgian and French forces in the coastal zone near Nieuport and a considerable chunk of the BEF – he knew his forces were numerically weaker. British divisions had twelve battalions of (roughly) a thousand men, while German divisions had only nine battalions of around 750 men each. British artillery was also considerably more powerful than that of its opponents, with over 3,000 barrels against just 1,100 German guns.[33] Rupprecht dealt with the pressure remarkably well. Usually to be found wearing the drab grey uniform of a Bavarian general (complete with silver collar patches), Rupprecht avoided the opulent displays of royal power favoured by the Kaiser. He was wise enough to leave much of the operational control of his forces to his impressive Chief of Staff, General Hermann von Kuhl, who had served him loyally since 1915.[34]

Working diligently and efficiently, Kuhl gradually readied Rupprecht's divisions for battle. He recorded that from the beginning of July, 'there were increasing signs that an attack was imminent':

> Railways were extended, battery positions increased, the trenches were manned with greater numbers. But still no attack followed. The situation in Crown Prince Rupprecht's Army Group was serious and caused its commander considerable worry. With anxiety he had to look at other sectors of the front, to the areas of Lens, Arras and St Quentin, where an enemy attack could be expected at any time, even if it took the form of a secondary attack.

All spare men and guns had been sent north to Flanders, but the Crown Prince watched his whole sector carefully. Ominously Sixth Army (which held the front opposite Arras) was reporting the arrival of railway guns and a detachment of tanks, leading them to conclude that they too would face an attack. Nevertheless, Rupprecht felt that Flanders would remain the principal focus of British efforts for the time being. A reliable agent in Amsterdam had reported that a 'general attack' would begin soon. He watched and waited.[35]

On 21 June, Ludendorff arrived at Courtrai for a meeting with Kuhl and the other senior officers. Using the large map that was pinned to the walls, Lossberg briefed them on the general situation. There were fifteen German divisions in the line as opposed to twenty enemy ones. They had twelve divisions behind the front – including those used to mount counter-attacks – while they estimated that another fifteen or so enemy divisions were in reserve. On the sectors that were most under threat (particularly the canal zone at Boesinghe), they had only left small detachments to hold the front line. In terms of artillery, they possessed 389 batteries against over 700 enemy ones – a clear disadvantage, but one which Ludendorff believed did not count for too much. 'The munitions situation was not splendid', he admitted, 'but if it came to battle, the Army would be supplied with everything it needed; nothing then needed to be kept back.' He also knew that they had far fewer aircraft than their opponents, but once the battle began further reserves could be sent to the front as required.[36]

Lossberg issued his defensive orders on 27 June. The key problem was trying to avoid the deluge of enemy shellfire that would herald any attack. 'The strength of the defence lies in concealment from enemy observation', he stressed. 'It is not possible to hold trenches, shelters, fixed machine-gun nests, and battery positions during a preliminary bombardment prior to a big offensive. To attempt it exhausts the troops, causes heavy losses, and is only work in vain.' Therefore, Lossberg wanted the defenders to understand that dugouts were merely 'man-traps', and as soon as a bombardment began, German units were to evacuate them and, if possible, move forward and be ready to fight in the open. Given the depth of German positions, counter-attacking at the right time was essential. 'The quicker the counter-attack is delivered, the greater the advantage given.' Once the enemy had established a workable defence and was supported by artillery, counter-attacks would usually fail. Therefore, it was imperative to deliver them independently and without waiting for orders from above. This was the essence of what Lossberg called 'the offensive defence'.[37]

More discussions continued over the coming days. At a meeting on 30 June, Rupprecht considered the possibility (that his staff officers had raised) of withdrawing in order to 'avoid the first blows' of any British offensive. However, when this was examined – with the Field Marshal and his staff poring over maps of their front – it was realized that to do this successfully, Fourth Army would have to give up its entire position, in all its depth, including much of the precious high ground, which Rupprecht was not minded to do. Their rearmost line (Flanders III) was, in any case, still incomplete. 'The local commanders', recorded Kuhl, 'agreed that the present trench system was suited to defence by artillery and infantry and that the collaboration of both arms and the plan for engaging the reserves had been well prepared. The advantages to be expected from a planned withdrawal were not found to be so many as to outweigh the disadvantages to our defence organisation which might have resulted.'[38] Therefore, the matter was settled: they would stand their ground.

The decision to hold fast did not mean, however, that the Germans would await their fate impassively. As the warning signs of an offensive in Flanders became more urgent, Lossberg realized that if Allied forces could seize a bridgehead over the Yser and drive along the coast – as Haig was indeed planning – then there was a danger that the whole German front could be, as he put it, 'unrolled'. It was decided to mount a spoiling attack to throw the enemy back east of Nieuport, and thus secure the coastal zone. At 5.30 on the morning of 10 July, under a heavy artillery and smoke bombardment, assault detachments of German marines surged forward.[39] Within three hours, they had broken into the British line, killed or captured most of the defenders, and wiped out the bridgehead over the Yser River, which would have been the jumping-off point for an offensive along the coast. Orders were rapidly issued for a British counter-attack, but once the blood had cooled, it was mercifully cancelled – the local commander protesting vigorously that such a rushed reaction would usually result in heavy losses for no result. While Haig brushed off concerns that this had damaged his offensive plans – telling Robertson that his artillery would soon blow the enemy 'out of his position as effectively as he blew us out of ours' – it was a stark reminder of how dangerous the Germans remained in this sector. The Battle for Flanders had well and truly begun.[40]

5.

'Under Constant Fire'

This was not just drum fire; it was as though Hell itself had slipped its bonds . . . It was as though the enemy was announcing to the world: Here we come and we are going to prevail.

Hermann von Kuhl[1]

16–30 July 1917

Considering how important the preliminary bombardment was, it is surprising that it did not even make the agenda of General Gough's first meeting in late May.[2] What kind of bombardment would precede the attack was one of the most vital questions that faced British commanders on the Western Front. Several months earlier, prior to the Battle of Arras, General Sir Edmund Allenby, Third Army commander, had argued vigorously with Haig about diverting from their long-established lengthy artillery preparation. He was of the opinion that they should fire a much shorter, so-called 'hurricane' bombardment spread over just forty-eight hours, thus gaining the element of surprise. It would aim not to destroy the German defences, but to neutralize them for long enough to get the infantry across no-man's-land. But Haig, worried lest this fail to suppress the enemy defences or prove too much of a strain on the guns, would not risk it and they opted for a more conventional four-day bombardment instead.[3]

As for Gough, his thoughts on artillery remained aligned to Haig's. At the army conference in which Allenby unveiled his plans for the 'hurricane' bombardment, Gough apparently 'expressed doubts' about the wisdom of veering away from longer preparation, and prior to Third Ypres he never seems to have considered anything else.[4] Perhaps the depth and strength of the German position in Flanders, as well as the impossibility of surprise, meant that a 'hurricane' bombardment was never a viable alternative anyway. Gough originally wanted a nine-day bombardment; beginning on 16 July and reaching its climax just before his attack went in on 25 July. However, because of repeated postponements to the offensive, it would eventually stretch to two weeks – the longest preliminary bombardment in the BEF's history. Millions of shells would be fired in a brutal, pulverizing display of firepower that would be the last great preliminary bombardment of the Western Front.[5]

The scale of Gough's artillery resources was staggering. In the weeks leading up to the attack, nearly 3,000 guns were brought up to the front: over 2,000 field guns (mainly 18-pounders and 4.5-inch howitzers), 718 medium pieces and 281 heavy guns. They were supplied with over 4.2 million shells.[6] In theory, such a preponderance of artillery should have been sufficient. On the Somme the previous year, the British had only been able to muster half as many guns, with a critical shortage of heavy howitzers with which to support the attack. In Flanders the BEF could boast not only many more heavy guns and an almost unlimited supply of shells, but they were also employing state-of-the-art gunnery techniques. Yet the length and depth of front that Gough's artillery had to bombard were considerable. Taken with Second Army, which would extend the attack to the south, the front was fifteen miles long – Messines had been just over nine miles – and in most places the defences were several miles deep. Suppressing or destroying such a vast zone of defences, including hundreds of almost indestructible pillboxes, would be very difficult. Moreover, they had to do all this while dominating or driving away the German batteries that ringed the Salient. In all, the Germans could muster somewhere between 1,000 and 1,500 guns – not as many as their opponents certainly – but enough to pose a serious threat to any attacking infantry.[7]

Getting all the guns into position was an engineering problem of the highest order. Artillery had to be deployed at night, while teams of pioneers worked tirelessly to construct the timber platforms that prevented them from sinking into the soft Flanders mud. They had to do this under harassing fire from the German batteries and their eagle-eyed observers who scanned the Salient for any signs of movement.[8] Batteries were hidden, as far as possible, in the myriad small copses or farm buildings that dotted the front, while those in the open had to make do with camouflage screens that were erected to try and block muzzle flashes, which would have given their position away.[9] To complicate matters further, mustard gas made its first appearance on 12 July, during what seemed like a routine gas bombardment of Ypres. When Fifth Army's Chemical Adviser, Captain G. W. Monier-Williams, investigated the scene, he found shell fragments from German 77mm field guns painted with unusual green and yellow crosses. The symptoms of those affected by this new gas were equally novel:

> First, a tendency to sneeze, with gradually increasing nose and throat irritation. Later on, in some instances as much as six or eight hours after exposure to the gas, intense and very painful irritation and inflammation of the eyes, accompanied by free discharge of mucus from the nostrils and occasional fits of vomiting.

When Monier-Williams examined many of the wounded, they all shared 'intense and painful irritation of the eyes', with the skin being blistered in places. Furthermore, officers who had handled fragments of shell were also suffering, having developed painful blisters and swelling of the hands within six hours of exposure. Monier-Williams did not know what weapon had been employed, but it would not take long for troops to christen it 'mustard gas' after its pungent smell.[10] Sadly this would only be the first of an increasing number of gas bombardments at Ypres.[11]

For an offensive on this scale, almost everything needed to be done: roads constructed; supplies moved up; telephone wires laid; cables buried, and so on. For the drivers who were the lifeblood of the Army, the Ypres Salient was, without doubt, the most unpopular sector of the Western Front. Almost every major road had been zeroed in on by enemy guns and the key junctions – such as Birr Cross-roads and Hellfire Corner – soon became pockmarked by shell holes and littered with dead horses and burnt-out wagons. Because the ground was so flat, most of the supplies had to move up at night, which meant that after dark the roads around Ypres became jammed with transport, lorries and trucks all trying to get to their destinations, and back again, as soon as was earthly possible. The Ypres–Poperinge road was one particularly lethal section. Straight and narrow 'as the way to heaven, to those who ran the gauntlet in the shell-riven darkness it seemed rather the road to hell', remembered one officer. 'Abandoned wagons, corpses of men, dead and wounded horses and mules lined the scenes of their labours; limbs and bodies sticking in rigid and grotesque pathos out of the mud of the shell-holes were the grim companions of their toil.'[12]

The sight of Ypres with its ruined Cloth Hall blanched white in the moonlight, and its abandoned streets haunted by shadows, would always stick in the memory of those who saw it. Frank Mellish, a subaltern with the RFA, remembered that Ypres was 'never a healthy place to linger in'. 'If one wanted a nerve-tonic one could get it at any time by taking a trip through the Menin Gate and once one decided on doing this there was no standing on the order of going – one went! I have run faster through that City than [Roger] Bannister ever did the mile, and that complete with gas-mask on chest and tin-hat on head!'[13] Another junior officer, Huntly Gordon (serving with 112 Brigade RFA), had only recently arrived in France – Passchendaele would be his first battle – but he quickly grasped what they were up against. At the appointed time (11 p.m.) he led a convoy of a dozen wagons up to the front, loaded down with ammunition, creaking under the strain. The traffic was heavy as usual; 'G. S. wagons, ambulances, lorries, water-carts, buses full of infantry, guns, everything imaginable'. After being shelled and running into 'a nasty belt of gas', the convoy, minus three horses – all killed by shell splinters – finally arrived in Ypres. But Gordon did not tarry. He led his men swiftly past the Menin Gate (which had long since been destroyed, existing merely as a gap in the stone ramparts of the town) and then, setting off at hundred-yard intervals at a brisk pace, the column went along the Menin Road into the belly of the Salient.[14]

At the same time as hundreds of tons of supplies were moved up to the front and issued to the men, many other tasks remained to be completed. Communication equipment, including thousands of miles of cable, needed to be taken up the line and then connected to the telephone exchanges. Captain F. A. Sclater, a signal officer with XIV Corps at Boesinghe, looked after the cable that linked up the artillery batteries. On his sector there were eight routes, buried six feet under ground and, with a bit of luck, immune to everything but the biggest shells. Shortly before the preliminary bombardment was about to begin, one of his heavy-artillery exchanges (camouflaged in a ruined cottage) came under heavy and sustained shelling. With up to eighty lines of cable running into the exchange, its destruction might have made the forthcoming bombardment extremely difficult. Fortunately, the circuits survived intact. They had been buried under a floor of concrete, and despite taking many direct hits (with the house rolling about 'like a ship') the exchange was still functioning on 31 July when the attack went in.[15]

For headquarters staff there may have been less physical toil than endured by the Tommies up the line, but the imminent offensive produced its own kind of pressure. According to Paul Maze, La Lovie was now 'charged with tension'. Every night he lay in his tent and listened to the 'rattle of lines of men trailing howitzers to their positions'; and the 'incessant roar of lorries' driving up to the front weighed down with ammunition.[16] Gough's Chief of Staff, Neill Malcolm, estimated that at one point his office was dealing with over 500,000 words a day over telegraph wire, and he himself took a couple of flights over the Salient, both of which were marred by what could have been potentially fatal accidents. In his first flight his aircraft was forced down by engine failure, and on the second a strut broke on landing.[17]

In the air the Allies enjoyed a notable numerical advantage. From Armentières to the sea they could muster over 800 aircraft – against about 600 German machines (only a third of which were single-seat fighters).[18] Major-General Hugh Trenchard, commanding the Royal Flying Corps, on 7 July issued his orders for the forthcoming battle. The main task was to make sure that as few enemy aircraft as possible were allowed to fly over the British front lines – so he authorized aggressive offensive patrols right across the Salient, pushing back any enemy fighters, and providing space for his other aircraft to complete their reconnaissance duties unimpeded. At the same time specially selected squadrons were tasked with bombing enemy targets: aerodromes and headquarters; railway junctions and roads; trenches and dugouts – all in line with his offensive policy that he was convinced would give them mastery of the skies above Ypres.[19]

By the time the bombardment began on 16 July, Trenchard's air offensive was already several days old. His squadrons attacked enemy ground targets and tussled with the German Air Service in large-scale, whirling dogfights that were watched by troops right across the line. One day, Arthur Sambrook, serving in the Royal Engineers at Messines, recorded seeing *Jagdgeschwader* 1, led by the legendary Baron Manfred von Richthofen (then on fifty-two kills). His aircraft 'were conspicuous in their scarlet coloured wings and fuselage, and fights between them and the de Havilland machines of our Air Force were frequent and exciting to watch'. He also witnessed the destruction of a number of enemy observation balloons that towered over the Salient. 'At first would be seen a wisp of black smoke, then a small flame from the balloon, which would begin to crump up and sink, until the whole was a flaming mass, plunging earthwards, leaving a pillar of black smoke which remained upright in the air for several minutes . . . The conditions were ideal for this sort of activity: a lot of white fleecy clouds drifting slowly along, hiding the aircraft while they stalked their targets.'[20]

The Germans understood how vital the coming days would be. On 19 July, Major-General von Hoeppner, commanding the German Air Service, issued a general order acknowledging the seriousness of the situation. 'In the last few days, enemy fighter pilots have appeared in overwhelmingly superior strength, against which our Jagdstaffeln have been unable to act.' He was confident that the ratio of kills to losses was still in Germany's favour, but the coming offensive would undoubtedly be a stern test. 'I have confidence in the entire German Air Service and in this: that the airmen of the Fourth Army, above all the Jagdgeschwader and the Jagdstaffeln, will thin the ranks of the enemy squadrons and defeat them.' Orders were issued on the urgent need to shoot down enemy observation balloons and 'keep the attack zone free of enemy aircraft'.[21] Accordingly, German air strength was gradually increased in the Flanders sector. In mid-May there had been only thirteen air squadrons in Fourth Army, but by the time the offensive opened at the end of July, this had been increased to eighty.[22]

In London, War Cabinet wrangling over the Flanders offensive continued almost to Zero Day. Robertson wrote to Haig on 18 July updating him on the meetings of the War Policy Committee, which had still given no formal approval to the attack. 'I understand however that the War Cabinet are now in favour of your plans', the CIGS hastened to assure Haig, 'and I have daily been expecting that they would tell me so, but up to the present they have not done so.' Unsurprisingly Lloyd George remained inflexibly opposed to a new offensive in France and continued to look towards his 'Italian venture'. Robertson had twice told him that time was 'running short' and that Fifth Army's preparations would soon be complete, but this produced little urgency from the Prime Minister. Evidently there were still concerns about the ambition of what Haig was proposing and a 'fear', as Robertson explained, that 'you might endeavour to push on further than you were justified pending further artillery preparation'. He reminded Haig that 'it is well understood that the extent of the advance must, roughly speaking, be limited by the assistance of the guns until such times as a real breakthrough occurs' and that if this 'step by step system of advance' was maintained, then there would be real support for his operations.[23]

Haig replied, impatiently, three days later, a tone of frustration and anger detectable in his words. 'It is somewhat startling at this advanced stage of preparations to learn that the War Cabinet had not then yet determined whether my attack was to be permitted to proceed.' He reminded the CIGS that the importance of this operation had been recognized by the War Office as early as November 1916, and the urgency of clearing the Belgian coast was communicated to him directly on 1 December. Evidently, thought Haig, the Cabinet 'do not understand what is entailed by preparation for an attack under existing conditions, or what the effect – material and moral – would be of altering plans once preparations are in full swing'. Moreover, he regretted to learn that his judgement and knowledge of conditions ('even on the depth to which each advance should be pushed') were not trusted; it was, he felt, very important that 'such matters should be left to the Commander on the spot'.[24]

Haig and Robertson's correspondence was, for both men, unsatisfactory and frustrating, as they circled each other without dealing with the other's point. Robertson had tried, yet again, to remind Haig that support for his operation was *directly conditional on how it was being conducted* and that the Cabinet would only consent to a 'step-by-step' advance being undertaken to avoid unnecessary losses. Haig – who envisaged a swift breakthrough *à la Nivelle* – failed to spot this distinction and referred back to decisions made in November and December 1916 about the need to attack in Flanders. Because he felt, instinctively, that how the operation was conducted was none of the Cabinet's business, he seemingly failed to appreciate what Robertson was saying. Thus it came back to the unresolved issues over how the attack was to be conducted. Was it to be a major breakthrough, a decisive 'battle of rupture' aiming to push the infantry through the deep belt of German defences in a matter of hours, or was it to be a limited, 'step-by-step' attack on the lines of Messines?[25] Haig seems to have either fudged it or failed to spot the distinction. He urged Gough to make a decisive advance, while at the same time telling the War Cabinet that his attack might unfold in a series of stages, and to Lloyd George's eternal shame he did not press the matter. Meanwhile the offensive, now seemingly with a life of its own, crept ever closer to fulfilment.

In Germany, the political crisis had not been solved by the appointment of Georg Michaelis as Imperial Chancellor. On 19 July, three days after Gough's artillery had begun pounding the German front line, the Reichstag formally passed its Peace Resolution. 'Germany took up arms to maintain her freedom and independence and to defend her territorial possessions. The Reichstag is striving for a peace of understanding and the permanent reconciliation of the nations.' It demanded an end to the 'embitterment of nations' and called for freedom of the seas and economic cooperation, while promising that the German Government would work towards the establishment of 'international legal machinery'. However, as long as Germany was threatened 'with robbery and oppression', it would 'stand together as one man and endure and fight on until her right and that of her allies to life and freedom' was secure.[26]

When GHQ's intelligence department got wind of the political developments in Berlin, hopes were raised that Germany was on the verge of collapse. Not much was known about the new man in charge (Charteris admitting that they were 'rather at sea about Michaelis'), but it did not prevent optimism from rising, once again, at GHQ.[27] Charteris's intelligence summary for 22 July confidently predicted that Michaelis would be forced to seek some kind of 'compromise peace' before the end of the year. Yet GHQ seemed to miss the real lesson of the political troubles in the Reich, which was the growing polarization of politics in Germany and the takeover of key positions by those on the right who rejected any so-called 'peace of under-standing'.[28] The appointment of Michaelis was not a symbol that Germany was ready to modify her war aims; it was, on the contrary, an indication that the military rulers of Germany would do whatever was necessary to continue to prosecute the war with all the ruthless aggression they could muster.

The political machinations in Berlin would have seemed a long way off to those German troops in the Salient as they prepared – once again – to face the *Materialschlacht*. Gough's batteries were now bring-ing down a curtain of shellfire on the German lines, columns of smoke and dust rising from the landscape like small, smouldering volcanoes. 'The increased activity of enemy artillery in recent days, the increase in systematic destructive fire and batteries being moved to within close proximity all point to the imminent start of the attack', recorded the war diary of Group Ypres on 17 July. 'Our front line – particularly in the sector of the 17th Infantry Division – has become a crater field. The enemy has systematically shelled the rear positions, command posts and batteries, and they have homed in on roads and important positions in the rear areas . . . The battle in Flan-ders has now begun.'[29] Within days German intelligence had identified the opposing British divisions and warned its units of what it would be facing, including 29th ('a very good attack division), 51st (an 'elite Scottish division'), and 11th and 15th ('first-class attack divisions').[30]

Every day Fritz von Lossberg ascended an observation tower that had been constructed in the grounds of his headquarters where he could survey the battlefield. Through the lenses of his binoculars, he could clearly make out the enormous preparations for the coming offensive. 'In many places the enemy artillery were wheel to wheel', he wrote, with 'tremendous ammunition dumps' stacked near their gun positions. His defensive arrangements were not yet complete, so he requested a further two heavy and four light ammunition trains from OHL. Once they had been shunted up, he directed his guns to engage British artillery, and do everything they could to disrupt their preparations and make life as difficult as possible for them.[31] Between 13 and 19 July the German Fourth Army fired 583,000 shells. The following week its consumption would hit 870,000 – causing nervous staff officers some unease about how much ammunition they were firing off.[32]

Day after day, night after night, the impact of thousands of shells rocked the Flanders battlefield, bursting in thudding explosions that sent showers of earth up into the air. Men who had long got used to the endless rumbling of artillery fire at the front felt that something different was happening now: the bombardment was bigger and more frightening than anything they had ever experienced. In the front German defensive zone – up to 3,000 yards in – the fury of the bombardment was at its worst. Most of the barbed wire was torn to pieces and many of the front-line trenches were pulverized beyond recognition.[33] One soldier who saw the destruction was Reserve Second Lieutenant Rau, of the 6th Company, Grenadier Regiment, which held the line around Hooge:

> Not a single communication trench was passable, the concrete pill-boxes all stood out clearly, making marvellous targets for the enemy. This meant that we had to move out of them and take cover in the craters, which themselves were under constant fire. Unfortunately the water table was so high that they soon filled with water, ruling out all thoughts of a rest, no matter how short. Ceaseless rain,

gas attacks, constant raiding and patrol activity, the need to lug forward stores and build wire obstacles by night wore our men out
physically and lowered their morale badly.

Getting supplies, and even orders, to the men in the trenches was
almost impossible. Telephone lines were invariably cut, which meant
that the front battalions had to rely on runners, who often became
casualties of the 'iron rain' that swept across the battlefield. For those
in the front line there would be no relief until the attack came.[34]

German casualties during the bombardment were not inconsiderable. Within days of reaching the front, 235th Division, which held
the line southeast of Saint-Julien, had sustained such severe losses
that it was withdrawn on 1 August.[35] One witness, a soldier from
455 Infantry Regiment, vividly described the horrors they encountered when they moved up to the front. 'The situation is melancholy.
Our company has suffered heavy losses during the one day we have
been here. At the present moment we are in the support trench, a
few hundred metres behind the front line. The English shell the
entire area incessantly with the heaviest guns and the ground is one
mass of shell holes, some of them large enough to build houses in.'
His company were due to move up to the front line the following
day, but they were already exhausted, having to survive on one
water-bottle each for a week because no supplies could reach them
through the shellfire. 'Death lies in wait for us', he wrote, 'like a fox
for its prey.'[36]

Despite the furious bombardment, much of the German defensive
position remained stubbornly intact. Pillboxes were impervious to
all but the heaviest calibres and forced the British to bring up special
armour-piercing ammunition to try and crack them open.[37] In the
tangled, broken woodland of the Gheluvelt Plateau, many of the
pillboxes remained hidden or protected by fallen trees and under-
growth, so the British found it almost impossible to target them all.
Their garrisons may have been shocked and stunned by the intensity
of the shelling, but crucially they would still be able to resist whenever Zero Hour came. More ominously, the German batteries massed
on the reverse slope of the Gheluvelt Plateau remained highly active.

II Corps's Intelligence Summary, dated 25 July, recorded that the enemy artillery observation was 'very keen, and any movement in the front and support lines draws heavy shelling immediately'.[38]

In spite of the disadvantages British guns laboured under, and the casualties that rose every day, Fifth Army's gun crews gradually gained an edge over their opponents. 'Under the enemy's powerful artillery and mortar fire, the German infantry suffered terribly, but the artillery was also in a difficult position', recorded the German Official History. 'Due to the persistent, greatly increased action, towards the end of July the signs of exhaustion could be observed in a greater number of batteries. The losses in men and equipment were considerable. Amongst the heavy field howitzers, the losses amounted to 50 per cent.'[39] In Group Wytschaete, Reinhard Lewald's battery (part of 12th Division) had been 'shot to pieces' by 28 July, with all their guns being knocked out by accurate British counter-battery fire. It was, he recorded, 'incredibly hard work' getting 'the shattered guns out in two nights of pouring rain and heavy shelling'.[40] On 25 July, Crown Prince Rupprecht was handed a report from Karl Dieffenbach (GOC Group Wytschaete) calling his attention to the loss of guns from British counter-battery fire. Half their heavy guns, 30 per cent of their howitzers, 17 per cent of their mortars and 10 per cent of their 10cm guns had already been destroyed.[41] There was nothing left to do but keep up as much counter-battery and harassing fire as they could, while, wherever possible, pulling batteries out of range to save them for the forthcoming push.

The difficulties experienced by the British in bringing guns and supplies up to the battlefield were mirrored on the German side. 'However many new guns we send up – and we do so every night; however many we repair – and we repair them night and day – we cannot keep up to the number which we ought to have', complained a German soldier, Rudolf Binding.[42] For Johann Schärdel, part of a signalling company in a concrete bunker just off the Menin Road, the intensity of artillery fire was almost indescribable. The worst scenes, he remembered, were around the high ground at Gheluvelt, where many field batteries were deployed and attracted much enemy fire.

We could not imagine how it was possible to bring up ammunition
on this heavily shelled approach road – it could certainly only have
been in frantic, life-or-death journeys. An ammunition wagon that
had been shot to pieces lay in front of the bunker in the middle of the
road, and in front of that, there were horses, still in their traces with
their bodies ripped open, and the fallen drivers. In the ditches of the
road, there were bodies who had been horrendously mutilated. One
of the dead had his face severed from the back of his head by a grenade splinter, in such a way that it was only hanging on from his chin
and stared back at us, a horrifically contorted, bloodless yellow mask.
How can one endure such a sight for weeks on end? Dying loses its
horror when it is one's constant companion every day and night.[43]

Working furiously, in between the breaks in the firing, Schärdel and
his men roved over the ruins of Gheluvelt trying 'to mend the wires
that were repeatedly shredded, and which led to the regimental command post'. When they were not in search of broken wires, they
returned to the telephone exchange in their cramped bunker and
plugged calls in, waiting for the day of the assault.

The intensity of the shellfire increased inexorably as the day of
attack drew near, straining men's nerves to breaking point. 28 July
was one of the worst days. According to German sources, the *Trom-
melfeuer* ('drumfire') continued without end, with shells being targeted
at the front line, as well as at German field headquarters and artillery
dumps – even moving trains – while the skies were filled with British
pilots scouring the landscape for anything to bomb.[44] Fourth Army
did what it could. That day (28 July) its guns fired off the contents of
nineteen ammunition trains. Crown Prince Rupprecht described the
artillery activity on his front as being of 'extraordinary violence'.
Even at the height of the Somme fighting the previous summer, a German army would not have used more than eight ammunition trains
per day, and here they were using more than double – such was the
intensity of shellfire in the Salient.[45] At a meeting in Courtrai that day,
the Chief of Staff of the neighbouring Sixth Army, Major Stapff,
argued that they should make a spoiling attack on the right flank of
the enemy, from the German positions at Estaires over the River Lys.

But Kuhl, surveying the maps at Fourth Army Headquarters, was unconvinced. In order to produce a stunning blow it would be necessary to attack further north, perhaps around Bailleul or Hazebrouck, but he doubted whether there were sufficient forces available.[46]

While the staff of Rupprecht's Army Group pondered on whether to mount offensive operations, their final defensive arrangements were being completed. German reserves had now been deployed into position and given their orders on when and how they were to move forward. One German soldier, serving with 62 Infantry Regiment (part of 12th Division – one of Group Wytschaete's *Eingreif* divisions), recorded his thoughts as his battalion made their way, via a series of railway journeys, from Hamburg to Tourcoing. The day they reached Courtrai was particularly depressing. 'Hospital train after hospital train meets us. Damaged guns are carried homewards to remind people of the war.' Any Belgian citizens they met were sullen and silent, stubbornly gazing at the hated conquerors as they rolled by. And then finally they reached the front. 'We saw flashes of the guns in the sky, and many a one felt his courage melt away.' Inevitably it was raining so they hauled on their packs and set out on the long and perilous march into the trenches near Gheluvelt. 'All night the district is illuminated with fire.'[47]

During the last days of July, the counter-battery struggle grew in intensity. British and German gunners were now engaged in a merciless duel for control of the Salient; for whoever mastered the guns would dominate the ground. It would be one of the most brutal artillery battles of the war, with British batteries, parked in exposed low-lying ground, exchanging fire with Germans guns, most of which were shielded by the ridgelines. Artillery spotting from the air certainly helped, but low cloud and poor weather prevented the RFC from being as effective as Trenchard would have liked, and the British came under heavy retaliatory fire almost every day. As the war diary of Group Ypres noted on 29 July: 'Our artillery continued to fight enemy batteries and battery positions with vigour . . . Again and again, particularly in the early hours of the morning, the enemy trenches and assembly areas sustained a combination of armed attacks and waves of destructive fire.'[48]

Behind the front the final movement orders were being received and long files of troops, bowed down with equipment, were making their way into the trenches as the guns, now more angry than ever, pounded their targets. The offensive had been scheduled to begin on 28 July, but a further three-day postponement was eventually sanctioned because Gough's preparations were still incomplete. Charteris recalled that Haig was 'very moody, but once a decision is made he will not give it another thought'.[49] There was nothing left but to trust in God and hope that the bombardment would work. Yet the weight of firepower that Gough was relying upon to unlock the German defences had one drawback: it was, quite literally, destroying the landscape. The delicate drainage system of Flanders, which kept water at bay, had already been badly damaged by three years of heavy fighting. But now, with what Gough was throwing at it, it was beginning to fail. Whatever else the British needed, they urgently required a period of dry weather in which to break out of the Salient. Unfortunately, fate conspired against them. As Gough's divisions were readying to go forward, heavy clouds were already beginning to form over the battlefield and weather reports were warning that rain was on the way. Perhaps it was already too late to start such an enormous campaign. Maybe Charteris had been right after all – maybe it was too late to accomplish anything?

6.

'A Perfect Bloody Curse'

The first strike is always the worst.

Albrecht von Thaer[1]

31 July–5 August 1917

In the early hours of 31 July, Fritz von Lossberg ascended his observation tower and peered out at the darkened horizon, which flickered with the bright flashes of artillery fire. The preliminary bombardment, which had been going on for the last fortnight, seemed to be reaching a climax. Lossberg had seen much as a soldier, but this was, without doubt, the heaviest display of firepower he had ever witnessed.[2] At the front, German soldiers, crouched in their trenches and dugouts, awaited the oncoming storm. Johann Schärdel, serving with 6th Bavarian Reserve Division, would never forget that night, which was 'burned indelibly' in his mind. He was sleeping in a bunker along the Menin Road, but woke, feverish and restless. 'The usual rolling of the front had increased enormously,' he wrote, 'and it penetrated the thick walls of the concrete block like the thundering of passing express trains. Barely a word was spoken. Everyone just listened in tense anticipation to what was happening. Outside on the road [was] the splintering crash of grenades. Now the chamber was full of men who did not belong to us. They stood and crouched there motionlessly, probably waiting until they could go out again.'[3]

At that moment two French and four British corps, with another three under Plumer's command in Second Army, were poised to move forward. Zero Hour was what they had all been dreading for weeks now; men with grey faces under tin helmets that had been carefully plastered with mud to dull any reflection, tightly gripping their rifles, bayonets fixed. Zero Hour would be 3.50 a.m. The decision to opt for such an early start – to try to offset the advantages possessed by the enemy in observation – meant that the battlefield was in darkness when the attack went ahead. The weather was overcast and misty, with thick banks of cloud down to 500 feet in places, which remained stubbornly in place all day. Unfortunately, this meant that the RFC was unable to play a major role in the battle. Selected bombing and strafing missions did go ahead, but the main programme for 'continuous offensive patrols' at 8,000 feet had to be scrapped. Thus the approach routes to the battlefield, those that would be used by Germany's reserves (and which had been identified beforehand by RFC headquarters), went unobserved.[4] Therefore, one element of Gough's plan had already been nullified even before his divisions were out of their trenches. It was an ominous start to the grand offensive.

As soon as the creeping barrage roared into life at Zero Hour – a dark-blue wall of smoke and earth, splashed with red – the first attacking waves scrambled out of their trenches or filtered past breastworks and advanced towards their objectives. 'There had been firing all the night, but at the moment of Zero every gun began to speak', wrote Lieutenant W. B. St Leger of 2/Coldstream Guards (Guards Division). 'The whole horizon to the north east, east and south east, was lit up by one continuous dancing flame composed of jagged flashes of bursting shells.'[5] Across most of the central and northern sections of the Salient – from Westhoek up to Steenstraat – the attacking waves quickly overran the German outpost positions. On the left flank, two French divisions cleared their objectives without prohibitive casualties – the extra time and effort spent on bringing up more guns paying off as the *poilus* secured the northern flank.[6] Likewise, Lord Cavan's XIV Corps took its objectives on time, aided by the collapse of the German position east of the Yser Canal several days earlier. As a result, the Guards Division was able to move on to its second objective by as early as 5 a.m.[7]

In the centre it was much the same story. The two attacking divisions of Sir Ivor Maxse's XVIII Corps were able to follow the creeping barrage and secure their objectives without prohibitive loss.

On the left, the men of 51st (Highland) Division made excellent progress, finding the enemy front-line trenches in most cases 'almost obliterated' by the artillery. Isolated strongpoints posed little problem. 'Whenever a point of resistance disclosed itself,' wrote the divisional history, 'it was attacked immediately by the troops with great dash – not, however, by wild frontal expensive charges, but by the skilful use of ground and their weapons, in accordance with their training.'[8] A young subaltern, Edmund Blunden, serving with 11/ Royal Sussex (39th Division), remembered how 'We rose, scrambled ahead, found No Man's Land a comparatively good surface, were amazed at the puny tags and rags of once multiplicative German wire, and blundered over the once feared trench behind them without seeing that it was a trench.' Fortunately, the German front line – what was left of it – seemed to have been abandoned, so Blunden's men cautiously crept forward. 'German dead, so obvious at every yard of a 1916 battlefield, were hardly to be seen.'[9]

Things were not, however, always so promising. Some of the fiercest fighting that day took place on the front of Herbert Watts's XIX Corps, which extended the attack between Wieltje and the Ypres–Roulers railway. Here the ground was open, gradually rising to the Pilckem Ridge, and was dotted with fortified farm buildings and dull grey pillboxes. Again two divisions would make the assault, 55th and 15th, supported by forty-eight tanks. The attack largely succeeded in reaching the second objective on time, although the village of Frezenberg and the Pommern Redoubt held out.[10] In its report on the action of 31 July, 55th Division complained that it faced pillboxes that 'were quite undamaged in spite of the bombardment by heavy artillery. The concrete was scarcely chipped. A direct hit by a 5.9 on the back of Uhlan Farm failed to make any impression.'[11] Because they had not been destroyed, they would have to be taken out, one at a time, by the infantry using a combination of fire and movement tactics. As the Highland Division had already shown, if specially trained sections were able to suppress and then outflank each pillbox, then they could be neutralized without affecting the pace of the advance. But this always relied upon the gallantry and initiative of officers and men, and the campaign in Flanders would be littered with examples of individuals taking on pillboxes on their own; usually by creeping up to them and throwing grenades through the firing slit, while bayoneting any Germans that tried to escape. Of the sixty-one Victoria Crosses that were awarded for conspicuous gallantry during the battle, more than forty were given to individual attacks on enemy pillboxes or machine-gun nests.[12]

The fight for the first objective was, on the whole, an infantry battle, but 136 tanks had been deployed to support the advance on to the Black and Green Lines. Although only two failed to reach their deployment areas in time for Zero Hour – something of a minor miracle given the ground conditions and incessant shellfire – tanks struggled to make an impact that day. In a report on the action of III Tank Brigade, which supported XIX Corps, the ground was described as being 'as bad as it could have been for a Tank operation', thus confirming the worst fears of the Tank Corps. 'The rain on the 29th July on the top of the heavy "crumping" turned the ground into an absolute swamp with no firm bottom to it . . . Even if a Tank gets over this ground it can only do so at its slowest speed.' Nevertheless, one machine, *Crusader*, helped a battalion of Gordon Highlanders advance to the Black Line by 'dealing with snipers, concrete MG emplacements and strongpoints, which were very numerous . . . Many concrete emplacements were dealt with by 6-pounders, which drove the enemy into the open where our infantry were ready for them with Lewis Guns.' Another tank, *Challenger*, patrolled parts of the Black Line all day, opening fire 'on anything that looked like a MG emplacement'.[13]

Tanks were particularly useful if gaps appeared in the artillery barrage and allowed German troops to recover or if barbed-wire entanglements remained intact. Lance Corporal H. S. Taylor of 1/10th King's Liverpool Regiment (55th Division) went forward that morning only to find his battalion 'hung up' outside their first objective, Capricorn Trench:

> This was still occupied, the wire intact, and there was a machine gun firing from a pill-box immediately in front of us, the combined [effect] of which made any further progress extremely doubtful. The

situation was remedied only a few minutes later when a Tank arrived and . . . disposed of the machine gun and the occupants of Capricorn, at the same time flattening two tracks in the barbed wire, but after crossing over in our direction it was knocked out by a field gun when only a few yards to our left on the slightly higher ground.[14]

Such an experience was typical. Mark IVs had a top speed of 4 mph, but the boggy ground brought their already leisurely pace to a wounded crawl and made them highly vulnerable. Indeed, 31 July would be one of the worst days in the history of the Tank Corps. About half of the total number of tanks fought with some success that day, but the rest became casualties, from either mechanical failure, getting ditched or being knocked out by shellfire.[15]

The problem of coordinating infantry and armour was especially acute at the most crucial point of Fifth Army's attack – on the Gheluvelt Plateau. Indeed, the ground on the southern sector was probably the worst on the entire battlefield. Sir Claud Jacob's II Corps had to take a series of German lines that lay close together and were well supported by artillery batteries on the reverse slope of the ridge. Given the difficulty of the task, Jacob deployed three of his divisions (8th, 24th and 30th) in the firing line, hoping to mass as much combat power as possible. He was also able to call upon 'A' and 'B' Battalions of II Tank Brigade, with forty-eight tanks (and another twenty-four in reserve), to help them secure the second, third and (if possible) fourth objectives. Yet the assault of II Corps was only able to make relatively minor gains; the tanks, in particular, being unable to get very far. Because of the awful ground, it was only possible to use three 'narrow avenues of approach', which left them at the mercy of entrenched German gunners and observers. Of the sixteen vehicles that were to be launched at Zero Hour, three 'were knocked out by shell fire, either at the Starting Point, or before reaching it, and one had mechanical trouble and could not start'. Of the remaining twelve, only four machines were able to engage the enemy, the other eight either suffering direct hits or being ditched.[16]

Only on the left was the attack able to make any sizeable progress. 8th Division overran its first objective on schedule, before setting off

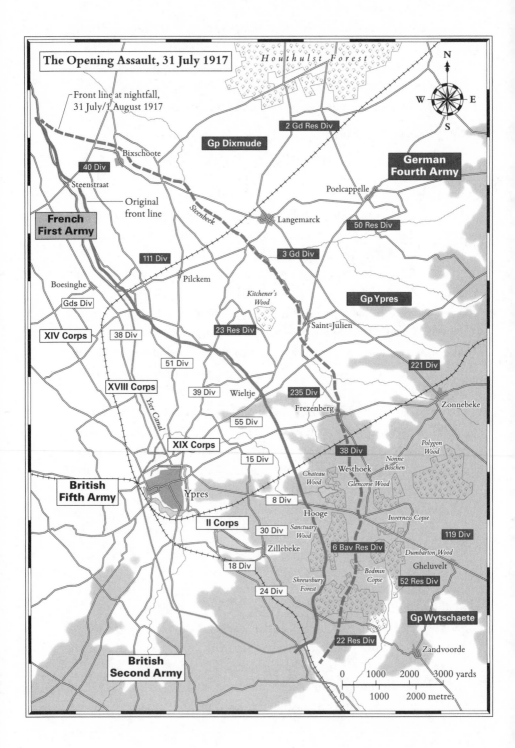

The Opening Assault, 31 July 1917

Front line at nightfall, 31 July/1 August 1917

Original front line

Houthulst Forest

Gp Dixmude

German Fourth Army

2 Gd Res Div

Bixschoote

40 Div

Steenstraat

Poelcappelle

French First Army

111 Div

Steenbeek

Langemarck

50 Res Div

Boesinghe

Pilckem

3 Gd Div

Gds Div

Kitchener's Wood

Gp Ypres

XIV Corps

38 Div

23 Res Div

Saint-Julien

51 Div

221 Div

XVIII Corps

39 Div

Wieltje

235 Div

Zonnebeke

55 Div

Frezenberg

Yser Canal

XIX Corps

15 Div

38 Div

Polygon Wood

Nonne Böschen

Westhoek

British Fifth Army

Ypres

8 Div

Chateau Wood

Glencorse Wood

Inverness Copse

Hooge

II Corps

30 Div

Sanctuary Wood

119 Div

Zillebeke

6 Bav Res Div

Dumbarton Wood

Gheluvelt

18 Div

Bodmin Copse

52 Res Div

24 Div

Shrewsbury Forest

Gp Wytschaete

22 Res Div

Zandvoorde

British Second Army

0   1000   2000   3000 yards

0   1000   2000 metres

for the Black Line on the Westhoek Ridge, only to be stopped by flanking fire from its right.[17] What had happened was that 30th and 24th Divisions, which should have captured Sanctuary Wood and Shrewsbury Forest, had been stopped dead. One after-action report mentioned bogs in 'which men in some instances fell waist high', causing them to 'lose' the creeping barrage. By the time they had secured their first objective and were ready to move on to the second, the artillery support was too far away to recall.[18] Throughout the day, repeated efforts were made to get forward. The experience of 21 Brigade (30th Division), which faced the southern edge of Sanctuary Wood, was symptomatic of what went wrong. One of the assaulting battalions, 19/Manchesters, was caught by enemy fire as it tried to leave its assembly trenches, with grave consequences for the subsequent attack:

> Almost immediately after Zero these entrances became choked by wounded men and others trying to get into the tunnel. The out-going troops were very much hampered in their movements and were only able to get out by ones and twos at a time; this made the assembly in the open difficult, especially as it was still dark and there was a heavy barrage on the British Front Line. Small parties pushed out into No Man's Land in order to get out of the enemy's barrage line, the result was that these two companies were unable to form up in their battle formations and cohesion was lost from the start.

By this point, the battalion was trying to make up for lost time, but heavy shellfire blocked its progress, and allowed the enemy enough time to re-man their strongpoints and machine-gun posts.[19] A reserve division, 18th, was sent forward to secure the Green Line, but found it impossible to reach its forming-up trenches and the attack was abandoned.[20] Unfortunately, the objectives of II Corps, which had been critical to the whole plan, were now – for the moment – out of reach.

Behind the German lines, scraps of information and wild rumours were circulating about what was happening. Johann Schärdel, still sheltering in his concrete bunker, watched in horror as it began to fill

up with casualties, 'who lay and stood in the narrow corridors in
blood-soaked bandages':

> It was impossible to get outside without stepping over casualties and
> pools of coagulated blood. The survivors of a direct hit on a banda-
> ging station that had been jam-packed with casualties and medical staff
> were brought in on stretchers. Most of them were severely wounded,
> and [their rescuers] had risked their own lives to pull them out of
> the rubble of the station. Now the rescued men lay splinted and
> rebandaged [*sic*] in front of the regiment's combat bunker, barely pro-
> tected by the concrete side walls. Clumps of dirt and the dust from
> impacts trickled down continuously from above on to the wounded
> and dying through the brushwood mesh, which served only to shield
> them from the view of aircraft.

The wounded were eager to talk about what they had seen and heard. It
was said that a Prussian unit, sent to relieve the Bavarians, had failed
completely and given themselves up, but no one knew whether it was
true or not. 'One talked about a new type of grenade that hurled
burning liquid and made all resistance impossible . . . A machine
gunner, who was covered in dirt all over, came with what remained
of his weapon, in which a grenade splinter had ripped a large hole in
the cooler.'[21]

All morning the defenders had been engaged in a desperate struggle for survival. The foremost trenches had been garrisoned very
lightly, often by just a handful of machine-gunners, with the majority of the defending troops echeloned in depth and deployed in a kind
of 'chequerboard' pattern, with each strongpoint offering mutual
support.[22] As soon as the British bombardment opened, red flares
began fizzing into the sky, as German units urgently requested protective barrages, but in the murky fog many could not be seen,
leaving the infantry on their own. Across most of the front the
advanced outposts could do little to stem the attacking onslaught.
Around Hooge, the men of 17 Reserve Infantry Regiment (6th
Bavarian Reserve Division) endured heavy drumfire at Zero Hour,
forcing the weak companies in the front line to make a fighting
retreat to their reserve position.[23] At Westhoek, the front-line

positions were 'simply overwhelmed' by the attackers. No officer of II Battalion, 95 Infantry Regiment (38th Division), came back from the front line and only a handful of battered survivors were able to find their way back to the regiment's main position, reporting the 'heroic struggle' in the outpost zone.[24]

Out at the front, German front-line battalions, and their supports, tried to stem the advance, mounting local counter-attacks through curtains of artillery splinters, barrages of long-range machine-gun fire, and predatory passing aircraft. That day there were countless acts of reckless bravery, including the example of Anton Liedl, serving with 17 Reserve Infantry Regiment, who was awarded a Silver Military Merit Medal. He volunteered to maintain contact between his company and battalion headquarters, and made the journey four times, 'heedless of danger and fatigue', until he collapsed from exhaustion.[25] On the Westhoek Ridge, Lieutenant Schmeichel took command of his battery (after his commander was killed) and, almost singlehandedly, destroyed three tanks. Similarly, another junior officer, Lieutenant Heimann, distinguished himself by holding on to his guns, despite being surrounded by attacking infantry. Further to the north, at Pilckem, 23rd Reserve Division was on the point of being relieved when the attack was launched. Major Johannes Scheffer (Commanding Officer III Battalion, 392 Reserve Infantry Regiment), his Adjutant, and Captain Himstedt (1 Lehr Regiment) were all killed after leading a counter-attack armed only with hand grenades.[26]

Supporting units were fed into the fighting as soon as they became available, and did much to slow the British advance, despite suffering from communication and coordination problems brought on by the collapse of the signal networks across the battlefield. At Langemarck, 3rd Guard Division had been sent to relieve 23rd Reserve Division, but had only completed part of its deployment when British troops broke through the Albrecht Line. By 'continuous close quarter fighting', the division was able to hold its ground for most of the morning until shortages of ammunition left them with no choice but to fall back.[27] On the crucial southern sector at Gheluvelt, 52nd Reserve Division had been moved forward as early as five o'clock to reinforce Bavarian troops on the Menin Road. During the advance it sustained 'heavy losses', and 'it was only with difficulty that the waves were able to get through the heavy fire and gas-filled hollows and reach the west edge of the Herenthage Park [the grounds of a ruined chateau southeast of Hooge], where the 4th Company entered the battle . . .' Fighting continued for several hours, but the advance began to slow, 'the enemy having to pay in bloody sacrifices for every inch of ground gained'. Here the Germans ran out of ammunition and hand grenades, and by the time they had re-established communication with their supporting artillery batteries the British had already begun to entrench.[28]

As the morning wore on, news gradually trickled back to the German Fourth Army on the progress of the battle. Although the situation remained confused, with fog and low-lying cloud blanketing much of the battlefield, German aircraft were able to identify the approximate location of their front-line units and provide Fourth Army with a reasonably accurate picture of what was going on.[29] It was evident that the main assault had been delivered, with enemy forces breaking into most of their front-line positions along Groups Wytschaete, Ypres and Dixmude, although in most cases the second line remained intact.[30] German commanders instinctively recognized that now was the moment to deploy the *Eingreif* divisions that lay poised behind the battlefield, ready to intervene, in line with their defensive doctrine.[31] In the north, 2nd Guard Reserve Division was given a warning order at 5 a.m., before moving out to their assembly areas, south of Houthulst Forest, an hour later. In the crucial central sector commanded by Group Ypres, two *Eingreif* divisions were available – 50th Reserve and 221st – and shortly after midday they were ordered to move against the flanks of the British advance between Zonnebeke and Langemarck. In addition to the two regiments from 119th Division (behind Group Wytschaete), which were despatched to Group Ypres, an additional division (79th Reserve) was sent off in the direction of Westroosebeke, and would begin to arrive around five o'clock that evening.[32]

With German reserves moving up, the crisis of the battle was now approaching. A key element of Gough's plan was to try and push as far as possible into the German defences, and shortly after 8 a.m. three reserve brigades from XVIII and XIX Corps began to 'leapfrog' on to the German third position. Yet just getting through the wreckage of no-man's-land was extremely difficult, with the attacking battalions having to run the gauntlet between flurries of shellfire and strong-points that seemed to spring to life again after not being properly 'mopped up' earlier in the day. Lieutenant-Colonel Edward Riddell (officer commanding 1/Cambridgeshires, 39th Division) recorded that as they approached the second objective (the Black Line) – the men shaken out into 'artillery formation' to prevent them from bunching up – they were 'getting it hot and strong, guns and machine-guns':

> But the men never wavered. The officers led on. A signal, and the pla-
> toons split up into sections in file and headed on for St Julien, now lost
> in the smoke of the shell-burst, now coming in view again; shaken for
> the moment as shells exploded amongst them, then reforming, but ever
> advancing steadily and slowly as if nothing unusual had happened.[33]

Worryingly, by the time they reached their objectives, the reserve brigades were exhausted and dangerously exposed. With II Corps coming under intensive counter-attack, it was unclear how long they would be able to hold their ground.

By midday the battle began to tilt – noticeably and irrevocably – in Germany's favour. Paul Maze went forward to find out what was going on, and managed to cross the Steenbeek before running into a heavy barrage. 'The fight had now definitely developed into a new phase', he wrote. 'I felt the pressure of German counter-attacks coming from several quarters, where obviously the progress of our troops was checked, particularly round St Julien, where the fighting was most severe.'[34] Unfortunately, the difficulties of communicating on the battlefield meant that British divisional commanders had only a patchy understanding of what was going on. In 55th Division, communications ran back to Wieltje, and as it was impossible to use visual signalling, runners had to be employed – taking between one and two hours to carry messages the 3,000 yards to the nearest signalling station.[35] Ominously, at one o'clock XIX Corps reported that enemy troops were 'reinforcing [the] Green Line and a large number of infantry [were] going along the Passchendaele Ridge'. Evidently the *Eingreif* divisions were beginning to arrive on the battlefield.[36]

Crucially the contact aeroplanes of the RFC – those despatched to locate infantry positions – were seldom seen and could offer little warning of the impending counter-attack. In any case, infantry were understandably reluctant to mark their positions with flares for fear of attracting enemy aircraft or artillery, giving those few aircraft that did make it over the battlefield an almost impossible job.[37] Lieutenant J. S. Walthew, a pilot with 4 Squadron, was ordered to discover where 'two Divisions had got to' but found flying conditions to be almost impossible. 'I was unable to fly at even a respectable height owing to the clouds, in fact most of the time I was up at about 500 feet. As soon as we got over the lines, where an extraordinarily intense barrage was being put up, we were under continuous machine-gun fire from the Huns.' Walthew had only been in the air for ten minutes when a bullet pierced his fuel tank, and, with petrol flooding all over his legs, he was fortunate to land at a nearby aerodrome without bursting into flames. 'It was a great misfortune having a bad day as otherwise the whole push could have been greatly improved', he wrote afterwards.[38]

As the British had already found out, deploying units on to the battlefield, and then trying to manoeuvre around it, was not easy. British artillery was still trying to seal off the Salient with long-range barrage fire and this badly interfered with the progress of German reinforcements. Personal accounts of those soldiers who served in the *Eingreif* divisions that day are replete with the confusion of battle, and the horror of trying to move forward into what must have been a terrifying and lethal environment. Moreover, they had almost no information on their precise objectives and little coordination with the units already in the line. For example, Reserve Second Lieutenant Alfred Wohlenberg of 77 Reserve Infantry Regiment, part of 2nd Guard Reserve Division (which was assembling on the northern edge of the battlefield), tried to conduct a mounted reconnaissance that afternoon – to sketch out where his division was to counter-attack – but the whole thing was hopeless. His horse ('a miserable looking nag') was terrified of the shelling and reared up constantly; one of his party got stuck in a shell hole and lost his horse; his map dissolved in the mud and rain; and he eventually stumbled into the wrong regimental headquarters having got hope-lessly lost.[39]

Despite the difficulties of deploying on the fire-swept battlefield, the *Eingreif* divisions found themselves up against opponents in an equally precarious situation. In the crucial central sector, the British advance had bogged down around midday, with the reserve brigades scattered by heavy shelling and dislocated by growing enemy pres-sure. 1/Cambridgeshires (118 Brigade) gallantly held off a number of counter-attacks; the first, shortly after midday, was repulsed 'thanks to stout hearts, well-sited trenches, and the number of Lewis and machine-guns salved from tanks'. Yet this would be only a temporary reprieve, and by the late afternoon the entire brigade was beginning to retire.[40] On the Westhoek Ridge, the positions of 8th Division – the only division of II Corps to meet any kind of success – gradually crumbled in the face of renewed attacks, despite the best efforts of Brigadier-General Clifford Coffin (GOC 25 Brigade), who won a Victoria Cross for his gallantry that day. Forty-seven years old and recently promoted, Coffin provided a remarkable example of leader-ship and courage. 'With a coolness and intrepidity which put new life and resolution into all he met, he went about from shell-hole to shell-hole, organizing the defence of the position gained and urging on his troops to new and willing efforts', wrote the divisional history.[41]

British battalions showed remarkable tenacity trying to hold on to their advanced positions, but once one began to pull back, it was inevitable that the others would have to do the same. When they got into position, the *Eingreif* divisions from Group Ypres (50th Reserve and 221st Divisions) were able to make significant progress, retaking sections of the Wilhelm Line, 'with the bayonet and grenade', and sweeping the British back, in most cases, to the line of the Steenbeek, the sluggish stream that ran parallel to Fifth Army's front line.[42] By late afternoon it was known that they had retaken the German third line (the Wilhelm Line) and were pursuing the retreating enemy back towards the second (Albrecht Line). Although some battalion com-manders wanted to keep going, to throw the enemy back even further, Freiherr von Stein at Group Ypres thought better of it. Cas-ualties had been heavy, the troops were exhausted, and he had few reserves left to feed into the battle. Accordingly, he ordered his men to hold the line of the Steenbeek up to Saint-Julien and dig in on the Albrecht Position. For the moment at least, the battle had ended.[43]

Sometime around 4 p.m. the sky clouded over and it started to rain. Soon large drops of water were splashing off tin helmets and forming in puddles on the blasted ground. German regimental histories recall the troops pressing their attacks up to their knees in mud.[44] Yet the *Eingreif* divisions had done their work and played a crucial role in blunting Fifth Army's attack. Gough's corps commanders met their chief at La Lovie at a quarter to eight that evening, with Neill Malcolm welcoming them inside. The men came in, took off their caps, and shook the rain from their capes. Shortly afterwards Gough entered the room. He looked around at their glum faces and sat down, his first words summing up the disappointment on their faces.

'What a perfect bloody curse this rain is!'[45]

Outside it was raining heavily. Long streams of water streaked down the windows of the chateau and squalls battered against the glass as daylight began to fade. The meeting lasted an hour. Gough asked his commanders to tell him how the day had gone, and Jacob, who began, stated that 30th Division had been unable to capture its first objective.[46] Moreover, there was little chance his other divisions would be able to make further gains at the moment. The best that they could hope for was to recover the ground lost in counter-attacks over the next few days. The other corps had fared better and it was decided to try and push them on to the Green Line (the third objective) by 4 August.

Gough had achieved a success, of sorts. Despite his gloom over the weather, the Fifth Army commander was encouraged by what they had achieved. The attack was 'decidedly successful', he felt, only spoilt by the arrival of the rain, which 'soon destroyed all hopes of success'.[47] It was evident that things had not gone to plan on the right, where II Corps had struggled, but elsewhere Fifth Army had advanced about 3,000 yards, taking its first and second objectives on time and without what seemed like prohibitive casualties. Once returns from the battlefield had been collected, total casualties in

Fifth and Second Armies (between 31 July and 3 August) amounted to 31,850.[48] Heavy enough certainly, but mercifully much fewer than had greeted the infamous first day on the Somme the previous year, the greatest disaster in the British Army's history, when 57,000 casualties had been sustained, including over 19,000 dead.[49] This was really where the good news ended, however, and the series of assumptions upon which Gough had planned his assault had proved incorrect, or, at least, seriously flawed. His attempt to drive as deep as possible into the German line had not proved feasible and any troops that had pushed on further than the second objective had been swept back by the *Eingreif* divisions. Thus it seemed that John Davidson's warnings prior to the attack had proved correct and that some other way was required. There was simply no chance that infantry could move, at speed and at distance, through such a layered defensive position. It needed to be bitten off, *one trench at a time*.

For the troops who fought there, the difficulties at Ypres seemed, in some ways, greater than those of 1916. 'It was the Somme over again, except that a Somme battle fought knee-deep in marsh was so much the worse', wrote Charles Carrington, a veteran of both battles.[50] According to the historian of the Welsh Guards, C. H. Dudley Ward, the men found the experience of fighting in the Salient uniquely depressing. From their point of view, seizure of ground did not bring an end to their troubles, only new ones, or, as he put it, 'the capture of one ridge always exposed another on which the enemy was firmly established'.[51] And there was something else, another factor, that made Ypres more dispiriting than the Somme (and something which Edmund Blunden had noticed too): there were fewer dead Germans to be seen on the battlefield – proof that the bulk of their manpower had not been in the front trenches at the time of the attack. Gough may have tried to deliver the knockout blow on 31 July, but that evening there was a sense that, somehow, the Germans had evaded it.

For the German Army, on the contrary, the mood could not have been more different. At the headquarters of Army Group Rupprecht in Courtrai, a full review of the situation was held at midnight. 'The first day of major combat was over', reported Group Ypres. 'Its end result was this: the major offensive that had been prepared with the utmost care for months and equipped with all available resources, and which was carried out with unprecedented force with double superiority in infantry and triple superiority in artillery, had failed utterly.'[52] The British may have managed to penetrate up to three kilometres on a front of sixteen kilometres, but the appalling weather conditions and the continued hold on the Gheluvelt Plateau ensured there was little possibility of a breakthrough. Although not all counter-attacks had been successful and losses had been 'severe', General von Kuhl was confident that the 'momentum of the assault had been broken'.[53]

Lossberg prepared a detailed brief that evening and was pleased to report 'the favourable outcome of the first great defensive struggle'. 'The attack met with strong resistance', he noted. 'A bloody melee, swaying back and forth, but in which our plucky infantry, well supported by our brave artillery, won the upper hand.' After continuous, heavy combat, their troops fought with 'dogged courage'; whenever ground was lost, much of it was soon retaken.[54] In Group Wytschaete, the staff officer Albrecht von Thaer was also pleased. As far as he could tell, they had only lost 'insignificant ground'. 'In any case,' he added, 'in light of the huge efforts on the part of the enemy, it has generally proceeded well and we can thank God if it continues in the same vein.' He continued:

> Of course there is always lots to do, day and night. One gets dead tired. The heavy rain today is a godsend for our troops because the soft, sodden ground hampers the English offensive considerably; it is more of an impediment for the English than it is for us and we could do with the break, to reorganize our groups, replace worn troops with fresh ones. However, it is of course awful for our soldiers to lie there in the water out in the open, especially for the countless injured whose return transport is only happening little by little.[55]

German losses had been heavy. Between 21 and 31 July Fourth Army sustained about 30,000 casualties, including 9,000 missing in action, with thirty-five guns being lost.[56] It had also been extremely expensive in munitions. Field batteries would have fired (on average) about 300 rounds per day during July, but on the first day of the offensive, this soared to over 1,200.[57] It was estimated that on 31 July Fourth

Army's batteries fired off the equivalent of twenty-seven ammunition trains – almost *quadruple* what had been regarded as heavy consumption on the Somme. This was the reality of the *Materialschlacht*.[58]

But could the battle continue? Haig was in a typically bullish mood on the morning of 1 August. He sent one of his liaison officers to tell Pétain that his idea of doing 'nothing serious' on the Western Front until the Americans turned up 'suited the Germans admirably' because it would have allowed them to concentrate all their reserves against Russia. 'In my opinion now is the critical moment of the war,' he added, 'and the French must attack as strongly as possible and as soon as possible so as to co-operate with the British in dealing the Enemy as strong a blow as possible.' Charteris had given him the highlights from an examination of prisoners taken the day before, with the encouraging news that up to 15 per cent of the total 'bag' were from the class of 1918 with a lower morale 'than any lot previously captured'.[59] Buoyed by this news, Haig met Gough and Malcolm at La Lovie the following day. Once again he emphasized the importance of the Broodseinde–Passchendaele Ridge (effectively the high ground on Gough's right) and told the Fifth Army commander that his 'main effort' must be devoted to seizing it. Until this was secured, it would not be possible to push further on with his centre. 'I also told him to have patience', Haig recorded, 'and not put in his infantry attack until after 2 or 3 days fine weather', to allow enough time for the guns to be brought up and the ground to dry out.[60]

Yet the rain kept falling. With the exception of 5 August, which saw the skies temporarily clear, rain fell continuously until 6 August, effectively bringing the offensive to a premature halt. 'Frightful weather. The worst experienced this year. Put a stop to everything except gun fire', wrote A. H. Roberts, a pioneer with 39th Division, on 3 August. 'Our Division is going back, which is something to be thankful for', he noted the following day. 'The sooner we get out of this the better.'[61] Given such appalling weather, it was perhaps inevitable that questions would be asked as to why men were fighting in such aquatic conditions. The weather station at Vlamertinge (just two miles from Ypres) recorded over 21mm of rain on 1 August and nearly 10mm two days later. In the month as a whole, 127mm of rain fell – 57mm more than average (with particularly heavy deluges on 14 and 26 August). Although it has been suggested that, to a certain extent, the heavy rainfall could have been foreseen, in reality there was no way such a terrific deluge could have been predicted by Haig and GHQ. It was the most remarkable spell of weather of the whole war.[62]

By 4 August, with the battlefield inundated, it was evident that any hope for an early resumption of the offensive was premature. That day, owing to the appalling weather, Gough cancelled his orders for the continuation of the attack and began relieving his front-line divisions. It was a decision that no one wanted to take, but it was impossible to keep men in the line, in such atrocious conditions, for any longer. At Montreuil, Charteris was convinced that the rain had saved the Germans from a crushing defeat. 'Every day's delay tells against us', he opined, pacing up and down his office. 'We lose, hour by hour, the advantage of attack.' The Germans could reinforce and reorganize, while they, on the other hand, could do nothing but wait. That morning he went up to the front line, his boots squelching into the mud, and found every brook 'swollen' and the ground 'a quagmire'. In spite of this the mood of the men was 'cheerful, amazingly so'.[63] For the British the long journey up to the Passchendaele Ridge was just beginning.

7.

'Like the Black Hole of Calcutta'

I remember running like a hare and dodging about to avoid
shells, which was absurd. You might as well try to dodge the
raindrops in a thunderstorm.

John Nettleton[1]

6–18 August 1917

It was not until 6 August that the rain finally stopped and the sun
appeared through the banks of dark cloud, shining wanly upon a
landscape that was almost indescribable. Brown earth turned up like
newly ploughed fields; broken coils of wire; clumps of dead bodies;
scattered bits of equipment, rifles, helmets, and shell fragments.
Across it were hundreds of silver moons – reflections of the dull sky
from the shell holes that pockmarked the landscape. 'The ground
very much resembled that of the Somme, every yard being churned
up by shells, the only difference was that many of the holes were a
good deal bigger. Both sides had evidently been using an extraordinary amount of big stuff', remembered Private G. Carter, who moved
up to the front with his field ambulance on 6 August. 'Fritz's lines
were unrecognisable as trenches for they were merely a line of shell
holes with an occasional bit of sand bagging or riveting showing. At
intervals along the support lines, Fritz had built strong block houses
of reinforced concrete and these stood comparatively unharmed.'[2]

Troops moving up to the line could now only do so via a thin network of duckboard tracks that had been laid across the sodden
landscape. German gunners already had most of the major lanes and
crossroads marked out, and their aerial observers quickly spotted the

duckboards that looked like thin white ribbons of a spider's web from the air. Moving along these narrow, precarious wooden paths became one of the enduring memories of the battle for British and Imperial soldiers: conveyor-belts of fear and terror that took them from the (relative) safety of the rear lines, all the way into the front, where there was no possibility of sleep or rest, only uncertainty and, inevitably, sheer terror. For Lieutenant John Nettleton of 2/Rifle Brigade (8th Division) there was always something 'particularly nerve-wracking' about 'plodding along a duckboard track in the middle of a long file of men and hearing the Boche shelling the track a few hundred yards ahead. You couldn't stop – there were always more troops coming up behind you – and you just had to go on, praying fervently that the shelling would stop before you had to walk into it. It always made me feel as though my stomach had fallen out.'[3]

The rain may have caused a temporary halt to Fifth Army's operations, but General Gough was determined to capture those objectives that had eluded him on 31 July. At a conference on 7 August, it was agreed that II Corps would try to secure the Black Line in the next day or two, depending on the state of the ground.[4] Two divisions would make the assault: 18th Division striking towards Inverness Copse and Glencorse Wood; while 25th Division, on its left, pushed into the village of Westhoek. Conditions for the infantry were – to use the Official History's euphemistic phrase – 'most trying'. It had been extraordinarily difficult to move up enough guns to support the attack and no counter-battery fire had been possible for several days owing to the persistent rain. Gough's intelligence officers were also warning that the enemy had reinforced their lines – another division had been spotted along the Roulers railway. Moreover, the two attacking divisions had already been at the front for the best part of a week, after taking over the line between 1 and 4 August. The troops were tired, wet through and thoroughly exhausted.[5]

Getting enough men and supplies to the front line, and making sure routes across the battlefield were kept open, was a logistical problem of the highest order. Because everything had to be brought up from the rear lines, there was almost always a shortage of food and water. British troops were thus forced to live on what Kenneth Page, a battery officer, called a 'very unpleasant diet' of bully beef, hard biscuits and stale bread. What water that did make it up the line was usually housed in two-gallon petrol tins, which inevitably tasted of petrol, and was a source of constant complaint.[6] Brigadier-General C. Godby, the Chief Engineer of II Corps, recorded the constant struggle to keep every-thing moving in his daily progress reports. On 3 August most of the main roads in his sector were closed for lorries for twenty-four hours because of the 'continual rain'. The route to Westhoek was 'said to be little better than a mud road'. Over the following week he marshalled a small army of engineers and Chinese labourers on what seemed like an endless list of jobs: the filling in of shell holes; the construction of shelters and dugouts; the maintenance of pumping installations and water tanks, and so on. By the week ending 4 August his corps work-shop at Busseboom had constructed 2,100 trench boards, 312 yards of mule tracks, ten latrines, over 8,000 pit props, and ten bridges that could take heavy artillery. Whenever time could be spared, Godby also directed the salvage and recovery of ditched tanks, but in this case bad weather 'rendered operations nearly impossible'.[7]

The attack finally went ahead in the early hours of 10 August; a heavy downpour several days earlier causing yet another delay. 18th Division found the enemy waiting for them, putting down a heavy barrage as they went over the top. 'The waves at the extreme end shrivelled under the intense rifle and machine-gun fire that burst out in front and on the flank', wrote the divisional historian. 'Few men escaped unhurt. Those who did sheltered in scattered shell-holes, and trickled back eventually to our original front line.'[8] The chief success of the day was the capture of Westhoek by 25th Division, which managed to hold on to their gains against fierce counter-attacks. Communication was particularly diffi-cult that day. Smoke and dust from the shelling made visual signalling almost impossible; runners were frequently killed or wounded; and cap-tured pillboxes regularly came under direct artillery fire. It was, wrote one witness, 'like the black hole of Calcutta'.[9]

Given the severe handicaps the British were operating under, the results of 10 August were, in some respects, quite encouraging. Yet Fifth Army would find restarting the attack in anything approaching favourable conditions to be almost impossible. The rain and wet, combined with the strength of the German defensive position, meant that by mid-August the British had, effectively, been stopped in their tracks. The weather continued to play havoc with Gough's plans, and he could only look up at the dark sky and curse their atrocious luck. The Fifth Army commander originally wanted major operations to resume on 13 August, but, after a request from Claud Jacob for more time to consolidate his position on the Gheluvelt Plateau, Gough agreed to a twenty-four-hour postponement. Yet rain, and more rain, kept coming down: 18mm fell on 14 August, another 8mm the following day, leaving Gough with no choice but to delay the attack until daybreak on 16 August.[10] The basic outline for the attack (subsequently known as the Battle of Langemarck) was for II and XIX Corps to push on to the German Third Line between Polygon Wood and the Zonnebeke Spur. This would entail an advance of about 1,500 yards. The northern flank would be secured by XVIII and XIV Corps, which would make a shorter advance to Langemarck. On their left, the French First Army would push on towards Langewaade and Merckem.[11]

Preparations for the attack were inevitably far from ideal. The ground was sodden and torn up by the almost continuous shellfire, which meant that in places proper forming-up trenches could not be dug, leaving the infantry exposed in no-man's-land. Moreover, the ground was so wet that tanks could not be deployed, so the attacking companies would be on their own. Indeed, in most places, just getting up to the front line was trial enough. For John Nettleton, serving on the staff of 8th Division in II Corps's sector, 16 August was 'a bad day'; one of the worst he ever lived through. He was given responsibility for guiding an attacking battalion (2/Royal Berkshires) to their jumping-off position in time for Zero Hour at 4.45 a.m. The battalion had to be led from Birr Crossroads up Bellewaarde Ridge and then up on to the high ground at Westhoek. But this would not be easy:

> Even at home, in peacetime conditions, troops moving across country in single file in the dark almost always lose touch. Here, with the broken ground and under shellfire most of the time, keeping touch was an impossibility. The delay caused by one casualty, or even by men ducking and falling about when a shell comes near, is enough to

break the line and once it is broken it is extremely difficult to catch up. The slightest check is cumulative and, even on a road, the back of a column can be running and still be left behind. And here you couldn't run, even if you wanted to.

Nettleton did his best. He stationed teams armed with red-light torches on the reverse slope of Westhoek Ridge to act as markers (with strict instructions to flash their torches from 11 p.m. till the battalion turned up). He was allocated sixteen guides (one per platoon) and told the commanding officer how important it was 'that every man should keep in touch with the man in front of him'. Yet the battalion still got lost. Despite leading the column as slowly as he dared, with frequent pauses, it took Nettleton most of the night to reach their destination (the red-light teams having given up long ago). When they finally reached Westhoek Ridge, Nettleton found that only one company had followed him. He retraced his steps, splashing through the mud and sludge, and eventually found the 'missing sheep' with twenty minutes to go before Zero Hour.[12]

Nettleton's account of the difficulties of getting the attacking battalions into the correct positions was mirrored across the front of that dripping wet night of 15/16 August. The sheer logistical challenges posed by the battlefield made even simple deployments incredibly taxing. Brigadier-General G. H. B. Freeth, commander of 167 Brigade (56th Division), made a number of urgent representations to higher command for the attack to be postponed because of the grave difficulties he was having in getting his brigade into position. Not only was the ground 'almost impassable', but one of his supporting units (3/London) had already been 'on the move' for three nights. Moreover, the two attacking battalions 'would have less than 24 hours to study the ground – a matter of great difficulty at any time owing to the continuous shelling, the lack of thorough reconnaissance, time for arranging details and studying orders, and the absence of efficient means of communication in the forward area'. As a prelude to a major attack, things could hardly have been worse.[13]

When Zero Hour came the attack verged, in places, on a fiasco, and Freeth's warnings about the lack of time for preparation were proved perfectly sound. The southern and central attacking corps, II and XIX, achieved almost nothing. For 56th Division, supposed to form a southern defensive flank, the initial advance progressed smoothly, with small holding parties of the enemy fleeing before the attacking brigades, but when they ran into a 'broad belt of mud', about thirty yards across and up to five feet deep, the attackers 'lost' their barrage. Isolated German strongpoints remained in action and held up repeated attempts to get forward. At a brigade inquest several days later, the reasons for the failure were spelled out bluntly. 'The time available for preparation and reconnaissance was insufficient. There was not time to get objectives etc., fully into the heads of officers, NCOs and men, and the assembly prior to the assault was carried out with some difficulty in consequence.'[14]

It was even worse in the centre, where H. E. Watts's XIX Corps was to push forward across a mile of open ground towards Gravenstafel. Attacking side by side, 16th (Irish) and 36th (Ulster) Divisions, were to fight their way through a forbidding maze of mutually supporting pillboxes and ruined farms. Yet the attacking divisions were already well below fighting strength on the day of the assault, having been in the line for a fortnight (during which a considerable proportion of their manpower was occupied in carrying parties and manual labour).[15] Cyril Falls, the Ulster divisional historian, noted grimly that 'The story of the attack, alas! is not a long one.' As soon as the men went 'over the top', they were met with heavy machine-gun fire from a number of key strongpoints across the front, including Gallipoli Farm, Schuler Farm, Hindu Cott and Border House. These 'seemed to be entirely unaffected by the pounding of many weeks' and were, in some cases, considerable fortifications in their own right, containing up to six different compartments. 'The ground was a veritable quagmire', Falls continued. 'The "mopping-up" system was found to be impossible. The concrete works had to be fought for; they could not be passed by and left to "moppers up" in rear.'[16]

British and French divisions had fared better on the left sector of the attack, pushing forward across the flooded Steenbeek and taking Langemarck, but the cost had been disastrous – over 15,000 casualties, proving, yet again, how dangerous the German Army remained.[17] On

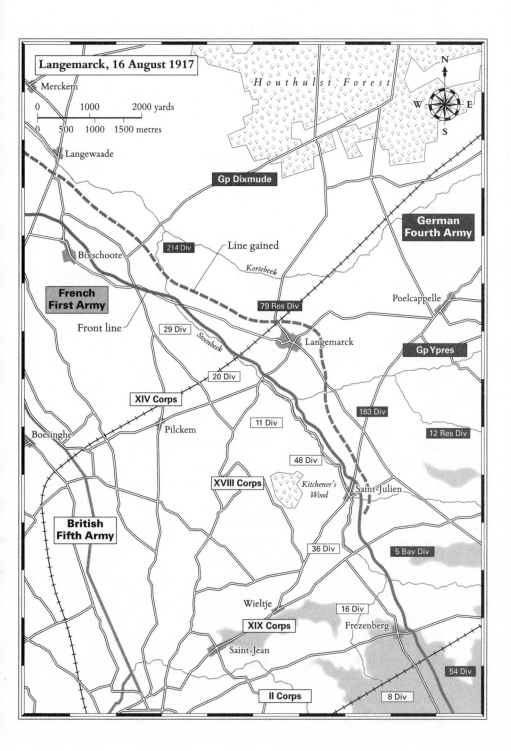

Langemarck, 16 August 1917

Merckem

0 — 1000 — 2000 yards
0 — 500 — 1000 — 1500 metres

H o u t h u l s t   F o r e s t

N
W · E
S

Langewaade

Gp Dixmude

German Fourth Army

214 Div

Line gained

Kortebeek

Bixschoote

French First Army

79 Res Div

Poelcappelle

Front line

29 Div

Steenbeek

Langemarck

Gp Ypres

20 Div

XIV Corps

183 Div

Pilckem

11 Div

12 Res Div

48 Div

Boesinghe

XVIII Corps

Kitchener's Wood

Saint-Julien

British Fifth Army

36 Div

5 Bav Div

Wieltje

16 Div

XIX Corps

Frezenberg

Saint-Jean

54 Div

II Corps

8 Div

this northern part of the battlefield, Lieutenant-Colonel R. J. Clarke's battalion, 1/4th Royal Berkshires (48th Division), were in action. He described what happened in a letter to his mother several days later:

> The attack pushed on in spite of all the difficulties. The Hun chief defences here are a series of concrete gun-pits and shelters, very strongly made, and well scattered, so that each helps the others, and the MG fire was heavy. One of them was surrounded with water and marsh except one pathway to it. They will keep out all but the largest shells and hold about 20/30 men each. We found them very useful after we had taken a few! The Brigade did well and especially the Bucks. We were in reserve, though some of the companies got in for part of the fighting and did well. We found the Bavarians opposite us and they fought well, there was none of that low moral[e] that you read about. We had never met it yet in any of our fighting though the Division who were in the line 3 days previously were a different lot from all accounts. The ground was so bad that the tanks could not move to help us. If they had, we should have taken all our objectives.[18]

For the Germans it was an entirely different story. The defenders had undoubtedly suffered badly from the wind and rain and slushy conditions, but when the attack came, it was easier to lie in shell holes or crouch in bunkers and pick off the attacking waves than it was to try and cross the flooded battlefield. The British attack had been heralded by an 'extremely violent' barrage that crashed down upon their positions, followed shortly thereafter by the infantry trailing in its wake. 'On both sides of the Staden–Boesinghe railway they broke into the German positions', recorded the German Official History. 'North of the railway they crossed the Steenbeek up to Bixschoote and pushed German troops back from the east bank of the Kortebeek. South of the railway they took Langemarck, claimed parts of St Julien and even penetrated into Poelcappelle.' In the northern sector, German units were unable to push the attackers back, and although there was fierce fighting for the village of Langemarck, the British were able to hold on.[19]

On the crucial southern sector, things were much more satisfactory, and the *Eingreif* divisions proved their effectiveness once again. Shortly after 9 a.m. three regiments of 12th Reserve Division launched a counter-attack against the 16th and 36th Divisions, which had made only precarious advances towards their objectives. Because the RFC had been unable to spot the Germans as they assembled, the exhausted Irishmen were taken by surprise when columns of enemy infantry came up over the Zonnebeke Spur and overran their forward positions. Within an hour, most of the advance parties had been killed or pushed back to their original starting line.[20] Despite their success, the *Eingreif* divisions seem to have encountered similar problems to 31 July – namely a lack of information about their objectives and a difficulty in moving forward. A junior officer, Schmidt (who was serving with the reserve regiment of 5th Bavarian Division), left a description of what happened that afternoon. 'Nothing is known from the front', he wrote. 'Scant and muddled news of the injured is flowing in. Where is the battalion now? Has the counter-attack been successful?' Eventually an advance was ordered:

> There is a hellfire across the whole terrain. Building a telephone wire is futile. There is no visibility for transmitting a message by signal lamp. But something needs to happen . . . We run like lunatics between the house-high mushrooms of exploded shells. Where are we now? Keep on going; it's definitely the right direction. We are bound to come across Germans or Tommies. Behind a hedge in a somewhat less flame-ridden stretch we catch our breath. We need to orientate ourselves! We have to make sure that we continue in a westerly direction! Out of the sheaf of fire!

They managed to reach their I Battalion, the field-grey soldiers strung out along the Wilhelm *Stellung* – the third German line – which was again under heavy shellfire, where they lay in support. That day Schmidt's regiment captured three officers and 157 men of 36th Division. As the Ulstermen were being shepherded to the rear, he found an officer crouching in a ditch, unable to move. 'His round, watery blue eyes in his clean-shaven face speak in wonderment at how quickly it has all happened.' They took the officer with them and a few minutes later found out that the counter-attack had been successful.[21]

Air and artillery support had been crucial to the defensive effort. *Jagdgeschwader* 1 shot down sixteen enemy aircraft that day, including the fifty-eighth victim of Manfred von Richthofen, who came upon a flight of Nieuport Scouts during a routine patrol. 'After a long chase, I attacked an opponent and after a short fight I shot up his engine and fuel tank.' The aircraft – piloted by Second Lieutenant W. H. T. Williams of 29 Squadron – went into a spin and crashed somewhere over Houthulst Forest, at the northern edge of the battlefield.[22] On the ground, German guns fired off a 'tremendous' number of shells, which the historian Werner Beumelburg credited for their dogged resistance. He estimated that over 269,000 shells had been fired by German batteries on 16 August. If the British are presumed to have used about double that, then the total number of shells on that day alone would have exceeded all those fired in the entire Franco-Prussian War of 1870–71.[23] With only nine trains in reserve for the entire Army Group, Crown Prince Rupprecht was understandably concerned at whether they could keep this kind of profligacy up. Yet the line, or what was left of it, held. When Rupprecht saw some English prisoners, they told him that they would prefer it if their own officers had been shot, rather than go through the slaughter![24]

One of those involved in the artillery battle was Reinhard Lewald, who returned to his battery on 9 August. He had recently attended a three-week shooting course at Maubeuge, and was not looking forward to coming back into the Salient. His battery position was 'not exactly brilliant':

> Two guns are at a shattered homestead on the eastern edge of the Hollebusch [a forested area north of Becelaere]. The third gun is about 200 metres forward of Hollebusch itself. We cannot dig stands or ammunition stores in the earth, because we immediately hit groundwater. The area is so marshy, in the continuous rain, that we need to perpetually improve the route to the battery with stones to get the ammunition in and to pull out the guns. The battery is not yet detected by the enemy, but the whole area is under fire day and night from evil explosive shells, which is very unpleasant for us in our meagre accommodation of corrugated iron huts.[25]

On 16 August the battery fired as many shells as the barrels would stand. 'The enemy has suffered terrible losses', Lewald wrote. By that afternoon the British had spotted his guns and were directing heavy counter-battery fire against them, so he ordered his men to pull out temporarily in order to escape the worst of it. When they returned later on, they found a cratered, smoking mess. 'Trenches have been created that one could put a whole mortar platoon in.' Even worse, the shelling had struck a war cemetery, so that 'dozens of bodies' were torn out of the ground. Several of their shelters had also been struck by direct hits. But, fortunately, Lewald and his men, with their precious guns, had survived.[26]

The Battle of Langemarck had been a significant victory for Fourth Army, and German commanders were understandably elated at how things were progressing. 'To the leaders and teams who prepared and fostered the fight and contended successfully for victory, I give thanks and credit', read an order of the day from General Sixt von Armin. He particularly credited the work of the stretcher-bearers and medical orderlies whose 'spirited conduct and tireless activity' had made it possible to get the wounded back from the front lines within a relatively short period of time. 'The doctors who applied themselves to their difficult task with the utmost dedication at the troop dressing stations, main dressing stations and field hospitals, the entire nursing staff, and the entire medical vehicle and ambulance service detachment also deserve full credit for their fruitful cooperation.'[27] It was clear to von Armin who was winning the battle.

In London the atmosphere remained tense. As early as 3 August, the War Cabinet had raised the subject of whether the offensive had 'realised the hopes anticipated of it', with Robertson working furiously to dampen down any signs of an imminent revolt.[28] Haig wrote a report on 'the battle of 31 July 1917', which was passed to the War Cabinet on 4 August. He regarded the results of the battle as being 'most satisfactory'. Moreover, he was confident that the objectives they had gained thus far would 'facilitate very greatly' the preparations for a subsequent advance once the ground had dried up.[29] Nevertheless, the pressure on Haig was increasing. Robertson wrote to him on 9 August, updating him on Lloyd George's support for an Allied General Staff, an idea which had been dusted off at a meeting with the French and Italians on 7–8 August. The Prime Minister had tried a version of this before, during the infamous Calais conference in February, but he was evidently still anxious for some kind of unified military staff. 'As the French keep rubbing in that it is necessary to have a Central Staff at Paris I can see Lloyd George in the future wanting to agree to some organization so as to put the matter in French hands and to take it out of mine', Robertson wrote grimly. 'However we shall see all about this.'[30]

Despite the stuttering beginning to the offensive, Haig was in no mood to reconsider his plans for the remainder of the year, and Robertson's growing unease made little impression upon him. He was determined to reassert his authority and remind London how important it was to persevere with his operation, which, he was sure, was bound to lead to positive results. 'You already know my views', he replied to Robertson on 13 August. 'Briefly, this being the decisive point, the only *sound* policy is for the Government to support me *whole heartedly*, and concentrate all possible resources here. And do it *now* while there is time, instead of continuing to discuss other enterprises.' Haig repeated his well-worn refrain that the enemy could only be beaten if he was given adequate support. An 'occasional glance at our daily intelligence summaries would convince even the most sceptical of the truth of what I write', and moreover 'I have been in the field now for 3 years and know what I am writing about.'[31]

Haig remained buoyant about the prospects for future success. In part this was because of what had happened at Hill 70, north of Lens in Artois, where the Canadian Corps had been in action. On 15 August, 1st and 2nd Canadian Divisions launched a diversionary 'bite-and-hold' attack on the high ground overlooking the town. The operation had originally been scheduled for the beginning of August, but the awful weather resulted in repeated postponements until the middle of the month. Supported by a brutal artillery bombardment, and with thoughtful, precise and detailed planning, Canadian troops managed to seize the high ground, dig in, and wait for the inevitable German response. Over the next ten days, the ground around Lens became a hecatomb of slaughter as German units were drawn into a vicious fight to recapture the high ground. In total over 9,000 Canadians would be killed or wounded in what was only a 'diversionary attack'.[32] Yet it achieved its aim. Seven German divisions had fought at Hill 70 and suffered up to 20,000 casualties. It was a perfect example of attritional warfare in action.[33]

The slaughter at Lens was, for Haig at least, an indication that the Germans were close to breaking. The intelligence coming from Charteris's office only seemed to confirm what he had always suspected. The German Army was evidently struggling to hold its ground: some units had been broken by the fighting; younger soldiers were now being drafted in earlier than anticipated; and it was thought that enemy divisions were being used up on the Flanders sector much quicker than they had been on the Somme. Haig, therefore, remained bullish about the prospects of the war, telling his senior staff officers on 19 August that '*if we can keep up our effort*, final victory may be won by December'.[34] Yet not everyone shared his confidence. At the War Office in London, Robertson's own intelligence sources left him with a much less sanguine interpretation of German weakness, and in his letter of 13 August Haig chided the CIGS for issuing 'pessimistic estimates' that jarred with his own assessments on the state of the German Army. 'They do, I feel sure, much harm and cause many in authority to take a pessimistic outlook when a contrary view, based on equally good information, would go far to help the nation on to victory', he added, not entirely helpfully.[35]

The truth was that while much of the intelligence GHQ received was not in itself inaccurate (even if less positive news tended to be downplayed), Haig was at fault for reading too much into it and forcing it to fit his own preconceptions. Relying heavily upon prisoner examinations – a notoriously unreliable source – Haig was convinced that many German divisions were either worn out by constant combat or on the verge of a catastrophic collapse in morale.[36] By this stage even Charteris – supposedly the 'high priest' of Haig's offensive doctrine – was disagreeing with his commander-in-chief. On 18 August, Charteris authored a report that predicted Germany could only stand the strain of current operations for a maximum of twelve months provided fighting was maintained '*at its present intensity*'. When Haig got hold of it, he went 'much further', reporting to the War Office that the time was 'fast approaching when Germany will be unable to maintain her armies at their present numerical strength'.[37] For Haig, as he had repeatedly told his superiors, there must be no let-up in the offensive.

This was the moment when the Prime Minister should have acted. Maurice Hankey was convinced that Lloyd George should have pressed for a searching re-examination of the offensive sometime in the middle of the month. The continuation of operations was always dependent upon results, and given the modest returns so far, Downing Street would have been more than justified in looking again at what was happening in Flanders.[38] That Haig was allowed to continue his attacks has always been a matter of debate and controversy. Lloyd George would later claim – loudly and persistently – that he had been deceived, and that the War Cabinet never received the full, unvarnished truth about what was happening on the battlefields of Ypres.[39] There was certainly something to this (and indeed the Prime Minister suffered from a lack of crucial information on occasions), but it should not be taken too far. Ultimately, at this critical moment in Britain's war effort, Lloyd George was found wanting. If he really believed there was a viable alternative to the Western Front, then he had to take advantage of Haig's misfortune and act upon it. His failure to do so would haunt him for the rest of his life.

The first mention of the Flanders operation at the War Cabinet was on 2 August, with Robertson doing little to illuminate his colleagues on its progress. He had, he said, 'little to add to what had appeared in the press' and that 'we had achieved all our objectives' across two thirds of the front.[40] While the subject was raised briefly the following day (and after Haig's first despatch was circulated), it was not until 17 August that the Western Front was discussed again in any detail, with the Director of Military Intelligence, Major-General Sir George Macdonogh, reporting on the recent attack at Langemarck. It had been 'completely successful' on the left, but elsewhere 'strong opposition' had been encountered with the enemy still occupying the high ground. Macdonogh was encouraged by 'signs of weakening' in German reserves, but admitted that the weather was 'bad' and, owing to the nature of the ground, it was unlikely they would capture particularly large batches of prisoners. Casualties since 31 July were over 45,000.[41]

Macdonogh's report, when stripped of its War Office gloss, revealed a number of things: Haig's attacks had not been entirely successful; the Germans were still resisting fiercely; the enemy remained in possession of the crucial high ground; and casualties had been heavy. Yet Lloyd George failed to act upon this sobering information. When Hankey pressed him on it, he found him to be curiously lethargic and 'unresponsive'.[42] Still smarting from the tiring arguments of June and July, and distracted by other business (including Smuts's important memorandum on the organization of air operations, which was delivered on 17 August), the Prime Minister seems to have let his focus slip when, arguably, it should have been resolutely directed on the Salient. Instead Lloyd George dealt with business as it came in – railway unrest, war risks insurance, the output of heavy guns, reserves of wheat, and so on – while struggling with persistent neuralgia that frayed his temper. It was little wonder that during August he spent a considerable amount of time at one of his country retreats, Great Walstead in Sussex, which provided a much-needed, albeit temporary, respite from the crushing pressures of London.[43]

Haig sent his second despatch on the battle to the War Cabinet on 21 August. He was keen to explain why no breakthrough had been achieved and why the Government must keep faith with his plans. 'For several days after the date of my last report', he wrote, 'the weather continued so unfavourable that a renewal of the advance in Flanders was impossible.' This 'unavoidable delay' allowed time for the enemy to bring up reinforcements and launch 'heavy counter-attacks' against his forces. Nevertheless, Fifth Army had gained important ground, and any further advance up towards the crest at Broodseinde would mean undeniable progress – gaining 'valuable advantages of position' and going 'a long way' to break down the enemy's 'power of resistance'. After repeating his 'conclusive evidence' of German decline – drawn from Charteris's report – Haig admitted that the battle was likely to continue 'for some weeks yet'. There was, therefore, only one thing to do: 'to continue to press the enemy in Flanders without intermission and to the fullest extent of our power; and, if complete success is not gained before winter sets in, to renew the attack at the earliest possible moment next year'.[44]

Haig's continued wish to go on was, to some extent, understandable – he was, after all, a proud man – but it paid little attention to how quickly the Flanders operation was descending into Somme-like conditions. Langemarck had been taken, but the push on the crucial high

ground at Gheluvelt had stalled badly and there was no indication of
when Fifth Army would get going again. But both Haig and Gough
saw little to reproach themselves for. Haig was concerned at the poor
ground conditions and felt that more time should have been allowed
for artillery preparation (time which he could have granted had he
been so minded), while Gough took solace in blaming his own men.[45]
At a conference at La Lovie on 17 August, the Fifth Army commander made it clear that he wanted investigations into 'the causes of
troops failing in certain instances to hold the ground they had gained'.
If they had withdrawn without sufficient cause, he wanted officers
and NCOs court-martialled.[46]

Yet if Gough's account is to be believed, he was not an unthinking
martinet devoted to the offensive at all costs. According to his memoirs, the Fifth Army commander lost faith in the Flanders operation
sometime in late August. Apparently, he went to see Haig and told him
that the offensive must be called off, only for the Commander-in-Chief
to ignore him and insist that the British must bear this 'heavy burden'
on their own.[47] Whether Gough really made such a strong representa-
tion is unclear. It has been suggested that this was subsequently invented
to put him in a better light, when he was fighting to restore his reputation, and there is probably much in this.[48] Gough had never been one to
shy away from maintaining an offensive, even if it was unlikely to succeed, and he continued ordering attacks (to 'straighten the line') until
the second week of September. The reality was that Gough was never
likely to abandon the mission he had been given in Flanders. There was
simply too much at stake, both personally and professionally, for him
to back down.[49] So on it went: the endless columns of mud-splattered
infantry making their way to the front on thin, wobbly duckboards;
the 'iron rain' of shellfire that never stopped; the rushed attacks on narrow fronts pressed forward with hope and gallantry, but little chance
of success. The enduring image of Passchendaele was being created.

It took days, in some cases weeks, to recover all the wounded from
the attack on 16 August. Army doctors and nurses at the Advanced
Dressing Stations witnessed the worst scenes as men, or what was left of
them, were brought in. Captain Martin Littlewood, a Royal Army
Medical Corps doctor with 15th (Scottish) Division, was charged with

running a dressing station near Potijze Château (on the eastern outskirts of Ypres). It was tiring and dangerous work. On 18 August one of his men was hit in the doorway with 'a piece of hot shell'. Littlewood's diary entry for the following day conveys the monotonous horror of daily life in the Salient:

> Heavy crumps all round us, some very near. Another man hit in the doorway. This went on from 11.30 a.m. to midnight. Intense barrage of 5.9's on road. One ambulance car knocked out at noon. Three stretcher dumps round us blown up. Some 70 of them in matchwood [*sic*]. Three direct hits on building. Amputated leg of Lieutenant Templeton. At midnight a dump set alight 500 yards down road, mostly smoke bombs and Very lights [flares].[50]

Littlewood struggled to keep his own spirits up, but no matter how bad conditions in the chateau got, he was always amazed at how stalwart were those who were carried in to see him. On 24 August a sergeant in the Royal Inniskilling Fusiliers was stretchered in, heavily wounded, his uniform plastered with mud. He had lain in a shell hole for nine days. Another Irishman whom he treated had been on the battlefield for eleven days. He had been tending two wounded men, and it was only when they died that he made his way, crawling, back to his lines. Such was the fate of the wounded on the Flanders battlefield.

Given such awful conditions, it is little wonder that morale began to suffer. 16 August was more than just another failed offensive; it seemed to become a tipping point, which badly affected Fifth Army's mood and dented whatever remaining confidence was left in its commander. The experience of the Irish divisions was particularly heartbreaking. For Philip Gibbs, an official war correspondent, the 'general opinion' after the battle was that they had been 'the victims of atrocious staff-work, tragic in its consequences'. Moreover he found both officers and men 'violent in their denunciation of the Fifth Army for having put their men into the attack after those thirteen days of heavy shelling', and then 'cast [them] aside like old shoes'.[51] Cyril Falls, writing about 36th Division, which had suffered so badly that day, vented similar frustration, contrasting the division's experience at Messines (when it had been in Second Army), with the operations under Gough's command.

The system of liaison was practised by the Second Army as in no other. General Harington's car stopped at every door, and the cheerful young staff officers, who knew every communication trench on the Army front, who drank with company commanders in their front-line dug-outs before coming back to tea with a Brigadier, or with General [Oliver] Nugent [GOC 36th Ulster Division] at his Headquarters, formed a very real link between the Higher Command and the troops ... The difficulties at Ypres were infinitely greater than at Messines; that everyone recognised. But in the former case they did not appear to be met with quite the precision, care, and forethought of the latter. The private soldier felt a difference.[52]

There were other indications too that morale was beginning to suffer. An army postal censor reported in late August that there was 'a feeling of uncertainty as to the progress of our arms to an ultimate victory, and a growing inclination to believe that military enterprise must give place to political ingenuity'.[53]

Notwithstanding the growing unease, the offensive – what was left of it – went on. At his conference on 17 August, Gough discussed plans for a new, and hopefully decisive, attack scheduled for 25 August. Before that could take place, it was essential to 'straighten the line' and secure all those objectives that had not fallen in the last attack, so a series of minor operations were sanctioned: XVIII Corps on 19 August; II Corps on 21 August; and XIX Corps on 22 August. Once these attacks had been successfully concluded, Fifth Army would then, hopefully, be in a position to mount more decisive operations.[54] The mood of Gough's commanders remains unclear – no dissent was recorded – but there must have been a sense of dreadful monotony about ordering yet more attacks against strongpoints and woods that should have fallen on the first day, but were still resisting strongly. 'We must be careful not to waste Divisions', Gough warned his commanders, 'or we should run short of troops.' Yet the Fifth Army commander was committing one of the cardinal sins of war on the Western Front, one, moreover, that he had already committed earlier in the year at Bullecourt: ordering attacks on narrow fronts without flanking support and without enough time to prepare effectively. It would be his last chance.

1. The British Prime Minister, David Lloyd George. He promised to deliver a 'knock out blow' against Germany, but was deeply opposed to Haig's offensive in Flanders. His failure to stop the battle would haunt him for the rest of his life.

2. Field Marshal Sir Douglas Haig, Commander-in-Chief of the BEF, was convinced that the war could be won in Flanders, but proved unable to achieve decisive victory in 1917.

3. General Sir William Robertson, Chief of the Imperial General Staff, was a bluff and no-nonsense soldier, but found himself caught between Lloyd George's opposition to an attack in Flanders and Haig's determination to mount a decisive operation.

4. Kaiser Wilhelm II (*centre*) studying maps at the German High Command with Field Marshal Paul von Hindenburg (*left*) and General Erich Ludendorff (*right*). Despite remarkable operational success in 1916–17, Germany ultimately proved unable to secure lasting strategic gains.

5. Crown Prince Rupprecht of Bavaria, commander of Germany's northern Army Group. He would have liked to pre-empt the British offensive in Flanders with a spoiling attack, but shortages of manpower and ammunition ruled it out.

6. General Sir Hubert Gough,
commander of the British
Fifth Army, was chosen to lead
the main assault at Ypres. A
'thruster', he was loyal to Haig
but distrusted by the rest of
the army.

7. British stretcher-bearers pose for a photograph in the ruins of Pilckem during the first day of the battle, 31 July 1917.

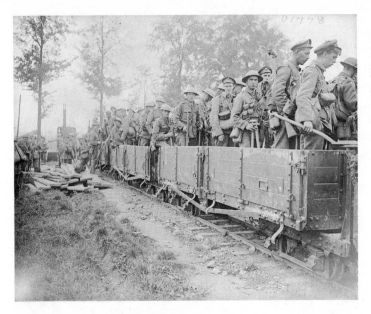

8. Men of a pioneer battalion getting out of light railway trucks, Brielen, outside Ypres, 31 July 1917.

9. 'If I were asked to name the heroes of the Third Battle of Ypres, my vote would go to the pack horses which brought up the field artillery ammunition.' Pack mules loaded up with shells move up to the front somewhere near Ypres, 1 August 1917.

10. British troops moving forward over shell-torn ground near Pilckem, 16 August 1917, during the ill-fated Battle of Langemarck.

11. Crown Prince Rupprecht distributing medals in Flanders. By the autumn of 1917, the German High Command admitted that the circumstances in Flanders 'exceeded the horror of anything previously experienced'.

12. Kaiser Wilhelm II pays a visit to Flanders, August 1917 (presumably along the coastal sector). From the left the front three men are Crown Prince Rupprecht, the Kaiser, and Sixt von Armin (Chief of Staff of the German Fourth Army).

13. Wounded German soldiers at the command post of 19 Infantry Regiment, somewhere near Ypres, August 1917.

14. Soldiers of 5th Bavarian Division in trenches near Gravenstafel, August 1917. The division took a key role in repulsing British attacks during the Battle of Langemarck.

15. General Sir Herbert Plumer, commander of the British Second Army, took over the main assault from Gough in late August 1917. His care and attention to detail were legendary. He would become perhaps the most beloved and successful British general of the war.

16. A shell bursts near a party of British stretcher-bearers and German prisoners near Zillebeke, during the Battle of the Menin Road, 20 September 1917.

17. The view from Stirling Castle (a strongpoint south of the Menin Road) on 23 September 1917, showing derelict tanks amid a sea of shell holes. In the distance lies Sanctuary Wood, the scene of fierce fighting on 31 July.

18. The bodies of German soldiers lying outside a group of concrete blockhouses near Zonnebeke, 23 September 1917. By 1917 British infantry were trained and equipped to deal with such strongpoints, but attacking them always required great courage. Of the sixty-one Victoria Crosses that were awarded during the battle, over forty were for individual attacks on enemy pillboxes.

19. A German bombing patrol, with messenger dog, probably taken in late September 1917.

20. A German observation patrol, September 1917. German counter-attacking tactics were dependent upon good observation of the battlefield, but this was frequently not possible because of mist, rain, smoke and dust.

21. Men of the West Yorkshire Regiment shelter in a captured German pillbox along the St Julien–Gravenstafel road during the Battle of Polygon Wood.

22. Royal Field Artillery ammunition limbers moving up the Menin Road, 26 September 1917. The Menin Road was a vital logistics route throughout the battle, but was regularly swept by heavy fire.

23. Aerial view of Polygon Wood, 5 September 1917. By the time it was captured by Australian soldiers on 26 September, the wood had been reduced to nothing but 'charred and splintered stumps standing about three or four feet high . . . totally devoid of any life'.

24. German prisoners captured during the Battle of Polygon Wood, 26 September 1917. The man facing the camera is showing the classic 'thousand yard stare' common to those who have faced extreme trauma.

25. A group of German prisoners make their way through the ruins of Ypres on 27 September 1917 after being captured on the Tower Hamlets Spur. The Battle of Polygon Wood was the second 'step' taken by Plumer and illustrated, yet again, how effective 'bite and hold' could be.

26. The headquarters of 3rd Australian Division in the ramparts of Ypres. Sir John Monash, the commander, described it as being 'like the underground workings of mines, narrow tunnels, broadening out here and there into little chambers, the whole lit by electric light'.

27. 24/Australian Battalion dug-in on the Broodseinde Ridge, 5 October 1917. The Battle of Broodseinde was one of the most successful battles of the campaign and provoked panic in the German High Command.

28. Senior German officers, including Sixt von Armin (*centre, looking up*) and Field Marshal Hindenburg (*second from right*), meet some of their men after the Battle of Broodseinde. By early October the German High Command admitted that it could do nothing to stop properly executed limited attacks.

29. A German soldier takes the opportunity to snooze in the entrance to a blockhouse, somewhere in the Ypres Salient.

30. German troops and transports in the village of De Ruiter, southwest of Roulers, sometime in the autumn of 1917.

31. British 60-pounder guns firing in the mud near Langemarck, 12 October 1917. Despite herculean efforts, it was not possible to move enough guns and shells forward to support the assault on Passchendaele.

32. Dead and wounded Australians in a cutting along the Ypres–Roulers railway, 12 October 1917. This was taken by the Australian official photographer, Frank Hurley, who described coming across an 'awful sight: a party of ten or so telephone men all blown to bits'.

33. Captain Clarence Jeffries (of 34/Australian Battalion) was awarded a posthumous Victoria Cross for his actions on 12 October 1917 during the doomed push towards Passchendaele. After taking out a number of pillboxes, he was shot and killed.

34. Troops of 10 Australian Brigade drying their clothes on 14 October, two days after the abortive First Battle of Passchendaele. After spearheading the attacks since late September, the fighting on 12 October marked the end of Australia and New Zealand's involvement in the battle.

35. Sir Arthur Currie with his staff at the headquarters of the Canadian Corps at Poperinge. When Currie was asked to take the Passchendaele Ridge he was unimpressed, reportedly saying that it 'was not worth a drop of blood' and would cost 16,000 casualties.

36. Canadian success at Passchendaele was dependent upon painstaking (and frequently backbreaking) logistical preparation. Canadian pioneers carrying trench mats pass German prisoners on the Passchendaele battlefield.

37. Wounded Canadians take cover behind a pillbox, November 1917.

38. 'The worst place in the world'. A Canadian soldier attempts to cross the Flanders battlefield. To capture the Passchendaele Ridge in such conditions was arguably Canada's finest achievement during the First World War.

39. The Cloth Hall, Ypres, lit by moonlight. For those who served in the Salient, the march past the eerie ruins of the town was an unforgettable rite of passage.

Trümmer der Kirche von Passchendaele.

40. View of Passchendaele church in the summer of 1917 before it was completely razed during the fighting for the village.

41. 'The defenders cowered in their water-filled craters without protection from the weather, hungry and freezing, continually exposed to the overwhelming enemy artillery fire.' A photograph taken in April 1918 showing the terrible ground conditions in which the later stages of the battle were fought. This was what the Germans called the *Trichterfeld* ('crater field').

42. Tyne Cot CWGC Cemetery. Lying on the outskirts of
Passchendaele, Tyne Cot is the largest Commonwealth war
cemetery in the world, with almost 12,000 servicemen
commemorated or buried within its walls. The Cross of
Sacrifice (centre) is built upon the ruins of an imposing German
pillbox that was captured in October 1917. When King George
V visited Flanders in 1922, he asked poignantly whether there
could be 'more potent advocates of peace upon earth through
the years to come than this massed multitude of silent witnesses
to the desolation of war'.

8.

'A Question of Concentration'

The P. M. is obviously puzzled, as his predecessor was, how far the Government is justified in interfering with a military operation.

Sir Maurice Hankey[1]

19 August–5 September 1917

On the morning of 20 August the Kaiser travelled to Waregem, southwest of Ghent, following an inspection of the defences of Heligoland. Crown Prince Rupprecht, Sixt von Armin and Fritz von Lossberg were there to meet him, standing solemnly in a line as the Kaiser's entourage arrived. After a troop inspection, Wilhelm II gave what one aide called an 'excessively long speech . . . much of which was completely incomprehensible to his audience'.[2] At lunch, the discussion turned to the situation at the front and the renewal of heavy fighting in the Ypres Salient. Sixt von Armin admitted that Fourth Army had already lost 84,000 men in the last two months, but the Kaiser 'did not seem unduly impressed'. Rupprecht, evidently unsatisfied with this response, tried to emphasize how difficult things were becoming. 'I did not fail to tell him that our losses are very significant in Flanders.' There were not enough reserves, he said, and those that arrived were of poor quality, meaning that another winter of war was unthinkable. His mood was not helped by the beaming optimism of the Chief of Naval Staff, Admiral von Holtzendorff, who was in the Kaiser's party, and assured Rupprecht that the U-boat campaign would force England out of the war by the end of October. At this point, Rupprecht just smiled. 'The men of the navy are dangerous optimists!'[3]

According to Rupprecht's Chief of Staff, Hermann von Kuhl, the repulse of the renewed British attacks in mid-August marked the end of the first stage of the battle. 'The British target was quite clear', he remarked. 'It was their intention to take the high ground east and north of Ypres as a spring-board for a break-through into the Flanders plain.' This had failed, but the fighting strength of numerous divisions had been worn down to dangerous levels and 'it was already proving difficult within the entire area of Crown Prince Rupprecht's Army Group to replace them promptly' with fresh troops. By 20 August, seventeen divisions had been exhausted by the fighting in Flanders and in order to hold the front, they had to engage in an increasingly frantic balancing act, moving worn-out units to quiet sectors, while their replacements were shunted north. However, as the battle dragged on 'such an exchange became ever more difficult, especially when it became necessary to back each division in the Flanders line with a counter-attack division'. Moreover, the Canadian assault at Lens, which sucked in five extra divisions, meant that Rupprecht's plans to relieve fought-out troops at Ypres had to be scrapped altogether.[4]

Elsewhere, bad news seemed to be multiplying rapidly. On the day the Kaiser visited Belgium, the long-awaited French operation at Verdun took place, with attacks on both banks of the River Meuse. Utilizing nearly 1,800 guns and almost unlimited stocks of ammunition, four French corps were involved in the attack, which aimed to retake Hill 304 and Mort Homme. Although the fighting was hard, and the terrain was hilly and wooded (thus reducing the effect of artillery), the operation achieved its objectives with 'only' 14,000 French casualties. German losses were probably roughly equal – including over 10,000 men taken prisoner. On 29 August, President Poincaré visited Pétain and bestowed upon him the *Grand Croix* of the *Légion d'honneur*, thanking him for 're-establishing our military position before Verdun'. Gradually, but inexorably, the French were recovering their offensive spirit. Morale remained fragile and in need of constant management, but it was clear the French Army was once again able to conduct limited, and effective, military operations.[5]

The Italians were also on the offensive. A day before the French attack at Verdun, General Luigi Cadorna, the Italian Commander-in-Chief, pushed his divisions forward on the Isonzo – the river that ran along the Austrian and Italian border where they had fought each other since 1915. The battle – the Eleventh Battle of the Isonzo – marked, up till that point, the culmination of Italy's war against the Austro-Hungarian Empire. Italian forces blew a hole eight kilometres deep across a sixteen-kilometre front and captured 30,000 prisoners and 145 guns.[6] Austrian losses were over 100,000, leaving the Chief of the General Staff, Arz von Straußenburg, with no option but to plead for German help. Although both Hindenburg and Ludendorff were initially loath to send German troops to bail out the Austrians, they eventually agreed that a proposed counter-attack on the Isonzo was feasible, and a number of difficulties could be overcome, if sufficient time was allowed for preparation. Because the terrain was so mountainous, troops would need special training, pack animals, and enough time to get into their deployment areas. Hindenburg ordered the creation of a new army, Fourteenth Army, and scraped together seven divisions for the proposed operation; now scheduled for sometime in the middle of October.[7]

Meanwhile in Flanders, Gough's 'line-straightening' operations commenced on 19 August with a dashing raid by seven tanks along the Saint-Julien to Poelcappelle road, which was still, just about, passable. Under the cover of a smoke screen, the tanks were able to silence a number of strongpoints that had previously held up an entire division, capturing crowds of Germans as they did so.[8] What became known as the 'Cockcroft action' – named after one of the pillboxes that had been captured – was a remarkable exercise in ingenuity and imagination. 'It seemed a big gamble as to whether the Tanks would be heard approaching the Steenbeek at Saint-Julien, crossing the Steenbeek, and getting into position at the Starting Point by Zero Hour' (within 400 yards of the enemy), recorded an after-action report. Machine-gun and artillery fire, as well as low-flying aircraft, had been ordered for two hours before the attack to drown out the noise of the approaching tanks and it seemed to work. Making straight up the Poelcappelle road, G.43, the tank commanded by Second Lieutenant Coutts led the attack into heavy machine-gun fire. As he reported later, they 'replied vigorously, and after ¼ hour between 30 and 50 of the enemy ran out from the buildings of the Cockcroft: killed a good many, got badly ditched on side of the road . . ."[9]

The success on 19 August energized morale in the flagging Tank Corps, but it did little to increase any lingering enthusiasm they had for operating in Flanders. As early as 2 August, as he watched the rain come down, Brigadier-General Hugh Elles suggested to Fifth Army that their remaining tanks should be withdrawn and used together in a surprise assault on better ground. The following day, Lieutenant-Colonel J. F. C. Fuller also reported that, from 'a tank point of view', the battle 'may be considered dead'. Furthermore, to continue to use tanks in such circumstances would 'only lead to good machines and better personnel being thrown away'.[10] By this point, staff officers in the Tank Corps were devising a plan for a major tank raid – what would eventually become the Battle of Cambrai in November 1917 – and were understandably chafed at being asked to work in such soggy conditions. What they wanted, they told GHQ time and again, was good firm ground, not torn to pieces by endless shelling, and the element of surprise. Give them that and they would really show what tanks could do.

Renewed attacks by XVIII and XIX Corps on 22 August were able to gain several hundred yards of ground, but German pillboxes and ruined farmhouses were proving, in places, almost impossible to dislodge. Their names are now largely forgotten, but then they were infamous, dark places reeking of death and misery: Potsdam, Vampir, Borry and Gallipoli Farms, Hindu Cott and Hill 35 to name a few. Despite the ground being 'practically a swamp', eighteen tanks were scraped together for the attack. Four machines of 'C' Battalion tried to drive down the Frezenberg–Zonnebeke road, but it had been so heavily shelled as to be almost indistinguishable from the surrounding mud. One tank was hit by shellfire, and the remaining three all ditched. Although six tanks from 'F' Battalion were able to assist in cleaning up some snipers and machine-guns, it had been yet another sobering day for the Tank Corps.[11]

The battle was now deteriorating into a brutal attritional slog: lone groups of infantrymen slipping and sliding across a squelching

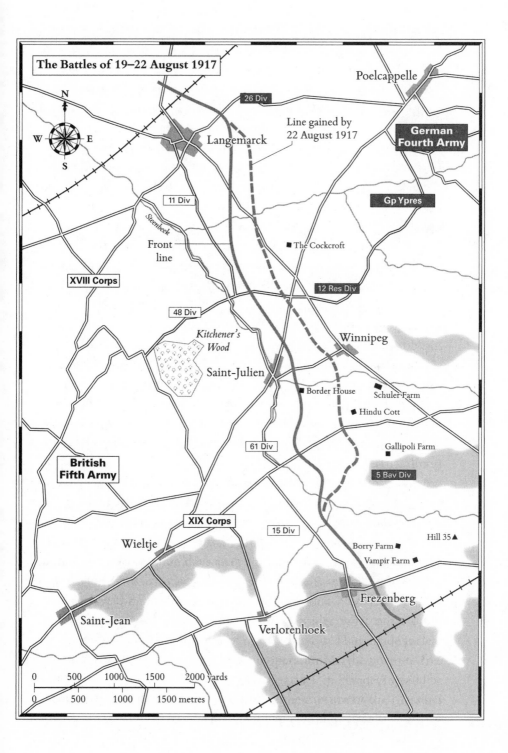

The Battles of 19–22 August 1917

N
W — E
S

26 Div

Poelcappelle

Langemarck

Line gained by
22 August 1917

German
Fourth Army

Gp Ypres

11 Div

Steenbeek

Front
line

The Cockcroft

XVIII Corps

12 Res Div

48 Div

*Kitchener's
Wood*

Winnipeg

Saint-Julien

Border House

Schuler Farm

Hindu Cott

61 Div

Gallipoli Farm

British
Fifth Army

5 Bav Div

XIX Corps

15 Div

Hill 35 ▲

Wieltje

Borry Farm

Vampir Farm

Frezenberg

Saint-Jean

Verlorenhoek

| 0 | 500 | 1000 | 1500 | 2000 yards |

| 0 | 500 | 1000 | 1500 metres |

sea of mud as the rattle of German machine-guns pattered out and another attack went to ground. Symptomatic of the deadlock was the struggle on the Gheluvelt Plateau, which by the last weeks of August had distilled into a series of vicious battles surrounding Inverness Copse and Glencorse Wood (two shattered woods off the Menin Road that had already resisted a series of major British assaults). On 22 August, Major-General V. A. Couper's 14th (Light) Division led a renewed attempt to seize control of this shattered ground. Over the next three days, Couper's division found itself engaged in one of the most brutal, seesawing struggles of the entire battle, as it became clear that the German Army was not going to give up without a fight.[12] The problem that Couper encountered was a familiar one: his division did not contain enough combat power to take and hold ground in such difficult conditions – particularly when their flanks were 'in the air' and they were under constant pressure from machine-guns on the higher ground around Glencorse Wood.

Four battalions made the initial assault, but such was the level of enemy resistance, and the difficulty of moving through the tangled wasteland, that two more battalions were fed into the mix over the coming days. A subsequent investigation concluded that the initial attack failed to secure all its objectives 'owing to casualties and the broken nature of the ground'. This meant that the final objective 'was reached by only small detached parties who were too weak and scattered to resist the immediate counter-attacks made by the enemy on both flanks'.[13] An account of what happened was recorded by Captain George Rawlence of 6/Duke of Cornwall's Light Infantry (14th Division). They started their march to the line, down the dreaded Menin Road, at 1 a.m. on the morning of 22 August. 'We had an awful time', he remembered. 'The Hun was smashing it to pieces and mixing gas shells with the bombardment. I had to order gas masks on and you can imagine what it was like; pitch dark, glass goggles, which continually fogged with the heat of one's body to look through, great holes in the road and shells bursting all round.' They made one attack, but then in came the enemy counter-attacks, 'again and again rushing up his storm troops in motors and throwing them in recklessly, all the while keeping up a terrific artillery fire'.[14]

Rawlence's men were eventually relieved on 25 August. 'We are all absolutely done [in] and one feels in that condition when all the events of the past few days appear like a far away dream', he admitted.

> You see we were on the go at all hours and dropped off to sleep on the floor when opportunity offered. Yesterday [24 August] was the worst day of all . . . The battle raged backwards and forwards all day and finally finished[,] we having given way about 200 yards, but still holding the crest of the ridge and well over it. Two fresh battalions of ours came up then and pushed through us and on into the line we had held during the morning, finding practically nothing but dead and wounded Boche in front of them.

Yet no matter how hard they fought, 14th Division just could not hold on to Inverness Copse. That day elements of 34th and 32nd German Divisions finally cleared the battered remains of the wood, leaving Jacob's II Corps with nothing to show for three days of ceaseless, draining combat. It was, in a sense, an apt summation of the Battle of Flanders as a whole.

The loss of Inverness Copse, after so much blood had been spilled, inevitably provoked a bout of introspection. According to Brigadier-General P. R. Wood, whose 43 Brigade had taken the brunt of British casualties, the failure was 'entirely a question of concentration'. For him, the key lesson was the importance of overwhelming force. Where 'the objective is, though small, of the highest tactical importance and possession is necessary to facilitate future operations, it is wiser and cheaper in the long run to make dead certain of getting it by employing at least 50% greater strength to capture and hold it than would normally be deemed sufficient in the case of an attack forming part of a larger operation on a broad front'. He recommended battalions being deployed in depth, thus 'ensuring greater driving power' with enough strength to resist counter-attacks. Moreover, only one brigade (of four battalions) had been initially tasked with the mission, while six battalions had eventually been drawn into the fighting. 'Had these 6 battalions been available from the first, so that their full weight could have been brought to bear, instead of being thrown into the fight piecemeal,' Wood noted, 'I am certain that complete success would have resulted.'[15] He had put his finger on something. The British were slipping back into old habits: a lack of preparation; inadequate time for reconnaissance and planning; little or no coordination with flanking units; rushed, penny-packet attacks; heavy losses for little gain. The curse of the Somme was returning.

In stark contrast to the urgent investigations then underway into British failure, there was a recognition that the fighting in late August brought out the best in the German Army. Theodor Oechsler, an NCO with 23 Reserve Infantry Regiment (12th Reserve Division), was personally congratulated by General von Armin after capturing an entire tank crew on 22 August, when he was deployed around Saint-Julien. He described what it was like to come under heavy shellfire and then face the clanking iron monsters that threatened to overrun their position:

> Early at 6 o'clock, the hellish artillery fire began, and the resulting smoke was such that we barely had a few metres of visibility in our craters. Yet we all waited for a visible attack. Finally, the English stormed forward, and we greeted them with our rifles, in such a way that those who weren't dead surged back in retreat. We had barely accomplished this when we saw a tank approaching us on the road behind us. Threatened by the tank, we left our craters and found a suitable place behind the road. Suddenly, to our delight, the tank got stuck in a crater and could not go any farther. Together with Lieutenant Schulz and Musketeer Krügel from the same company, I attacked the monster. But it was in vain! We used hand grenades and rifles – we used everything. But there was not a single hole. The crew was also firing continuously with the guns that were there. I ignited a charge comprising six hand grenades under the gun, but this did not help either.

Later that evening, Oechsler and his men crawled up to the tank again. After sliding several grenades through a small opening they found in its armour, Oechsler shouted, 'Get out of the box, or it'll explode!' Immediately the small side hatch opened and the eight crewmen clambered out as quickly as they could, begging for mercy.[16]

At Courtrai, Crown Prince Rupprecht felt an enormous sense of

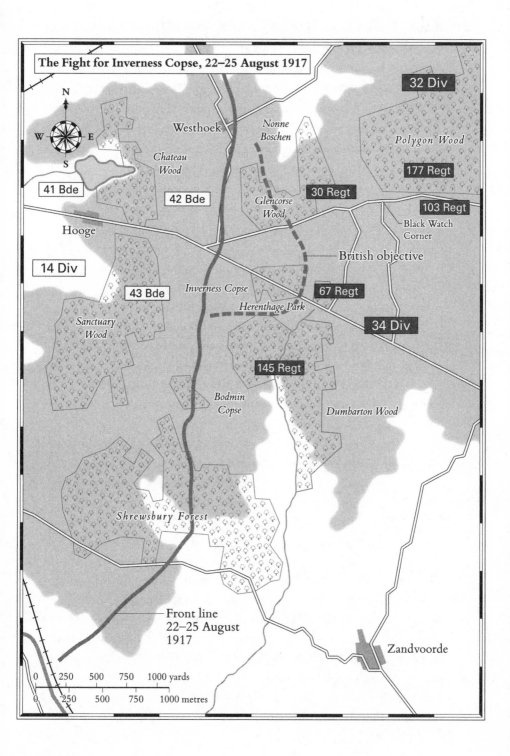

The Fight for Inverness Copse, 22–25 August 1917

pride in how well his units were coping, particularly given what they were up against. The fighting on 22 August, he noted, 'lasted into the night'. So heavy was the demand for shells that his reserve had shrunk to only seven ammunition trains.[17] Nevertheless, he was confident that morale was holding. On the morning of 24 August, he met some officers and men of 5th Bavarian Division, which had fought at the Battle of Langemarck.

> All officers I spoke to emphasized that our excellent infantry feel superior to the English. During our counter-attacks, the English often hardly defended themselves while English troops previously bore up even against a wall of fire. Apparently even officers knelt down with hands held aloft and surrendered without a struggle. Generally our troops desire to be allowed to attack. As painful as it is for each soldier to remain in the defence, our method is the right one . . .[18]

In Group Wytschaete, Albrecht von Thaer was of a similar opinion. 'Yesterday's battle, on the whole, went well', he wrote in his diary for 23 August. His losses were significant, but he felt they were fewer than last year on the Somme, owing to better organization, and more artillery and ammunition. 'Accordingly, the mood of the troops is far better than in the previous year.'[19]

The use of combat reserves, to seal off enemy penetrations and strike back at key moments, remained at the heart of German defensive tactics. Two days after Inverness Copse had been recaptured, Fourth Army issued a report on how such reserves should be handled, which distilled the lessons of recent fighting. Stress was laid upon organization and preparation, as well as the vital need to avoid getting battered by the artillery fire that swept the Salient. Reconnaissance could 'never be thorough enough', even during heavy artillery bombardments. Troops 'must be rested as far as possible in the days before their expected deployment'. Assembly points had to be located 'outside the main zone of fire' and, if possible, in improved accommodation to protect against the weather. Battalions should practise together 'at least two or three times' and ensure close contact and liaison were maintained between the *Eingreif* divisions and the units they would support in the line. A key point, which the document stressed, was the importance of not assembling troops too far forward. 'A minor loss of time in the counter-strike will be amply compensated by the division's greater freshness for combat'. If these precautions were taken, Fourth Army was confident all counter-attacks would have 'good prospects of success', and in the last days of August this seemed to be borne out.[20]

Back in London, David Lloyd George was in a positive mood, writing to Robertson on 26 August: 'The Italian attack seems to be developing well, and judging by the reports . . . there are great possibilities in it if fully and promptly exploited.' The Prime Minister had still not given up on his wish to circumvent the Western Front, and Cadorna's success on the Isonzo electrified him. After reading reports from the British liaison officer in Italy, Major-General Delmé-Radcliffe, he was convinced that Austrian demoralization might herald 'a signal military victory' on that front.[21] For Lloyd George, news of this success was energizing and tantalizing – an alluring glimpse of what could be achieved away from the Western Front and the muddy killing grounds where Haig's army continued to flounder.

Yet Lloyd George's belief in the Italian Army would prove, like his naive faith in Nivelle, to be dangerously misplaced. Delmé-Radcliffe was 'long on gossip and short on crisp assessment', while his consistent and unabashed optimism on the state of the Italian war effort masked serious deficiencies.[22] Far from being on the cusp of a decisive triumph, Italian soldiers were suffering from a catalogue of weary problems: poor morale and exhaustion; a lack of heavy artillery and ammunition; and corrupt, brutal and frequently incompetent commanders. Yet pacing around Downing Street, reading reports and grumbling to his secretary, Lloyd George saw none of this. For him, the Italian Front offered the possibility of decisive success without the blood cost of the Western Front (or at least without British blood). Screwing up his courage, he pressed Robertson to act urgently, reminding him of the 'enormous responsibility' not to lose this 'promising opening'. 'Do you not think that a new situation has arisen there which requires immediate action on the part of the Allies to support the Italian attack, make up their deficiencies and enable them to convert the Austrian retreat into a rout?' he asked.

For the CIGS, who no doubt read the letter with a furrowed brow, this was yet more unhelpful meddling by an amateur strategist with no idea of the practical difficulties of moving hundreds of heavy guns to the Italian Alps. He was determined to stop it. At a meeting of the War Cabinet the following day (27 August), Robertson's Director of Military Operations, Sir Frederick Maurice, delivered the bad news. 'The only way by which he could assist the Italians with a sufficient number of guns to have an effective result was by withdrawing them from the Ypres operations.' Furthermore, sending the guns would mean the abandonment of the Flanders campaign – something, it must be admitted, that was very much on Lloyd George's agenda – and this would have a 'disastrous' effect on British Army morale. The best they could do, he suggested, was to keep attacking in Belgium, where they could 'really afford the most direct assistance to the Italians'.[23] Robertson continued this rearguard action before the War Cabinet on 28 August, lecturing those present on 'the history of events during the last eight or nine months'. After taking the War Cabinet through the long, tortuous story of Allied policy since the winter, he proclaimed that it would be 'false strategy to close down the offensive on the Western Front in order to give General Cadorna support which would only reach him too late to be effective'.[24]

Despite Robertson's dour refusal to countenance Lloyd George's wishes, the Prime Minister would not let go. At an inter-Allied conference on 4 September – which Haig attended – the question of sending guns to the Italians was raised again. The French commander, Ferdinand Foch, who was present in London, suggested that 100 medium guns could be made available. The usual military protests were made, but, ultimately, the political imperative of supporting an ally won out, and Haig was told to review his artillery situation and, if possible, send up to fifty of General Anthoine's guns to the Italians. Although Lloyd George seemed to have made some progress, it was hardly a major victory. Haig was only mollified with the promise that Pétain would replace these before his next major push. Moreover, fifty guns might eventually reach General Cadorna, but this was hardly the decisive shift in Allied strategy that the Prime Minister desired. Yet again, his military commanders had proved stubbornly resistant to his charms; it was almost as if he were stuck in mud.[25]

In Flanders, matters were coming to a head. As in 1916, the British kept battering away. Gough launched further attacks on 27 August, with Maxse's XVIII Corps pushing on to the Langemarck–Gheluvelt Line (the Wilhelm position), but running into the same problems again and again. 'The weather conditions were wretched', noted an after-action report. 'Rain fell in torrents the previous night and continued to fall on the day of the operation after Zero Hour.' So bad was the ground that the infantry of the two attacking divisions (48th and 11th) would probably have been unable to keep up with the barrage had it proceeded at a much slower rate. As it was, even covering 100 yards every eight minutes – half the speed of the barrage on 31 July – the covering fire soon left the struggling infantry behind. The report continued:

> The attacking waves at once found the going almost impossible. The Boche, at first, showed every inclination to surrender, but directly they took in the situation and saw that our troops could not move, they picked up their rifles again and took full advantage of the unequal contest, at the same time training every machine gun on our men as they struggled in the mud.[26]

The result was predictable. Although some minor gains were made against a handful of strongpoints, elsewhere the infantry were shot down in droves. Evidently Fifth Army was no nearer to realizing the kind of decisive success that Haig's 'northern operation' clearly demanded.

It was the same story on Maxse's right flank, where XIX Corps continued to toil. The attack of 61st Division was supposed to have been preceded by a discharge of smoke candles – to shield the first waves from enemy observation – but by the time they went 'over the top', a 'driving wind' prevented them from being lit. The creeping barrage moved at the same, gradual pace as in XVIII Corps, but, as the war diary recorded, 'it is clear that the state of the ground, cut up with shell-holes full of water, and all slippery with mud, made it impossible for our leading lines to keep in touch, and on approaching the enemy trenches they were met by a heavy fire from the direction of Gallipoli, Keir Farm, and Martha House'. Junior officers tried to rally their men, but it was no good. Weapons became clogged in mud and refused to fire; many of the attackers fell into shell holes and drowned; a third of the men and half of the officers were hit. The advance came to a standstill about 100 yards in front of the enemy trenches.[27]

The assault of 61st Division was perhaps one of the worst examples of a failed attack at Third Ypres. The combination of heavy rainfall and mist, poor artillery support and treacherous ground meant that it was almost inevitable the attacking infantry would be slaughtered. It was extraordinarily difficult to manoeuvre across no-man's-land, meaning that 'fire and movement' tactics were hardly possible; and, in any case, with enemy strongpoints able to fire at will the leading waves were decimated. When Arthur Gould Lee, a pilot with 46 Squadron, finally got airborne on 1 September (many squadrons having been grounded for days), he was astonished at the sight of the battlefield, now covered with thousands of bodies. He flew along the front line east of Ypres trying to 'work out where British territory ended or German began', but could not see anything. He only spotted the infantry after noticing 'little groups of white blobs', which he realized were the faces of men on the ground. 'I suppose their uniforms are so smothered in mud that they've become part of the landscape. It's just not conceivable how human beings can exist in such a swamp, let alone fight in it.'[28]

By the end of the month Fifth Army had fought itself out. In the week ending 24 August, Gough's forces had suffered almost 17,000 casualties and for very little gain.[29] 'Until the weather improves', lamented Neill Malcolm on 28 August, 'all dates mentioned in the Conference notes . . . of the 26th August may be taken as being in abeyance.' Gough had originally wanted XIV, XVIII and XIX Corps to continue their attacks in the direction of the Green Line towards Poelcappelle, but this was now out of the question. Any further operations would depend upon good reconnaissance – which was unlikely given such stormy weather – and getting enough guns up to the line of the Steenbeek. In XVIII Corps Ivor Maxse was already struggling to get enough artillery into range of his objectives, and he was 'doubtful whether he could find sufficient gun positions' to support any further attacks. The army commander had no choice but to let go. Until such time as the weather improved, he urged his corps to 'proceed with the capture of tactical points with a view to improving the line and gaining a good "jumping-off" position for future operations'. He also wished to draw 'special attention' to extending tracks and roads in the forward area, pumping out flooded dugouts, and improving captured pillboxes wherever possible.[30]

Sir Hubert Gough, the man who had been brought in to achieve Haig's breakthrough, cut a frustrated figure. On 2 September he issued a memorandum on the 'evidence of recent operations' and the 'dangerous tendency' of troops to give up ground to German counter-attacks. 'Nothing could be worse', he stated. 'If such action becomes general throughout an Army that Army will never achieve success and will lose a great deal.' Moreover, troops who retire 'not only cause unnecessary losses to their comrades and their Country but bring dishonour to their arms and their nation'. For Gough, this was 'not due to any lack of fighting spirit', but rather to a want of training and a failure to utilize enough rifle fire to repulse the 'inevitable' counter-attacks. He urged his officers to 'stick it out' and consolidate captured trenches thoroughly, while impressing upon their subordinates the importance of 'courage, resolution and the offensive spirit'. He ended with a blunt reminder to his men: 'The Bosch [sic] cannot stop the British soldier if the latter means to advance.'[31]

Gough's tendency to blame his own men when things went wrong was hardly new; indeed, throughout 1915 and 1916 he had done much the same thing. When attacks failed, often because of inadequate time to prepare or a lack of artillery, Gough usually lost no time in sacking one or two commanders.[32] That even determined troops could not advance into the teeth of unsuppressed machine-gun fire and heavy shelling, particularly across such treacherous, wet ground, seemed to make little impression upon him. Moreover, he was at a loss to know how to deal with the German counter-attacking tactics that were proving so disruptive. He would, however, find that his time was running out. On 23 August the lack of progress forced Haig to postpone the amphibious landing – which was supposed to link up with the breakout from Ypres – and now, for all his faults, he was determined to make other changes as well.[33]

On 25 August the Commander-in-Chief paid a visit to Second Army headquarters at Cassel and told General Plumer that he would have responsibility for a renewed push on to the Gheluvelt Plateau.[34] At the same time, Gough was warned that he was not to attempt any operation 'on a great scale' until Second Army was ready to lead the new attack, and that any operations should be 'methodical and well combined'.[35] Accordingly, the ground occupied by II Corps (up to the Ypres–Roulers railway) would now come under Plumer's jurisdiction. Such a change of heart must have been difficult for Haig, who had placed such faith in his protégé, but it was becoming increasingly clear that Fifth Army's morale was plummeting and that a new commander was needed.[36] And in Belgium there was only one option: Sir Herbert Plumer, the experienced campaigner whose cautious plans and limited advances Haig had spurned earlier in the year. Plumer, who had hitherto been maintaining Gough's right flank, was perhaps expecting Haig's call – yet he seemed to have no thoughts of *Schadenfreude*. He was always a loyal subordinate, firm and clear in his own mind, and buttressed by a powerful Christian faith. He did not accept without conditions, however. He told Haig, clearly and firmly, that he would need three weeks to prepare. Haig, whose options were narrowing by the day, had little choice but to accept.[37]

From his headquarters in the medieval hill town of Cassel, General Plumer tried to work out some way of squaring the circle; how to make a meaningful and sustainable advance in such a difficult environment. As early as 12 August he had written a set of tactical notes recommending progressively shorter advances or bounds (employing fresh troops for each one), with regular halts to ensure areas were 'thoroughly cleared' and troops readied for the next stage.[38] Plumer seemed to have grasped the essence of German defensive tactics: 'the farther we penetrate his line, the stronger and more

organised we find him; the farther we penetrate his line, the weaker
and more disorganized we are liable to become'. Therefore, he recommended that proportionally more troops be allotted to the furthest
objectives, so that they would be strong enough to repulse the inevitable enemy counter-strokes. Moreover, any advance could only be
successful if the artillery preparation, and the creeping barrage, were
deeper and more thorough than ever before, with the heavier batteries focused on locating and destroying enemy guns. 'This is the real
road to the infantry success', he believed, 'and the enemy is well aware
of it.'[39]

Capturing the Gheluvelt Plateau would entail an advance of about
4,000 yards up one of the most heavily defended sectors on the Western Front. Plumer wanted to do this in four 'steps' (each of around
1,000 yards and taking place every six days), which would allow Second Army to master the ridge, while also enabling Fifth Army to
advance on their left towards the Zonnebeke–Gravenstafel Spurs.
Once these objectives had been secured, it was hoped that a final
assault on the Passchendaele–Staden Ridge could be mounted (after
which opportunities for exploitation might occur).[40] Second Army
issued Operation Order No. 4 on 1 September, which outlined how
the first step would be conducted.[41] The attack would secure the
southern section of the Passchendaele Ridge from Broodseinde down
to Hollebeke, including the high ground at Polderhoek and Tower
Hamlets. Two corps would make the main assault: X Corps and I
ANZAC Corps, driving through the Albrecht Line towards Polygon Wood and Gheluvelt. The flanks would be secured by IX Corps
in the south, while Fifth Army extended the attack to the north by
pushing on to the Wilhelm Line. The operation consisted of three
separate stages – Red, Blue and Green Lines – but it would not be a
deep advance. On the contrary, Plumer's plans were straight out of
his 'bite-and-hold' manual: exhaustive preparation for a strictly limited push forward – no more than 1,500 yards in – covered all the way
by his guns.

Much depended on the artillery. While tanks had been employed
in numbers for Gough's operations, they would have little role in
Plumer's plan. I Tank Brigade was tasked with securing a series of

strongpoints on the Saint-Julien to Poelcappelle road, but elsewhere the infantry would make do without them.[42] Instead, they would rely on a formidable preliminary bombardment to 'break down obstacles which are impassable for infantry' (while, as far as possible, not creating new ones); to isolate the enemy's front-line troops and batteries from their supplies (particularly food); to teach the enemy 'to lie at the bottom of his shell holes or dugouts whenever any barrages are going on'; and to 'carry out observed destructive shoots on hostile batteries'. When Zero Hour came, five creeping barrages – about 1,000 yards in depth – would cover the advancing troops, sweeping the ground in front of them with an invincible wall of shrapnel and high explosive. Once their objectives had been secured, standing barrages would be fired on enemy counter-attacks or possible approach routes to ensure German reserves were wholly engaged.[43] In order to achieve this, Second Army would need a prodigious amount of guns and ammunition. For the seven-day preliminary bombardment, and to ensure the attack was thoroughly supported, General Plumer requested (and then received) over 1,800 guns (principally 18-pounders, but also significant numbers of heavier howitzers to take on German bunkers) and upwards of 3.5 million shells.[44] Gough's haphazard thrusting was now to be replaced by order and method. Firepower would trump manoeuvre. The first step would go in on 20 September.

9.

'An Introduction to Hard Work'

*The physical capability of the infantry depends undoubtedly
not so much on the distance traversed as on the intensity of
the hostile fire to which they are subjected.*

Sir Herbert Plumer[1]

6–19 September 1917

Fresh troops were now coming into the line. Watts's XIX Corps was
relieved by Sir Edward Fanshawe's V Corps on 7 September, while
further south X Corps and I ANZAC Corps relieved Sir Claud
Jacob's battered divisions, and occupied the front between Westhoek
and Shrewsbury Forest. British and French troops had opened the
attack on 31 July and fought throughout August, but the next phase
of the battle would be spearheaded by troops from Australia and New
Zealand. After being given their 'baptism of fire' at Gallipoli, the
Anzacs had gradually been concentrated on the Western Front
throughout 1916. Now they were organized into two corps, I and II
ANZAC, which were commanded by Lieutenant-Generals Sir William Birdwood and Sir Alexander Godley respectively.

Like all those who came into the Salient, the Anzacs did so with
mixed feelings. While they had, for the most part, enjoyed a long
period of rest and training since the spring and were ready to go into
action, some units grumbled about the amount of hard fighting they
had endured. 4th Australian Division, in particular, was struggling
to absorb over 9,000 new recruits after being heavily engaged at both
Bullecourt and Messines, with reports of young soldiers running in
the face of the enemy or going absent without leave.[2] Edward Lynch,

a nineteen-year-old from Sydney, was serving with the 'Fighting Fourth' and complained about being in the line constantly. 'When word came about the move, some of the men very decidedly voiced their opinions that the army heads had broken faith with our division', he wrote. In a sober, disgruntled mood, they moved by motor-bus to Westhoek, where they went into reserve.[3]

The fragile mood in 4th Division was not particularly widespread, but it was often said that the Anzacs were poorly disciplined. A British Royal Engineer, Arthur Sambrook, remembered sharing a camp with the men of 3rd Australian Division at Neuve Eglise. 'This camp could not be mistaken for an establishment of His Majesty's Brigade of Guards', he noted sourly. Apparently the only person 'who kept up the Guards' tradition in behaviour and smartness' was their Company Sergeant Major, John Mitchinson, 'whose blood pressure went up every time he saw the Aussies on parade':

> Our turnout was better than that of our camp maters [*sic*]: we always went on parade with all our uniform on. Our Australian companions came on half-dressed, and stood in some sort of a line, with pipes and cigarettes and plenty of conversation going on; their company officers never walked up and down the ranks inspecting them, having a good idea what they looked like from the first glance at the front rank. With the smoking and tobacco chewing indulged in there was more spit than polish, and when they were required to march off the officers just said, 'OK chaps, we'll get going.'[4]

To make matters even worse, the Australians were – at least when compared to their British cousins – very well paid. Tommies looked upon the Australians' six shillings a day with jealousy and envy (no doubt doing so while they jingled what was left of their shilling a day wage in their pockets).

For their part, the Australians prided themselves on their sometimes slovenly appearance: a loose-fitting jacket with their traditional felt hat looped over the left side. Charles Bean, who wrote the official Australian history of the war, noted that the uniform of the AIF may have struck some people as dull – a pea-soup shade of khaki with brass buttons oxidized to a drab black to prevent reflection – but it was 'designed for one subject only – that of being serviceable for war'.[5] The same could have been said of the 'diggers' themselves. They were, to a man, convinced that they were better fighters than their brethren from the Mother Country, and regarded the British obsession with 'spit and polish' as mere unnecessary 'bull' that was more trouble than it was worth. And while the Australian soldier would gain a reputation for ill-discipline and insubordination, even Haig was forced to admit that the BEF had few better fighters than the men from the southern hemisphere. When the Commander-in-Chief reviewed 2nd and 5th Australian Divisions on 29 August, he was at pains to stress how pleased he was with their demeanour, noting that they could not have marched any better 'if they had received years of peace training'.[6]

Second Army had issued a pamphlet on the enemy's new defensive methods and this formed the basis of a 'progressive method of teaching' whereby platoons and sections 'were practised constantly in the new formations and tactics'. 'Concurrently with the musketry training, careful attention was paid to training in discipline and in the use of the auxiliary platoon weapons – the bayonet, Lewis gun, rifle grenade, and hand grenade.'[7] In 4th Australian Division, training was 'energetically carried out' throughout September, mainly in how to deal with the shell hole defence they were coming up against. Long route marches through the countryside, close-order drill, tactical training and musketry all kept the men busy.[8] Lieutenant Ben Champion, a native of Stanmore, New South Wales (serving with 53/Battalion), who had rejoined his battalion at Poperinge, saw for himself how much was being done. 'As an introduction to hard work . . . we had a 15-mile route march with packs up, and now the Battalion is in splendid condition', he wrote. It would be the same across the two Anzac corps.[9]

A curious lull now seemed to fall upon the ragged Flanders battlefield. The endless columns of trucks and infantry, despatch riders and working parties, still came up and down, and Ypres remained a bustling centre of activity – even if it was still being shelled and bombed from the air – but the intensity of the previous months had gone. While small-scale attacks still continued in places – such as XIX Corps's operations at Borry Farm on 6 September and 6th

Division's attack on Hill 35 four days later – all minor operations were cancelled by GHQ on 10 September.[10] More encouragingly, the weather had steadily improved since late August. Warm winds and clear skies meant that, finally, the sodden battlefield could begin to dry out. 'In appearance it changed from a morass to a desert', wrote Charles Bean. Westhoek Ridge, in particular, with its shattered farm buildings and battered pillboxes, even reminded some Anzacs of the craggy Libyan Desert, where they had trained prior to deploying on the Western Front.[11]

Behind the lines, in fields covered with white canvas bell-tents, British and Dominion troops enjoyed a temporary respite from the offensive. Charles Carrington, a junior officer with 1/5th Royal Warwickshire Regiment (48th Division), spent September near Saint-Omer, 'in rich rolling country with golden harvest weather and comfortable billets'. 'We spent long happy easy days luxuriating in the sun, glad to be alive, more concerned with the Divisional Football Cup than with the war, but quite concerned with incorporating our drafts of new recruits – conscripts now and just as good soldiers as the old volunteers.'[12] 'If it had not been for the growl of the guns, an occasional shell in Poperinge while we were bargaining for greengages, or the perseverance of the enemy airmen, who dropped bombs somewhere in the neighbourhood each fine night, we might have forgotten the war completely', recorded W. H. L. Watson, who was serving with the Tank Corps. 'There were walks through the pine-woods, canters over the heath, thrilling football matches against our rivals, little expeditions to Bailleul for fish, or Cassel for a pleasant dinner in the cool of the evening.'[13]

It was an old joke that the sun always shone in the Salient whenever the British were not attacking, and September 1917 was no different. 'The weather during this time was simply glorious,' remembered Captain James McCudden of 56 Squadron, 'and we always had plenty of spare time, so we thoroughly enjoyed it.' When not airborne McCudden and his fellow pilots spent their time either in the mess playing cards and listening to the gramophone or outside hitting a tennis ball around a pole – a game known as 'bumple-puppy'. When it was hot they would bathe in a stream near their aerodrome, and if it rained they would catch lifts into nearby towns, principally Saint-Omer, and spend their wages in the teashops on filling French pastries.[14] Such an existence may have sounded idyllic, but the life of a pilot on the Western Front could sometimes be measured in hours. On 6 September, while flying his SE5, McCudden encountered two new types of enemy aircraft, the Fokker Triplane and the Pfalz Scout. Although nothing came of this encounter ('we manoeuvred around for a while, and the Huns did most of the shooting'), he was disappointed with the performance of his Lewis gun and spent the next few days trying to get the interrupter gear to work properly.[15] He was right to be concerned; five days earlier Manfred von Richthofen, flying one of the newly arrived Triplanes, shot down a British observation aircraft somewhere over Zonnebeke. On 3 September *Jasta* 11 recorded 11 kills in a single day – a stark illustration of how costly it was to maintain a continual air presence against such formidable opponents.[16]

Squadrons of German bombers also carried out regular sorties over the British lines. The number of dead and wounded from these raids may have been relatively inconsiderable – particularly when compared to the scores of casualties coming from the battlefield – but the loss of control of the air over the rear areas was an increasing concern to RFC headquarters. Over 600 tons of bombs were dropped by German aircraft against targets as far west as Saint-Omer between July and November 1917.[17] Camouflaged tents were ordered by Second Army on 15 September – in place of their highly visible white ones – and Major-General Hugh Trenchard authorized day-bombing of German aerodromes, as well as an intensive effort against German railway communications and troop accommodation, in the days before the renewal of the offensive.[18] When commanders complained about the air raids, Haig and Trenchard were nonplussed. Both were convinced that the aggressive aerial posture taken by the RFC was the right one and should be maintained at all costs. It was very difficult to detect incoming aircraft, particularly at night, and they felt that precious resources should be directed against enemy infrastructure rather than defensive patrols. The British just had to get on with it.

Despite daily losses in the air, the work of the Corps squadrons of the RFC continued unabated as they prepared to support the renewed offensive. Every day, hundreds of aerial photographs were taken of the battlefield, processed, analysed and then sent off to the corps and divisional headquarters for dissemination. In September alone the RFC exposed over 14,500 photographic plates and distributed almost 350,000 prints.[19] Trenchard, who regularly updated Haig on 'the work of the Flying Corps', was extremely proud of what his squadrons were doing. He visited Montreuil on 28 August and impressed the Commander-in-Chief with the latest photographs. Haig wrote in his diary:

> Our photographs now show distinctly the 'shell holes' which the Enemy has turned into a position. The paths made by men walking in rear of those occupied, first caught our attention. After a most careful examination of the photo, it would seem that the system of defence was exactly on the lines directed in General Sixt von Armin's pamphlet on 'The Construction of Defence Positions' . . .[20]

This was the reality of the front line in the Ypres Salient – rough positions strung between shell holes and anchored around pillboxes – presenting the attacker with a much more complex problem than the old linear defences had done earlier in the war.

Three weeks were set aside for the renewed attack and it was prepared with all the care and attention to detail that was Second Army's hallmark. The huge transfer of guns from Fifth Army meant that new roads and paths had to be built, while light railways were constructed to bring up tons of supplies from the railheads all the way to the front.[21] In I ANZAC Corps, dumps of road metal and road planks were made every 100 yards, with larger dumps every 1,000 yards, and all roads were divided into sections under suitable officers. 'The whole terrain consists of a mass of shell craters and as the German liquid [mustard] gas clings in these craters for 24 hours or more, we have had more men knocked out by this gas than by shell fire, which practically never ceases', recorded I ANZAC Corps's Chief Engineer, Brigadier-General A. C. Joly de Lotbinière.[22] Nevertheless, by 18 September most of the key sections of road and track had been laid – providing firm foundations for the subsequent attack.

In the attacking units, orders were thorough and wide-ranging, laying out in frequently exhaustive detail how the attack was to proceed.[23] In I ANZAC Corps, the front had been thoroughly reconnoitred and all ranks were familiar with the contours of the ground over which they would advance. A large model of the battlefield had been constructed behind the lines at the village of Busseboom and battalions were shunted in to see it throughout the month. 'Every detail is marked to exact size, Fritz trenches, cement pillboxes and dugouts marked, and the likely positions of machine guns', remembered Ben Champion who saw the model on 6 September. 'This huge scale map has been compiled from thousands of aerial photographs and has taken engineers a month to construct. We had it explained to us by competent officers and thoroughly memorised it and can now visualise the area when reading our maps.'[24] Message forms (with helpful maps printed on the back) were also distributed down to company level, while pioneers worked tirelessly to put up the thousands of signposts and lay the miles of tapes that would guide the battalions into the right positions. For the attacking infantry, coloured patches were even fixed to soldiers' helmets to denote which objective – red, blue or green – they had been assigned to take.[25]

All attacking units were routinely briefed on the nature of the artillery support they would receive, because timing needed to be perfect. At Zero Hour (5.40 a.m.) a creeping barrage would crash out 150 yards in front of the leading waves and begin to advance after three minutes. It then 'walked forward' exactly 200 yards, taking eight minutes to do so, before slowing down and moving at a rate of 100 yards every six minutes until the Red Line (the first objective, on the other side of Glencorse Wood and along the Hanebeek stream) was reached. There it would halt for forty-five minutes to allow the attacking brigades enough time to consolidate their gains, 'mop up' their sectors, and make sure the 'leapfrogging' battalions were ready to go. At the appointed time, it would advance on to the Blue Line (the second objective, which ran along the western edge of Polygon Wood and included most of the Wilhelm Line), covering 100 yards every eight minutes. There it would halt, as Plumer had decreed, for a longer period of time (two hours) before pushing on to the Green

Line (the final objective, a shorter advance further into Polygon Wood) at the standard rate of 100 yards every eight minutes. At each halt smoke would be fired to shield the attackers from observation and allow time for officers and men to reorganize.[26] Nothing would be left to chance this time.

In contrast to the frenetic activity on the British side of the line, there was a sense of suspended animation among the German defenders. 'My deepest conviction is that the Battle of Flanders is at an end', wrote General von Kuhl on 15 September. He had telephoned Sixt von Armin at Fourth Army and briefed him on the latest intelligence reports. German observers had detected the movement of an English division, with supporting artillery, away from the coastal sector – indicating that no attack from Nieuport was imminent. Surely if an offensive was to be continued from the Ypres Salient, then the British would need to remain in strength along the coast? A captured RFC pilot who crash-landed near Lille had also declared that the Flanders offensive was all but over. Although von Kuhl could not say for sure, and he insisted that 'caution should still be exercised', he was confident that they had seen through the worst of the summer offensive.[27]

By September 1917 German intelligence was drawn from a variety of sources, some more reliable than others, including aerial reconnaissance, spies and agents in France and Belgium, and wireless intercepts. Prisoner interrogation remained – like it did in the British Army – the easiest and most direct method of gauging enemy intentions. On 11 September, Albrecht von Thaer recorded a new process for the interrogation of British personnel which may not have been 'exactly dignified and chivalrous', but was 'practical' and seemed to work:

> When they are delivered, they are first taken to a cell where they encounter another English officer who was captured some time before them and who is very interested in hearing what their fellow officers are doing over there and whether there is another offensive on its way etc. However, this is not a real captured English officer, but a

German agent who speaks English like it is his mother tongue and knows the conditions over there exactly. For this purpose he is wearing an English officer's uniform.[28]

This was only part of a systematic process of prisoner interrogation that the German Army engaged in, which focused on ways to make prisoners feel at ease and relaxed, whereby they would be more likely to divulge important information.[29] For an army on the defensive, being able to second-guess the enemy's intentions was of the highest importance.

Whether Kuhl was right was the subject of intense debate at Rupprecht's headquarters in the first half of September. Fourth Army regularly submitted assessments to its Army Group on the likelihood of a renewed offensive, but came to no firm conclusions. On the one hand, there was no doubt that something was going on around Ypres, but what it meant, and whether it was the prelude to a major resumption of operations, was unclear. The number of active enemy artillery batteries was undoubtedly lower than before, but new bridges had been built over the Yser Canal and the Kortebeek (north of Langemarck), which could have been jumping-off points for a new attack. Behind the front the rail network had also been extended, most noticeably in front of Groups Dixmude and Ypres. Also of note was the increase in camp buildings and accommodation northwest of Ypres and in the vicinity of Dunkirk. Some argued that a new attack was coming, probably against Group Ypres, but also spreading as far north as Merckem and south to Hollebeke, but others disagreed. The combination of fine weather with little enemy activity meant that the British must surely have given up, particularly given how late it was getting in the year? In truth, German intelligence was unsure.[30]

For the time being the battle seemed to have ended. With the sudden cessation of activity, Fritz von Lossberg, exhausted from overwork, fell sick with influenza in mid-September. For others, the pause brought on not illness, but introspection. 'It is boring here', mused Albrecht von Thaer, 'you sit and wait and rack your brains thinking about what the enemy is going to do.' He wanted the British to attack again, 'otherwise it would be a sign that they want to wait until the spring for the Americans'.[31] By the first week of September artillery activity had dropped off noticeably and Crown Prince Rupprecht was reporting that the combat activities of his main groups were 'extremely low'. He had received intelligence that 1st Australian Division had been transferred to Egypt, which could, as he wrote in his diary, 'indicate that the British want to shift the focus of their military activity to Syria and Mesopotamia'. Indeed, the Flanders sector became so quiet that, on 12 September, Rupprecht, like Kuhl, had come to the conclusion that the battle was over.[32]

For both sides, the cessation of major operations at Ypres allowed for the relief of those infantry and artillery units that had been heavily engaged. The railway junction at Thourout was busy throughout September with the movement of thousands of field-grey-clothed German soldiers in and out of the Salient. 27th Infantry Division, which had suffered terribly from artillery fire on the Wilhelm Line, was relieved by 2nd Guard Reserve Division, east of Saint-Julien, on 11 September, and 3rd Reserve Division (one of the counter-attacking divisions on 16 August) was replaced by 236th Division.[33] This was part of a wholesale reorganization of the front. After three months of intensive combat, III Bavarian Corps, which had commanded Group Ypres, was relieved on 10 September, the men marching out to Mariakerke (a suburb of Ghent) for a well-deserved rest. They were replaced by the Guard Corps, an elite formation commanded by Lieutenant-General Ferdinand von Quast.[34]

It was not just the men that needed replacing. The enormous expenditure of artillery ammunition – which in September could reach 400,000 rounds per day across the whole Ypres sector – put gun barrels under intensive strain. Between 31 July and 25 September, Group Ypres had to replace 1,775 field and 1,250 heavy guns due to wear and tear.[35] In Group Wytschaete, the artillery had played a major role in the failure of the renewed British attacks on the Gheluvelt Plateau, and many units were in urgent need of refitting. Reinhard Lewald's battery had done their part – supporting the counter-attack at Inverness Copse on 24 August with 'heavy destructive fire' throughout the night, the guns 'firing continuously' until they ran out of ammunition. Two guns were hit by counter-battery fire on 28 August and over the following week they were regularly deluged with heavy shellfire as the British searched out artillery positions and approach routes; anywhere where guns were likely to be found. According to Lewald's diary, when they received orders to pull out on 11 September, their battery was in need of a thorough overhaul, they no longer had enough men for gun crews, and were desperately short of horses. They were, in a word, exhausted.[36]

They moved out at dawn on 13 September and headed for Jurbise, near the city of Mons. They were sent to an artillery training ground where their battery would be 'restored to full combat power' with new guns, new crews and fresh horses. To their surprise and delight they were stationed in a vacant castle – the owner having fled to Paris at the beginning of the war. Lewald recorded:

> Large beautiful halls with precious furniture and beautiful living rooms. Each man has a four-poster bed. Around the castle there are magnificent facilities and a deer park of several hundred acres. Beside the castle stand the ruins of a great abbey from the Fourteenth Century. The views from the castle, on the wide lawns of the park, are wonderful. In addition, there is idyllic rest and wonderful weather.

Lewald described their surroundings as like being in 'Wonderland'. After spending months on the Flanders front, with its mud and death, the sense of relief was overwhelming. There, in the 'marvellous autumn weather', his men spent quiet days; hunting, shooting and riding – perhaps wondering if the battles in Flanders had come to an end.[37]

A period of extended quiet on the Western Front was just what the First Quartermaster-General, Erich Ludendorff, wanted. After returning from Belgium in late August – during which he had a lucky escape from a train crash – Ludendorff slipped back into his old habits.[38] At Kreuznach, he followed a strict routine that was only rarely interrupted. He was usually at his desk by 8 a.m., and worked for an hour before Hindenburg turned up. The Kaiser arrived at midday, and they would spend some time talking about the military situation and any urgent issues that had arisen overnight. This would continue until breakfast (at 1 p.m.), which was usually finished within three quarters of an hour. Ludendorff's only break from the crushing burden of work was a daily stroll that he would take, usually along-side Hindenburg, between their villa – a former home of Emperor Wilhelm I – and the Oranienhof hotel, where General Headquarters was based. Sometimes locals would come and give the men gifts or flowers, which they would gratefully accept, but usually they were left to themselves. Ludendorff then returned to his desk and worked until eight o'clock, when dinner was served. He would remain at OHL, overseeing Germany's war effort, until midnight or 1 a.m.[39]

Ludendorff sometimes gave the impression of being a man whose emotions were frozen hard: an inarticulate soldier incapable of warmth and feeling; but sometimes he let the mask slip. On 5 September he received news that his stepson, Lieutenant Franz Pernet, a fighter pilot with *Jagdstaffel* 2, had been shot down over the English Channel; his body washed up on the Dutch coast several days later. Ludendorff immediately travelled to Baden Baden, where his wife was in mourning, remarking that Pernet had been 'like a real son to him'.[40] Yet there was no time to grieve – Ludendorff was required to manage a war on multiple fronts. On 1 September the German Eighth Army mounted a major offensive on the Eastern Front to cross the River Dvina and seize the old Hanseatic port of Riga. One of Germany's most formidable soldiers, General Oscar von Hutier, was put in charge of the operation and delivered stunning success, cross-ing the river and inflicting upwards of 25,000 casualties on the Russians. German losses were just over 4,000 men – a further indica-tion of why the war on the Eastern Front was coming to what looked like its natural end.[41]

The success at Riga meant that Ludendorff could devote more time to the planned Italian offensive. Mountain training was organ-ized for the divisions allocated to Italy, while they were also equipped with everything they would need: engineering units and trench mortar sections; aeroplanes and balloons; motor and horse trans-port.[42] Turning to the Western Front, the renewal of British preparations at Ypres was a growing concern, even if the German High Command was unsure of what it signified. 'The Crown Prince was not alone in his anxiety', admitted Ludendorff, even if he could offer no succour, other than to tell him that he had to 'get along on his own resources'.[43] Ludendorff was convinced, whatever anyone said, that the line would hold. Any available German reserves had already been earmarked for Italy, so OHL could do little else but urge its commanders to hold firm. A renewed emphasis was placed on 'patriotic instruction' for the troops', utilizing a series of 'welfare officers' (*Wohlfahrts-Offiziere*) to deal with complaints and direct the men to suitable reading material. They were to make sure Germany's soldiers and civilians were aware of what was at stake and how important it was to show sufficient fighting spirit and self-sacrifice.[44]

Whether Ludendorff's so-called 'patriotic instruction' would be enough remained to be seen. Obviously it could do nothing to remedy the poor food, lack of leave and exhausting conditions that wore men down, although it seems that some aspects of the programme, including evening talks with free beer, were especially popular.[45] On 10 September, Rudolf Binding was appointed one of the divisional 'welfare officers' who were supposed to help gauge the mood of the troops. He had been handed a copy of Ludendorff's order of 31 July 1917, in which he warned against 'pessimism and revolution-mongering', particularly on the home front, which was 'absorbed by humdrum preoccupations, and hardly understands either the greatness of the situation or the sufferings of the Army and the Fleet'. Therefore, lecturing officers must constantly 'foster and maintain affection for the Kaiser and the reigning princes and the strong German sentiment for the Fatherland' to revive 'confidence in victory'. Binding approved of the scheme ('wars are won or lost by letters from home'), but felt that it would take a lot of time and offer little reward. Whenever officers asked men how they were getting on, the response was lukewarm; often just a shrug and a mumbled 'all right'.[46]

The German Army may not have suffered from anything like the chronic instability of the Russian Army or the mutinies that flared up in certain French divisions, but there were undoubted low points. Records have survived for 26th Division, which fought at Langemarck between 16 August and 4 September and suffered heavy losses from artillery fire. Divisional morale seems to have been battered by service in Flanders, and subsequently it was plagued by a number of

disciplinary incidents. For example, four soldiers of 121 Infantry
Regiment were condemned for 'mutiny and aggravated insubordination' after refusing to march up to the line, and there seem to have
been long-standing problems with 'brawling, plundering, disobedi-
ence and theft'. The division's record was eventually so poor that it
was transferred to the Italian Front, seeing action in the fighting at
Caporetto.[47] Other incidents seem to have been dealt with in-house,
although how widespread this was is difficult to say. Elements of 6th
Bavarian Reserve Division underwent some kind of mutiny during
its service in Flanders in June and July 1917. While garrisoning the
second line, the men were subject to intensive artillery fire that caused
heavy casualties and resulted in morale breaking down. One of its
officers, Johann Schärdel, recorded his regimental commander being
'deeply shaken' at what had gone on in the 10th company of 22 Regiment. Standing before his men, hardly being able to speak for 'shame
and excitement', the commanding officer reminded them of 'the
indelible disgrace of mutiny'. Yet the men went unpunished.[48]

Events were now moving quickly, bringing Fourth Army's enforced
idyll to an end. When General von Kuhl had predicted the end of the
Battle of Flanders, the guns of Second Army had already started their
preliminary bombardment. It would continue in varying severity,
with regular practice barrages and feints, until shortly before the
attack began. Anxiously huddled in their pillboxes or concrete
emplacements, the German defenders waited – faces white, hands
shaking – as the shells burst upon them. It was like being tortured on
the rack, never knowing when it was going to end. Indeed, the British
seemed to take an almost sadistic pleasure in ratcheting up the pressure, and then releasing it, as they searched the battlefield for German
positions. 'All the blockhouses and pillboxes were engaged systematically', wrote Captain Schwilden of 15 Reserve Infantry Regiment
(2nd Guard Reserve Division), deployed around Gravenstafel:

> Prior to 20 September five [pillboxes] were destroyed by direct hits
> and, in addition, the British artillery kept bringing down huge con-
> centrations of fire along the entire front line and the rear areas. In the
> early morning they would start slowly, then build up to drum fire

during the space of an hour. We could easily deduce that an infantry assault would not be long in coming. The companies were put on the highest state of alert and reminded that it was their bounden duty to hold their forward positions in the event of an attack, regardless of what might transpire.[49]

In places the German line seemed perilously thin. Between Boesinghe and Hollebeke there were only six front-line divisions, another three *Eingreif* divisions behind them, with two in army reserve. Only 752 guns were available across the entire front – less than half of what Plumer could call on for his operation.[50] Moreover, in the crucial central section of the line, on the Gheluvelt Plateau, the German positions were held by three worn-out divisions: 9th Reserve; Bavarian Ersatz; and 121st Division. By the time Plumer's attack began, they had already been in the line for three weeks and were in urgent need of relief. For them, 20 September 1917 would be one of the worst days of the war.[51] Plumer was finally ready.

IO.

'A Stunning Pandemonium'

You do not know what Flanders means. Flanders means endless
endurance. Flanders means blood and scraps of human bodies. Flanders
means heroic courage and faithfulness unto death!

Unknown German soldier[1]

20–25 September 1917

The day of the assault had finally arrived, and with it – almost
inevitably – wet weather. At La Lovie, General Gough (whose Fifth
Army had now been relegated to covering Plumer's left flank) was so
disturbed by the rain that around midnight he got in touch with
Plumer and suggested postponing the attack. After consulting his
corps commanders, who gave a mixed response, the Second Army
commander decided to go ahead.[2] It was a tortuous decision. To order
the attack in uncertain weather was bad enough, but the alternative
was even less edifying. Orders countermanding the operation would
have to be sent out immediately, while other plans were drafted. The
front-line units could not remain in the trenches indefinitely, and
would probably need relief within a day or two, raising the prospect
that any surprise would be lost. In the back of Plumer's mind was
undoubtedly the worst possible outcome: a confused, partial attack,
with some units standing down, but others – perhaps because they
had not received confirmation – going ahead as originally planned.
That was unthinkable. It was all or nothing.

It was in the early hours of 20 September that German front-line
commanders began to have their worst fears confirmed. Shortly before
3 a.m. – over two hours before Zero Hour – a bedraggled Australian

officer was brought into the headquarters of 121st German Division south of Zonnebeke. He had been captured while moving into position with his company, somewhere along the outpost line of 2nd Australian Division. He became separated from his men and ran into a German patrol, who quickly seized him and shunted him off to the nearest headquarters. Although he tried to destroy his papers, his interrogators found operation orders on him confirming that two Australian divisions were about to launch an assault astride the Ypres–Menin road. Within minutes a general warning order was sent out via wireless and divisional artillery batteries were told to lay down 'annihilating' fire on the Australian positions.[3]

It was now a race against the clock to see who would react first and whether there was enough time for the German defenders to pre-empt the incoming assault. Although 2nd Australian Division came under bombardment several minutes before Zero Hour – presumably because of the intelligence leak – it was not heavy enough to dislocate the impending attack. In those places where German shells were falling, at least one unit went 'over the top' early in order to avoid the shellfire.[4] And then at 5.40 a.m. the tension, which had been gradually building across the front, was rudely broken by the storm of shellfire that lashed down upon the tortured battlefield. Archibald Gordon MacGregor, a signals officer with 27 Brigade (9th Scottish Division), remembered the opening of the barrage being 'awe-inspiring', with guns lined up 'axle to axle' along the frontage of their sector. It was, he wrote, 'a stunning pandemonium'.[5] There was one gun or howitzer for every *five yards* of front, producing an intensity of fire that was at least double what had supported Gough's assault on 31 July.[6] The Battle of Menin Road (as it would subsequently be christened) unfolded, for the most part, as Plumer had planned. The wall of shellfire escorted the attacking divisions on to their objectives and kept the Germans at arm's length; a shield of fire through which nothing could pass.

Behind the smoke and dust of the creeping barrage, the attack was getting underway. The northern flank was secured by Fifth Army, with five divisions going 'over the top' from V, XVIII and XIV Corps. Given the difficulties of crossing what had been such a blasted, flooded wasteland, the attack was remarkably successful. There was bitter fighting around Hill 35 and a section of the Wilhelm Line known as 'Pheasant Trench' (where the tanks were largely ineffective), but the speed and swiftness of the advance seem to have taken the defenders by surprise.[7] In 9th Division, the South African Brigade captured Borry Farm and Potsdam House, two heavily defended locations that had held up the British advance in this area for the best part of two months. 'The hostile infantry showed very little fight in the open', it was reported, 'but where they held blockhouses they used machine guns until they found themselves surrounded . . . The prisoners were in all cases greatly demoralised by our heavy artillery fire.'[8] An examination of Germans captured that morning revealed that while many had been warned to expect an attack, no specific instructions had been given. Furthermore, the assault 'surprised them by its quickness and they were able to offer little resistance'.[9]

The stunning effect of Plumer's mass of artillery was particularly evident in the main assault by I ANZAC Corps, with 1st and 2nd Australian Divisions attacking side by side. In 7/Battalion (2nd Division) Lieutenant Alexander Hollyhoke went forward with his men, following what he called 'a wall of dust and fumes, intermingled with shell bursts' as the creeping barrage chewed up the ground in front of them. Far from being overawed by the spectacle, Hollyhoke's men took it in their stride, lighting pipes or cigarettes and 'advancing steadily behind the barrage with a cheerful smile on their faces'.

> Here and there a dead German was seen – killed by the barrage or a shot from the advancing troops. Prisoners, cowed and broken, began to come in in groups, or crouched in shell holes until sent to the rear. Short sharp fights were often carried out by small parties of troops around 'pill boxes' or concrete German blockhouses left intact or only slightly damaged by shell fire. A bomb or two in the entrance generally reduced the occupants to surrender. During the whole advance there was the continual swish, swish, of shells overhead – some high, some low – some indeed too low. With shells bursting around, many indeed were narrow escapes. Most men were hit at times by flying pieces of high explosive or shrapnel. Unless a man was badly hit all went eagerly on.[10]

Hollyhoke's men did what they were there to do: take the furthest objective (the Green Line), 'mop up' their sectors, and then consolidate. The barrage then halted for two hours to give them enough time to dig a new line and establish communication with the rear.

It was a similar story across I ANZAC Corps. Places that had been fought over for months had now fallen, including the shattered remnants of Glencorse Wood and a small copse known as Nonne Boschen. Although some resistance was encountered at Black Watch Corner (at the southwestern tip of Polygon Wood), elsewhere Australian troops were able to subdue enemy pillboxes and pick their way through what remained of the German defences. 'The enemy did not show the resistance that was expected, and in no case did he hold out in pockets in rear of our advancing lines', a report later noted.[11] In 2nd Division it was concluded that there were a number of reasons why the attack had been so successful, including extensive training; the physical fitness of the men; thorough reconnaissance; the 'systematic establishment of battle dumps' and lines of approach at the front; the depth of the artillery and machine-gun barrage; and the urgency with which the attacking battalions went forward: 'the men followed the artillery barrage so closely and rushed each position so quickly that the enemy had not time, in most cases, to open fire.' Moreover, because many of the Germans in shell holes and trenches had been 'dazed' by the artillery fire, they could put up only 'feeble' resistance.[12]

Further to the south, the attack of X Corps, striking on to the Gheluvelt Plateau, proceeded on schedule, despite hard fighting. 'Heavy rain had fallen during the night making movement over the cratered ground very difficult', recorded the war diary of 39th Division. 'At dawn a steady drizzle was still coming down whilst a thick mist and low clouds, combined with a strong wind, made observation and aerial reconnaissance almost impossible.' When the troops went over the top, they were met with heavy gunfire from a number of concrete blockhouses and machine-gun emplacements. These had to be taken out 'by a series of determined rushes covered by Lewis Gun and Rifle Grenade fire'. By 6 a.m. the division was on the Red Line (the western edge of Bulgar Wood), and a little over two hours later the supporting units had 'leapfrogged' on to their second objective (having cleared most of the wood) and were busy digging in.[13] Elsewhere, 23rd Division encountered heavy resistance getting through Inverness Copse and a string of undamaged German bunkers along the Menin Road. Although casualties were heavy, 'so thoroughly did each man know his individual task that formations and direction still continued to be well maintained and each section made independently for its own objective on the Blue Line'. Consolidation continued, in spite of sniper fire, for the rest of the day.[14]

It was on this sector that two of the most outstanding feats of bravery during the entire battle took place. William Burman, a twenty-year-old NCO with 16/Rifle Brigade (39th Division), won the Victoria Cross during the advance across no-man's-land. Burman's Company Commander was astonished at what happened:

> Sergeant Burman is the finest fellow that ever lived, standing only 5ft 4in, but with the heart of a lion, knowing no fear. When we had gone halfway to our objective, a machine-gun opened fire at us from 30 yd range in a shell-hole position, and my poor fellows were falling down everywhere. Sgt Burman went on all alone in face of what appeared to be certain death, killed the three gunners and captured the gun, saving, by his gallant deed, the lives of his chums behind and allowing the company to continue to advance. He carried the gun all the way to the final objective, and turned it on the retiring enemy, and his courage and fortitude throughout were amazing to see.[15]

The second VC was won by Corporal Ernest Egerton of 16/Sherwood Foresters, who took out an enemy strongpoint almost singlehandedly in what his commanding officer called 'the most reckless piece of gallantry I ever saw'. In the confusion of the advance, a German pillbox had been missed, but Egerton – who was mourning the death of his elder brother, killed in August – ran forward seeking revenge. 'I first shot the man who was firing the gun', he remembered; 'then I shot the second, who was waiting with another belt of cartridges, and I also shot the third man who was a bomber.' With that the German garrison, stunned by the ferocity of the attack, shuffled out, their hands in the air.[16] Elsewhere, 41st Division had cleared its first objective by 7.47 a.m. (pushing on to the Albrecht Line); had secured the Blue Line by 10.15 a.m. (crossing over the Basseevillebeek stream); and by eleven o'clock observers had spotted British troops on the Tower Hamlets Ridge.[17] Now the most crucial part of the battle began: the German response.

The *Eingreif* divisions had been assembled and readied to go forward by 8 a.m., but they were unable to intervene as planned. The almost complete collapse of communication at the front meant that it was impossible to gain a detailed picture of what was going on. Moreover, pilots of the RFC had been in the skies above the Salient as soon as it was light and proved highly effective at interfering with German plans. More than 28,000 rounds of ammunition were fired and over sixty bombs were dropped on ground targets that day, including columns of infantry marching to the front, artillery batteries and machine-gun nests. Unlike 16 August, when bad weather had effectively prevented aerial observers from pinpointing German reserves, British aircraft were able to provide vital information on the movement of the *Eingreif* divisions, which were so crucial to the second phase of the battle. Air reports notified British artillery of at least eight counter-attacks, including at Zonnebeke at 8.30 a.m., Polygon Wood at 10.20 a.m. and east of Zandvoorde at 2–2.30 p.m.[18] Using 'zone calls', the aircraft were able to direct devastating shellfire on to their targets and, according to the German Official History, 'cripple the momentum of the reserves'.[19]

It was only in the afternoon that the full-scale counter-attacks, which were so critical to Germany's defensive tactics, were able to make any headway. From about two o'clock, ominous reports of 'enemy concentrations' began coming into British divisional and corps headquarters. Elements of three reserve divisions, 16th Bavarian, 236th and 234th, were marching to the front from the direction of Menin, Moorslede and Westroosebeke. This had been anticipated by Second Army intelligence and artillery barrages were immediately ordered on the likely deployment areas with every available medium and heavy gun, while long-range machine-gun fire added to the maelstrom of steel that came down. By 5 p.m. the *Eingreif* divisions had arrived on the battlefield, but could do little to dent the

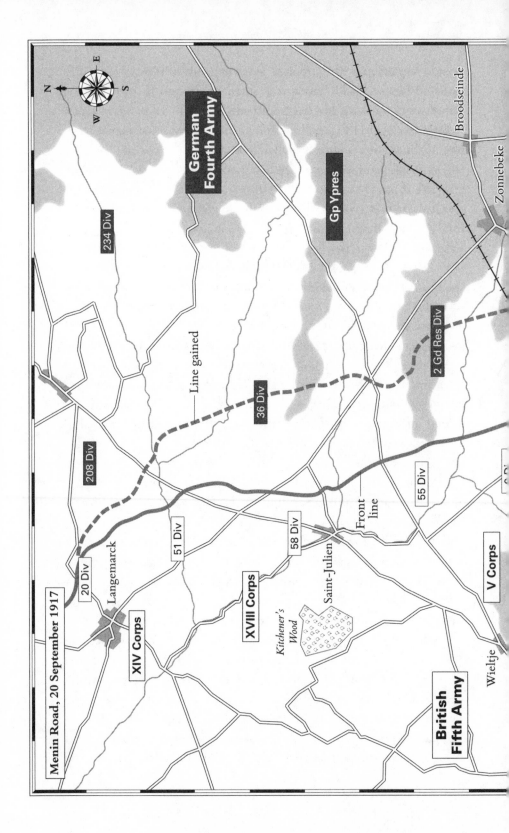

Menin Road, 20 September 1917

N E S W

German Fourth Army

234 Div

Line gained

36 Div

208 Div

Gp Ypres

2 Gd Res Div

Broodseinde

Zonnebeke

20 Div

Langemarck

XIV Corps

51 Div

XVIII Corps

58 Div

Saint-Julien

Kitchener's Wood

Front line

55 Div

V Corps

Wieltje

British Fifth Army

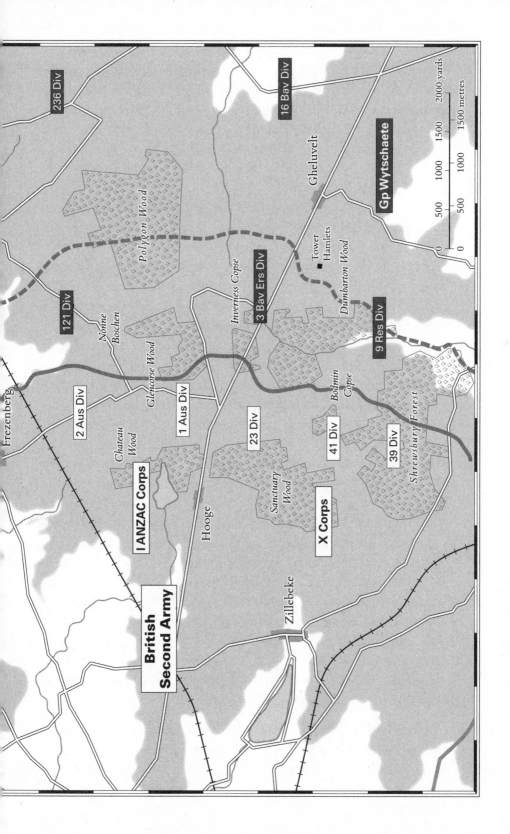

storm of fire in front of them. When they moved forward into the open, they were torn apart, with whole sections being brutally wiped from the battlefield under an enormous weight of firepower.[20] 'They managed to push back the British at different points and retake some important terrain features,' noted the German Official History, 'but in general, the attacks against already secured opponents had only limited success.'[21]

Such curt, official language underplays the horror and carnage of what happened that afternoon. In contrast to the elegant theory of flexible and effective counter-attacks flooding against an enemy that had already been weakened and overstretched, the *Eingreif* divisions were frequently poorly prepared, lacking orders and clear objectives, and running up against an enemy that was well dug in. A German soldier, Kleine, left a brief description of what it was like to be in one of the counter-attack divisions that day. He was a member of 459 Infantry Regiment, part of 236th Division, and when his regiment tried to make its assault, it found the whole area swept by fire. 'In attempting to get forward and close with the enemy on the slopes to the front, our assault companies and their supporting battery suffered severe casualties.' A direct hit on their command post wiped out fourteen of his comrades; he was wounded in the groin by a fragment of shell, while a corporal lost his mind and began rushing around in blind panic, foaming at the mouth. Although they were able to make some minor gains around Schuler Farm (600 yards east of Saint-Julien on the Zonnebeke–Langemarck road), where they pushed back 55th Division, it had been a terrible day.[22]

This combination of confusion and carnage seems to have been a common experience. 11 Infantry Regiment (part of 16th Bavarian Division) had received reports at 11.30 a.m. that the Wilhelm Line had been overrun and that the enemy was already digging in. What happened over the next six hours, recorded in a series of breathless despatches, illustrated some of the difficulties that German units had in trying to respond to Plumer's advance.

> 11.30: Terrain to the west and south of Becelaere as far as the Polder-
> hoek Ridge under a heavy barrage from the enemy.

14.10: Reconnaissance patrols [have been] sent out [and] attack will be continued after clarification.

14.30: III Battalion, 21 Infantry Regiment, reports that the enemy is just east of the Wilhelm position without being fired on at all. The Wilhelm position itself is held firmly. [There is] a very large number of English machine-guns close together; only a flanking attack can be carried out from the northeast; a frontal attack is not currently possible with the severely shrunken battalion. Battalion had sustained heavy losses and has lost many machine-guns.

15.45: Message received that the enemy is holding the Wilhelm position with powerful forces; artillery support [is] essential for any further advance.

16.00: Regiment again telephones the reserve brigade and requests artillery fire, otherwise attack [is] not possible, as it has been established beyond doubt that the Wilhelm position is held by the English.

17.30: Report that the Wilhelm position is definitely held firmly by the enemy, and that the enemy is working there openly and without being fired on at all. Formations are still intermingled. The penetrating effect of artillery is a prerequisite of a successful attack. Stretcher-bearers are urgently requested.[23]

It was evident that 20 September would be unlike 31 July or 16 August. This time there would be no overstretched or vulnerable British forces ripe for swift and decisive counter-attacks. Now they were ready: dug in and well-supported by artillery.

Haig, watching events at GHQ, was delighted. 'All reports show that Enemy's losses have been *most severe*', he wrote in his diary, 'about 20,000.'[24] Although British losses were not inconsiderable, there was a sense that a signal victory had been achieved. Apart from in a handful of locations – around Schuler Farm and Tower Hamlets – both Second and Fifth Armies had been able to secure their objectives (including Inverness Copse, Glencorse Wood and large sections of the Wilhelm Line) and, crucially, hold on to them, doing enormous damage to the *Eingreif* divisions as they did so. It had certainly not been an easy battle, but they were – inexorably and doggedly – inching their way up the high ground. Indeed, General Plumer had seemingly done the impossible: reversed the tactical dilemma that he had faced in late August. This time the further the *Eingreif* divisions advanced, the more disorganized they became and the stiffer the resistance they faced. *Plumer had turned their famed defence-in-depth totally on its head.*

'Menin Road battle. Big British success. The woods carried', reported *The Times* on the morning of Friday, 21 September. 'Great success was achieved by our troops east of Ypres yesterday on an eight-mile front athwart the Ypres–Menin road. Positions of considerable military importance were won, heavy casualties were inflicted on the enemy, and more than 2,000 prisoners were taken.'[25] More details emerged over the coming days. On 22 September *The Times* detailed the number and variety of troops that had taken part: Australians at Glencorse Wood; North Country regiments at Inverness Copse; Scottish and South African units at Vampir and Borry Farms; and West Lancashire Territorials at Iberian Farm. Moreover, it was evident that an important success had been achieved. German prisoners spoke of the 'overwhelming character of our artillery fire and the brilliance of the infantry advance' and, according to the 'special correspondent', the whole attack was 'as perfectly prepared as was the brilliant Messines success, which, of all operations in this war, it most closely resembles'.[26]

Within hours of the battle, staff officers at GHQ were analysing what could be learnt from it. 'The fighting during the last three days has been more severe than was expected', wrote Charteris on 23 September. 'The German methods were precisely as predicted; no attempt to support the front line but well-organized immediate counter-attacks.' He reckoned that eleven separate counter-attacks had been delivered by German forces opposite Fifth and Second Armies, with all but one being repulsed.[27] At Cassel, Second Army quickly produced its own set of comments on the battle. While there was much to be encouraged about – including the pace of the barrage ('suitable'); the 'great value' of laying out tapes and 'well-prepared tracks' to guide the infantry; and the use of flares to signal to passing aircraft – Plumer's Chief of Staff, Tim Harington, also emphasized the need for better training. 'It becomes more and more evident that greater stress must be laid on training in open warfare to encourage initiative and power of leading in the ranks of Junior N.C.O.s and Privates, which are so necessary when Officers become casualties.'[28]

Aside from the tactical issues that emerged from the fighting, there was the larger question of whether Plumer's methods had worked. Was Menin Road an example of how the battle should have been fought since 31 July? Did it prove that Second Army's 'step-by-step' approach was better than Gough's more ambitious attacks on a wider front? Plumer has certainly received many of the plaudits that have been denied to Gough. Historians have generally viewed his more limited, artillery-heavy, approach as the only viable tactical response to the awful conditions in the Salient.[29] Yet doubts have occasionally surfaced. The historians Robin Prior and Trevor Wilson argue that Menin Road was not the unqualified success its proponents have claimed, rather 'a triumph over adversity'. They suggest that Plumer's methods secured only limited amounts of ground at too high a price in casualties. At Menin Road 21,000 men were killed or wounded for a gain of just over five square miles (or 3,800 casualties per square mile) – roughly equivalent to what the enemy had lost. When this is compared with the results of 31 July, Menin Road seems curiously expensive. For example, according to Prior and Wilson, Gough's much maligned opening attack gained eighteen square miles for the loss of about 1,500 casualties per square mile.[30] This was less than half what Plumer had sustained on 20 September – *so what was going on?*

Gough's defenders have always argued that his main assault on 31 July has never been given the recognition it deserved. According to Gough's biographer, Fifth Army 'fought its way forward over ground and defences no less formidable than that on the ridge', and did so with less artillery and across a wider front.[31] Moreover, Gough's attack held out the possibility of exploitation and breakthrough, whereas Plumer's *modus operandi* permitted nothing of the sort. Because Plumer's objectives were subordinated to what the artillery could cover, there was no possibility that the plan could be amended or diverted, no matter how favourable the situation. Arguing along these lines, Prior and Wilson state that the reason why Plumer's operations have been perceived as more successful was their context: 'Gough's accomplishment on 31 July has been judged, not in terms of a limited advance even though that was all he was attempting, but of the large expectations of a breakthrough to the Belgian coast, which Haig had aroused.' Plumer's operations, on the contrary, held 'no such expectations'. Therefore, Menin Road was hardly the unblemished triumph that Second Army proclaimed it to be.[32]

Yet there was more to Menin Road than such a cold exercise in statistics. The attack on 31 July may have gained more ground than 20 September, but much of that had been abandoned by the German Army before the attack went in – in line with the theory of defence-in-depth. On the contrary, *the battlefield over which Plumer's men advanced in late September was ground that the German Army very much intended to fight over and could less afford to lose*. Furthermore, that repeated attacks by the full weight of Germany's counter-attack divisions had failed to dent Plumer's advance was highly disconcerting. Whereas on 31 July British units had been swept back from their foremost gains, this had not happened on 20 September, bringing into sharp focus the effectiveness of German defensive tactics. Indeed, the German reaction to events on the Menin Road was far sharper and more worried than it had been on 31 July. Then Gough's attack had been greeted with relief and pride in what German regiments, and their defensive tactics, had accomplished. On 20 September, on the contrary, there was no such pleasure, only dark, worried concern.[33] Because German commanders, whether they admitted it or not, were *scared* of General Plumer.

The shock of Menin Road produced a sudden sense of anxiety within the German High Command. Although Fourth Army reports glossed over the results of the battle and insisted that everything was all right, Crown Prince Rupprecht was not so sure. 'We are making the old mistake of underestimating the strength of our enemy again and again,' he wrote, angrily, as news came in of the attack. He admitted that he had been as much to blame as anyone ('I too believed this time that, owing to their heavy losses, the English were no longer capable of renewing the great battle in Flanders'), having been totally deceived by the preparations for the new offensive. 'Uncertainty about the intentions of the enemy, and the dependency of counter-measures thereon, is precisely one of the main disadvantages of defence', he concluded gloomily. His Chief of Staff, General von Kuhl (who had made the same mistake), was away in Kreuznach for a meeting at OHL, and when he returned he could offer little to lighten the mood. The Army Group was crying out for replacement horses, but none could be provided; nor could an increase in their oat rations. They were also warned that 'extreme economy' should be exercised in the consumption of gasoline – and these restrictions would most likely remain in force until the spring. 'I'm afraid we are still far away from peace', Rupprecht wrote, in some despair, that evening.[34]

On 22 September, following a series of further counter-attacks around Tower Hamlets, which failed to wipe out the British gains, Kuhl ordered Fourth Army to review its defensive tactics urgently. It had been observed that the British were now placing less emphasis on artillery fire on the front lines, but on interfering with the movement of reserves in the rear of the combat zone – seemingly a reaction to how important the *Eingreif* divisions had now become. Furthermore, captured documents revealed that the British were adopting new methods in their attacks. In each brigade, three battalions would advance 'in equally strong waves', while a fourth, in reserve, would leapfrog ahead if circumstances permitted. Then they would dig in and hold the front with a deeply layered series of machine-guns, all the time protected by a strong, standing barrage. Thus, although there might be no breakthrough, the British could still be certain of achieving limited gains of ground. In response to this, Kuhl made three main recommendations. Firstly, German artillery must be reinforced. Secondly, 'frequent offensive attempts' – essentially strong raids – should force the British to man their front line in greater strength and provoke them into unwise moves. And, finally, the *Eingreif* divisions should make 'accelerated' counter-attacks against enemy penetrations.[35]

Of all the people who should have been mightily impressed with Menin Road, Lloyd George remained curiously unmoved. From his perspective he had heard it all before and approached any news from GHQ as invariably tainted and corrupt. After spending the morning of 24 September in London discussing the war in the Middle East – where General Sir Edmund Allenby was gearing up for a major offensive against the Turks at Gaza – Lloyd George crossed the Channel and headed to the Western Front.[36] When he arrived, he found the atmosphere at GHQ one of 'unmistakeable exaltation'. Haig was 'radiant'; Charteris 'glowed with victory'; while Kiggell 'had the air of a silent craftsman, whose plans, designed and worked out by his art in the seclusion of his workshop, were turning out well'. After Lloyd George had become sick of hearing about the 'visible deterioration' of the prisoners they were capturing, he told Haig that he wanted to see some for himself. He was eventually presented with 'a weedy lot' of Germans and seemed reasonably convinced; although he would later claim that GHQ had specifically ordered all 'able-bodied specimens' removed before his arrival.[37]

According to Maurice Hankey, Lloyd George's visit to GHQ in late September was really the last time that he could have intervened and stopped the battle. But because he encountered 'the usual optimism, emphasized by the picture of steady, remorseless execution of the plan', there was, he claimed, little to justify stopping the offensive. One of the problems was that War Office news tended to be positive with 'a considerable lag between events and the arrival of unofficial information which sometimes helps to elucidate the official reports'; meaning that by the time Lloyd George had heard contradictory rumours, events had moved on.[38] It was, from his perspective, unfortunate that he happened to visit GHQ just when the British had achieved their greatest success since Messines, which did much to nullify the Prime Minister's dry scepticism. It was becoming clear – no matter how much Lloyd George nagged or grumbled – that Haig was not going to call off his offensive unless *directly ordered* to do so. Therefore, if Lloyd George was going to reclaim control of Britain's war effort, then he needed to grasp the nettle as tightly as possible.

From Montreuil, Lloyd George went on to Paris to discuss what looked like a promising glint of light in the international situation. On 19 September, London received a cable from its Ambassador in Spain, Sir Arthur Hardinge, which seemed to offer tantalizing hope of dramatic developments. 'Minister of State says he had heard through a Spanish diplomatic representative that [the] German Government would be glad to make a communication to ourselves relative to peace.' Apparently this feeler, which came from 'a very exalted personage' in

Germany, had been put out to gauge whether His Majesty's Government would be willing to listen to a suggestion for peace.[39] This was an overture by the new German Foreign Secretary, Richard von Kühlmann, who had been authorized to see whether Britain would enter into talks about the possible restoration of Belgium, in return for giving Germany a free hand in Russia and returning her African colonies, which had been seized at the beginning of the war.

The question for Britain was whether a compromise peace with Germany was either possible or desirable. The War Cabinet was unsure of what approach to adopt, agreeable in some quarters to abandoning Russia to her fate, but wary of the effect on Britain's other allies. In the end nothing came of the so-called 'Kühlmann peace kite'. Both Haig and Robertson were opposed to doing anything other than keeping on fighting, and Lloyd George was caught domestically in his own rhetoric of the 'knock out blow', which compromised his search for a way out of the slaughter. At a meeting of the War Cabinet on 27 September, shortly after the Prime Minister had returned from France, it was agreed that Britain's allies must be consulted and on 6 October the Foreign Office informed the relevant ambassadors in London. As might have been feared, their response was lukewarm. The consensus view was that the possibility of a separate peace should be dismissed out of hand. Furthermore, any kind of 'round table discussion' should only occur once 'the main objects of the Allied efforts had already been secured'.[40] Three days later, von Kühlmann, recognizing that there was no chance of splitting the Allies, reminded the Reichstag that Germany would never abandon her territorial claims in the west – principally Alsace–Lorraine – thus leaving any possibility of a negotiated peace in ruins.[41]

The failure of the Kühlmann peace note meant that the war in the west would continue into the following year. Above the Salient, sweeping dogfights took place between British and German fighters for control of the air, where no quarter was given, nor any expected. In what would become one of the most celebrated aerial duels of the war, Werner Voss, the German prodigy from *Jagdstaffel* 10 (with forty-seven kills), was shot down by Lieutenant Arthur Rhys Davids on 23 September. Voss was ambushed by a patrol of six SE5s of

56 Squadron led by James McCudden. As he later recalled: 'The triplane was still circling round in the midst of six S.E.'s, who were all
firing at it as opportunity offered, and at one time I noted the triplane
in the apex of a cone of tracer bullets from at least five machines
simultaneously, and each machine had two guns.' By choosing to
stand and fight – when he could have sped away in retreat – Voss
showed an extraordinary level of dedication and bravery, even fool-
hardiness, but once he did the outcome was inevitable. After about
ten minutes of frantic air combat – when most of the SE5s received
bullet damage – Voss's plane was hit and it went down in a steep dive,
hitting the ground and disappearing 'into a thousand fragments'.[42]

On the ground, no time was lost in preparing for General Plumer's
second step. As before all major offensives, a daunting engineering
and logistical effort was required to build the new roads and tracks
that would allow the advance to continue. Fortunately, the weather
improved and clear skies, with the accompanying choking dust,
meant that Second Army's engineers and pioneer units, labourers and
drivers, were able to get to work. In I ANZAC Corps every spare
man – pioneers, field companies and reserves – were 'employed in
pushing forward roads, tramlines, mule tracks[,] duckwalks [*sic*] and
water supplies'. According to the Chief Engineer:

> The country we are passing over is one sea of shell holes which are filled
> with water in the valleys. Our roads therefore, when crossing valleys,
> are floating. We put down a foundation of fascines, hurdles etc., and laid
> planking on these. The original country roads in the battle zone have
> totally disappeared in many cases, but as a rule we try to follow these
> lines of road, and some road metal is found in the shell holes, and the
> local people when making the roads must have selected the best lines i.e.,
> as far as solidity of ground was concerned. As a rule the greater propor-
> tion of our forward roads must be built of planking as this means quicker
> work and we could not get sufficient metal up for metal roads.[43]

They did all this under intermittent, sometimes heavy, artillery fire.
That month the construction parties from I ANZAC Corps suffered
at least 550 casualties. It was deadly, but vital, work. Sweat would
save blood.

II.

'War with a Big W'

There is not a bit of cover anywhere, not a tree or dug-out of
any description. Nothing but mud and dead.

Stanley Roberts[1]

26 September–3 October 1917

Following the Battle of Menin Road, Haig was eager to strike again
as soon as possible. 'In view of the fine weather which our weather
experts think is likely to last for a week,' he wrote on 21 September, 'it
is most desirable to take full advantage of it, and of the superiority
which we have now gained, for the time being, over the enemy's aeroplanes and artillery.'[2] It had been arranged with General Plumer that
Second Army would attack again, with I ANZAC Corps capturing
the whole of Polygon Wood and Zonnebeke, while units on its flanks
continued to advance in line. Should this be successful, a third step
could then take place towards the main ridge at Broodseinde and the
Gravenstafel Spur.[3] Haig was determined to keep going, come what
may. 'My plan is to press the Ypres offensive as vigorously as possible',
he noted on 23 September. There was all to play for.[4]

Plumer's second step – the Battle of Polygon Wood – opened at
5.50 a.m. on 26 September. It had been prepared in the same intricate
manner as his other battles and produced much the same result. Once
again two Australian divisions, 4th and 5th, would make the main
assault, pushing forward about 1,200 yards towards the Flanders I line
south of Zonnebeke, while clearing the main obstacle on this part of
the front: Polygon Wood. Lieutenant Sinclair Hunt, a former school
teacher from Croydon, New South Wales, was part of 55/Battalion

(5th Division) as it made its way up the line the evening before the attack. They were led in silence by a group of guides, who had taped out the route they would follow to their jumping-off point, which lay at the southwestern tip of Polygon Wood. What had once been a pleasant young forest was now 'totally devoid of any life'. Not even green young saplings could survive in such a blasted place, which was regularly swept by heavy fire. 'The whole road appeared like a forest of charred and splintered stumps standing about three or four feet high', Hunt remembered. Every so often a flare would fizzle up from the German positions, causing them to crouch and freeze 'so that Fritz would have no idea of what was happening'.[5]

Once they were in position – lying in shell holes or scrapes in the ground – they waited for the moment to attack. The German defenders seemed to have sensed something was up. Flares were fired 'with unusual frequency' and soon a scattering of shells fell along Hunt's sector, causing some casualties, but fortunately missing most of the attacking waves. Gradually the minutes ticked down.

> A fog had fallen and we could see Fritz flares only hazily through it. Ten minutes, a man rose here and there to tighten a belt or to stretch his cramped limbs. Three – the fog was more dense, and sections became very restless as they quietly fixed bayonets and prepared to advance. A gun behind boomed louder than the rest, suddenly the whole earth seemed to burst into a seething bubbling roaring centre of eruption and as at the touch of an enchantresser's [sic] wand, out of the ground sprang a mass of men in little worm like columns – each wriggling its way forward to a sparkling shouting seething line of earth, fire and smoke in front of them.

After seventy-five yards they saw their first Germans, just bodies 'chewed up by the barrage'. After 100 yards they ran into 'a platoon of scared Fritzes', hurrying towards them with their hands in the air. They soon reached the great mound at the far side of Polygon Wood (the 'Butte', which was once used for musketry training by the Belgian Army), cleared out a dugout, and then re-formed their platoons for the next stage of the attack.

Charles Bean would later call the artillery barrage on 26 September 'the most perfect that ever protected Australian troops', crashing out in front of them 'like a Gippsland bushfire'.[6] As it moved on to the second objective, perfectly on time, Hunt and his men followed as closely as they could ('the boys hugged it to a yard'). There were occasional short rounds – including one that just missed Hunt and failed to explode – but they did not dent the eagerness of the men to close with the enemy. 'Before the last shot fell on a Pill Box it was swarming with "Aussies" who scrambled all over it looking for "Flues" or ventilators through which to drop a bomb. Fritz, however, did not want any coaxing in most cases, but ran out with hands up at the first call and shewed [sic] no signs of fight. Indeed we found the rifles in most of the "Boxes" without even bayonets fixed.' Hunt was elated at what they had done. 'The advance itself was the finest we had ever experienced', he said proudly. 'The artillery barrage was so perfect and we followed it so close, that it was simply a matter of walking into the positions and commencing to dig in.'[7]

On the left, advancing towards the Flanders I line at Molenaarelst-hoek, 4th Australian Division made good progress. 'The barrage fell at the appointed time, 5.50 a.m., and lifting three minutes later our troops commenced to advance moving close under it. Distances were adjusted between waves after all troops were in advance of our front line', recorded an after-action report. Although the morning was misty and visibility difficult, which meant officers had to rely on their compasses to keep direction, the fury of the bombardment cleared all before it. 'The density and power of the Barrage had a very demoralising effect on the enemy as evidenced by his abject terror, and willingness to surrender', recorded Lieutenant-Colonel Harold Paul, the commanding officer of 49/Battalion. 'A few isolated cases occurred where snipers did use their rifles, but they were promptly dealt with.'[8] By 7.15 a.m. 16/Battalion was on the first objective (the Red Line) and within an hour 'leapfrogging' troops were on the Blue Line with German soldiers 'surrendering freely'.[9]

More problematic were the operations on the flanks, where the barrage was less dense and ground more difficult to cross. In the north V Corps achieved most of its objectives, but fell short of reaching Hill 40, a German position north of Zonnebeke, which remained in enemy hands. The attack had gone largely to plan, but after the infantry were held up by the Zonnebeke stream, they lost touch with the creeping barrage and suffered accordingly – machine-gun fire stop-ping the attack about 600 yards from the final objective.[10] In X Corps, on the southern flank, the situation was more precarious, in part because of a heavy German spoiling attack that had gone in the pre-vious day. 33rd Division had already sustained about 5,000 casualties and had been fighting for over twenty-four hours when Zero Hour came. The division was hastily reorganized, with the reserve brigade (19 Brigade) reinforcing the attacking waves, which swept forward that morning 'with extreme bitterness'.[11] Fortunately, 15 Australian Brigade helped to re-establish the line and push on to their objec-tives at the far side of Polygon Wood. The fighting in this shattered, broken woodland was incredibly bitter.

It was here where two Victoria Crosses were won: Sergeant Jack Dwyer (4/Australian Machine-Gun Company) and Private Patrick Joseph Bugden (31/Battalion). Dwyer, in charge of a Vickers machine-gun team, won his for leading the defence of the position throughout 26 and 27 September. Oblivious to danger, moving from shell hole to shell hole, directing machine-gun fire against the numer-ous counter-attacks that came through the blasted remains of the wood, he showed remarkable bravery, not to mention uncommon luck. At one point, his machine-gun was destroyed by a direct hit from an artillery shell, so he gathered his team and led them back through the enemy barrage, where they were able to bring up one of their reserve guns. 'Paddy' Bugden showed a similar level of bravery, but unfortunately he was not as lucky. He went out into no-man's-land at least five times to aid the wounded, but on the final occasion he was mortally wounded by a shell splinter. He was just twenty years old.[12]

Further heavy fighting broke out around the bastion of Tower Hamlets, which anchored the German southern flank in Flanders, and had already resisted numerous attacks. 39th Division, deployed about 1,000 yards south of the Menin Road, made 'rapid progress' after going 'over the top'. Although the right half of the division was delayed by poor ground conditions, elsewhere the attacking infantry overran their objectives on time. An after-action report noted that 'The opposition met with on the Western slopes of the Tower Hamlets Ridge was speedily disposed of. Our troops advanced through Tower Hamlets and over the high ground in its vicinity with but few casualties, and our objective on their Brigade front was gained according to the scheduled time.' On the right, the boggy ground, combined with enfilade fire from German strongpoints to the south (most notably a position known as the Quadrilateral), ensured that progress came to a halt – and it was necessary to pull back in places and form a defensive flank. Nevertheless, 39th Division's hold on the high ground was secure; not even concentrated artillery bombardments and two separate counter-attacks could dislodge it. The second, which advanced shortly before 7 p.m., was 'crushed by combined artillery and machine-gun fire'.[13]

The second phase of the battle, when the *Eingreif* divisions tried to launch their counter-attacks, was eerily similar to the events of 20 September. British aircraft had been scouring the battlefield for targets for most of the day, machine-gunning and bombing enemy concentrations, while also watching out for any German batteries that disclosed themselves. Their most important contribution, however, came in the early afternoon, when they began to notice the tell-tale signs of German units moving up: columns of infantry, trucks and horses crowding the roads southeast of Zandvoorde. Probable assembly areas, crossroads and junctions, were then subjected to heavy artillery fire.[14] Three formations were ordered forward: 17th Division on the southern sector against X Corps; 236th Division against I ANZAC Corps; and 4th Bavarian Division along the front of V Corps.[15]

Captain Caspari (II Battalion, 75 Infantry Regiment) was in 17th Division and had been directed to move towards the break-in south of Polygon Wood. His description of how they tried (and failed) to intervene was typical of what happened on that grim afternoon. They received news of the renewed attack at 10.30 a.m. and were immediately ordered forward, but they could only pick their way 'tortuously and painfully' because of the heavy drumfire. With communications torn to pieces, it was 1 p.m. before they were in their assembly positions, ready to go forward. Their advance was something out of a nightmare:

Everywhere the explosions of high explosive shells and the effect of smoke shells was reducing visibility, making breathing difficult and stinging our eyes. It was impossible to follow a set route, or to

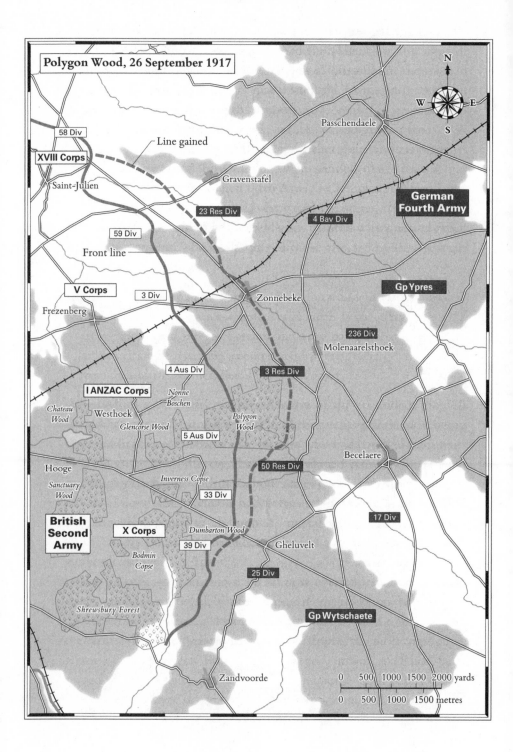

Polygon Wood, 26 September 1917

maintain separation between individuals or groups of men. Commanders just led their men stumbling in a westerly direction through
the roaring grey-black wall of the barrage, which was periodically lit
up with flashes. Watching out for the places where the fire was falling
most densely, attempts were made to pass weaker points, skirting
wired-off battery positions, swamps and hedgerows, looking for
crossing points across swollen streams.

Incredibly, Caspari's men managed to close with the British positions
around Polderhoek Château, but found all the approaches swept by
machine-gun and mortar fire. When they tried to get forward, either
individually or in groups, they were all shot down. 'It was beyond
human endurance', he noted painfully.[16]

Other units fared similarly. 459 Infantry Regiment (of 236th Division) was ordered forward at 12.55, but could make little progress
against the Australians. The men crept forward, rifles in hand, each
carrying two sandbags full of hand grenades, but came under heavy
artillery and machine-gun fire, which rapidly brought their advance
to a halt. Courageously they kept going, their faces 'covered with
dust and sweat; for the sun was burning down from the sky':

> If only visibility wasn't so good and the terrain not so flat and level,
> allowing the English to see everything over many miles! Advancing
> on this churned-up ground is becoming slower and slower. But every-
> one is gritting their teeth. For what is at stake is to bring relief to our
> embattled brothers ahead. So far losses among the advance party are
> moderate, but now that they have arrived at the level of Broodseinde,
> the enemy puts a final protective line of fire in front of our infantry.
> So the counter-attack has been detected. Geysers the size of houses
> consisting of soil, metal splinters and rocks erupt everywhere. It is as
> if giant invisible fists were pounding, clobbering everything without
> mercy. Everyone who hasn't been hit yet looks for a gap in the horrible
> wall of fire, half insane from breathlessness and terror.[17]

459 Infantry Regiment's attack failed as surely as all the others had.
They lost 550 men in a matter of hours. Likewise, the final counter-
attack, made by Bavarian troops, was repulsed in the same brutal

manner. 'The enemy, who appeared to have suffered severely from our artillery fire during their advance, were badly disorganised and were met by our troops in the open with the bayonet and easily dispersed', recorded V Corps.[18]

Polygon Wood had been a success, with another 1,200-yard advance, but casualties were beginning to rise. Together Fifth and Second Armies sustained 15,375 casualties on 26 September; about 25 per cent fewer than Menin Road, but as they had occurred on a significantly shorter frontage (8,500 yards compared to 14,500 on 20 September) and within fewer divisions (seven versus eleven), they were proportionally greater.[19] The attacking divisions at Polygon Wood sustained about 4,400 casualties per square mile of ground gained – about 15 per cent higher than Menin Road.[20] This illustrated not only the diminishing scale of returns that each subsequent 'step' would encounter, but also how effective German combat units remained. Moreover, the counter-battery struggle was being lost. German shelling had caused continuous losses throughout the afternoon. The case of 2/5th Lincolnshire Regiment (59th Division) illustrates how intensive some of the bombardments were. That morning they attacked a line of strongpoints on the Wieltje–Gravenstafel road, German troops showing 'very little fight' and surrendering in droves as soon as the leading lines closed with their positions. Nevertheless, the Lincolns were subject to heavy and continuous bombardment once they had secured their final objective, particularly around captured pillboxes, which 'came in for rough treatment'. When they were withdrawn from the fighting, the battalion recorded only ten officers and 275 other ranks fit for duty out of a total strength of twenty-one officers and 563 men – a casualty rate of over 51 per cent.[21]

The Reverend Edward Tanner, a chaplain attached to 2/Worcestershire Regiment (33rd Division), spent 26 September at a dressing station on the Menin Road and described the heartbreaking scenes as men – those wounded in mind as well as body – were brought in:

> All through the day the flow of wounded through the Aid Post had been uninterrupted, and the floor was just one mass of mutilated, writhing humans. It was terrible to look at and I was only too glad

that I had my attention taken off it by other things. On one occasion
during that afternoon I made a note of what I saw. The bunks on
the floor were crowded with some of the worst cases we had had. One
young KRR [King's Royal Rifle Corps] of 19 years had [his] face
lacerated and caked with blood. All he could say was 'Shoot me,
Doctor. Shoot me please. Do shoot me.' He died soon after he left
the Aid Post. Just inside the door was a man with a wrist broken and
artery pierced by a splinter. Blood was pouring on the ground and a
tourniquet had to be applied. Two sitting cases were crouching on
the bench near the door. These two had been too frightened to go
down the day before on the stretchers and now we could not send
them as other cases were of far greater urgency. Another young
KRR was lying with one side absolutely lacerated with splinter
wounds. His tunic had been almost shot away. One man lay just
inside the doorway unconscious. A bullet had pierced his brain.

For Tanner, the most difficult cases to deal with were those who had
lost their minds on the battlefield and were suffering from 'shell shock'.
There were a range of different symptoms on display: a Highlander
who was 'absolutely demented – shouting at the top of his voice the
most utter nonsense and waving his arms and legs'; a man too old for
active service who 'hung about all day in the doorway trembling from
head to foot'; and two others, young boys, 'shaking from head to foot
and cowering down every time a shell came over'.[22] This was the price
of Plumer's advances: shredded bodies and shattered minds.

The attackers may have sustained significant losses, but the defenders
found Polygon Wood to be far from comfortable. Indeed, the success
of Plumer's methods produced yet more anxiety at Fourth Army
headquarters. Counter-attacks had been launched, but had regained
little ground, and casualties, as always, had been heavy. German
losses between 11 and 30 September amounted to over 38,500 men,
including 9,700 who were listed as missing (many undoubtedly being
captured).[23] Some regiments had been hit particularly hard. The history of 229 Reserve Infantry Regiment, which fought just north of
the Menin Road, recorded that its time at Polygon Wood was the

heaviest fighting it experienced during the war. Between 19 and
28 September forty-three officers and 1,109 NCOs and other ranks
were killed and over 1,000 wounded.[24] Two regiments of 4th Bavarian Division, which had counter-attacked around Zonnebeke, had
fared equally badly, losing forty officers and 1,300 other ranks in a
single day with nothing to show for it.[25]

In some units, morale seemed to be breaking down. Against the
Australians, 3rd and 50th Reserve Divisions had sustained heavy
losses, with the former suffering a number of desertions prior to the
battle. On 26 September, one platoon surrendered as a whole unit,
while another company refused to go forward into the line (with
Allied intelligence estimating that this was probably due to a high
percentage of *Landsturm* men and pressed Polish troops in its ranks).[26]
Observing the battle from his bunker in Group Wytschaete, Albrecht
von Thaer was almost beside himself with grief. 'We are living
through truly abominable days', he wrote in his diary on 28 September. Studying reports from the battlefield, bent over a dozen maps, he
was beginning to understand how effective Plumer's attacks were,
and how limited their response could be. His account was one of the
clearest and most powerful descriptions of what 'bite and hold' was
really like for those German commanders tasked with defeating it:

> I no longer have any idea of what should be undertaken against the
> English. They set themselves a fairly limited objective for their
> attacks: to advance only by about 500 to 1,000 metres, albeit across
> quite a wide front. In front of this area and deep into our zone, there
> is such devastating English fire that no being can survive in it. Then,
> under the protection of this fire, and without sustaining many losses
> of their own, they simply move into the field of corpses and quickly
> install themselves there. Our counter-attacks must first get through
> the rapid wave of fire, and then behind it they find a fixed phalanx
> with machine guns, and they collapse in ruins. The last few days have
> brought us the bitterest losses of life here. Early in the day before
> yesterday, when one of our divisions was severely attacked, I imme-
> diately ordered a fresh new division from the rear to carry out a
> counter-strike and provide relief. Even when advancing through the

terrible fire, it lost a great number of men, and afterwards it could not go one step farther forward. Of course, the English have also suffered losses, but probably not as many in this process. This is primarily an artillery battle. The English have three times as many guns and six times the quantity of ammunition. So our dear soldiers die off. One constantly keeps thinking: if we deploy more men at the front from the start, then these personnel will obviously also be annihilated; but having a thin front line and strong reserves coming from the rear – which is our current approach – will no longer do, either.[27]

Thaer was left to pray for 'good, inventive ideas'; anything that would help them cope with the situation they were facing, now that the English, as he put it, 'have given up their famous penetration tactics'. The only hope, he felt, was for the mass employment of tanks, but the German Army had none of them. 'Lossberg does not really know what to do, either', he lamented. 'Ludendorff will be coming tomorrow morning, and he wants to talk to us, but he will not know of any panacea, either.'[28]

Ludendorff, overseeing things at the Supreme Command, may not have been as squeamish as Thaer, but he was also at a loss as to how they should respond to Plumer's tactics. On 30 September he reported to the General Staff that the 'latest British attacks – artillery barrage, smoke and machine-gun fire against our massed divisions on a comparatively narrow front – are almost irresistible'.[29] He was so worried at these new developments that he returned to Belgium and met with senior officers to discuss what could be done. 'Our defensive tactics had to be developed further, somehow or other', he wrote. 'We were all agreed on that.'

> The only thing was, it was so infinitely difficult to hit on the right remedy. We could proceed only by careful experiment. The proposals of the officers on the spot tended rather in the direction of our former tactics; they amounted to a slight, but only a slight, reinforcement of our front lines, and the abandonment of the counter-attack by the counter-attack divisions, local counter-attacks being substituted for this. These local counter-attacks were to be brought close up and spread over a wide front, before the enemy's attack began. So, while the front line was to be held rather more densely once more, in order to gain in power, the whole battle-field was to be given more depth than ever.[30]

However, in order for this to work, OHL would need to supply more men, in the form of a second division behind every front-line division, which Ludendorff called 'an unheard-of expenditure of force'. It was agreed to bolster the front-line garrisons, move support and reserve units closer in – so they could intervene more quickly – and deploy extra machine-guns in the forward zone to try and break up any attack in its early stages.[31] It was also arranged that a spoiling attack would be mounted on the morning of 4 October, to try and secure important observation points southwest of Zonnebeke.[32]

The truth was that there were no perfect solutions to the 'bite-and-hold' tactics they were coming up against. Putting more men in the trenches was hardly ideal, but given that British artillery fire was now falling deeper into the German defensive zone, there may have been no alternative.[33] Fourth Army orders, issued on 30 September, urged the importance of forcing the British to place more men in the trenches, so they could be targeted by German artillery.[34] Yet how to deploy the *Eingreif* divisions remained the great question. Because it took them some time to get assembled, they tended to deploy on the battlefield only after the British had been given a chance to dig in, which was usually by the afternoon. As had been seen on 20 and 26 September, if the British were allowed enough time to get organized, there was very little the *Eingreif* divisions could do about it. Therefore, it was agreed to hold them back until a day or two later and then make a more systematic and better-organized counter-attack where, it was hoped, these handicaps could be avoided. While this was not an outright rejection of defence-in-depth, it was an acknowledgement that modifications were required if the Fourth Army was to stand any chance of defeating Plumer's limited advances.[35]

Accordingly, orders were issued to the front-line units updating them on the need to adapt their defensive organization. For example, 5th Guard Infantry Brigade (4th Guard Division), which went into the line around Zonnebeke, was issued with orders on 29 September warning them of further British attacks:

> At the Commanders' conference today, mention was made on all sides
> of the fact that the counter-attacks of reserve and storm divisions

usually come too late in cases of a hostile attack with a limited objective, and that the losses caused in this way are out of proportion to the success gained. In many cases the counter-attack hardly reached the front line then held; heavy casualties were suffered and the whole thing was a failure, as our enemy contented himself with the objective already gained. His gain in ground was secured by his numberless machine guns, which he immediately built in, and by his protective waves following close behind the attackers, who dug themselves in under the latter's protection.

Therefore, defending units were ordered to strengthen their front-line garrisons and, if possible, mount quick spoiling raids as the enemy was preparing to attack. Eight companies would hold the front, while the rest of the regiment were moved 'outside the principal zone of fire', ready to intervene whenever possible. Whether this would work remained unclear – only time would tell.[36]

Given the events of 20 and 26 September, everyone knew that a renewed assault was only days away. On the British side of the line, a series of major reliefs took place as reinforcements came up. II ANZAC Corps occupied the line from the Ypres–Roulers railway, on the left of I ANZAC, up to where it met XVIII Corps. At a conference on 28 September, Haig urged his generals to prepare to exploit success after the next attack, which would go in on 4 October.[37] They were to take the eastern edge of the Gheluvelt Plateau, including the important village of Broodseinde. 'I am of opinion that the enemy is tottering,' he told them – his voice betraying more emotion than usual – 'and that a good vigorous blow might lead to decisive results.' He anticipated that should they destroy or interrupt the junction at Roulers for up to forty-eight hours, there might be a debacle 'because the enemy would then have to rely on only one railway line for the supply of his troops between Ghent and the sea'.[38]

Were the British on the verge of a major breakthrough? Was there a possibility that cavalry could now be employed in masses? Notwithstanding the success of the last two attacks, both Plumer and Gough were not so sure and expressed their reservations to Haig in the days after Polygon Wood. Although happy with the success so far, they were of the opinion (correctly, as it turned out) that the high ground at

Passchendaele along to Westroosebeke would have to be secured before any further exploitation could take place, and this would entail perhaps two or three further 'steps' of 1,500 yards each. And, of course, after each step it would be necessary to rebuild the roads and tracks, move the artillery forward, and bring up more reinforcements, which would all take precious time.[39] Haig – perhaps reading these notes with a furrowed brow – met them at Second Army Headquarters on 2 October and 'pointed out how favourable the situation was and how necessary it was to have all the necessary means for exploiting any success . . . should the situation admit'. 'Both Gough and Plumer acquiesced in my views', Haig went on to say, 'and arranged wholeheartedly to give effect to them when the time came.'[40]

When the time came. Gough and Plumer could perhaps be forgiven for acquiescing in Haig's renewed optimism, knowing full well that a breakthrough was not imminent. They had seen this before: a limited success that had been based upon exhaustive preparation and phenomenal firepower causing Haig to find new faith in dramatic breakthrough operations. As they already knew, it was best to nod in agreement and get on with the job in hand. At Second Army Headquarters, General Plumer continued in his usual style; what Tim Harington likened to that of a director of a 'large corporation'. In the spirit of a board of directors' meeting, Plumer would sit at the head of a large table, which could be extended out a considerable length, in order to accommodate as many commanders and staff officers as possible. Before their plans were finalized, Plumer always asked whether everyone was in agreement. Harington remembered one meeting, just after Polygon Wood, during which 'there had been a long series of arguments, covering a good part of the morning between corps commanders, their general staff officers and artillery generals, as to boundaries for attack and overlapping barrages and responsibilities concerning adjoining formations'. According to Harington:

> The conference had temporarily broken up into small groups, but after a time it became obvious that they were ready to report and all re-assembled around a long table. General Plumer, from his seat at the head, sitting erect with his back to the main window, could see by

the attention and the expressions on the faces of his corps commanders and staff officers that unanimity had been reached on the last of the points in question. He then said, 'Have you reached an agreement that is satisfactory?' and after a rather general expression he proceeded deliberately to take an individual poll of his corps commanders.

For Harington, this was why Second Army received such 'extraordinary co-operation and determined adherence to plans agreed upon, and unswerving loyalty and cheerful support for all of those in responsible places in his Army'.[41]

As Cassel buzzed with staff officers and reverberated with the sound of telephones, a mass movement of men was underway. 3rd Australian Division, the lead element of Sir Alexander Godley's II ANZAC Corps, marched into Ypres on the evening of 29 September. They made what was by now a familiar journey through the ghostly streets, passing the ruins of the Cloth Hall, before marching out to the trenches. 'The night was dull and cloudy and obscured the young moon, the roads were congested with heavy traffic, ammunition and ration limbers, an occasional field gun or howitzer, together with moving troops made frequent stops a necessity', recalled Lieutenant-Colonel Henry Goddard, Commanding Officer of 35/ Battalion. As the long lines of infantry passed the shells of buildings in silence, Goddard could only wonder at the scale of its 'pre-war beauty', now smashed by enemy artillery. 'It made us feel that War with a big W was in progress and that it meant Work with a bigger W before the job of knocking out the Hun would be complete.' They passed the ramparts of the town, crossed the moat, and then headed off, on the Zonnebeke road, up to the line.[42]

Ypres had been bad enough – particularly as the column narrowly escaped a bomb thrown from a passing German aircraft – but once they left the (relative) safety of the town, the sense of being exposed to enemy guns became overwhelming. Indeed, as if in some kind of Dante-esque nightmare, the further the Australians descended into the Salient, the worse it got. Goddard went on:

We passed that well known spot Hell Fire Corner, nor did we linger in passing. It was very noticeable how the drivers of the mule teams as they neared this spot whipped up their mounts and cleared it at breakneck speed. The country, or as much as we could see, presented a miserable spectacle. What trees remained were blasted and the debris of overturned wagons and other vehicles as well as the few battered houses were sufficient evidence of what had occurred through the whole length of this road.

Two guides led them, by platoons, towards their positions. 'Mud, mud, mud, we sank over our boot-tops, then to our knees, and being heavily leaden with packs, etc., our progress was sadly impeded.' Machine-gun bullets occasionally whistled overhead. The smell of rotting flesh and bodies crept into the nose and made men gag. Their trenches were hardly worthy of the name, being shallow, badly sighted ditches with no wire or shelters of any kind. They would need their wits about them when daylight came.

Their divisional commander, Major-General Sir John Monash, set up his headquarters in the town. 'I am writing in a dugout, in the eastern ramparts of Ypres, close to the Menin Gate', he told his wife on the evening of 1 October. 'For three years it has been dying a lingering death, and now there is nothing left of its fine streets, its great square, its Cathedral, the historical Cloth Hall, its avenues, and boulevards of fine mansions', only 'a charred collection of pitiable ruins'. Although Monash's living quarters were certainly more comfortable than the trenches, they were hardly luxurious:

> It is in every respect like the underground workings of mines, narrow tunnels, broadening out here and there into little chambers, the whole lit by electric light, run by my own portable electric plant. It is cold and dank and over run by rats and mice, and altogether smelly and disagreeable, but here I shall have to stay for nearly 3 weeks. Myself, A.D.C.'s Staff, clerks, signallers, cooks, batmen and attached officers are tucked away all over the place, in little cabins, recesses, and dugouts.

Monash's mess was in a small cabin (he described it as being akin to a tramp steamer), with very little room to move and always noisy from the constant traffic. 'It is one enormous medley of military activity', he noted, comparing it to the traffic on Elizabeth Street in

Melbourne, 'for an hour after the last race on Cup Day, multiplied ten fold'.[43] He had just three days to prepare his division for their biggest battle since Messines Ridge.

Intelligence soon began to filter in of the changes that the Germans had made to their defensive tactics. Lieutenant Charles Carrington (1/5th Royal Warwicks, 48th Division) led his company up to their assembly positions at dusk on 3 October. He was 'miserable beyond belief', likening the feeling to that which must 'envelop criminals in the condemned cell' before their execution. 'There was much routine work to be done,' he remembered, 'which I did in an unreal mood as if it were a game, a piece of play-acting. My true self had been filled with the presentiment that this was the end, that I was marked to die or be crushed in the military machine . . .' He had been handed the latest intelligence reports just as he was about to leave, which left him cold. 'Two German companies were now holding the front I was to attack with one' – an indication of how the Germans were thickening up their front line after Polygon Wood. The company eventually reached their assigned sector in the darkness – somewhere past what had once been the Langemarck–Gheluvelt line.[44]

Carrington was only one of thousands of officers and men moving up to the front that evening; each one having to deal with his own fears and worries. At Zero Hour the following morning (timed for 6 a.m.), Second Army would go, once more, into battle. Four corps would make the assault from the Tower Hamlets Ridge to just north of Gravenstafel (a total frontage of 9,700 yards). I and II ANZAC Corps would make the main assault against the Broodseinde Ridge, while X Corps advanced deeper into the Gheluvelt Plateau and Fifth Army covered the flank in the north. Whereas the Battle of Menin Road had been preceded by several days' heavy bombardment, there would be no such preparation before Broodseinde. Although an intensive effort was made to silence enemy gun batteries, a massed barrage would open the assault at Zero Hour, hoping to gain the element of surprise.[45] What happened the following day would be the climactic moment of the Flanders campaign: a brutal attack that would smash up the German defence and raise the prospect, distant though it had once seemed, that Haig might actually achieve his objectives.

12.

'An Overwhelming Blow'

He is staggering, and we are all praying for the weather to keep up;
so that we can keep on hitting him . . . everything depends upon the
rapidity with which we can bring up the guns.

Sir John Monash[1]

4–8 October 1917

4 October 1917 dawned with another of those miserable rain-filled mornings, filled with anxiety. The ground was wet and slippery; visibility was low; and a thick drizzle saturated the air. By 5.30 a.m. most of the assaulting brigades were in their assembly positions, the men lying out in no-man's-land behind their jumping-off tapes, bayonets fixed.[2] All seemed to be well, but at twenty minutes to Zero, German batteries began firing – in support of their pre-planned spoiling attack – and shells started falling on the forward positions of the Australian divisions around Zonnebeke. While this could have caused panic and chaos, the men stayed firm: hugging the ground as closely as possible; doing what they could for those who had been hit; and praying that the shelling would pass. In some sectors, battalion commanders ordered their men to move forward, out of their assembly positions, to avoid the worst of it, as they waited for the moment to attack.[3]

At 6 a.m., when the British artillery opened fire, it appeared to eyewitnesses that 'a wall of flame' had descended on the German trenches.[4] Behind the explosions, and the plumes of dirt, the attacking infantrymen got up and moved out, no doubt lighting a cigarette as they did so. The barrage was 'of such weight and density as to belittle anything we had seen on the Somme', wrote Lieutenant

Charles Carrington, who had gone into the line the previous evening convinced he was going to die. The chief difficulty, he noted, 'was to identify any place whatever on the ground, even after days spent studying large-scale maps, air photographs, and the "Corps Model"'. It was almost impossible to be certain of your location, or where your objective was, amid 'a lunar landscape of shell-craters, one touching another, filled with water or with sludgy clay that could almost wrench the boots off your feet'. His men struggled to keep direction, veering off to the left and taking a neighbouring battalion's objective. For Carrington, writing in his retirement, it was with some amazement to find that historians had elevated the battle (known as Broodseinde) 'into a tactical masterpiece like Messines'. For him, 'it was just all-in wrestling in the mud'.[5]

On the frontage of I and II ANZAC Corps, the men moved out, often in sections, walking carefully in single file along the lips of shell craters, while covered by a screen of skirmishers. 'Through the roar of the guns and bursting shells could be heard the whining of bullets going over from a line of Vickers guns not far behind us', remembered Private H. G. Hartnett of 2/Battalion (1st Australian Division). 'In no time the battalions in front of us were forming a line and were moving off to attack. Strange to say very few casualties had been sustained around us, despite the heavy shellfire.' Soon afterwards they met batches of German prisoners coming in and quickly relieved them of any weapons or souvenirs they might have been carrying. 'As soon as they were released they ran to the stretchers on which lay our wounded and stood in pairs at the end of each.'[6] After encountering only 'slight' opposition, his brigade reached their final objective at 9.45 a.m. and busily started digging in.[7]

The most difficult task of the day fell to II ANZAC Corps, with 3rd Australian Division and the New Zealand Division having to secure the Gravenstafel and Zonnebeke Spurs, the last area of high ground before the Passchendaele Ridge. Here, the infantry went forward as quickly as they could. The New Zealanders had to cross the Hanebeek, a small stream that had been turned into a broad swamp, which slowed them down and left them exposed to German artillery. Fortunately the ground was so soft that many of the shells buried themselves before exploding; showering the men in freezing cold, smoking water, but luckily saving them heavy losses.[8] Soon fire started coming from the blockhouses and pillboxes that remained intact; the intermittent sound of machine-guns filled the air as the attackers went through their routines: suppressing fire; hurling off flurries of rifle grenades or trench mortar bombs, while designated teams worked around the obstacles and silenced them, often at the point of the bayonet.

Eight Victoria Crosses were won that day, including those of two Australians, Lance Corporal Walter Peeler and Sergeant Lewis McGee (of 37 and 40/Battalions respectively). Both men showed enormous courage in taking on enemy blockhouses and pillboxes singlehandedly. McGee's company were just 100 yards from their final objective when they came under heavy fire from a German position known as Hamburg Redoubt. 'This pillbox contained a number of the enemy, who had their machine-gun in a recess on top of the fort, and were firing straight at B Company, the machine-gun bullets cutting the tops of the shell-holes where our men were taking cover.' McGee sprinted fifty yards and 'in the face of certain death' shot the crew with his revolver.[9] His counterpart, Walter Peeler, showed the same single-minded determination. As his battalion went forward, they came up against small teams of German machine-gunners and snipers who could have wreaked havoc on the Australian infantry. Peeler killed about thirty of the enemy as he darted from shell hole to shell hole, firing his Lewis gun from the hip. 'I never saw the faces of those I killed', he later admitted. 'They were just men in an enemy uniform. It was simply them or me.'[10]

It would be, in the main, an infantry and artillery battle. The RFC could only assist in limited ways, with the high winds and low clouds, which were down to 400 feet in places, meaning that only forty-nine 'zone calls' were made (as opposed to 394 on 20 September). Although these resulted in twenty-six targets being destroyed, much more could have been achieved had the weather been better.[11] As for the tanks, 4 October was undoubtedly encouraging, albeit as only a handful of machines had been parcelled out across the front, there was a limit to what they could do. Most notably, eleven machines of 'D' Battalion, I Tank Brigade, cooperated with XVIII Corps in its advance towards the ruined village of Poelcappelle. The tanks helped the infantry to get forward, using their 6-pounders to smother pillboxes and demolish the few farm buildings still standing, before withdrawing, largely intact. The attack was also noticeable for the close cooperation with the infantry and the high standard of tank driving, which enabled objectives to be seized without heavy loss.[12]

For the embattled defenders, the situation was desperate. In places German troops surrendered; in others they fought hard and had to be snuffed out one section at a time. Both 6th Bavarian and 10th Ersatz Divisions (deployed around Poelcappelle) were seriously under-strength, with reports that the average company contained as few as between fifty and 100 rifles (as opposed to 200 men at full strength). Although they were able to offer strong resistance as the British struggled to cross the Stroombeek, elsewhere they were unable to stem the advance and had to fall back.[13] Walter Rappolt, an NCO with I Guard Foot Artillery Regiment, spent the morning with his battery in constant action, firing 'annihilation' and 'blocking' barrages without stopping; having to shout to make himself understood. He remembered seeing a German soldier stagger back from the front line about 6.30 that morning, 'looking more like an animal than a human being, with a grey face . . . eyes wide open, barefoot, trousers and jacket torn, heavily bleeding from a wound in his arm'. They took in the straggler, bandaged his wound, and gave him a cup of coffee. After a while the man began to open up and explain what had happened. 'Gradually he is regaining his senses and gives us the shocking news that most of his comrades were taken prisoner and that there is scarcely anything in front of us. They had repulsed three waves of the British. The fourth broke through . . .'[14]

As for those Prussian units that had been assigned to retake the higher ground southwest of Zonnebeke, they found themselves in the worst possible place at the worst possible time. Their attack had been scheduled to go ahead at 6.10 a.m., but as they were about to go forward, they were engulfed in a nightmare of dust, smoke and shell splinters as Second Army's opening bombardment streaked down from the sky. According to the history of 4th Guard Infantry Division:

> At 5.55 a.m., shortly before our infantry was due to march in, a fire-storm unlike any previously experienced erupted. The whole earth of Flanders shook and seemed to be on fire . . . What were the horrors of Verdun and of the Somme in comparison to this hugely increased exertion of force? The powerful thunder of battle could be heard in the most remote corners of Belgium. It was as if the enemy wanted to tell the whole world: we are coming, we will force victory! But they did not defeat us! They misjudged us! Even if they bombarded our troops with millions of shells from thousands of batteries . . . so that mathematically not a single speck of land was left that hadn't been hit, they failed to destroy one thing: the courage of our front-line troops.[15]

The brutal truth, of course, was that courage could be vaporized as easily as men's bodies in the ensuing maelstrom. 212 Reserve Infantry Regiment, which was supposed to lead the attack, was torn to pieces. It sustained over 1,000 casualties that morning, with reports indicating that some of the assaulting companies lost 95 per cent of their effective strength. It was little wonder that German bodies carpeted whole sectors of the battlefield.[16]

By midday the battle, for what it's worth, was over. Second Army had reached most of the Red Line by 8 a.m., and after a pause of one to two hours (which was mainly devoted to 'mopping up' the captured positions) had marched on to the Blue Line, which was consolidated shortly after one o'clock. Another 'bite' of 1,200 yards had been made in the German line, with over 4,000 prisoners being escorted to the rear. Although a number of counter-attacks had been launched against the newly won positions, the Germans found themselves up against well-drilled machine-gun and rifle fire that scattered their columns as quickly as they came up. Out to the north, XVIII and XIV Corps of Fifth Army had secured the left flank and captured the village of Poelcappelle.[17] Whether it would have been possible to go further remained unclear. Although in places subsequent, albeit modest, gains were made (such as XVIII Corps, which pushed on another 500 yards), it was generally considered that any deviation from the plan would have been too risky. The Germans still had eight divisions in close reserve and it was known that their positions on the Flanders II and III lines were largely intact, which made any kind of 'rush' against them highly improbable. It was probably for the best that Second Army decided to sit tight.[18]

There may have been no dramatic exploitation, but Broodseinde appeared to be a stunning success, and within weeks news was being relayed across the empire of the 'greatest victory of the war'.[19] German dead were everywhere: scattered by heavy shelling; torn to pieces inside caved-in pillboxes; or cut down by machine-gun fire like slaughtered cattle. Second Army intelligence recorded how evidence of German demoralization and disorganization was everywhere. Prisoners had been taken from nearly every company of the defending divisions; their wireless stations were now 'significantly silent'; and no 'serious counter-attack with large forces' had been made. 'His machine-gun and rifle fire is erratic and his artillery continues to change rearward and to the flanks', it concluded. There were also 'abnormal train movements' as the Germans desperately tried to relieve shattered divisions and thousands of wounded, and bring fresh troops into the line.[20] For Lieutenant-General Sir William Birdwood, whose corps (I ANZAC) had taken the village of Broodseinde, there could be 'no doubt as to the completeness and importance' of their success. 'The Germans, who had recently been holding their front line in vastly increased strength, not only suffered heavily, but had lost one of their most vital positions on the Western Front; and this despite their knowledge that the blow was coming.'[21]

Predictably, perhaps, there have always been those who remain to be convinced by the victorious tales that emerged from Broodseinde. Lloyd George was supposed to have scoffed at Haig's 'victory' and, more recently, the historians Robin Prior and Trevor Wilson have asked whether the battle really 'constituted a model of irresistible progress'.[22] They claim that some of its apparent success was undoubtedly down to 'ill-judgement and sheer bad luck on the part of the enemy' – such as the ill-fated spoiling attack at Zonnebeke – that was unlikely to reoccur in subsequent operations. Moreover, Plumer had benefited from the dry weather throughout the preceding month,

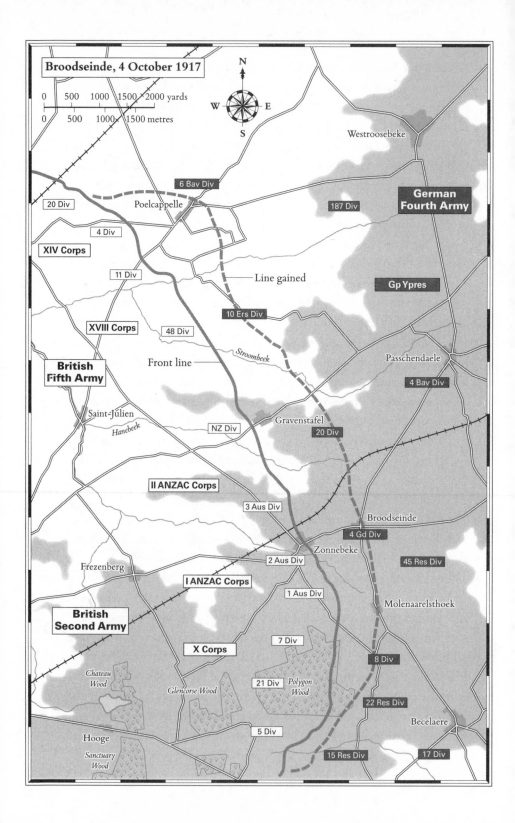

Broodseinde, 4 October 1917

which would soon be replaced by the usual autumn rains. Given that the British were now overlooking an ominous stretch of low-lying ground before Passchendaele (where the Ravebeek drained into the Stroombeek), it was highly likely that any more bad weather would inundate the battlefield and make significant progress all but impossible. Even more worryingly, Broodseinde did nothing to address the fundamental problem that British attacks were getting narrower and narrower as they drove towards the high ground at Passchendaele. The further they pushed into the re-entrant, the more exposed they would become to German artillery batteries on either side.

A number of objections can be raised to these criticisms. Yes, the British certainly benefited from running into a German counter-attack at Zero Hour, but such is the fate of war. Indeed, given the appalling luck they had experienced since the beginning of the offensive (particularly with the weather), they were surely due a slice of good fortune. It was true that every day brought the winter closer (and reduced the chance of significant progress), but Plumer had been ordered to try and push on and he did his best. As for the problem of fighting on narrower and narrower frontages, it was true that this was hardly ideal, but then what possible tactic was ideal in Flanders in October 1917? It was a question of what else Second Army could have done. It could either continue along those lines or revert back to the wider and deeper 'penetration' attacks that had caused such frustration on 31 July and throughout the August battles.

Whether Plumer made all the correct decisions or not will remain a point of conjecture, but, nonetheless, Broodseinde deserves to be recognized as a major success and, in hindsight, would be the highpoint of the Flanders offensive. Charles Bean sensed as much. He argued that it was one of the most decisive and 'cleanest' victories ever won on the Western Front; one moreover that 'has never been fully recognised except by the commanders and forces that took part'. 'An overwhelming blow had been struck,' he wrote, 'and both sides knew it.' Broodseinde was the third such strike in fifteen days, driving the Germans away from one of their most important positions in the Salient, and doing so in the full knowledge it was coming.[23] As with all military operations, the only thing that really mattered was *its impact on the enemy*, and this was undoubtedly severe (as Bean fully realized). The German Official History called the battle 'a considerable success' for the British and detailed the sense of resignation, verging on despair, which took hold of the German command in Flanders as they realized that their 'new combat methods' (i.e. the heavier manning of the front line) had been ineffective. 'All the counter-attack divisions behind the Ypres Group and the Wytschaete Group had had to be used', it noted. 'The Army High Command came to the conclusion that there was no means by which the positions could be held against the overpowering enemy superiority in artillery and infantry. Loss of ground in these heavy attacks was unavoidable.'[24]

The intensity of artillery fire at Broodseinde was testament to how hard the German Army was fighting to maintain its hold on the high ground. That day Fourth Army fired off the contents of thirty ammunition trains – surpassing the total for 31 July – and claiming the record for the highest amount of German shells fired during the battle.[25] 'Here in Flanders, the battle continues with an intensity that increases with every day. Inconceivable artillery fire rages incessantly', wrote Major-General Karl Dieffenbach, the commander of Group Wytschaete (in a letter to his family):

> On Thursday [4 October], they attacked again with twelve divisions. Our brave compatriots, the 25th Infantry Division, occupied the most important ground. They did not cede an inch of it and repelled the last attack on Gheluvelt around midnight. Next to this, the enemy was able to penetrate, to a depth of 2.2 kilometres in one spot, but the Mecklenburg Division [17th Division], deployed to carry out a counter-attack, was able to repulse them in a desperate struggle, so that they were only able to hold on to 1 kilometre of ground on my outermost right flank. The acts of heroism of our troops up there defy description; one has to see it with one's own eyes. We expect another four great days of battle, after which the plains of Flanders will be an impassable swamp. And the English will not achieve their goal in these plains.[26]

Like Dieffenbach, some German observers crowed about the relatively modest amount of ground that had been gained by the enemy –

seemingly missing the point of Plumer's 'bite-and-hold' tactics – but there was no doubt that the German Army was being placed under enormous strain.[27]

German casualties for 4 October had been heavy. Somewhat predictably, the thickening of the front line with extra troops had only resulted in greater losses and dislocation for those units unfortunate enough to be deployed. At Becelaere, no battalion of 8th Division came out of the line more than 300 strong, with some battalions being reduced to fewer than 100 men.[28] 4th Guard Division had lost eighty-six officers and 2,700 other ranks killed, wounded or missing in a matter of days.[29] In the two infantry regiments of 20th Division that faced the New Zealanders, there were over 2,000 casualties (about 42 per cent of their nominal strength).[30] According to captured prisoners, the division had 'an exceptionally high percentage of casualties' and was 'practically wiped out', with companies being reduced from 120 men to as few as twenty-four. In total it lost 257 dead, 878 wounded and 2,588 missing between 29 September and 9 October.[31] Indeed, some Australian battalions, particularly those in 3rd Division, ran into crowds of German soldiers who surrendered freely. The ground over which they advanced was also, quite literally, covered with enemy dead and wounded. For example, 37/Battalion, which advanced along the northern edge of Zonnebeke, captured 420 German prisoners and counted 350 dead in their sector alone (roughly 500 yards square).[32]

For the German High Command, the Battle of Broodseinde was just the latest in a series of major battles and it seemed the worst of all. It was, what one German historian has called, '*der schwarze Tag*', 'the black day of 4 October'.[33] At OHL, Ludendorff met the first reports of the battle with barely concealed despair. 'It was extraordinarily severe,' he wrote, 'and again we came through it only with enormous loss. It was evident that the idea of holding the front line more densely, adopted at my last visit to the front in September, was not the remedy.'[34] Within days, he had met with Sixt von Armin and discussed further defensive positions that needed to be constructed to keep the British at bay. He also requested opinions on what amount of ground could be safely given up without imperilling the U-boat bases on the coast. A major counter-attack against the British right at Gheluvelt had been mooted, but a lack of men and shortages of ammunition had prevented it from going ahead. Therefore, if they could not attack or redeploy, the Germans had to find some other way of enduring what was coming.[35]

After 4 October, Ludendorff recognized immediately that there would have to be tactical changes. Without bothering to ask the opinion of his senior commanders, he ordered a return to defence-in-depth with a greater emphasis on machine-gunners to hold the front. Fourth Army should form an 'advance zone' between the enemy's position and the German front line (known as the *Vorfeld*). 'The enemy would have to cross this strip in making his attack, and our artillery would have time to get on to him before he could reach our main line of resistance.'[36] Essentially (as explained by General von Kuhl), this meant that the 'cratered area in front of the trenches, to a depth of 500 to 1,000 metres, was considered an outpost zone and held by a thin chain of posts and a few machine guns'. When attacked, those in the outpost zone were to retreat back to the main defensive line, after which artillery would lay down a 'destructive curtain barrage'. This, it was hoped, would give the *Eingreif* divisions enough time to get into position, while also giving 'our own artillery the opportunity to smash the enemy in the outpost zone'. The only problem with this tactic was that it was not always clear when to retreat to the main defensive line – *was the enemy making a major attack or just a local raid?* – and those soldiers in the outpost zone tended to suffer (somewhat understandably) from a sense of abandonment and desperation, resulting in earlier retreats than was always desirable. As Kuhl noted ruefully, a 'completely fool-proof method did not exist'.[37]

Ludendorff issued further remarks on 9 October. He believed the recent failures had been primarily the result of an 'inappropriate deployment' of the *Eingreif* divisions, and he blamed penny-packeting, premature or delayed orders, unclear objectives and a lack of coordination with supporting artillery. Front-line units had the responsibility of ejecting the enemy from their sectors, and the *Eingreif* divisions would only become involved if they failed to do this. It was essential that they only launch counter-attacks if they were properly coordinated and supported, and *'concentrated and swift'*. The *'art of command'*, he stressed, 'comprises *sparing* deployment of the *Eingreif* divisions and the *maintenance of their fighting strength'*.[38] While this was all well and good, such fine distinctions tended to melt away in the chaos and confusion of battle. As Albrecht von Thaer could have told him, it was almost impossible to make the correct judgements on when and how counter-attack divisions should be employed. Communication broke down, and units became isolated or confused, meaning that commanders found it virtually impossible not to prematurely deploy their reserves or squander them under the enormous weight of fire on the battlefield. Indeed, at this point in the war, the only thing that would stop the British was the weather – what Rupprecht called 'their most effective ally' – and this, once again, would come to the defenders' aid.[39]

Predictably, the mood at GHQ surged again after Broodseinde. Although there remained a sense of frustration that the gains could not be exploited further, Haig and his staff were well pleased. 'Today was a very important success', wrote the Field Marshal, 'and we had a great fortune in that the Enemy had concentrated such a large number of divisions just at the moment of our attack with the very intense artillery barrage.' Never one to allow an opportunity to slip, Haig met his army commanders on the afternoon of 4 October and decided that the next attack would go in two days earlier than planned (on 8 October). Haig was confident the enemy's divisions had been fully engaged and that they had few reserves remaining. He believed that now was the moment to increase the tempo of operations, and he pressed Plumer to take another step towards the village of Passchendaele. *Now was the moment to push on and take the high ground.*[40]

Those who saw Haig at this time got a sense of a man who was determined not to let go, cost what it may. 'I saw Haig at most week-ends during those anxious months', wrote his chaplain, George Duncan. 'Acutely distressed as he must have been by the set-back to his plans and the mounting casualty lists, it was not his way to give open expression to his thoughts on such matters.' At other times he was more loquacious. One day, at lunch, the conversation turned to a divisional commander who was apparently 'showing himself restless and dispirited' – a not uncommon occurrence in the Salient – when Haig turned to Duncan and looked him straight in the eyes.

'*The fellow hasn't the faith to see that we can go through the enemy and beat them . . .*' he said, before returning to his lunch.[41]

Others were less sanguine. Charteris, whose optimism always paled in comparison to his chief's, felt the burden grow as the offensive staggered on. 'The casualties are awful', he had written a day after Polygon Wood; 'one cannot dare to think of them. The temptation to stop is so great, but the obviously correct thing for the nation is to go on.' After Broodseinde, he had all but given up hope of the offensive achieving anything. 'We are far enough on now to stop for the winter', he wrote on 5 October, 'and there is much to be said for that. Unless we get fine weather for all this month, there is now no chance of clearing the coast.'[42]

There was a sense, both then and ever since, that the campaign should have been called off after Broodseinde. The British had won a clear victory, taking the Gravenstafel Ridge, the last rise before Passchendaele, and in the face of worsening weather and awful ground, maybe they should have stayed put and been content with what had been achieved.[43] Charteris thought as much, but Haig, as bullish as ever, wanted to carry on. He was convinced that should they gain the Passchendaele Ridge, then 'the enemy will be forced to withdraw from the Dixmude front and Foret d'Houthoulst [*sic*] because he cannot risk his troops being cut off in that area'.[44] Therefore, plans were hurriedly drafted for a series of three more bounds, in quick succession (that would take place on 9, 12 and 14 October). Second Army would push on to the Passchendaele Ridge, with Fifth Army offering flanking support in the north, aiming to break the Flanders I Line at Spriet, before taking the village of Westroosebeke.[45]

Such an ambitious series of operations, at such a late stage of the year, should have roused serious concerns. Yet Haig's subordinates, from Plumer all the way downwards, offered little dissent to what GHQ was now proposing: three major assaults in just six days. The Second Army commander, who had hitherto taken barely a wrong step in the battle, was content to carry on. His Chief of Staff, Tim

Harington, later claimed that 'he never gave a thought to stopping and turning back' and that, in any case, there was nowhere for his troops to winter (other than on the Passchendaele Ridge).[46] Further down the chain of command, Sir Alexander Godley (GOC II ANZAC Corps), who would play a prominent role in the next step, was equally enthusiastic. There is no doubt, he told Sir James Allen, the New Zealand Minister of Defence, that 'the Boche is becoming very demoralised, and if the weather will only hold up for a bit longer and we can deliver a few more blows before the winter sets in, it will go a very long way towards the end'.[47]

Given what would happen next – and the horrors that would engulf Plumer's divisions on 9 and 12 October – the question of whether the offensive should have been called off after Broodseinde is worth exploring. Haig's apologists have always cited Tim Harington's view that there was no choice; that it was absolutely necessary to command the heights of Passchendaele, thus denying them to the enemy and also securing higher, drier ground from where the British could spend the winter (and from where a renewed push in 1918 could be launched).[48] Moreover, given the crushing success of 4 October, surely it was worth pushing on, even at heavy cost, to break what remained of the German Army? For John Terraine, Haig's greatest defender, the reasons for continuing were 'complex': a desire to exploit recent success; to maintain the initiative over the enemy; and to grasp at the possibility – faint though it might be – 'of hammering Germany to her knees before the end of the year'.[49] Therefore, the Passchendaele Ridge had to be captured at all costs.

Yet the painful truth was that the Passchendaele Ridge did *not* need to be captured, or at least was not worth the heavy losses that taking it would entail. It was true that the Gravenstafel Ridge – which the British had just overrun – was not as high as Passchendaele (and certainly did not overlook open countryside to the northeast), but there was only a handful of metres in it, and, moreover, holding the Gravenstafel would have been, in many respects, no more difficult than holding on to Passchendaele; indeed, it might have been significantly easier. Between the two ridges lay perhaps the worst stretch of ground on the entire battlefield, where the Ravebeek drained into the Stroombeek. The farms here – Waterfields, Marsh Bottom and Peter Pan (among others with suitably aquatic-sounding names) – lay in a flooded morass overlooked by heavily wired German positions on the Bellevue Spur, which guarded the western approaches to Passchendaele. This ground was a significant obstacle in its own right and would have served as an excellent no-man's-land. Moreover, Passchendaele Ridge was virtually indefensible. When it was finally captured in November 1917, a detailed appraisal admitted that the newly won positions were hugely disadvantageous. Front-line troops could 'now be shelled from any point on an arc of 240 degrees'; there was 'no cover for supports or close reserves'; it was only with 'great difficulty' that supplies could be moved up; and it was almost impossible to reinforce the garrison in an emergency.[50] Yet, increasingly for Haig, Passchendaele assumed a significance that surpassed its mere importance on a map.

Haig's desire to push onwards was not just a response to success on the battlefield, or a feeling that the Germans were cracking, but was also a reaction to growing unease in London, and a need to give them something, *anything*. The previous day he had received a 'great bombshell' from Robertson threatening to bring his offensive to a premature halt. At a conference in Boulogne on 25 September it had been agreed 'in principle' that the BEF would take over more of the front line from the French Army, thus drawing off Haig's reserves and making any kind of concentrated effort in Flanders almost impossible.[51] Haig was not happy, muttering unkindly that 'Robertson comes badly out of this' and complaining that he had not been kept informed of these developments.[52] But Haig must have known this would happen. Support for his 'northern operation' had always been tenuous at best and now the failure to progress was inevitably bringing the spotlight back on to GHQ. The truth was that Lloyd George was still determined to undermine the Flanders campaign, and by now he had decided that the only way to do that was to remove the weapon from Haig's hand.

The Field Marshal, doggedly as ever, fought his corner. Downing Street had requested an appreciation of the role of British forces in the event of Russia being knocked out of the war (as part of the discussions over the Kühlmann peace note), so Haig duly obliged. Addressed to Robertson (and dated 8 October), it covered familiar ground: the lack of any strategic alternative to defeating the German Army; the danger of undertaking 'any of the various indirect means' of attacking the Central Powers; the 'good progress' that had been achieved at Ypres; the draining effect of sustained combat on Germany's divisions; and so on. Haig concluded that the offensive must be maintained for the remainder of the autumn, which would give 'excellent prospects of decisive success' for the following year, but only if the British threw their full weight into the Western Front. Even if Russia failed over the coming months (and the Germans were able to shuttle divisions to France), he had no doubt that the accession of America to the war would provide enough combat power to defeat Germany's forces in 1918.[53]

In some respects, there was much to recommend in Haig's memorandum. Germany's armed forces *were* the key centre of gravity for the Central Powers, and when they failed, so would the Austrians and the Turks. While the elimination of Russia from the war would enable sizeable reinforcements to be sent west, Haig guessed correctly that it would not provide a *decisive* superiority on the Western Front (as would be shown in 1918). Yet Haig's appreciation of the situation raised the question of whether it was still either possible or desirable to maintain the offensive in Flanders, and here he was on stickier ground. 'I have every hope of being able to continue it for several weeks still and of gaining results which will add very greatly to the enemy's losses in men and moral[e], and place us in a far better position to resume an offensive in the spring', he noted rather hopefully. Moreover, he was pleased that they would end the year 'with practically all the observation points originally held by the enemy in our possession'. Yet Haig would not have appreciated being reminded that his offensive had not been launched simply to wear down German divisions, or secure key observation points, *but to liberate the Belgian coast and achieve a strategic decision*. In this it had failed.

Once again, Haig seems to have been oblivious to the awkward

contradiction in his way of making war: the tension between con-
ducting breakthrough operations aimed at securing huge sweeps of
ground, and more limited 'bite-and-hold' attacks that were designed
to chew up German divisions. As Pétain had long noted, in the context of 1917 the Allies could only hope to achieve any kind of success
with avowedly attritional methods: using artillery-heavy, limited
attacks to wear down German formations while exposing their own
units as little as possible. But Haig had never been entirely converted
to this way of thinking, and saw his 'northern operation' as being
primarily about seizing ground. Had he wanted to operate on a more
limited, attritional basis – something his commanders had repeatedly
argued for – then it would have been much better to conduct a series
of operations on the lines of the Canadian attack at Hill 70. Indeed, if
you wanted to wear down the enemy, then Flanders was, arguably,
the worst place to do this, given the German advantages in holding
the high ground, and in forcing the British to occupy a shell-ridden
swamp.

As for Robertson, his room for manoeuvre shrank with every
week that passed, having to endure frequent clashes with the Prime
Minister. 'He is out for my blood very much these days', he complained to Haig on 9 October.[54] Lloyd George was still heartily sick
of the military advice he was receiving, but was now more inclined
to do something about it. He was increasingly bent on some kind of
unified military command, or at least an inter-Allied council that
would take a common view of strategic questions, and allow him to
bypass Haig and Robertson. He attended four meetings of the War
Policy Committee between 3 and 11 October and repeated, yet again,
his belief that Britain should 'make every effort to detach from Germany her Allies, beginning with Turkey', which would require
'adequate military assistance' and a viable plan to defeat the Ottoman
Empire.[55] He also convened a special Council of War on 10 October
and invited Sir John French (former Commander-in-Chief of the
BEF) and Sir Henry Wilson (GOC Eastern Command) to address it;
both of them could be relied upon to stick the knife into their former
colleagues.[56]

For all of Lloyd George's frantic efforts, he achieved very little.

Robertson fought him all the way, insisting that any attempt to knock Turkey out of the war (as the Prime Minister was urging) was fraught with difficulty and was, in any case, logistically unviable.[57] He also made it clear that French and Wilson's involvement revealed – as it did – a lack of confidence in his advice, and, therefore, he would offer his resignation. The situation, which could have caused a Cabinet meltdown, eventually resulted in an awkward stalemate, with none of the underlying problems being resolved. Robertson was reassured – not entirely convincingly – that the War Cabinet's invitation to French and Wilson was merely like calling in an 'independent medical opinion' and that they were perfectly entitled to do it.[58] At the same time – like warring schoolchildren being separated by friends – Lord Curzon warned Lloyd George that any attempt to push Robertson out would probably result in the resignation of the Cabinet, including himself, Lord Derby (the Secretary of State for War) and Arthur Balfour (the Secretary of State for Foreign Affairs).[59] Lloyd George could do little other than fume impotently from the sidelines. On 11 October he predicted to his colleagues that the latest attack would fail and that 'he would call the War Cabinet's attention to this in three weeks' time'.[60] The Prime Minister was right. The Flanders offensive was now to enter its most infamous phase.

13.

'The Weakness of Haste'

Our dead were lying in heaps. It was the worst slaughter
I have ever seen.

Alexander Birnie[1]

9–12 October 1917

The success or failure of General Plumer's next steps would depend
upon logistics: in making sure the attacking battalions had everything they needed to take their objectives. Haig wanted the attack to
go ahead two days earlier than originally scheduled, but it was only
possible to advance the date by twenty-four hours because it started
raining again. Between the morning of 7 October and the date of the
attack two days later, 25mm of rain fell, which soaked the already
slippery battlefield and played havoc with the logistical and engineering arrangements upon which so much depended.[2] Postponing
the attack would have seemed sensible, but might have had serious
repercussions and, in any case, opinion was split. When Haig had tea
with Plumer on the afternoon of 8 October, he was told that Sir
Alexander Godley, whose corps (II ANZAC) would make the main
assault, had 'specially asked that there should be *no postponement*'. So
there it was; they would go ahead the following morning.[3]

Roads and tracks had to be driven forward as quickly as possible,
while existing ones required almost continuous repair work. The
Wieltje–Gravenstafel road was one particularly vital artery and was
maintained by field companies of Royal Engineers, who laboured on
what seemed an increasingly futile task. Timber – 'green and rough
cut straight from the saw' – was brought up and unloaded at the

railhead at Wieltje, and then, by whatever means available, taken up
to the line. The best method of road construction was to 'lay on an
approximately level prepared bed four or five lengthwise stringers, to
which were spiked broad stout beams making a continuous decking'.
Planks were then nailed on either side as 'wheel guards' to ensure slippery lorries kept on the straight and narrow path. While this certainly
helped to keep a steady trickle of movement going, German shelling
regularly brought it to a halt. Because the heavier howitzers could
only be dragged a few metres from the roads, they made tempting
targets, and on several occasions direct hits on their ammunition
dumps caused enormous craters to be torn in the surrounding area.[4]

Given the difficulties of reaching the gun positions, Second Army
had no choice but to rely on packhorses. Eight shells were hitched to
each animal (four on each side), and they were led up to the front
through a treacherous wasteland of mud and death. J. A. Whitehead, a
driver with the RFA (temporarily attached to 18th Division), recorded
what their daily routine was. Reveille was at midnight, a quick breakfast, before heading off to the ammunition dump, loading up their
horses' packs, and then, in single file ('with plenty of room in between
us, to avoid shells maiming or killing too many horses and drivers'),
making the five-mile journey up to the front. Inevitably there were
casualties and Whitehead admitted that their only objective 'was to
get more and more ammunition to the guns', even if it meant rolling
dead horses and men out of the way. By the time they returned to
their camp, they had to find the energy to clean everything, scrape the
mud off their boots and uniforms, and inspect and groom the horses.

The drudgery of such an existence inevitably took its toll on the
men's spirits. 'How we stood it, day after day, and week after week, I
do not know', he remembered. 'I do know that I slept hours walking
with my horses, or riding, to and from the guns, during those long,
weary, sloppy journeys.' Moreover:

> The surprising thing was that hardly any of us had to report sick dur-
> ing this time, but the sick parade increased when things quietened
> down. Otherwise our view was one huge mass of mud and water, a
> few remaining trunks of trees, and some duckboards that needed a

tight rope walker to keep balanced on, and then mud, mud, and more
mud. Many a time we should go plunging on with our pack horses,
and, suddenly, either a horse, or one of us would drop into a shell hole
up to our middle. We had then to scramble out, shake ourselves like
dogs, and carry on.[5]

'If I were asked to name the heroes of the Third Battle of Ypres',
wrote the gunner Frank Mellish, 'my vote would go to the pack
horses which brought up the field artillery ammunition . . . They
carried or pulled prodigious weights through country practically
devoid of roads or tracks, and more often than not they were up to
their hocks, and sometimes their bellies, in sticky mud. When shelling began there was just no means of getting them under cover and
they stood patiently until either they were hit or the shelling stopped.
They never seemed to panic and yet seemed grateful if anyone stood
near them during their ordeal.'[6]

The problems with engineering and logistics would ultimately
prove beyond both Fifth and Second Armies. Two tank battalions
had been brought in to assist the operations of General Gough, but
the awful ground prevented them from getting anywhere near the
front, while Plumer – never the Tank Brigade's warmest supporter –
did not even bother to send any up.[7] The harassed field companies,
working like ants, performed miracles of improvisation throughout
October, but it would not be enough. Too few guns could be dragged
into range, and those that could were often deployed in the open in
extremely precarious positions: half sunk in the glutinous mud,
which left their crews foraging desperately for anything – timber,
wooden crates, slabs of concrete – that could shore up their gun positions. Without reliable and solid firing platforms, they soon bogged
down after a few rounds had been fired, which meant that accuracy
suffered and the crews had to laboriously dig them out, reset them
and fire again – all under growing enemy counter-battery fire.
Ammunition shortages were another problem. While the heroism of
the pack mules and their drivers was remarkable, in no way could
they possibly meet the enormous demands for shells that a truly powerful preliminary bombardment and creeping barrage would require.[8]

'We dream of nothing else but ammunition in this blessed world', wrote Stanley Roberts, an NCO with the RFA. 'Those guns have tremendous appetites. It is impossible to find sufficient food for them, such gluttons are they.'[9]

For Plumer's fourth step, II ANZAC Corps would make the main assault, not with Australian or New Zealand units, but two British divisions, 49th and 66th, which had assembled around Frezenberg by the evening of 8 October. It was pouring with rain. They had two and a half miles to go to reach the front line. This should have taken no more than five hours, but some attacking battalions took almost twice as long, before collapsing, exhausted and soaked through, into their jumping-off positions, shortly before the attack began.[10] The urgent need to get as many guns as possible forward meant that infantry routes were neglected in the days before the assault, leaving the attacking battalions to rely upon inadequately maintained duck-boards that rapidly exhausted the men. Moreover, because priority had been given to the construction of single-track roads that could carry artillery, there were not enough double-track pathways to carry men and materials up and down the line, producing extra delay and what seemed like endless traffic congestion.[11]

On the other side of the line, the German Fourth Army may have been battered in the three previous assaults, but it still held on to most of the Flanders I Line and could boast strongly wired and heavily fortified positions on the Bellevue Spur, which guarded the western approaches to the village of Passchendaele. Here the defences were well thought out and covered with thickets of barbed wire, up to fifty feet deep in places. Multiple machine-guns were also dug in, mutually supporting and hidden behind the concrete walls of a dozen pillboxes.[12] Those divisions that had been in the line on 4 October had been relieved, with fresh units moved up, including 16th, 233rd and 195th Divisions (the latter having been hurried back to Flanders after being earmarked for service in Italy).[13] The crucial sector on the Passchendaele Ridge was given to 195th Division, which deployed three *Jäger* regiments with a reputation as elite troops. As well as being well-rested and motivated, the *Jäger* regiments also brought with them up to *twice* the number of machine-guns – both heavy and light – as standard German Army regiments had, meaning that they could produce a formidable volume of firepower should they be attacked. Perhaps on no other place on the battlefield would the British artillery bombardment be of such importance.[14]

When the strength of the German position was combined with wet weather and an increasingly exhausted attacking force, there was only going to be one outcome. The attack on 9 October (what would become known as the Battle of Poelcappelle) could not have been more different to the victory of Broodseinde; indeed it was reminiscent of the carnage at Langemarck on 16 August. There were no thunderous wall of shellfire (despite some observers being impressed by the spectacle); no impressive gains of ground; no carpeting of German bodies. There were, on the contrary, only patchy artillery support and a weak, tentative attack, as the British infantry slogged forward through a moonscape of mud. 'I had been frightened sometimes before, and windy; anxious very often', remembered Neville Hind of 1/Lancashire Fusiliers, who was in one of the attacking divisions that day. 'But never before, so far as I can now recollect, had I been so stunned, and stupefied, as to lose for some minutes all presence of mind . . . Earth and air seemed full of death.' He went on:

> The din of the massed artillery behind us, the continuous crash of exploding shells before us, great shoots of fire, and shot in the air above us, the rattle of machine guns in the German line, the bursting of shrapnel shells from the German guns; flashes of flame that seemed to swoop down from the air, as a hawk on its prey, and obliterate the men on whom they descended – it was through this kind of thing that we moved forward, across that desolate waste of mud and water and shell-holes – nothing else.

Hind pushed on with his battalion and managed to take one of the pillboxes that were holding them up, before suffering a 'terrific punch on the back'. He slid into a shell hole, shivering with shock, and realized that he had been hit by a sniper's bullet. Fortunately it had not punctured any major organs and he was soon evacuated to a casualty clearing station behind the line.[15]

Neville Hind was one of the lucky ones. He had a prized 'blighty' wound that would take him out of the war, but for thousands of others on that dark morning of 9 October, there would be no escape. 49th Division, which had somehow managed to get its attacking battalions into position via a *single* duckboard track (No. 5 track south of the Wieltje–Passchendaele road), marched into a killing zone. Attacking infantry failed to notice the artillery lifts every fifty yards (an indication of how unimpressive the creeping barrage was), while the German defenders were not forced to shelter in their dugouts, meaning that they could hold their shell holes in strength. The main obstacle across the front – the Ravebeek – was waist deep and impossible to cross under heavy fire. Rifles and Lewis guns were rendered ineffective by the liquid mud; communication to the forward battalions broke down; and effective German sniping caused a great deal of demoralization among the attackers.[16]

On the right, 66th Division experienced similar problems, with the approach march taking, in places, up to ten hours. When the attack finally went ahead, the division managed to get forward further than the units on its left, but the unsuppressed German defences on the higher ground at Bellevue, which had torn 49th Division's attack to pieces, began to enfilade its lines and cause heavy loss.[17] 'The whole world seemed to have erupted like a volcano: one had to fix one's mind on the necessity of going forward to reach the objective at all costs', wrote P. R. Hall, a private in 2/6th Manchesters. 'The whizz of bullets was startling but you knew that the ones you heard had already gone past. Shells one could hear coming and judge roughly how close they were – if very close just duck and carry on. The Minenwerfers were the worst. We did not hear them coming and they seemed to explode almost beneath one's feet.'[18] Although elements of the division managed to secure the Blue Line (the second objective), with parties even making it as far as the village of Passchendaele, local counter-attacks forced a retirement to the first objective by the early afternoon, leaving II ANZAC Corps with virtually nothing to show for such an enormous effort. Total casualties for the attacking divisions had been over 5,700 men – virtually destroying them as fighting formations.[19] Although the attack had met with more success in the north, with XIV Corps and the French

First Army advancing, successfully, towards the southern outskirts of Houthulst Forest (where the ground was much less cut up by shell-fire), elsewhere the attack had stalled. This was not 'bite and hold'; it was more like rush and grab.

German morale rose after the events of 9 October – the first real victory the Army had achieved since late August. Its defence had been thoroughly planned and ruthlessly executed, with the reintroduction of tried-and-tested tactics being totally vindicated. Indeed the events of the day offered further evidence that a more cautious approach offered the best chance of conserving German strength in the face of the numerical superiority of the enemy.[20] The defenders had to endure days of harassing fire, little food or water, and the risks of exposure and exhaustion in the cold, wet weather, but when they got their chance they extracted a terrible revenge. On the northern sector, 86 Fusilier Regiment (18th Division) found itself coming under intense attack, so three heavy machine-guns were hoisted on to the top of a bunker and loaded with ammunition. From there they could enfilade the whole line of advance. After waiting until the attacking infantry closed to within 500 metres of their positions, they opened fire, driving apart the attacking lines and forcing them to take cover in no-man's-land. In the course of the day those three machine-guns fired almost 16,000 rounds.[21]

Elsewhere there was close combat as the attackers broke into the main German position. West of Passchendaele, the men of 5 *Jäger* Regiment (195th Division) were in the line, desperately trying to hold off a furious onslaught. 'The weak line of defence in the section of the battalion is almost completely shot to pieces', noted its history. 'The assault of the English infantry surges across it in a rapid succession of waves . . . Isolated groups penetrate through the large gaps in the security line but are then stopped by autonomous and automatic fire from the infantrymen and machine-gunners that operate from the main line of defence. The coordinated attack dissolves into fierce fighting. All company sections battle with great tenacity.' In such a confused battle, it was essential that reserves were moved up quickly, but heavy harassing fire had all but isolated the front-line battalions, severing all telephone connections to the rear. Fortunately, after the

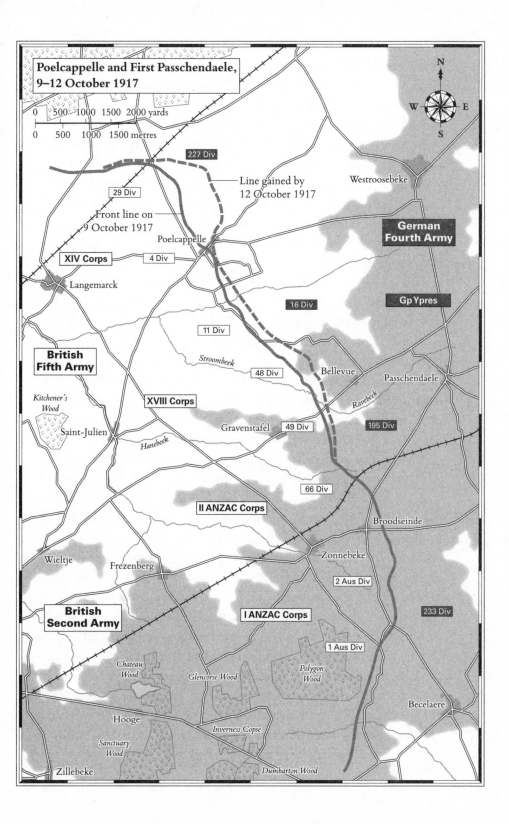

**Poelcappelle and First Passchendaele,
9–12 October 1917**

N
W   E
S

0   500   1000   1500   2000 yards

0   500   1000   1500 metres

227 Div

Westroosebeke

Line gained by
12 October 1917

29 Div

Front line on
9 October 1917

**German
Fourth Army**

Poelcappelle

XIV Corps   4 Div

16 Div

Gp Ypres

Langemarck

**British
Fifth Army**

11 Div

Stroombeek

48 Div

Bellevue

Passchendaele

Kitchener's
Wood

XVIII Corps

Ravebeek

Saint-Julien

Hanebeek

Gravenstafel   49 Div

195 Div

66 Div

II ANZAC Corps

Broodseinde

Wieltje   Frezenberg

Zonnebeke

**British
Second Army**

I ANZAC Corps

2 Aus Div

233 Div

Chateau
Wood

Glencorse Wood

Polygon
Wood

1 Aus Div

Becelaere

Hooge

Inverness Copse

Sanctuary
Wood

Zillebeke

Dumbarton Wood

heroic efforts of a signal section at the regimental command post, which had managed to flash out an emergency message before smoke obscured the whole battlefield, supporting units were able to move up and reinforce this crucial sector, sealing off any enemy penetrations.[22]

German artillery fire had also been highly accurate. One of those involved on 9 October was the battery officer Reinhard Lewald, who, by his own admission, was an uncommonly lucky soldier. He had been sent on a gunnery course shortly before the offensive began (thus missing the heavy fighting on 31 July) and had also received a fortnight's leave in late September (allowing him to escape the carnage of Plumer's first three steps). Yet his luck was changing. On the afternoon of 7 October he stepped off a train in Belgian Flanders, before rejoining his battery just in time for Poelcappelle. Although this would be an extremely hard-fought engagement, it was a clear-cut German victory. In the pouring rain, across shell-churned ground, they deployed their guns and were in position on the morning of 9 October, when Plumer's attack went in. That day the British fired 'an indescribable barrage' that heralded yet another major battle. 'Our losses are heavy, but the enemy breakthrough is destroyed', he wrote. 'They can only occupy a strip of muddy terrain.'[23]

Notwithstanding these encouragements, there was little sense of celebration at Army Group headquarters in Courtrai. Crown Prince Rupprecht worried constantly about his ability to maintain such an exhausting defence and reported to OHL (on the morning of 11 October) how difficult things were becoming. The intensity of operations between 4 and 9 October had put his Army Group under almost intolerable pressure. The contents of twenty-seven ammunition trains had been fired off at Poelcappelle, and Rupprecht worried about the overburdened railway system, which was struggling to keep up with the regular relief and reinforcement of front-line units.[24] Moreover, 'bringing the divisions up to strength was becoming more difficult. Fourth Army must adapt itself to manage with less strength.' Consequently, it might even be necessary to conduct a significant redeployment; giving up much of the coast and, presumably, the vital railway junction at Roulers. He issued orders that divisions that had not lost more than 1,800 men were to be kept in Flanders for the duration of the battle. For the moment, at least, relief was out of the question.[25]

The Germans may have successfully held their ground, but the intensity of the fighting wore units down. Group Ypres bore the brunt of the losses. In October its divisions sustained 3,851 dead, 15,202 wounded and 10,395 men missing in action. Of particular concern were the disproportionate losses in officers, with some regiments losing their commander, two battalion commanders and up to nine captains.[26] North of Poelcappelle, 18th Division, from Schleswig-Holstein, had failed badly, with none of its regiments being able to counter-attack properly.[27] Around Passchendaele, 195th Division suffered over 3,200 casualties between 7 and 13 October.[28] 'You, dear schoolboys who read about deeds of heroism; Germans sitting around tables enjoying a beer,' wrote Major Ludwig von Menges, the commanding officer of 4/Reserve *Jäger* Battalion (which had been in support that day), 'just think of all the blood that flowed; all that had to be performed whenever the Army Communiqué read: "Today, too, our troops beat off all British attacks in the Passchendaele area; their meagre gains of ground were recaptured from them."'[29]

The attack on 9 October may have been disastrous, but Plumer's fifth step would go ahead, as planned, on 12 October. Preparations for what would become the First Battle of Passchendaele were little better than they had been at Poelcappelle. The three-day interlude was in no way sufficient to give the attacking brigades a fighting chance of getting through and the artillery situation remained on the point of collapse. In II ANZAC Corps, most of its field batteries were now 'operating at half strength or less', with guns being either out of position, clogged in mud or starved of ammunition.[30] On 11 October, Major F. J. Rice's battery took over new positions in the wasteland about half a mile south of Langemarck. 'At this time these positions appeared to be undiscovered, but, as always in Flanders, digging down was impossible owing to reaching water so quickly, and the only protection was sandbags and corrugated iron.' The roads leading up to the position were in a 'terrible state', but further on, out towards the front line, they got even worse. 'Infantry officers told us more than once that they doubted if they could have dragged their way to their objectives even if there had been no enemy, the mud was so deep, and one heard stories of men, wounded and unwounded, being stuck in waterlogged shell holes for more than a day.'[31]

The attack on 12 October should never have gone ahead. While Haig and his commanders could, perhaps, be forgiven for ordering their divisions forward on 9 October – flush from the success of Broodseinde – there was no excuse for trying again just seventy-two hours later.[32] Haig, optimistic as ever, needed little encouragement to urge his generals on, and his diary for this period contains wildly inaccurate information on the results of the attacks. Even the offensively minded General Gough – whose Fifth Army continued to offer flanking support – thought that Second Army's objectives for the next offensive were 'too far distant'. When he warned Haig, the Commander-in-Chief was unimpressed, telling him bluntly that 'the enemy is now much weakened in moral[e] and lacks the desire to fight'.[33] Sadly, further down the chain of command, there was a similar, depressing lack of realism. While Birdwood at I ANZAC Corps counselled Plumer against any further advances, others seem to have had few concerns, with over-optimistic reports about how much ground had been taken doing much to cloud the issue. Alexander Godley, the commander of II ANZAC Corps, suffered from what the historian Andrew Macdonald has called a 'Passchendaele fixation': an obsession to take the high ground, safe in the knowledge that it was what Haig wanted, and its capture would surely result in his promotion. He told Sir John Monash, the commander of 3rd Australian Division – which would make the main assault – that it was his 'sacred duty' to fly the Australian flag from the ruins of the village.[34]

For his part, Monash was much less enamoured of the prospect facing him. 'Things now rushed. No time to prepare, refer to orders as we go along' was one instruction he dashed off to his brigadiers.[35] Not only was it almost impossible to bring up the number of guns and tons of ammunition they would need, but they also had to attack more formidable positions than had been the case on 4 October. It was evident that if the New Zealand Division failed to capture the

Bellevue Spur on their left, the Australians would be exposed to deadly enfilade fire and cut to pieces (as had happened to 66th Division). On 11 October, Monash pleaded with his superiors for a delay, perhaps just twenty-four hours, to give them more time to get ready for the assault. But it got him nowhere. Godley was all for pushing on, confident that his divisions would take the high ground. As for Plumer – for so long the Apostle of order and method on the battlefield – he was convinced that conditions were favourable and turned Monash's request down. They would attack, as scheduled, on 12 October.[36]

The role that Plumer played in this tragedy remains curious. He must have known that conditions were steadily deteriorating and that there was not enough time to prepare attacks properly. He had requested three weeks to mount his push on the Menin Road on 20 September, but now he was sanctioning attacks with intervals of five days and then, incredibly, *just three days*. Why he did not tell Haig, as he had done before, that there was no use pushing divisions forward without artillery supremacy and until all preparations had been completed remains unclear. He left no personal papers or memoirs, and, in any case, Tim Harington insisted they had done the right thing.[37] Possibly confusion or incomplete intelligence was to blame – it would have taken days to clarify exactly which positions were held and where units were situated – and it has been suggested that he was 'swept along by the tide of false optimism' that emanated from GHQ in its urgency to take the high ground.[38] Yet Plumer had never been one to take anything for granted. He had always been a 'soldier's general', steady and clear in his own mind about what needed to be done and fully aware of the lethality of the modern battlefield. So his failure to stand firm on the timing of the attacks, and the essential need for more preparation, can only have been down to a temporary and fateful loss of nerve; a tragic character flaw. Harington never admitted as much, but he was always highly sensitive to any accusation that they had been at fault at Third Ypres, which perhaps betrayed a lingering sense that something had gone wrong. So in those crucial, rushed days, their principles – which had proved so successful all year – were abandoned; trampled in the mud by a Commander-in-Chief who would simply not let go. Far from mounting considered and organized 'bite-and-hold' attacks, Haig had once again cast them aside in his elusive, quixotic quest for a breakthrough.

12 October dawned with high winds and a forecast of rain, which came in later, deluging the already sodden battlefield. Most of those at the front knew it was going to be a difficult day. Brigadier-General G. N. Johnston, artillery commander in the New Zealand Division, was so frustrated with the tiresome delays in getting men and material forward, and in deploying his guns, that he reported to both corps and division on 11 October that 'they could not depend on the artillery for the attack on the following day'.[39] Patrols had also discovered that the enemy defences were much less damaged than had been anticipated. At 5.30 a.m. on 11 October – just twenty-four hours before Zero Hour – Lieutenant-Colonel Geoffrey Smith, Commanding Officer of 2/Otago Regiment, despatched a worrying report to his brigade warning them of the strongly held blockhouses and swathes of barbed wire that confronted his battalion. Here the enemy held the high ground and manned (on his sector alone) six pillboxes, and no-man's-land was 'three parts filled with water'. He urgently requested a heavy artillery bombardment to clear the way, but this only went ahead during the afternoon, and then with negligible results.[40]

What followed on the morning of 12 October was a brutal lesson in warfare. A combination of poor artillery support, awful ground conditions, exhausted infantry and a formidable defence stopped the attacks just as effectively as they had on 9 October. The left flank of the main assault was supposed to be secured by men of 9th (Scottish) Division of XVIII Corps, but they progressed barely further than their start line. An after-action report listed a range of sobering conclusions. 'Brigades attacked on a much wider front than they have been accustomed to lately. The consequence was an increased difficulty in forming up correctly and in keeping correct direction.' Because the ground was so treacherous, the waves of infantry became strung out and 'lost' the barrage, thus suffering the 'usual consequences' of attacking without artillery support. Throughout the day communication almost entirely broke down. 'Wires were cut and visual [signalling] was difficult owing to gun flashes. Pigeons could not fly against the wind and the men in charge of the dogs became casualties.' Runners – those that were not killed – took hours to get from the front-line battalions to brigade headquarters, but the main problem, and one that other divisions noted, was the 'thinness and raggedness of the barrage':

> Batteries, moved forward since the last attack, encountered great difficulties and had many guns stuck in the mud. The exhausted state of some of the Brigades owing to casualties and severe weather undoubtedly militated against a good barrage. The lesson seems to be that too much stress cannot be laid on the necessity of constructing roads and railways expressly for the guns.[41]

Yet, in Flanders in October 1917, this was easier said than done. Across the front that day similar horrifying scenes were recorded and similar damning conclusions were drawn.

The main assault of II ANZAC Corps was to seize the highest part of the ridge, with Monash's 3rd Division taking the village while the New Zealanders, on their left, attacked the blood-soaked Bellevue Spur. Incredibly their orders demanded an advance, in places, of around 2,500 yards, and included those objectives that had been assigned on 9 October and which should have already been captured by 49th and 66th Divisions. They were supposed to push forward in three bounds: 1,000 yards to the Red Line; another 550 yards to the Blue Line; and a final advance of between 500 and 900 yards to the Green Line (which would take them to the outskirts of Passchendaele). The infantry were to be covered by a creeping barrage moving at an initial rate of 100 yards every four minutes, before slowing down, but even this would be too quick. As had been the case with most of the attacking units, preparations were sketchy and incomplete. In 9 Australian Brigade, for example, no buried cable had been laid further than brigade headquarters (over 2,000 yards from the firing line); there were no forward dumps of food, water and ammunition; and no operation orders had been written, leaving everything to be done face to face and at the last minute.[42]

In such appalling conditions, that the attack failed was hardly a surprise, more a foregone conclusion. The worst scenes were witnessed in front of the Bellevue Spur, where the New Zealand Division found itself unable to cross broad belts of barbed wire that had been left largely untouched by the bombardment. Given how wet the ground was, many of the shells sank into the soft mud, which dissipated the force of their explosions or prevented them from going off entirely. The New Zealanders had to pick their way over the detritus of the fighting of 9 October – including dead bodies, broken equipment, and the wounded – and do so while dodging their own shells, which frequently fell short and went off among their own struggling lines of infantry. When they had crested the main rise, they were met with vicious bursts of unsuppressed machine-gun and rifle fire, which cut down scores of men. The barbed wire, still uncut, was an impenetrable obstacle, leaving the survivors, alone and exposed, in a death-trap. 'Hun machine guns and snipers play havoc', recorded Private Ernest Langford of 2/Otago Regiment. 'Absolute Hell . . . Brigade practically wiped out.'[43]

Amid such awful carnage, acts of enormous courage and valour were commonplace. In 1/Otago Regiment, Second Lieutenants J. J. Bishop and N. F. Watson were both killed while throwing grenades through the loopholes of pillboxes; Captain C. H. Molloy was cut down as he led his company in a forlorn hope; while Second Lieutenant A. R. Cockerell managed to singlehandedly capture a pillbox and take forty enemy soldiers prisoner. Joined by one of his men, he kept going – head down, revolver in hand – and managed to silence another enemy blockhouse, taking another thirty-two prisoners.[44] But it was all to be in vain. Two supporting battalions, 1 and 2/Canterbury, tried to move up, but ran into the same nightmare of machine-gun and sniper fire that rapidly brought any forward movement to a dead stop. 'Party after party made the attempt from either flank,' recorded the regimental account, 'and though some got as close as fifteen yards from the pill-boxes, none succeeded in reaching them.'[45]

As for the Australians, things were little better. According to the war diary of 34/Battalion:

> The general condition of the terrain over which the men had to attack was one of the two primary causes for the non-success of the operation. This was in many cases, particularly on the left flank, a marsh

across the whole front, a succession of water-filled shell-holes, which not only reduced the rate of advance, but bunched the men together, endeavouring to find a track around the shell-holes. This gave the enemy splendid opportunities for his machine-gun fire.[46]

Lieutenant G. M. Carson of 33/Battalion was one of those who went forward that day. 'I nearly got blown to pieces scores of times', he remembered:

We went through a sheet of iron all night and in the morning it got worse. We attacked at 5.25 [a.m.] and fought all day at times we were bogged up to our arm pits and it took anything from an hour upwards to get out. Lots were *drowned* in the mud and water. The Bosch[e] gave us Hell but we managed to hold on to the little we had taken till night when we dug in.

Carson would win the Military Medal for his bravery in taking a German pillbox. 'I waddled up and couldn't get near it because it was held very strongly and it took one and a half hours to surround it. There were six guns and 30 Bosch[e] in it. I eventually got there but stayed only a few hours as we were compelled to get out.' He returned from battle with only two of his men still alive, and both of them were wounded.[47]

The Australians did what they could. 10 Brigade, on the left, only managed to reach their first objective along the Ravebeek Valley, but 9 Brigade, on the right, was able to advance all the way to the Blue Line, on the outskirts of Passchendaele. Showing enormous fighting spirit, three battalions were able to reach the second objective – a march of over 1,700 yards – against heavy resistance.[48] Here, on the highest part of the ridge, the 22-year-old commander of 'B' Company, 34/Battalion, Captain Clarence Jeffries, won a posthumous Victoria Cross for leading an attack on a series of pillboxes at Hillside Farm. Accompanied by Sergeant James Bruce (who had been a colleague of Jeffries' father back home and who had promised to keep an eye on the young officer), Jeffries organized a bombing party and outflanked the enemy position (capturing four machine-guns and thirty-five prisoners in the process). Later that day they did the same, running forward, almost into the teeth of German machine-gun fire, to capture a bunch of forty prisoners on the outskirts of Passchendaele. But in this final assault Jeffries fell to the ground, mortally wounded with a bullet in his stomach.[49]

Sadly 9 Brigade's heroics could not be maintained. The curse of communications meant that the advance was unknown to brigade headquarters for a number of hours. There was no buried cable and visual signalling was impossible in the smoke and mist, which left the battalions dependent upon their runners and a handful of surviving pigeons. It was impossible to hold on to the Blue Line without fresh and timely reinforcements, leaving the surviving officers in charge with an ominous decision. Their position on the forward slope of the ridge left them exposed to enemy machine-gun and artillery fire for most of the afternoon, including lethal enfilade fire from the Bellevue Spur; and, with no reserves in sight, eventually the order was given for the Blue Line to be given up. 9 Brigade's casualties had been appalling: forty-nine officers and 915 other ranks had been killed or wounded in the attack on Passchendaele.[50]

It did not take long for word to spread of the horrors that had befallen the Anzacs. Alexander Birnie of 12th Field Company Engineers (4th Australian Division) was one of those who was wounded that day. He wrote to his parents on 26 October telling them his story:

> My dear Mother and Father, here I am once more in England in peace and comfort with a bullet hole through my neck. If it had been an inch closer in I would now be lying out on the bloody Passchendaele Ridge with many hundreds of our good fellows who went West on that day – but you see it didn't so let me try and give you an account of how 750 men went over the top and less than 50 came back.

Birnie spent the day as a stretcher-bearer. 'It was heart breaking work', he remembered; 'one could do so little and there was so much to do . . . We could not carry men away but we dressed them, sometimes we simply had to hide in shell holes, it got so very hot.' Then he was shot by a sniper. 'Something red hot shot through my neck and I fell into a shell hole. I don't remember much more for a while until I heard poor old Steven say "Are you dead, Sir? Are you dead? God help those buggers if they've killed you."' But incredibly Birnie survived. He continued working among the dead and wounded, dodging flurries of shellfire and the odd burst of machine-gun fire. Despite his injuries he kept going, doling out vials of morphine for those with no chance of survival, and listening, with tears in his eyes, as they uttered their final words. When he eventually reached a dressing station, plastered with mud and blood, Birnie was utterly worn out. As he sat down to have his wound dressed, he remembered a verse from his childhood: 'It's not the fact that you're dead that counts, but only[:] how did you die.'[51]

Yet again the German defensive position on the Flanders I Line had proved incredibly tough. Exhaustion, fear and shock brought on by the endless bombardments may have shredded the nerves of the defenders, but when the time came, they resisted with every ounce of courage and determination they possessed. The true horror of what happened to the New Zealand and Australian battalions was revealed in the combat report of 6 *Jäger* Regiment, which held the Bellevue Spur. It recorded that:

Despite the heaviest of losses, the troops were in the best of spirits, probably mainly due to the first-rate impact of their guns and in view of the colossal losses among the English. The day was a particularly great day for the machine-guns. As sufficient ammunition was available, and delivered efficiently all day – during the course of this day alone, more than 130,000 rounds of machine-gun ammunition were delivered – all targets that presented themselves could be taken under continuous machine-gun fire. Some of the machine-guns fired up to 15,000 rounds. The consumption of [small arms] ammunition was very significant too. A corporal reports having fired 700 rounds. As the field of fire was often very wide, and as the English presented the most worthwhile mass targets all day long, the effect of the machine-guns was truly devastating for the enemy. It was probably above all thanks to the machine-guns that, despite an enemy incursion on both the right and the left side of our section, the enemy was neither able to roll up the flanks of the battalion, nor to turn its incursion into a breakthrough towards the back.

Working furiously, the *Jäger* battalions improvised rudimentary cleaning sections, where muddy weapons could be brought in, cleaned up, and then sent back out to the front line, making sure that the fire never slackened off. As if that were not bad enough, the combat report also recorded how the effect of artillery upon the struggling attackers was 'absolutely exquisite'. By letting off white flares they were able to direct shells to wherever they were needed, while also launching hundreds of mortar bombs, which caught 'the often concentrated enemy with direct fire'.[52]

Such an intensity of defensive firepower produced carnage. It was in front of the Bellevue Spur where some of the worst scenes were played out: doomed battalions slugging forward over heavy ground; lines of infantry getting cut down by brutal machine-gun fire; shell holes filled with brown muddy water, now washed red with blood. Colonel Hugh Stewart, a classics professor from Christchurch and commander of 2/Canterbury Regiment, was appalled at the dire vista in his sector. Over 600 dead New Zealanders lay in front of the German barbed wire at the Bellevue Spur and were strewn, like torn rags, along the Gravenstafel road. 'They had poured out their blood like water', he wrote bitterly, summing up the reasons why. 'As the obstacles were overwhelming, so the causes of failure are easy of analysis.' Certainly, the whole operation was rushed, without sufficient time to reconnoitre the ground and prepare adequately, but Stewart regarded these as only contributing factors. 'The reasons for our failure lay rather in the inevitable weakness of our artillery barrage, the nature of the ground, the strength of the machine-gun resistance from the pillboxes, and above all in the unbroken wire entanglements.'[53]

For Major-General Sir Andrew Russell, the New Zealand commander, 12 October was a bitter reminder of the need never to take anything for granted in war. 'Attacked this morning at daybreak', he wrote in his diary, 'we, and indeed all other divisions, were held up at the start by M.G. [fire]. Evidently the artillery preparation was insufficient, the barrage poor, and it goes to show the weakness of haste – our casualties are heavy.'[54] An astute soldier, meticulous and professional, Russell had worked hard to forge his division's reputation as elite troops who never failed. He visited the front several days later and saw for himself the strength of the German position. He realized that his attack had been rushed, but he still insisted his staff should have known and done something about it.[55] In total, Russell's division suffered 3,000 casualties, including nearly 1,000 dead – the only time in the war that they would not achieve their objectives and the single worst day in New Zealand's military history.[56]

Monash wrote to his wife on 18 October, bitter at the latest setback. 'Our men are being put into the hottest fighting and are being sacrificed in hare-brained ventures, like Bullecourt and Passchendaele, and there is no one in the War Cabinet to lift a voice in protest', he complained. He wrote again three days later, seemingly in a more collected frame of mind. Casualties were evidently still bothering him and he described in detail the system they had evolved for the evacuation of the wounded from the front lines to the Advanced Dressing Stations – almost as if he wanted to reassure himself that everything possible was being done. The average 'carry' from the battlefield was over 4,000 yards, with each casualty requiring sixteen stretcher-bearers to get him home (four relay teams of four). 'Of course, the whole of this enormous department is, relatively speaking, only a small side show in the running of big battle, but throughout every department of the work, both fighting and feeding up supplies, stores and ammunition, I strive to introduce similar systematic methods and order, so that there shall be no muddling, no overlapping, no cross purposes, and everybody has to know exactly what his job is, and when and where he has to do it.'[57] He was visibly relieved when he handed over his sector the following day, 22 October. The Anzacs were done.

14.

'Not Worth a Drop of Blood'

It was no longer trench warfare, but mud-hole warfare.

A. H. Atteridge[1]

13–25 October 1917

Day in, day out, the endless, dangerous monotony of life in the Ypres Salient went on. In mid-October, Lieutenant Godefroy Skelton was posted to a section of Royal Engineers deployed out at the northern edge of the Salient near Houthulst Forest. He had spent the summer at Second Army headquarters at Cassel, but now he found himself among the wilderness of the front. 'We had to live in bell tents in the open and the horse lines were a sea of mud', he noted. 'All was mud and shell holes . . . and the German pillboxes made of concrete in our lines were sinking in the mud and canting at all angles.' They were tasked with myriad jobs: building thick sandbag walls around captured pillboxes (to shelter their entrances from shellfire); keeping duckboard tracks in a good state of repair; marking tapes out in no-man's-land; and training their mules to carry packs of engineering supplies up to the front. When not in the line, Godefroy occasionally had to complete the 'painful task' of writing letters to the families of the men who had been killed under his command. It was a far cry from his time at Cassel, where he had lived 'in style at the largest hotel in town'.[2]

Working constantly in poor conditions, often over sodden, gas-poisoned ground, which meant long hours spent in his gas mask, it was little wonder that Godefroy soon began to feel on the verge of a nervous breakdown. 'I think at this time I was becoming "nervy",' he admitted, 'due to the strains and constant fear of death or wounding and the responsibilities of the work of the sappers and the large working parties of infantry.' When he reported to company or battalion headquarters, he found himself not wanting to leave, so he put off the moment when he would have to run the gauntlet between machine-gun and sniper fire, taking solace in whisky to help numb the senses. Indeed, Godefroy was not alone. Everyone who served in the Salient felt that they left something of themselves there; found themselves unable to stand the ravaged battlefield or the claustrophobic pillboxes they sheltered in, which may have been sprinkled with quicklime, but always smelt of the dead. Stanley Roberts, a driver with 49th Division – one of the divisions that had been shattered at Poelcappelle – believed that it was 'no longer a Darwinian survival of the fittest, but the survival of those who stay safely away from this terrible holocaust, whether in civilian occupation or comfortable billets, either at the Base or in England. The strongest, healthiest man cannot refuse death when a shell hits him and smashes his body to blood clots. My faith in war is wavering . . .'[3]

There was no doubt that the Ypres battlefield, with its toxic, gas-scarred moonscape, littered with mutually supporting pillboxes, proved immensely trying to men's morale. Shellfire was probably the worst thing that soldiers faced and it could take an enormous toll on their spirits. 'My wife sometimes asks me what shell-fire was like', recalled Lance Corporal H. S. Taylor (1/10th King's Liverpool Regiment):

It varied of course, differing between a barrage and individual shelling to a specific target. In the latter case you had a chance to run before the next shell arrived. The most hateful were the German Whizz-bangs, which as the name implies arrived without warning fired with a flat trajectory these small shells about 12 lbs., I think, sometimes came through the parapet, indeed I once saw a soldier wounded in this way and by some miracle not only had the shell failed to explode, but had lodged partly in his chest and he survived. 5.9's were unpleasant and accurate, to our disadvantage. One heavy howitzer shell was nicknamed a 'Jack Johnson', and another of that calibre a 'Coal-Box' because it left a very large pall of black smoke hanging about. Some big shells made a noise like a train going through a tunnel, others passing high overhead made a gentle whistle or a sort of swish. Shells coming in your direction made a different noise altogether, and even gave you a moment to take whatever shelter you might think would assist your further survival in a seemingly mad world.[4]

It never entirely stopped 'raining iron' in the Salient, but in those brief moments when the storm abated, men's thoughts centred on more prosaic matters: trying to ward off the crushing tiredness and stay awake; the constant itching from lice that roamed over their bodies; and when they would get hot food and water or when they would be relieved.

Given the lack of suitable trenches on the battlefield, it was inevitable that some men took shelter in hastily converted German pillboxes. But these were not enjoyable places to stay in, and could turn even the toughest of men into nervous wrecks. Victor Fagence, a Lewis gunner with 11/Queen's Royal West Surrey Regiment, had been wounded in the hand on the morning of 31 July and took refuge in a recently evacuated pillbox. Ominously, a 12-inch armour-piercing shell had come through the roof, but not exploded, which made Fagence understandably nervous about remaining. Yet he stayed where he was, reasoning that the shell had been fitted with a percussion fuse (not a timed one), so that it would not explode as long as it lay undisturbed. Yet this caused some panic when others joined him later that evening:

> All through the night there was a continuous stream of people coming to the 'pillbox' for shelter and it was necessary for us inside to shout out 'mind the dud shell on the floor, don't kick it for Christ's sake!' Fortunately no one did kick it or we would probably all have 'kicked the bucket' by being blown sky high.[5]

Unexploded ordnance was not the only thing that could be found in pillboxes. Major F. J. Rice, a battery commander with 18th Division, remembered taking cover in a bunker known as 'the Kennels' (near Saint-Julien), which was notorious for attracting shellfire. 'The floor of the pillbox was composed of duckboards on boxes in order to keep us clear of the filthy black water underneath, which was too deep and too foul to be baled', he remembered. 'If anyone trod on a loose board and disturbed the water the stench was indescribable, but it was the only concrete covering in the neighbourhood, so we stuck to it. Perhaps there were some Germans at the bottom of the water . . .'[6]

British and Dominion morale may have remained remarkably stable, even under the most inhospitable conditions, but it was particularly noticeable how nervous men became as their moment for relief drew nearer. According to Lieutenant Sinclair Hunt (55/Battalion AIF), the first few hours' walk after being relieved, when you would make your way back down the line, were particularly trying. 'It is then that the ugly feeling of fear grips hardest', he wrote.

> A hot walk becomes a steady jog, a steady jog becomes a run until some puffing hero declares he won't run another step for every Fritz in creation and the pace slackens. No barrage descends, some optimist declares he thinks we are pretty right now and wonders what the cooks will have for tea and whether the blankets and packs will be ready when we arrive. The pace becomes a swinging walk and long, long into that night and the next morning parties of weary fagged men limp along the roads resting here and there to get a cup of the finest coffee they ever tasted at some YMCA and often just before dawn throw themselves down upon some tent or hut floor to sleep the sleep of the just.[7]

As Lieutenant John Nettleton (2/Rifle Brigade) later recalled:

> one was always more windy coming down the line than going in. The nearer you were to safety, the worse luck it seemed to be hit. And when you were going on leave, it was worse still. Men who stood up to all sorts of horrors in the line, behaved like frightened rabbits when they were going on leave. It was a well-understood phenomenon and nobody thought the worse of you for it.[8]

Inevitably some men decided that their only salvation lay in leaving their units, going absent without leave or deserting entirely. The total number of British soldiers reported absent without leave rose steadily throughout 1917, peaking in December with 2,000 recorded cases. Australian soldiers seemed to be particularly affected by the intensity of fighting in Flanders. Despite only consisting of about 3.6 per cent of the nominal strength of the BEF, just short of 200 Australians were recorded as being absent in December 1917 (or about 10 per cent of the total number of deserters). Australian figures for both absence and desertion also hit a high in October – when fighting was at its fiercest.[9] Although there is no doubt that Australian and New Zealand combat performance remained high, it was a worrying indication of how draining Passchendaele was becoming. Even senior commanders did not escape lightly. Although they were spared the worst of the conditions of the battlefield, most did not live a life of chateau-bound luxury. The headquarters of II ANZAC Corps was at Ten Elms Camp near Poperinge. Admittedly, this was about five miles from the front line, but most staff officers lived in tents (as did the GOC, Sir Alexander Godley), which were draughty and highly vulnerable to enemy air raids.[10] As for I ANZAC Corps, its commander, Sir William Birdwood, made regular trips to the front line and suffered from painful swelling in his feet. 'Even though I wore good, thick boots, laced lightly to encourage circulation, I found that the many hours I had to spend tramping through icy mud turned my feet into blocks of ice, and gradually a couple of toes gave out and troubled me for years afterwards.'[11]

Despite the murderous shambles in front of Passchendaele, Haig was not yet willing to give up (or at least not entirely). At a major conference at Cassel on 13 October, which everyone seemed to attend – Kiggell, Charteris, Davidson, Plumer, Gough and assorted staff officers – the question of whether the offensive should continue was discussed. According to Haig, 'We all agreed that our attack should only be launched when there is a fair prospect of fine weather. When ground is dry no opposition which the Enemy has put up has been able to stop them.'[12] This might have been so, but the 'prospect of fine weather' seemed increasingly unlikely as the offensive dragged on deeper into the autumn. It was now getting inexorably colder and wetter with little hope for improvement. While the British had benefited from a better than usual September, October was worse than expected and the month was notable for heavy downpours on 7–8, 13, 17 and 24–26 October.[13] Yet this did not cause Haig to question whether he should give up; if anything it hardened his determination to see it through, whatever the cost.

In correspondence with John Charteris after the war, Haig would reaffirm that one of the reasons he maintained the offensive was to keep pressure off the French Army, which he then believed to be in an extremely fragile state. When he found out that Winston Churchill, then Chancellor of the Exchequer, had criticized him in the third volume of *The World Crisis*, Haig was unimpressed. 'It is impossible for Winston to know how the possibility of the French Army breaking up in 1917 *compelled me to go on attacking*.'[14] Therefore, according to Haig, his operation could only be judged after taking into account the weakness of his allies and the burden this placed on the BEF. Haig's claim would eventually become enshrined in the British Official History, with Sir James Edmonds writing of the 'persistent and urgent pleas of General Pétain to continue the Flanders operations in order to ensure that the flow of German reserves should be diverted from the French front'.[15]

The question of what influence French weakness (or perceived weakness) had on the continuation of the battle is an important one. Most historians have been sceptical of Haig's claims – seeing them as either a fabricated *ex post facto* justification or evidence of impaired memory. There is, indeed, little evidence that Pétain begged Haig to keep attacking.[16] Recently the historian Elizabeth Greenhalgh has described Haig's justifications as being 'completely false', citing French documents which reveal that in the build-up to the French Army's attack at Malmaison (which would take place on 23 October) Haig repeatedly asked for it to be brought forward – to as early as 5 October – to draw German units *away* from Flanders. Much to Haig's chagrin, Pétain, as cautious as ever, refused to be rushed.[17] Haig's own diary entries are clear on this point. On 26 September he told Robertson that he wanted to see the French commander about 'the importance of attacking without delay'. He summoned General Anthoine and asked him to get Pétain to do something 'to hold the

German divisions in their front'. Yet it was to no avail. After Haig was told that it would probably be mid-October before Pétain could attack, he was distraught, muttering that this would 'not help me' and that the French were 'not playing the game!'[18]

The reality was that Pétain had never been particularly keen on Haig's plans for Flanders, and had warned him about his over-confidence back in May. The thing that Pétain wanted, more than anything else, was for the British to take over more of the Western Front, which would have allowed him to relieve units and concentrate his forces for a number of carefully prepared limited attacks (at either Verdun or the Chemin des Dames). By the autumn of 1917, with Russia likely to exit the war imminently, Pétain's mind was already turning towards the possibility of having to conduct major *defensive* operations in 1918, hence his wish to conserve what forces they had. On 18 October, when the Allied general staffs met in Amiens, he asked the British to relieve his Sixth Army and told Haig that he 'was anxious that I should agree to the principle of taking over more line' – thus raising that perennial bugbear: how much frontage should be allocated to each army on the Western Front.[19] When Haig commented that this would probably force him to abandon his operation in Flanders, Pétain was nonplussed. Thus the two Commanders-in-Chief held diametrically opposing views on how to fight the war. Haig – always the compulsive gambler, throwing good money after bad – believed that changed circumstances merely reinforced his belief in offensive action. Pétain, on the contrary, showed a much more perceptive grasp of how the tide of war was changing and turning, ominously, against them.[20]

For the time being, then, Haig remained convinced that he was on the cusp of a decisive victory and that the enemy was close to breaking. When Major-General Macdonogh at the War Office disagreed with some of his most recent pronouncements on the state of the enemy (which had been drawn from prisoner interrogations), Haig was deeply affronted and complained loudly to Robertson.[21] The problem was that the Field Marshal had 'cried wolf' too many times before. Certainly, morale was low in a number of German divisions – Haig cited the 10th Bavarian and 79th Reserve Divisions as being particularly poor – but how much reliance could be placed upon the testimonies of individual prisoners or rumours about mutinous units? In any case, so what? This hardly meant that the whole German Army was on the brink of collapse. Robertson, as coolly as ever, wrote back to Haig on 18 October. For three years 'numerous optimistic prophecies and calculations . . . have been made by different people, and it is not too much to say that most of them have proved to be false'. Therefore, it was 'premature to assume that any great diminution of morale in the German armies has yet taken place'.[22]

The arguments over the state of morale in the German Army, and whether GHQ's assessments were accurate, rumbled on for the rest of the year. But they would become increasingly irrelevant to the last series of attacks that would be made on the Passchendaele Ridge. On 3 October, Haig had signalled that the next phase of operations would be conducted by the Canadian Corps, which had been holding the line around Lens. Having recently been involved in a sapping attritional battle at Hill 70, its commander, Lieutenant-General Sir Arthur Currie, was loath to put his corps through more combat, let alone in dreaded Flanders. It had been rumoured that they were being placed in Fifth Army, but Currie made it clear that he would, under no circumstances, serve under Gough, and Haig, reluctantly, went along with him. When Currie met Plumer on 13 October, a day after the attacks towards Passchendaele had met with such fierce resistance, he made it clear how unhappy he was. One look at the ground convinced him that the whole endeavour was futile. He is reported to have said that taking the Passchendaele Ridge would cost 16,000 casualties (and subsequent events would prove his forecast to be remarkably accurate). The blasted place was 'not worth a drop of blood', he swore. Plumer, always a sympathetic listener, had to agree, but shook his head slowly.

'My orders are clear.'[23]

News of Currie's unease did not take long to reach GHQ. 'It was not common for Haig to dicker with his generals', wrote the historian Tim Cook, 'but in this case he made an exception.[24] In stark contrast to how he treated his other – British – corps commanders, Haig felt it necessary to ask personally for Currie's help. Partly this was due to Haig's growing respect for the Canadian, but it also reflected Currie's position as head of what was, effectively, a small 'national army' with a '*de facto* veto over what Haig and British Army commanders could or could not ask the Canadian Corps to do'.[25] According to Major-General Archie Macdonell (GOC 1st Canadian Division), when Haig's car rolled up during a divisional meeting, Currie went outside to greet the Field Marshal, who was eager to put some kind of proposition to him. 'Haig was very earnest and very animated and after a halt during which he had failed to convince Currie, would take him by the arm and walk up and down with him in a very animated way and evidently full of argument.' Shortly afterwards, Haig addressed Currie's staff directly. He told them that Passchendaele had to be taken and that the Canadians were being asked to do it. He admitted that their commander was 'strongly opposed' to doing so.

'But I have succeeded in overcoming his scruples. Some day I hope to be able to tell you why this must be done, but in the mean time I ask you to take my word for it.'

Haig reassured the men that '*an unprecedented amount of artillery*' would support their attack.[26]

Sir Arthur Currie could not have been more unlike Haig. Hailing from a modest background in Strathroy, Ontario, Currie had been, successively, a teacher, insurance salesman, commander of militia and real-estate broker. Currie had joined the militia in 1897, and although he was prevented from serving in the South African War owing to an on-going stomach ailment – that would periodically resurface in France – he was a natural fit. Known as a disciplinarian, Currie approached war with an emphasis on professionalism and training, smart dress and attention to detail. Crucially, Currie 'never claimed to have all the answers', but read what he could, learnt off others, and understood that only hard-won experience would allow him to master his craft.[27] These traits would stand him in good stead as he embarked on a dizzying rise: brigadier-general in 1914; major-general in 1915; and lieutenant-general twenty-one months later. By the summer of 1917, Currie had become the foremost Canadian soldier in the empire – and the man whom Haig went to when he needed a favour.

Haig's reticence in telling Currie why the Passchendaele Ridge had to be taken was, in some respects, quite remarkable. For such an important operation to go ahead, employing some of the best troops in the empire, without a clear understanding of why objectives had to be secured and at such a late stage, was highly unusual. But Haig, as can be understood, was not keen to dwell on the matter or discuss it in more detail. When Currie asked him, again and again, why the ridge had to be taken, Haig would reply with the same infuriating phrase – *that some day he would tell Currie, but not now.*[28] The truth was that without it he had little to show for an offensive that had been conceived in over-optimism and which had failed to achieve its grandiose objectives. The Field Marshal had envisaged his forces sweeping towards the Flanders coast, but the grim truth was that Roulers and the Channel were as distant as ever. Without the ridge in his hands, Haig would have to go bareheaded back to the War Cabinet and beg for their forgiveness. Therefore, the capture of Passchendaele was not about breaking the line or fixing the enemy in place, or even gaining a better line for the winter – *it was about saving Haig's own skin.*

Haig may not have been open about his reasons for wanting Passchendaele taken, but his attitude towards Currie illustrated how important the Canadian Corps had become by 1917. The biggest overseas contingent of the BEF, it comprised four divisions with supporting artillery, engineering and medical units, and totalled over 8,000 officers and 106,000 other ranks (significantly bigger than the Australian and New Zealand contingents, which could field around 75,000 men combined).[29] Whereas British divisions would be shuffled around the front as was necessary, moving in and out of corps headquarters on a relatively regular basis, it was made clear to the British Government by Ottawa that Canadian public opinion would not stand for their divisions being treated in the same way. *Canadian divisions would stay together, and they would fight together.* Some British officers would grumble that this meant that the Canadians were more troublesome to deploy and less flexible than British units – and there was certainly some truth in this – but the benefits more than outweighed any drawbacks. Because Canadian troops operated together, not only did this help to generate a remarkable *esprit de corps* and cohesion, but it also made it easier to develop and promulgate new tactics and doctrine.

By 1917 the Canadian Corps had won a growing reputation for innovation and professionalism on the battlefield. By the time it attacked Vimy Ridge on 9 April, it had already pioneered the use of new platoon tactics, more effective counter-battery fire, machine-gun barrages and armoured cars.[30] Canadian units were also employing greater numbers of analysts and intelligence staff, and to a lower level, than their British counterparts and were making impressive efforts to integrate this with air power and artillery.[31] Utilizing a new centralized structure, the Counter-Battery Staff Office, the Canadian Corps was able to pool information on the location and movements of enemy guns and devise comprehensive measures for dealing with them. At Vimy, Canadian officers reckoned that they had pinpointed 176 out of 212 German guns on their front; a success rate of over 80 per cent.[32] Indeed, this excellence – more than anything else – showed why Haig had entrusted the capture of the Passchendaele Ridge to the Canadians. Their struggle to seize the high ground would be the last great act of the Third Battle of Ypres. If they could not take it, then no one could.

The German infantry of 'F' Company, 9/Grenadier Regiment (3rd Guard Division), went up to the front on 13 October, deploying from Keiberg north to the Ypres–Roulers railway line, just south of the village of Passchendaele. 'The weather is dreary', recorded the regimental history. 'Rain day and night. All paths have been destroyed.'

> As far as the eye can see, everything is a vast field of craters. Fusiliers will sink into the muddy ground up to their knees. The craters themselves are filled with muddy water, and only a few concrete blocks [pillboxes] that have escaped enemy bombardment so far offer miserable protection against the inclemency of the weather to small numbers. Most men lie wet and freezing in the craters, partly in water, and the tarpaulins they have pulled over their heads barely protect them against moisture from above. At the same time, any conspicuous movement must be avoided. For all day a swarm of

enemy aircraft continuously circles in the sky above, reporting any movement to their artillery. The heaviest harassing fire is continuously trained on the sea of craters . . .[33]

By October 1917 conditions on the Passchendaele Ridge were appalling. The village itself had been almost wiped from the map, and aerial photographs showed all too clearly the progressive destruction of buildings and roads. When he first saw it, 'lit by the glare of the morning sun', a soldier with 13 Reserve Infantry Regiment (13th Reserve Infantry Division) was amazed. 'The smashed walls reached up towards the sky, as did the wrecked and torn remains of the church . . . In all directions there was yawning emptiness, ruins, ruin and destruction.' There was little cover for the men, just endless shell holes – what they called the *Trichterfeld*, the 'crater field' – while battalion headquarters was housed in a ruined farmhouse that was terribly vulnerable to shellfire. It was from here that the next phase of the battle would be led: the desperate juggling act of trying to support the forward battalions as they fought off the attackers; working out where reserves should be sent; and then pressing forward from shell hole to shell hole through murderous drumfire.[34]

It was often said that the terrible ground conditions and appalling weather hampered the attackers far more than the defenders. General von Kuhl thought differently. For him the opposite was true. Because the ground water was just below the surface, German troops were left exposed on the battlefield; unable to build the trenches or dugouts that would have protected them from the unending 'iron rain'. While the landscape was dotted with concrete pillboxes and bunkers, these were magnets for enemy guns and soon became surrounded by shell holes and scattered with bodies – like battered ships amid a turbulent sea of mud. Kuhl described the situation German troops faced in stark terms:

The defenders cowered in their water-filled craters without protection from the weather, hungry and freezing, continually exposed to the overwhelming enemy artillery fire. Even the staffs of the forward units had no cover, except perhaps a thin corrugated-iron roof over their shell hole. Movement in the muddy soil was very difficult: men and horses sank into the slime; rifles and machine-guns, coated with mud, refused to function. Only rarely was it possible to supply the defenders with a hot meal. Distribution of orders in the forward area was difficult in the extreme as telephone and line communication had been shot to pieces. It was painful work for runners struggling through the mud.

For Kuhl the 'suffering, privation and exertions' his men endured were 'inexpressible'. 'No division', he lamented, 'could last more than a fortnight in this Hell.'[35]

It was not just men who struggled through the mud; horses were particularly vulnerable in such boggy conditions. On 18 October men of 8th Battery, Field Artillery Regiment (10th Bavarian Division), tried to reinforce the lines around Becelaere. According to Reserve Second Lieutenant Peistrup, they endured 'unspeakable difficulties' bringing up their guns. At the appointed time, their battery was to fire a thousand rounds of gas shell and then, as soon as was safe, move them back. But the ground was so awful that the exercise rapidly descended into a terrifying struggle for survival:

> As we prepared to move our guns, one of the limbers slid down into a huge shell crater. Officers and men attempted, in some cases up to their necks in icy water, to free the horses. Despite the greatest efforts this proved to be impossible, because the horses were trapped by the mud. There was nothing else for it but to put them out of their terrified misery with a revolver shot. Hardly one hundred metres further on, another team fell into a crater where, before it could be rescued, all the horses were drowned.[36]

The gunnery officer Reinhard Lewald went through a similar ordeal. 'We had another gun shot to hell', he wrote on 19 October. After two 'nice autumn days', when the battle seemed to have ended, renewed artillery fire picked up again as the Canadians began gearing up for their assault. 'Our battery is under almost continuous fire, and we are being fired upon with calibres up to 34cm. The terrain at our firing position is a single crater field. We can barely bring up our ammunition any more in the churned-up ground. Our horses – yet again, almost a quarter of which have been shot dead or wounded – are in danger of collapsing.'[37] This constant exposure to death, or near-death, presented soldiers with enormous psychological challenges, and it was not unusual to see men collapse under heavy fire, go screaming from shell hole to shell hole, until stilled by their comrades or wounded or killed. Others internalized their fear and kept going: reciting prayers or spells; holding good-luck tokens; or following well-worn routines that, they were convinced, helped them to navigate 'death's gray land' in the trenches.[38]

The *Flandernschlacht* did not just take a psychological toll on the men in the trenches. Their commanders could be equally depressed at having to send units into the maelstrom knowing that they were, in all probability, condemning them to death. Indeed, the fate of the *Eingreif* divisions, if, where and when to deploy them, caused many anxious moments in battlefield headquarters up and down the front. Albrecht von Thaer, who sent in many counter-attacks at Group Wytschaete, described the enormous responsibility he faced, as he worried constantly that he would make a mistake, with inevitably lethal consequences. 'It is simply terrible when one has to decide within a matter of a few minutes whether to send reserves to rescue the people at the front, which effectively means that, once again, some hundreds or thousands of men will march forward, mostly to their doom. I always tell myself that, in making decisions of this kind, I must exercise the same caution as I would if my brother or my son were in these columns. But what is the point of all that?' he asked. 'After all, can we not "turn back?"'[39]

Contrary to Haig's faith in an imminent collapse in enemy morale, the mood of German soldiers remained largely stable, if sorely tried, during this period.[40] Although there is no doubt that Flanders had become a byword for mud and death – 'the great Flemish human mill', as one soldier put it – German units continued to perform well throughout the summer and autumn.[41] According to Staff Sergeant Alfred Kleysteuber of 233 Reserve Infantry Regiment (195th Division), when notice came to embark for Flanders, 'the word flashed round the regiment like news of a death. Everywhere there were serious faces, because everybody knew that the fateful hour was upon them.' Yet the men detrained on time, arriving at Thielt – with the sky lit up, as usual, with artillery fire – one day before reaching Passchendaele to take their place in the line.[42] Not all units went into the 'mill' so easily, however. A company commander in 16 Bavarian Infantry Regiment (of the notoriously poor 10th Bavarian Division), who was captured by the British on 12 October, told his captors that his officers had 'great difficulty' in averting a mutiny when the men heard they were going back to Flanders. 'On the march, an Oberleutnant rode along the ranks and told the men to "close up" and not straggle; he was met with shouts of "Sauhund" [Bastard]', and warned that if he did it again he would be shot.[43]

The balance, as with all armies, was crucial. Units had to feel that their sacrifice was both proportional and fair; that they were being asked to do no more than others. Although some evidence filtered back to British intelligence of ill-feeling between the Bavarians and the Prussians, with those from South Germany being 'sacrificed', which increased levels of desertion, the Army held together reasonably well, bound by common discipline and patriotism, and the realization of how important it was to hold on.[44] Yet the commanders knew full well how exhausting the battle was becoming. According to a Fourth Army report, dated 21 October, the circumstances in Flanders 'exceeded the horror of anything previously experienced' by its troops. 'In the judgement of front-line soldiers who also served at Verdun and the Somme, the strength of the firestorm that preceded and accompanied the charges of the attackers in Flanders in 1917 was far greater than ever before.' As might have been expected, the demands this placed on the men – what the Official History called 'psychological tenacity' – were enormous. Cowering 'here and there in muddy craters behind obstacles that had been completely shot to pieces, exposed to fire and the elements and at all times aware of impending enemy attacks, as well as being exhausted owing to a lack of sleep and provisions, as they were only rarely delivered in adequate quantity and quality', the German soldier had to find the courage to keep going. 'The vast majority of German troops deployed in this battle', it concluded proudly, 'passed this nearly superhuman test of their resilience.'[45]

The intensity of the shellfire could drive men insane. According to the regimental history of 86 Fusilier Regiment, which fought throughout September and October, the bombardments it experienced at Ypres were different to those on the Somme, causing 'paralysing terror' among those subjected to it. 'The soldiers bury their faces in the mud and cling on to tree roots to stop themselves from involuntarily jumping up and running away like madmen. Others squat in the concrete blocks in passive desperation.' Being in a pillbox when shelling was going on was, as could be imagined, simply hellish. 'When the mud of Flanders splatters into the sky all around and the earth is grasped by spasms, then the block will sway up and down like a ship on the waves.' Although the walls and ceiling could withstand calibres up to 15cm, the detonations travelled through the concrete with 'harrowing effects'. Pillboxes could also be badly undermined by artillery fire, with shells slipping deep into the surrounding mud and then exploding beneath the ground, ripping open the floor and blowing to pieces anyone unfortunate enough to be inside. That was bad enough, but what men feared more than anything else was the whole pillbox being knocked on to its side, doorways facing the mud, trapping the occupants inside. It was little wonder that many men thought long and hard about whether to take shelter in those dark, claustrophobic, haunted caverns. *There were many ways to die in the Ypres Salient in that awful summer of 1917.*[46]

Someone who saw for himself how horribly unpredictable death could be was Walter Rappolt, an NCO with 1 Guard Foot Artillery Regiment. His battery spent most of the battle deployed around Becelaere (a mile and a half from the eastern edge of Polygon Wood), which was one of the most heavily shelled areas of the front. One of his worst experiences took place on 26 August when a telephonist called Meyer had the 'top of his skull blown off' by a shell splinter. Although the man sitting next to him was unharmed, he was 'deeply disturbed' by what had happened. Rappolt recorded how his commanding officer, Lieutenant Konig, tried to deal with the situation as quickly as possible. He 'took a piece of wood and removed part of the brain which was lying on the telephone' and cleaned up the mess. Rappolt admitted that he now faced 'a difficult task, to prevent my breakdown . . . It was only a moment before, that I had talked to that man.' The following day another horrific incident occurred when a shell cartridge got stuck in the breech of one of their 10cm guns. Their mechanic 'got tired of it' and in 'a touch of madness he took a mallet smacking it on the priming handle with the breech half open'. The result was a vicious flash, like a lightning strike. 'The shell burst from the gun, but at the back a tremendous explosion which caused terrible burns to the poor chap. His eyes were gone and he cried very much on his way to the first aid station. I do not know what happened to him.'[47]

How close did the German Army come to breaking during the Battle of Flanders? In truth, it came close, but not close enough. According to the German Medical History, eleven corps were deployed in total, sometimes for significant periods of time, and all would be affected by the horror of Third Ypres. Nineteen divisions arrived to replace 21 divisions in August; 12 arrived and 14 left the following month; 31 arrived and 18 left during October; and 11 arrived and 25 left in November. In all 100 infantry divisions were brought into Flanders, with 98 being relieved, between May and December 1917 – what was recognized as 'an extraordinary turnover of divisions'. Of these, 23 were deployed twice and one was even deployed three times.[48] According to official records, the 63 divisions that went into action between 10 July and 10 October sustained a total of 159,000 casualties, many of them caused by heavy artillery fire, including long-range howitzers, which searched the rear areas for ammunition dumps, billets and headquarters of any kind. There is little doubt that Third Ypres demanded a heavy and continuous commitment of troops, guns and supplies.[49]

It seems clear that the German Army had come through the fighting of July and August relatively intact. Although Fourth Army's casualties were not inconsiderable, there was a sense that the battle was proceeding in a largely manageable and stable way. At the beginning of August, Crown Prince Rupprecht favourably compared the battle with the Somme fighting of 1916. In Flanders, his divisions had lost, on average, between 1,500 and 2,000 men each, which contrasted with the figure of 4,000 for an average two-week tour on the Somme.

'While at that time the troops required a long recovery period for the exhaustion caused primarily by a lack of sleep because of their long deployment, the troops now recover significantly faster.'[50] This (relatively) comfortable situation did not last, however, and the Battle of Menin Road on 20 September ushered in the most harrowing phase of the fighting for the Germans. It was telling that the three worst periods of losses for the German Army in the summer of 1917 were the Battle of Messines (1–10 June), with 10,374 killed or missing and 12,614 wounded; Menin Road and Polygon Wood (21–30 September), with 7,821 dead and missing and 16,986 wounded; and Broodseinde and Poelcappelle (1–10 October) with 9,034 killed and missing and 14,217 wounded.[51]

By early October the German position in Flanders was becoming increasingly precarious, with congestion on the cramped railway network and a lack of reinforcements badly affecting both morale and combat effectiveness. The impact of Plumer's first three hammer blows produced a feeling of desperation, verging, in places, on panic, within the German High Command. 'Since the day before yesterday, Ludendorff rang me three times concerning orders,' complained Albrecht von Thaer on 11 October; 'Kuhl, Lossberg and other minor deities race to headquarters and to the troops in the staff car and also rage over there in the offices, and make everyone frantic and nervous. The nervousness from above surely does not make a good impression and does little to help . . .'[52] The same day, Rupprecht's diary entry also betrayed a growing sense of unease. 'Our troops along the main battle front in Flanders are still thoroughly mixed up and confusion reigns in the various formations.' He believed that the 'fighting ability' of the men was 'reducing all the time', primarily because of the 'oppressive superiority' of enemy guns. 'Because we are involved in a battle for time, there remains nothing for it, but repeatedly to give ground in order to force our opponents to waste time as they move their artillery forward.'[53]

Yet the moment of greatest danger had already passed. It was impossible for the British to maintain the impressive operational tempo that had been achieved between 20 September and 4 October, and rushed preparations, heavy rain and the sapping effects of operating across such a waterlogged, open battlefield eventually proved fatal to Haig's hopes. With renewed attacks on 9 and 12 October gaining little ground, the battle returned once more to the slower, more predictable affair that it had been throughout August. The conditions at the front were certainly awful and extremely exhausting, but Fourth Army could cope for the short period of time that remained for any offensive action to take place. On 21 October Ludendorff telephoned Rupprecht and told him that 'the main objective was to hold out for the next 14 days, and for that reason as much field artillery as possible had to be deployed at the main battle front', with frequent gas shoots at night to interfere with the enemy.[54] Although the Army Group commander felt that if the weather was better, attacks could continue into December, a major advance seemed more and more unlikely. By 24 October, two days before Currie's first step towards the heights of Passchendaele, OHL issued guidelines for the maintenance of their positions through the winter.[55]

Given the pressures on the Army, changes, both tactical and organizational, were imminent. The day after the victory at First Passchendaele, General Freiherr von Marschall travelled to Flanders, where he was to assume command of the newly formed Group Staden. Based on the Guard Reserve Corps, Group Staden was deployed between the Houthulst Forest and just south of Passchendaele, where it would play a major role in the final defensive actions in the Salient.[56] One look at the ground made it clear where the British would come from. 'The Passchendaele–Roulers railway line gave the English a favourable route for the attack, as south of it our front bent backwards . . . whereas north of the railway our line turned to the west and around Passchendaele', wrote Lieutenant E. Schaarschmidt of 126 Infantry Regiment (39th Division), who entered the line on 20 October. His men dug into the wet ground as best they could, scraping out foxholes that were covered over with wooden boards, tarpaulins or corrugated iron. It was hardly ideal, but it would have to do.[57]

As well as bringing in reinforcements, German defensive doctrine was rapidly being updated after the experiences of Flanders. On 23 October it was agreed to deploy an *Eingreif* division behind each

front-line division, forming a 'legion' of two divisions to a depth of
8,000 yards. The front-line commander was given authority over
both units to ensure they operated in tandem.[58] It was, in a sense, the
logical next step in the continual evolution of German tactics that
had been seen throughout 1917. Although this was, admittedly, a
greater commitment of manpower than OHL would have liked
(being the 'unheard-of expenditure of force' that Ludendorff had
warned about a month earlier), it seemed the only reliable way of
making sure that the British were kept at bay in the last weeks of the
battle.

It may not have felt like a victory, but by the time Canadian Corps
headquarters opened at Poperinge on 18 October, the German Army
had, effectively, already won the battle. It had held on for long
enough and, crucially, was still camped upon a significant area of
high ground, to make it to winter and the inevitable cessation of
major combat operations. Moreover, it had done what the *Westheer*
had been doing successfully since the failure of the Schlieffen Plan in
September 1914: holding the line in the west and thus allowing the
Central Powers to maintain freedom of manoeuvre; reinforcing
threatened fronts, and taking on the Russian Army in the east. Now
it was Italy's turn. On 24 October, Ludendorff's counter-attack on
the Isonzo River was launched and, like a thunderbolt, cracked open
the Italian Front. Such was the violence and rapidity of the Austro-
German assault – known as the Battle of Caporetto – that the Italian
forces disintegrated. Within four days, the Italian Second Army was
in full retreat after losing 60,000 prisoners and 500 guns.[59] It would be
one of the swiftest and most decisive operations of the war, leaving
further Italian participation in the conflict on a knife-edge. For the
Allies, 1917 had begun with unease, confusion and disaster, and it
looked like it was going to end that way as well.

15.

'Against the Iron Wall'

The enemy charged like a wild bull against the iron wall which
kept him from our submarine bases . . . But it held, although a faint
tremor ran through its foundations.

Erich Ludendorff[1]

26 October–10 November 1917

Sir Arthur Currie made no secret of his opposition to fighting in Flanders, but his professionalism and sense of duty meant that, once the orders were issued, he lost no time in getting his corps into the best possible position to launch its assault. Artillery would be crucial, yet the problem of how to get enough guns into position without them being destroyed by German batteries or bogged down in the mud was maddening. When Brigadier-General E. W. B. Morrison, Currie's head of artillery, inspected the front, he was horrified by what he encountered. There were supposed to be 250 heavy guns (used by the Australians and which the Canadians would take over), but he could only find 227, of which eighty-nine were already out of action. Regarding the field artillery, the situation was even worse. 306 18-pounders were supposed to be deployed within range, yet many of these were sunk up to their axles in mud and at least half were out of action.[2] Currie even caused a scene when he was late one day for a meeting with Haig, who was attending a conference at Poperinge. When Currie came in, mud still clinging to his uniform, a sour look on his face, he stared at Haig and demanded to know where his guns were.[3]

Currie's uncompromising attitude, combined with his absolute insistence that everything possible was done to ensure success, was commendable and, indeed, absolutely vital. But he could not work miracles. By the time the Canadian Corps launched its attack, it had been unable to get all its guns into position and had suffered heavily from the regular enemy bombing and strafing missions, which went on, with annoying regularity, every night. Mist and rain prevented observation of the battlefield and because the sound-ranging and flash-spotting sections – both of which were crucial for locating enemy batteries – had been unable to keep up with the advance, German guns were not subjected to the kind of intensive counter-battery fire that the Canadians had become used to. As a Canadian artillery report later noted, enemy guns kept up 'harassing fire on routes of approach, long distance fire on railheads and depots, concentrations on billets, battery areas and forming-up localities', which caused heavy casualties and continually delayed the work of repair and construction. Indeed, some were left wondering whether the German High Command truly realized how handicapped the attackers were, with British guns cramped in a narrow salient under little or no cover and dependent upon a few well-worn approach routes. Had the Germans made a really sustained effort to bombard the salient, they could have increased British and Canadian losses 'many fold' and may even have made future operations all but impossible.[4]

The first step involved 3rd and 4th Canadian Divisions making an advance of between 600 and 1,200 yards to the Red Line (the first of Currie's three objectives). On the left 3rd Division would take the high ground at Bellevue, while 4th Division, on the other side of the swollen Ravebeek, would aim for a 'tangle of shattered tree trunks' on the Ypres–Roulers railway known as Decline Copse.[5] The assaulting battalions moved up several days before – long, thin columns of troops making their way along the corduroy roads and duckboards, slick with rain; a *via dolorosa* through the trenches. In the sodden wilderness, with major landmarks and most trees having been erased from the surface of the earth, officers and men struggled to locate their positions, although they soon spotted the squat pillboxes, covered with earth or bricks, that blocked their way up the ridge. On 23 October, Lieutenant-Colonel G. F. McFarland, second-in-command of 4/Canadian Mounted Rifles, marched with his battalion to a forward position called Cluster House, where they would relieve Australian troops. 'The Anzacs were more than delighted to hand it over to us,' he wrote, 'because they had had a very dirty time. Cluster House was a series of pill-boxes on a low ridge, and a more desolate, god-forsaken place I never expect to see. The route to it was bath-matted all the way, which alone made it passable. The ground was simply a morass, pitted with shell-holes full of water, and getting off the bath-mat meant sinking to one's waist in the ooze.'[6]

One of McFarland's junior officers was Lieutenant Tom Rutherford of Owen Sound, Ontario. 'The trench we occupied was hardly worthy of the name', he remembered; 'just a broken down ditch with up to six inches of water in it.' On the morning before the attack, he slithered up and down his sector, binoculars in hand, trying to familiarize himself with the ground over which they would attack:

> The right flank of our company was in a little wood relatively much smaller than the Wolf Copse as it is called on the sketch-map in the 4th CMR History. It was elm trees about a foot through and, at that time of year, bare of leaves . . . Beyond Wolf Farm and the edge of the wood was what appeared to be an enemy pillbox covered on top and in front with broken bricks, apparently from Wolf Farm as the loose bricks had been gathered up around that area. Beyond this and about 300 yards to the right . . . and on the end of a small spur that dominated the whole area, was another very obvious pillbox.

Rutherford returned to his company headquarters (just 'a projection cut in the side of the trench and covered with some old boards') and arranged frontages and attack plans with the other subalterns, flinching as the occasional shell or mortar round exploded around their positions. They settled down that night with just 'a couple of hunks of bread' for their provisions and no water.[7] It was an inauspicious start to the renewed attack: *this was not like Vimy Ridge.*

The lack of water in the forward positions – when it lay everywhere around them in muddy pools – only added to the discomfort of the troops and, perhaps, their urgency to get going on the morning of 26 October. At Zero Hour (5.40 a.m.), in the chill dawn, the creeping barrage lifted and the leading lines, stiff with cold, caked with mud and filth, crept forward to their objectives through the drizzle and mist. The rows of barbed wire that had stopped the attacks on 9 and 12 October had now been blown away, but the attack only made slow, grudging progress. 8 Brigade (3rd Division), which pushed on past Wolf Copse, north of Bellevue, recorded that its front-line battalions were 'heavily and continuously shelled' during the night prior to the attack. When they went over the top – their helmets painted a dirty brown colour to prevent reflection – the enemy resisted as long as they could, with machine-gun and rifle fire being 'severe'.[8]

It was a hard, brutal day's fighting. 4/Canadian Mounted Rifles progressed just 500 yards in two hours, the men gradually mastering the pillboxes that littered their front.[9] 'At 5.45 the leading companies commenced to move forward, and the first line of pill-boxes was reached on time with the barrage', remembered Lieutenant-Colonel McFarland, who watched the attack go ahead. 'Here very serious casualties were inflicted upon our people, particularly among the officers who were picked off by snipers from the pill-boxes. Two garrisons of these strongpoints fought bravely, keeping their rifles and machine-guns in action until they were bayonetted or bombed.' Once they had re-formed, the battalion tried to push on to a second line of pillboxes, but 'such a devastating fire was poured upon them that they were completely held up'.[10] With units on either flank having been unable to keep pace, the battalion had little choice but to consolidate its gains and hope for the best. As for Tom Rutherford, he fell into a pool of water, three feet deep, and lost most of his equipment, before leading an assault on a pillbox that was blocking a neighbouring battalion. He later explained his success as down to being 'just crazy', 'fighting like a guerrilla', and being covered in mud, which made him difficult to spot.[11]

Similar acts of bravery helped the Canadians on to most of their objectives that day. The Canadian Corps would win nine Victoria Crosses between 26 October and 6 November, with three on the first day alone.[12] In 43/Battalion (the Cameron Highlanders of Canada), Lieutenant Robert Shankland led his platoon up the Bellevue Spur into a storm of machine-gun and sniper fire. 'When dawn broke sufficiently our men could be clearly seen moving slowly over the skyline and around the two formidable looking Pill Boxes on the

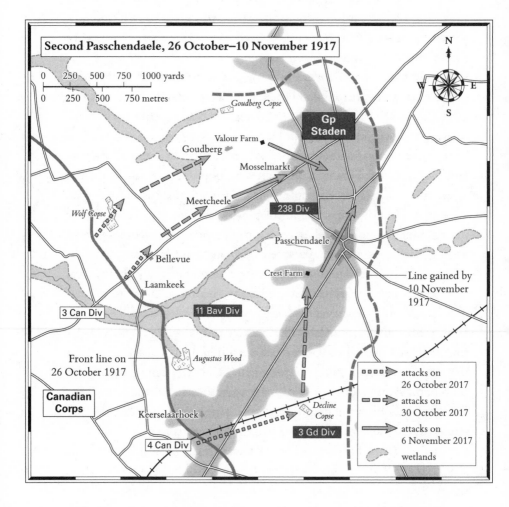

Second Passchendaele, 26 October–10 November 1917

0   250   500   750   1000 yards

0   250   500   750 metres

N
W   E
S

Goudberg Copse

Gp Staden

Valour Farm

Goudberg

Mosselmarkt

Meetcheele

238 Div

Wolf Copse

Passchendaele

Bellevue

Crest Farm

Laamkeek

Line gained by
10 November
1917

3 Can Div

11 Bav Div

Front line on
26 October 1917

Augustus Wood

Canadian
Corps

Keerselaarhoek

Decline
Copse

3 Gd Div

4 Can Div

attacks on
26 October 2017

attacks on
30 October 2017

attacks on
6 November 2017

wetlands

crest of the ridge', recorded the battalion war diary. Yet progress rapidly slowed, and as the morning wore on, more and more stragglers
began to turn up at battalion headquarters, having lost their officers
and become shaken by the intensity of the shelling. 58/Battalion, on
the right, had been held up by a strongpoint, which left Shankland
and his men in an exposed and increasingly dangerous position. All
the officers of 'C' and 'B' Companies had been hit and it was unclear
whether the battalion would be able to hang on. At ten o'clock Shankland returned to battalion headquarters and reported that he was
holding the ridge with about forty men, but they were 'suffering
considerable annoyance from snipers' and if their ammunition ran
out they would be unable to maintain their position. The Canadian
advance seemed to be on the point of failure.[13]

Rallying those men who had retreated back to headquarters, Shankland returned to the Bellevue Spur just in time. They were able to form
a defensive flank on the high ground, while a supporting company, 'A'
Company of 52/Battalion, led by Captain Christopher O'Kelly, took
the attack forward. Despite having to make their way through a nest of
fortified strongpoints, with flurries of shelling churning up the muddy
ground, O'Kelly's men cleared obstacle after obstacle. By concentrat-
ing their fire, from both rifle grenades and Lewis guns, on to each
pillbox in turn, they were able to temporarily blind the occupants.
While this was going on, flanking parties rushed up to each fortifica-
tion and threw in a handful of grenades, killing those inside and forcing
the survivors to surrender. In this way, O'Kelly managed to take out
six pillboxes, and capture 100 German prisoners and ten machine-guns.
Without such unfailing dedication to duty, it is likely that the opening
attack would have failed. Both Shankland and O'Kelly were awarded
the Victoria Cross for their part in taking the Bellevue Spur.[14]

The conditions were certainly a major handicap, but the German
Army deserves credit for what would become a textbook defensive
operation: gradually yielding ground whenever necessary; counter-
attacking whenever possible; and, most critically, regulating the pace
of the battle. To the south of Passchendaele stood 3rd Guard Infantry
Division, which had gone into the line on the night of 25 October.
When the Canadian barrage crashed down in 'a fiery sulphurous

cloud', the forward troops put into practice their new defensive doctrine, and began evacuating the *Vorfeld*, while sending off urgent requests for artillery support. 'Coloured flames are going up everywhere', recorded the history of 9/Grenadier Regiment:

> The German artillery starts its curtain fire immediately afterwards. Blow by blow, shot by shot. Communication is out of the question. The infantrymen are crouching in their craters, helplessly exposed to the fire. Added to this at all times, the English planes, against which the troops are practically powerless. They are still circling at low altitude above the shell holes, training their machine-guns at any sign of life. In defiance of fire and frequent burials by sliding earth, the infantry lie in their craters without the slightest movement that would give their line away. It is probably mainly thanks to this that the regiment isn't wiped out completely. Yet the enemy is still not attacking. Only heavy machine-gun fire from the right neighbouring section tells of the battle raging over there. Soon the news arrives that the enemy is advancing on Passchendaele north of the railway.[15]

At that moment, Paul von Kneussl's 11th Bavarian Division, which defended Passchendaele, was under heavy attack. It had been sent to Flanders on 20 October and entered the line with orders stating that the 'focus of the whole defence' lay in swift and 'ruthless counterattacks'. After hearing lectures on the latest enemy tactics and the state of the defence, each company was equipped with between two and three MG 08/15s, the lighter variant of the legendary German version of the Maxim machine-gun. Twelve light mortars and fourteen grenade launchers were also distributed per regiment – an impressive array of firepower that was meant to compensate for the declining number of combat soldiers in each infantry battalion (now around 650 men).[16] The performance of the Bavarians on 26 October was remarkable. Not only were they heavily outnumbered, but they also inflicted about twice the number of casualties upon their more numerous attackers than they themselves received.[17] Afterwards, a soldier called Grießenbeck described what happened: 'Dearest Father! On the 26th we had a very difficult day. After 3 days of drumfire, the English attacked our positions 4–6 times, overran them in one small section and had to be repulsed in desperate counter-attacks. We held our line without exception. The losses of the enemy are very large, but ours unfortunately no smaller.'[18]

The German Army may have gradually lost much of the high ground it had been occupying since the offensive began, but this did not necessarily prevent its artillery from being effective. The final stages of the offensive saw German batteries – clustered around Becelaere and southeast of Gheluvelt – employing increasing amounts of enfilade fire. Indeed, the further the British and Canadians pushed into the Salient, the more vulnerable they became to German guns that could flank their whole line of advance.[19] Second Army's artillery batteries shelled known points of concentration, making it difficult for German gunners, but never being able to completely silence the harassing fire, which continued day after day. 'The enemy assault columns were greeted by us with hellish artillery fire, and despite its vast use of ammunition, the enemy did not manage to silence our batteries', wrote Reinhard Lewald, whose battery was deployed a few hundred metres east of Passchendaele. That morning they had come under heavy gas bombardment, but fortunately the strong winds rendered it largely ineffective. 'As hard as it was for our batteries in the firing position in these days, we were not to find any peace in our place of accommodation, De Ruiter, where the relieved teams and horses were staying with limbers. For several days and nights, the place came under heavy fire, and it needed to be vacated.'[20]

As quickly as German batteries relocated, British aircraft were out trying to spot their new locations. Almost all the intelligence that came into Canadian Corps HQ regarding enemy gun positions and the effectiveness of counter-battery shoots came from aerial observation, although this was not made easy because of frequent engine failures, mist, and the appearance of predatory German *Jasta*s on the lookout for the slower, cumbersome observation aircraft.[21] Indeed, the ferocity of the aerial war in the final phases of the battle was as great as ever. On 27 October, following an improvement in the weather, aircraft of the RFC were out in force over the Salient. Over 200 targets were engaged in artillery 'zone calls' and nine German fighters were destroyed.[22] Unfortunately, that day the RFC was to lose one of its most highly regarded young pilots, Second Lieutenant Arthur Rhys Davids, the diminutive twenty-year-old who had shot down Werner Voss a month earlier. He was out on patrol when his formation spotted a group of six enemy aircraft near Roulers. Never one to shirk a fight, Rhys Davids immediately dived down upon an Albatros D.V, but was never seen again.[23]

The second phase of Currie's attack opened on 30 October. The objective was to continue the push along the two main roads to Passchendaele (which occupied slightly firmer ground) from Gravenstafel and Zonnebeke and then on to the Blue Line. They would take on the left, the Goudberg Spur; the houses at Meetcheele, in the centre; and the German strongpoint at Crest Farm, on the right.[24] The attack would be, in the main, a repeat of 26 October: an appalling struggle in a wilderness of mud, where survival was dependent upon good training and excellent leadership, but, above all, upon the trusty Lewis gun and rifle grenade. 4th Division took Crest Farm – a dark, brooding strongpoint bristling with machine-guns – with a combination of fire and movement tactics, while 3rd Division could only make grudging progress towards Meetcheele. Enemy snipers picked off officers and men alike from hidden positions, until they too were taken out by riflemen or bayoneted where they lay. Artillery support was hardly worthy of the name. 'The Field Guns were given an almost impossible task', noted the war diary of 49/Battalion (which led the assault on Furst Farm). 'As a result the barrage was short, irregular, and ineffective in preventing enemy retaliation with rifle and machine-gun fire.' 49/Battalion went into action with a total strength of twenty-one officers and 567 other ranks – by the end of the day just five officers and 140 other ranks remained unscathed.[25]

Such terrific losses would have been in vain had it not been for the remarkable tenacity of 5/Canadian Mounted Rifles, which was deployed on the extreme left of Currie's line. The attacking companies managed to skirt past Woodland Plantation, but then their pace slowed, the barrage was lost, and local enemy reserves began to muster.[26] Major George Pearkes, commanding 'C' Company, quickly realized how precarious their situation was. It was evident that both their flanks were 'hung up' and unlikely to recover soon, which left them exposed to heavy enfilade fire. Gathering the survivors together, Pearkes decided that half his men would push on to their primary objective, Vapour and Vanity Farms, while a second party, led by Lieutenant Allen Otty, would head out to the left, towards Source Farm, where enfilade fire was coming from (and which had been an objective of XVIII Corps on their left). With little more than a dozen men, Otty led the attack on Source Farm, crawling through the thick mud under heavy fire. When they got within range, they were able to silence the pillbox with a handful of Mills bombs. Although Otty was killed later that day, his leadership had been invaluable, allowing Pearkes to take Vapour Farm and secure the left flank. Pearkes was subsequently awarded a Victoria Cross for 'most conspicuous bravery'.[27]

The courage of the men of 5/Canadian Mounted Rifles, moving forward into certain death, and then holding on against what must have seemed like futile odds, would be one of the most incredible stories from the entire battle. It would help to turn the tide of what had been a dispiriting day and ensure that the Canadian Corps was now within touching distance of Passchendaele. 'We advanced again this morning, and present reports indicate all objectives in our hands', wrote Currie on 30 October. 'Today's fighting is very important, and I look for a very severe struggle. We have already broken up several very determined counter-attacks. As usual the flanks are giving us a little trouble.'[28] Currie's reference to 'the flanks' betrayed his frustration that the British were not able to keep up and that, once again, the Canadians seemed to be the only ones doing any fighting. On 26 October, Gough's Fifth Army had attacked on Currie's left – extending the attack out towards Houthulst Forest – while X Corps pushed further along the Gheluvelt Spur. Yet they met with little success. Together, XIV and XVIII Corps sustained over 5,000 casualties, with their battalions barely advancing further than their start lines. Although the men of 5th Division (in X Corps) were able to capture Polderhoek Château (about a mile southeast of Polygon Wood), they were forced to abandon their gains later that day at the cost of another 3,000 casualties.[29]

It was a similar, depressing story four days later. XVIII Corps attacked again on 30 October, pushing two divisions (58th and 63rd) forward and yet again failing to take its objectives. In 63rd (Royal Naval) Division, an intense enemy barrage fell 'right in the middle of the attacking troops', with some companies being 'practically wiped out' within the first five minutes. Yet again, gallant efforts were made to get forward. Some companies pushed on about 300 yards, before losing the barrage and then, inevitably, becoming exposed to heavy fire.[30] Such an appalling waste of life contributed to a growing sense that British units were simply being sacrificed for no purpose. 'The result of the battle was a repetition of what has been so frequently experienced when an attack is launched over waterlogged ground and deep mud', complained the war diary of XVIII Corps. 'The troops found it impossible to keep up with the barrage and, in fact, did not attempt to do so. Their efforts were mainly employed in endeavouring to extract each other out of the mud . . . This attack again demonstrated the fact that to expect troops to attack across deep and clinging mud is to expect the impossible.'[31] Yet doing the impossible was just what the Canadians *were* doing. Bit by bit, inch by inch, the Canadians were driving forward at the tip of a narrower and narrower sword. The penultimate attack would begin in seven days. Currie was now just one step away from the village of Passchendaele.

While the Canadians struggled on, momentous events were taking place on the Italian Front. David Lloyd George first heard about what would become known as the Battle of Caporetto on the morning of 27 October. He was at his house at Walton Heath in Surrey when he received the news via a telephone call from Maurice Hankey. After conveying initial reports of the disaster, Hankey said that the French were offering immediate help.[32] Soon after, a telegram arrived from Robertson advising that 'We must not get rattled over this business, but of course we must stop the rot if we can.'[33] Although the CIGS was in favour of waiting until the Italian Government formally requested troops, Lloyd George wanted something done immediately. He wired back:

> The loss of 650 guns is in itself a serious blow to the Alliance and unless the Italian morale is restored this movement may well end in overwhelming disaster. If we mean to exercise a dominating influence in

directing the course of the War we must do so in the way the Germans have secured control i.e., by helping to extricate Allies in trouble.[34]

Later that afternoon the War Office confirmed that two divisions had been despatched to Italy, to join four French ones that had already started moving. With some luck they would be on the Italian Front in two weeks.[35] Finally, the Prime Minister was sending sizeable reinforcements to the Italian Front, although not, of course, in the circumstances he would have wanted. Far from reinforcing a victorious strike at the vulnerable flank of Austria–Hungary, British and French troops were now engaged in a desperate rescue effort.

The true scale of the Italian disaster became clear over the coming days. At a meeting of the War Cabinet on 2 November, Major-General Sir Frederick Maurice read out an official enemy *communiqué* that boasted of 60,000 troops and 'great quantities of guns' being captured by Austro-German forces, which had cut off large parts of the Italian Third Army north of the Tagliamento. Potentially far-reaching changes in Allied command structure, which had been mooted all summer, now took on an added urgency; perhaps with the British taking over the northern half of the Western Front, and French GQG overseeing the rest, right down to the Adriatic, including the Italian sector. Accordingly, it had been proposed that Allied representatives would meet at Rapallo on the north Italian coast, to discuss the new arrangements, and salvage what they could from what seemed like a potentially mortal blow to the Italian war effort. That day, after furious behind-the-scenes negotiations, Lloyd George informed his colleagues that the French Government had accepted a preliminary scheme for the creation of a Supreme Inter-Allied Council, with Sir Henry Wilson being appointed as the British representative.[36]

The support for some form of inter-Allied council was, at least in part, because each belligerent hoped it would be a mechanism for the achievement of their own aims: for the French, to get the British to take over more of the Western Front; while Lloyd George trusted it would scupper the power and independence of the General Staff.[37] The following day, the British Prime Minister, dragging a reluctant Robertson with him, crossed the Channel and headed for Rapallo.

Over the course of two frantic days, the arrangements for the Supreme Inter-Allied Council were hammered out. In order to ensure 'better co-ordination of military action on the Western Front', the new council would be composed of the Prime Minister and a member of the government of each of the Allied powers, and entrusted with preparing recommendations for overall strategy. 'Sir William Robertson ostentatiously declined to attend the discussions on the Supreme Council', Lloyd George wrote acidly. 'His general sulkiness was apparent to all. He left the room with a flaunting stride . . . just stopping on the way for an instant to instruct Sir Maurice Hankey to make a note of the fact that he was not present during the discussions.'[38] The struggle between Robertson's immovable object and Lloyd George's unstoppable force would go on.

Meanwhile, as the rattled Allied leaders gradually coalesced on the need for unified command, the Flanders offensive was left to stagger on. Maurice Hankey, who had long ago warned Lloyd George to face up to his responsibility for the Ypres offensive, claimed that the Prime Minister let the battle go on in order to discredit Robertson and Haig and other so-called 'westerners'. If the battle continued, and so obviously failed to achieve its stated objectives, then Lloyd George – so he reasoned – would be strengthened in the coming battle over Allied command.[39] If that was true then it amounts to a gross abandonment of those who found themselves in the Salient, tasked with getting on to that blasted ridge, through the mud, rain, filth, darkness and endless shellfire. For his part, Currie just got on with it, arranging with General Plumer for Second Army to simulate attacks up and down the line on 6 November, while ordering preliminary barrages and surprise bombardments by all available guns and howitzers in the days leading up to the attack.[40]

After 30 October the weather improved, although a clinging mist continued to hamper the on-going search for German batteries and the ground remained as bad as ever. Inevitably guns were 'continually smothered in mud from bursting shell', and special care had to be taken to cover them up when not firing and keep working parts cleaned and oiled. Indeed, it was remarkable how well the field artillery stood up to repeated firing in such trying conditions. The Canadians found that almost all the wooden platforms disintegrated, sooner or later, in the cloying mud, although no effort was spared in trying to hold them together. It was found that a raft of 3-inch planks spiked to sleepers and supported on piles driven deep into the earth worked as well as could be expected, although when no wood was available, batteries had to make do with laying down a bed of sandbags, covered with a sheet of corrugated iron.[41] Shelter for the men who serviced the guns was, as might have been expected, rudimentary in the extreme. For Lieutenant H. L. Sheppard of 39th Battery, Canadian Field Artillery, they had to make do with scraping a shallow trench in the ground, building up a wall with sandbags filled with mud, and then stretching a tarpaulin across the top. 'You ate your meals in there and slept in there and it was only big enough, with three or four of us in there, if one fellow crawled over to get over to his side, the mud dropped off his boots into the other fellow's tea and it was almost unbelievable.'[42]

1st and 2nd Canadian Divisions moved up to the front on the night of 5/6 November, with orders to take the Green Line, which included the village of Passchendaele and the small hamlets of Mosselmarkt and Goudberg at its northern edge.[43] The conditions were as bad as ever. 'The whole countryside was a complete morass', wrote Magnus McIntyre Hood of 24/Battalion (2nd Division). 'It was impossible to move any artillery in the deep mud, because horses sank in it right up to their necks and had to be abandoned. For our infantry, the approach to the line had to be along duckboards of slats laid on top of the mud. They provided fairly secure footing, but to step off into the mud was fatal. Men fell into the morass and just disappeared.'[44] Given how treacherous the ground was becoming it was difficult to see how operations could proceed for much longer. 'The Belgian Front is the worst I have seen so far', remembered a stretcher-bearer, Private Andrew Coulter. 'Shell holes without number merge into one another and are so close together that walking among them is almost impossible. Nearly all are full of water of a green colour or tinged red with blood. Roads, except those kept in repair to bring up supplies, are completely obliterated.'[45]

Currie undoubtedly found the strain of seeing his corps put through such an ordeal to be deeply troubling, yet he persevered with his usual tenacity. 'The Australians tried to take it, the British tried to take it and now they had called on the Canadians' was how one veteran remembered a speech that he gave in the run-up to the attack.[46] Every night, after dinner, he would hold a meeting with his staff, who reported on how operations were proceeding. His leadership style was reminiscent of General Plumer's: professional and deeply consultative. According to Colonel William Rae, who worked at Canadian HQ, after listening to the reports Currie would then 'express his own views and his intentions for the future and it was open to anyone to put forward views, either in amplification or possibly, on some occasions, in criticism of the Corps Commander's own views'. After everything had been thrashed out, Currie made his final decision and 'left no one in any doubt whatever about what he wished to be done'.[47]

Despite the deteriorating situation, Currie was in no doubt that his men would take the ridge. 'It has got to be done', he told William Griesbach's 1 Brigade, standing on a table, with the battalions formed up in a square. 'It is going to be your business to make the final assault and capture the ridge. I promise you that you will not be called upon to advance – as you never will be – until everything has been done that can be done to clear the way for you.'[48]

Currie was as good as his word. In contrast to the artillery barrages that had preceded the attacks on 26 and 30 October, the creeping barrage on 6 November was a fearsome spectacle; a roaring typhoon of shells that blocked out the ridge in drifting smoke and smothered the German batteries around the Salient. For the assault that day, Currie managed to scrape together an 18-pounder for every eight metres of front and a howitzer for every 32 metres.[49] Together with batteries of heavy machine-guns, the artillery was organized into a formidable barrage consisting of seven layers – up to 700 yards in depth – that would fall in front of the attacking infantry. Moreover, because of the softness of the ground, it was decided that a significant percentage of shrapnel shells (with percussion fuses that detonated on contact) would be adjusted to explode in the air, hopefully just above the ground, where they would be more effective.[50]

At Zero Hour (6 a.m.) the barrage came down about 150 yards in front of the leading lines and began churning up the ground 100 yards every eight minutes – the by now standard speed of the creeping barrage at Third Ypres. On the left, 1st Division was to clear the northern part of the ridge. Griesbach had told his men that 'success lies always in snuggling up close to Brother Boche' and they did not let him down, clambering out of their trenches and following the creeping barrage as closely as they dared.[51] Major A. W. Sparling, commanding officer of 1/Battalion, reported that 'B', 'C' and 'D' Companies 'experienced very little resistance from the enemy until the first objective was reached', only isolated groups that were 'quickly disposed of'. There were no enemy wire and no major trench works to speak of, so most of the defenders had to make do with thin scrapes in the ground, just covered over with camouflage, and these were swiftly overrun. In Mosselmarkt the garrison could shelter in a series of cellars, but they seem to have been caught by the creeping barrage and were mostly wiped out.[52]

In 2nd Division's sector, the enemy's response was equally fitful. North of Passchendaele the men of 28/Battalion (Northwest) found the German counter-bombardment to be 'extremely heavy but erratic' – as if unsure of the battalion's location – while the soft state of the ground 'greatly localised' the effects of the shells, which plunged into the mud and water and frequently bogged down before exploding. 'On that particular day . . . it was safe to say that there wouldn't have been anybody come out of that show if the ground had been hard', remembered Private W. McCombie-Gilbert of 31/Battalion.[53] About 500 yards from their objective, the attackers were met with bursts of heavy machine-gun fire, but pressed on, slipping over the ground to outflank the defenders. The ground was 'strewn with dead', including a large number of Germans who had evidently dropped their weapons and fled at the first sight of the Canadians. The 'greater majority were found lying in heaps' – presumably killed by the bombardment.[54]

The capture of Passchendaele had been entrusted to 27/Battalion (City of Winnipeg). Private W. E. Turner was one of the soldiers who would make the assault. 'We were at the foot of the ridge and right in absolutely nothing but mud and water and nothing was dry at all', he remembered.

We were told to rest the best we could until time for jump off. I was so exhausted that I lay there right in that mud and I went sound asleep until the sergeant major came along and he shook me. He said, 'Come on, time to go.' We got just ahead of the front line fellows when the barrage started and it was really a wonderful barrage. Our training for Passchendaele had called for us to get right up close to it and we sure did. I don't know, we must have had some casualties but it was dark at the time and I don't know who was hit. You never know in a job like that what's going on any more than a few yards from you. Anyone who has had front line service will tell you that.[55]

As soon as the Canadians went forward, the defenders fired off their SOS flares, but the resulting barrage only came down after the attackers had cleared their jumping-off positions. 'Our men followed the barrage evenly and were well controlled by their leaders', recorded the battalion war diary. 'It was found that the enemy had been occupying a line of shell holes less than fifty yards in advance of our jumping off trench. The effectiveness of our barrage was shown by the fact it immediately put out of action the enemy MGs in his outpost lines.' The battalion pushed on across the flooded ground, advancing 'in lines of sections in single file' (rather than waves in extended order), which tended to reduce casualties and allow for greater control. 'The spirit and fighting qualities shown by the men was magnificent and the supervision and leadership exercised by the officers was of the highest standard', it was noted. 'All ranks made the assault with great dash.'[56] Under heavy machine-gun fire, they pushed on into the village of Passchendaele, clearing cellars and bayoneting any Germans who refused to surrender.

Against the Canadians was 11th Division, which had moved up to the front several days earlier, and would be all but destroyed in the subsequent fighting. A prisoner said that the attack 'was so rapid that they did not come into action, being captured in a concrete dugout'. Another said that the Canadian barrage was too heavy.[57] German dead were everywhere, particularly around the church, where a cluster of seventy-eight bodies was later recovered.[58] Despite brave and determined resistance, the Germans had no choice but to gradually fall back through the village. The men of I Battalion, 51 Infantry Regiment, met the attackers with 'lively machine-gun and rifle fire', but after being outflanked, they were forced to retreat. With heavy artillery fire blocking them off from their supporting units, it was almost impossible to mount a properly coordinated counter-attack. The problem was finding out what was going on. All telephone wires had been 'shot to shreds' and it was not even possible to be sure the village of Passchendaele remained in German hands. It was decided to organize small patrols, led by officers, to push on through the 'curtain fire' and find out for themselves. They soon ran into Canadian troops east of Passchendaele, confirming that it had fallen.[59]

By 8 a.m. reports were coming into Canadian Corps HQ that its men were established in the village. Private Turner, whose company pushed on through the battered, shell-torn streets, saw a bedraggled group of German soldiers retreating in panic, only to get stuck in a swamp at the far side of the ridge. 'We shouted to them to come back', he remembered, only for the Germans to ignore them and continue struggling through the mire. 'Things weren't too rough at the time and we weren't feeling too bad about it and we shouted for them to come back and they wouldn't, so there was nothing we could do, we had to finish them off.' Turner was in no doubt that they had no choice. 'The next day them fellows were up against you and you couldn't have any qualms about things like that under the circumstances.'[60]

German resistance in the village may have been snuffed out, but sporadic artillery fire continued for several hours, with shells plunging down and snipers' bullets whistling overhead. Consolidation was a slow, time-consuming and exhausting business, particularly in such an exposed position, and the Canadians suffered casualties for most of the afternoon. 'The utter hopelessness of our position was devastating', remembered Magnus McIntyre Hood; 'we lay there, in shell holes half-filled with water, and just waited for whatever would happen.' Suddenly there was a 'great crash, and blackness' as a shell burst a few feet from where he was crouched. He would wake up hours later in a hospital bed with spinal injuries.[61] Others were not so fortunate. Private Peter Robertson (27/Battalion) won a posthumous

Victoria Cross for his outstanding bravery that day: rushing a machine-gun nest during the attack and then bringing in two wounded men under fire. Just as he was about to return with his second casualty, he came under 'a veritable storm of bullets' and was killed.[62] Yet the Canadians held on. Currie had done it.

Had Passchendaele been lost with a month or two of the fighting season remaining it would have produced a significantly greater impact in Army Group headquarters in Courtrai than it actually did. Instead of being the beginning of a series of breakthrough operations, it only marked the final, stuttering phase of an offensive whose flame had gone out long ago. Fourth Army reported the news in typically sober style. 'After heavy and fluctuating fighting, Passchendaele remained in enemy hands in the evening. Faced with an extremely strong counter-attack by enemy infantry and artillery, our counter-attack was unsuccessful . . . Otherwise, our line is unchanged by yesterday's fighting.'[63] At Courtrai, Crown Prince Rupprecht acknowledged its loss, but doubted whether it was worth the trouble to recapture. After being told that he could not be supplied with fresh troops, he accepted that the line would have to remain where it was for the time being.[64]

The ridge may have fallen, but among German troops in the line, there was understandable pride in how hard they had fought. 'Today was another day of major combat across a vast front', wrote Reinhard Lewald. 'The fighting raged from early in the morning until late in the evening. Again, the English failed to break through our Flanders front. But in our divisional sector, where the heaviest fighting took place, the enemy finally managed to seize the high ground of Passchendaele and the village itself.' Lewald, whose divisional artillery had just won a special commendation, comforted himself with the thought that the enemy had suffered 'extremely heavy losses', and only made gains owing to 'vastly superior numbers'.[65]

For Sir Douglas Haig, the capture of Passchendaele and the securing of the ridge was the cause of a great deal of relief, albeit with a sense that the battle was still unfinished. 'Today was a very important success', he wrote in his diary. 'Passchendaele was taken as also were

Mosselmarkt and Goudberg. The whole position had been most methodically fortified. Yet our troops succeeded in capturing *all* their objectives early in the day with small loss – "under 700 men"!' Yet whatever pride he felt must have been tempered by the knowledge that his offensive was now at an end and he had run out of time. GHQ had received orders to send General Plumer to head Britain's deployment to Italy the day after Passchendaele had fallen. 'Was ever an Army Commander and his Staff sent off to another theatre of war in the middle of a battle?' Haig asked incredulously.[66] He installed Sir Henry Rawlinson in Plumer's place for the concluding operation on 10 November, when Currie's forces would strengthen their hold to the north of Passchendaele up to Hill 52, the highest point on the ridge.[67] As for Plumer, he seems to have taken the news stoically.

'You and I have got the sack,' he is said to have told Tim Harington, who would remain at his chief's side during their sojourn in Italy.[68]

Plumer called into Poperinge on the morning of 9 November to say farewell to Currie. The old man evidently found it difficult to remain composed. 'Was very much and visibly moved', wrote the Canadian in his diary.[69]

It was sometimes said that the Canadians had been given 'the almost impossible to do, and did it'.[70] But the cost, as always, had been paid in blood, in shattered bodies, and in families torn apart. Canadian losses in Flanders had been just as Currie had predicted – just shy of 16,000 battle casualties.[71] Whether the capture of the ridge justified the effort became a topic of almost immediate debate, although Currie tried to put a brave face on it in his reports back home. 'We were brought to this part of the battlefield for a special purpose', he wrote to Sir William Hearst, the Conservative Premier of Ontario, on 14 November:

> It was absolutely necessary to gain certain ground, and in order to make sure of it the Commander-in-Chief sent for the Canadians . . . The year 1917 has been a glorious year for the Canadian Corps. We have taken every objective from the enemy we started for and have not had a single reverse. Vimy, Arleux, Fresnoy, Avion, Hill 70 and Passchendaele all signify hard fought battles and notable victories. I know that no other Corps has had the same unbroken series of

successes. All this testifies to the discipline, training, leadership and fine fighting qualities of the Canadians. Words cannot express the pride one feels in being associated with such splendid soldiers. The only regret one has, and it is a very sincere one, is that one has lost so many gallant comrades, men whom a young country like Canada, or in fact any country, could ill afford to lose.[72]

As Currie had predicted, the losses sustained in taking the ridge would always overshadow the Canadian Corps's achievement of November 1917. Currie would even have to endure regular post-war criticisms that he had been too eager to sacrifice Canadian troops for dubious battlefield honours. His near-mutiny on being sent to Flanders, as well as his unyielding insistence on time and preparation before he attacked, was then either unknown or too operationally sensitive to be widely publicized. He even won a libel case in 1928, suing a Canadian newspaper for allegations that he had wasted the lives of his men in the final days of the war.[73]

The Canadian Corps would reach its peak operational effectiveness in the late summer and autumn of 1918, when it spearheaded the BEF's Hundred Days campaign and took a starring role in an unbroken series of victories that brought the German Army to the verge of total defeat.[74] Yet what the Canadians achieved at Passchendaele arguably surpassed anything they would do in 1918. According to the historian Daniel Dancocks, Passchendaele was 'at least the equal of any other victory they won on the Western Front'.[75] The ground at Third Ypres was, without doubt, the worst they would ever encounter; the enemy much stronger than they would face in 1918. Private Kenneth Foster, who served with 62/Battalion, felt that Passchendaele was 'without exception, one of the toughest engagements that the Canadian Corps ever went through', primarily because of the conditions in which it was fought. 'The battlefield was just one sea of mud and water', he remembered, 'which made it exceptionally difficult for all ranks, especially the Artillery Corps.' Moreover, guns and horses, as well as men, would simply disappear beneath the surface and never be seen again, 'for there were no trenches, just shell holes full of water'. For him, Passchendaele came 'top of the class'.[76]

Epilogue

History must give its verdict.

Sir Tim Harington[1]

On 11 November 1917, a day after the final attack at Passchendaele had petered out, a top-secret conference was held at the German Supreme Command (which had now moved to Mons in Belgium). The meeting had been called to discuss operations for the following year. The Bolshevik seizure of power in St Petersburg, or Petrograd, on 7 November meant that Russia had now, for all practicable purposes, exited the war, leaving German territorial ambitions in the east unopposed. The question remained about what could be done in the west; whether Germany should settle for a compromise peace – and the great shock this would be to a people who had been nourished on stories of victory for years – or strike a decisive blow. As might have been expected, the German military opted to stay true to its traditions. Hermann von Kuhl, who was present at the meeting, noted afterwards that 'There was no other choice.'[2] Germany would stake everything on a massive attack in the west, aiming to destroy the Allies before the Americans could intervene in strength. The U-boats had failed. Now Germany, once again, would place her fate in the hands of her Army.

The Spring Offensive, which finally opened on 21 March 1918, through a thick morning fog, was one of the worst days in the history of the British Army. The spearhead of Ludendorff's vast attack, comprising upwards of seventy divisions, spread across three armies and supported by over 6,000 guns, battered against the British line in a day of unremitting terror. Sir Hubert Gough's Fifth Army, which had been given the unenviable task of holding the southern sector of the front around Péronne, found itself being overrun. Of the twenty-one divisions that held the front line that day, nineteen had seen action at Third Ypres and had lost, in the words of the official historian, 'a large proportion of their best soldiers whose places had been filled, if filled at all, by raw drafts and transfers'.[3] Although Gough had been warning for months about poor defences and too few reserves, the collapse of his position demanded a scapegoat, and on 3 April Haig told the Fifth Army commander that he was being dismissed and must return to England immediately.[4]

It did not take long for the magnitude of the disaster, and the sheer scale of the German assault, to cause an urgent rethink about whether a renewed British offensive from Ypres would be possible. Sir Herbert Plumer, now back at Second Army after a winter in Italy, surveyed the British positions on the scarred Passchendaele Ridge, indefensible at the best of times, and wondered what they should do. When Tim Harington suggested that they withdraw, Plumer walked out of the room.

'I won't have it' was all he could say.

Shortly afterwards, the general returned, laying his hand on Harington's shoulder.

'You are right,' he said, with a heavy heart, 'issue the orders.'

Plumer hated to do it. 'It was a scene which I shall never forget', recalled Harington. 'There was the man, who by sheer determination and pluck had held the Ypres Salient for years against all comers and who had gained Messines and Passchendaele, being forced to withdraw.'[5]

That night British troops slipped silently off the Passchendaele Ridge. The ground that had been won at such cost was now left to the Germans – if they wanted it – while Second Army returned to its familiar haunts closer to the battered city of Ypres, where they were once again overlooked by those ghostly ridges. The loss of Passchendaele without a shot being fired seems, in many respects, to sum up the futility and utter pointlessness of the whole campaign at Ypres in the summer of 1917. In the end credits for Paul Gross's 2008 feature film, *Passchendaele*, a line of text notes how 'On October 26, 1917 the Canadian Corps entered the Battle of Passchendaele. Within a week they captured the ruined village at a cost of 5,000 lives . . . An enemy offensive the following spring recaptured the hard won ground in less than a week . . .'[6] If the ridge that had cost so much blood to conquer could be abandoned so quickly, then what was the point of it? Surely it would have been better not to have taken it in the first place?

Such a damning judgement on Third Ypres remains commonplace: the utterly futile ending to a thoroughly depressing and miserable campaign. But this question should be considered carefully – it would certainly not have been the view of those German commanders who had seen for themselves what the ridge meant. Although the battle was not particularly controversial in Germany, it was generally recognized as one of the worst ordeals of the war. In his order of the day, issued on 5 December 1917, Crown Prince Rupprecht hailed all those who had taken part in 'the most violent of all battles fought to date'. Eighty-six divisions had been rotated through Flanders, including twenty-two that had completed two tours, while most artillery units had been engaged at one time or another. For Rupprecht the outcome was an unqualified victory for the Fatherland. 'Despite the employment of immense quantities of men and materiel, the enemy achieved absolutely nothing.' The Army's courageous defence in Flanders allowed German units to conduct devastating blows against the Russians and Italians and stand on the brink of complete triumph.[7] Lossberg agreed, calling it 'the most formidable defensive battle of the war', and taking pride in the heroism of the German Army that 'fought doggedly' in a swampy crater field under the eyes of enemy aircraft for months on end.[8]

The story of a successful defensive battle that had all gone to plan (and which German memoirists were keen to propagate) should not deflect from how enormously difficult Third Ypres was for the German Army. Historians have tended to concentrate on the mistakes and weaknesses of the British High Command, and have sometimes downplayed the awful experience of the 'Flanders bloodbath' for the defenders.[9] Yet it should not be underestimated how sorely pressed the German Army became, particularly during September and October 1917. The sapping effects of operating in the open in such wet weather were bad enough, but the German soldier had to cope with

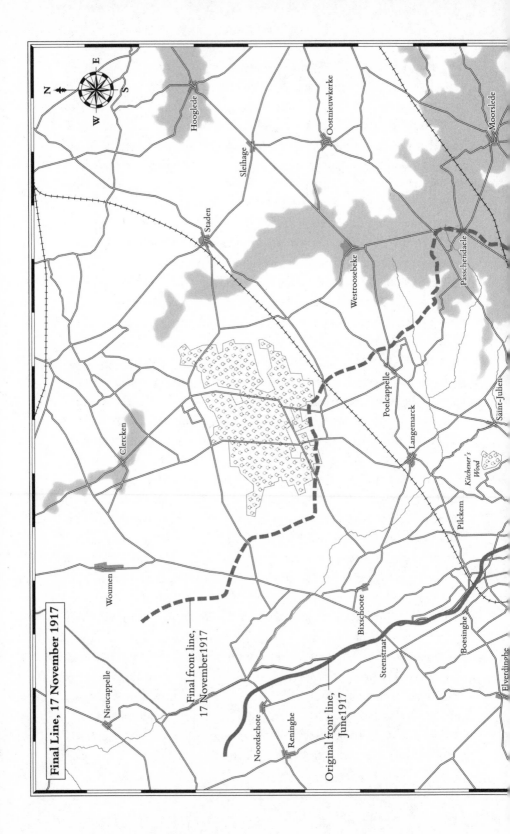

Final Line, 17 November 1917

Final front line,
17 November 1917

Original front line,
June 1917

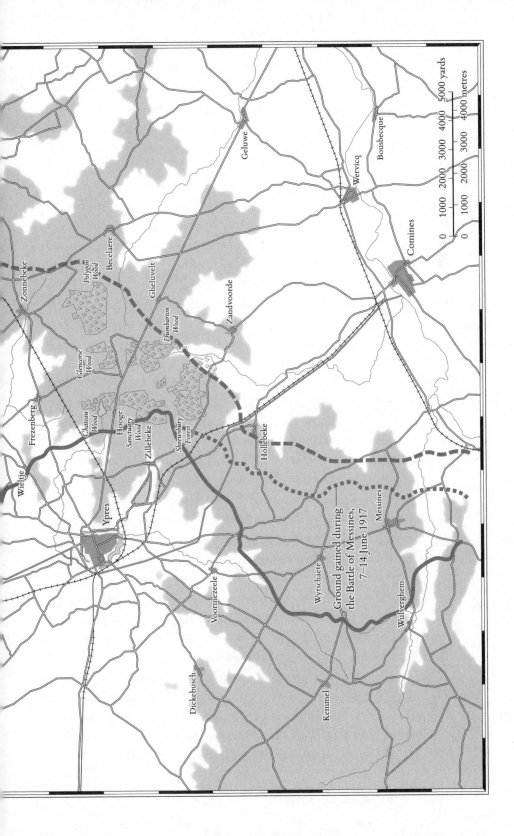

Ground gained during
the Battle of Messines,
7–14 June 1917

Zonnebeke
Becelaere
Polygon Wood
Gheluvelt
Geluwe
Dumbarton Wood
Zandvoorde
Wervicq
Bousbecque
Comines
Glencorse Wood
Frezenberg
Wieltje
Chateau Wood
Hooge
Sanctuary Wood
Zillebeke
Shrewsbury Forest
Hollebeke
Ypres
Voormezeele
Wytschaete
Messines
Dickebusch
Kemmel
Wulverghem

0   1000   2000   3000   4000   5000 yards
0   1000   2000   3000   4000 metres

the perils of seemingly endless drumfire, poison gas and low-flying aircraft, while surviving on what little food and water could be brought up to the front. Even the best units could be reduced to a shambling, lice-ridden bunch of stragglers after a few days on the battlefield. When 465 Infantry Regiment (238th Division) came out of the line on 30 October, no company was more than thirty strong. The sight of these 'emaciated, battered and filthy' men was almost too much for a Major Wilcke, who watched the thin columns trudge by. Shaking, with tears in his eyes, Wilcke took his helmet off with both hands and paid tribute to what he called the '*Helden von Passchendaele*' – the heroes of Passchendaele.[10]

There were few battles as mentally and physically challenging to the German Army as Flanders was in 1917. German tactics were highly effective in the early stages of the battle, when Gough's attempt to drive deep into the German line perfectly suited the use of the *Eingreif* divisions, but Plumer's adoption of limited 'bite-and-hold' attacks in September and October 1917 was much more difficult to resist. The significant challenges that faced German commanders in this phase of the fighting has, for too long, been either unknown or largely ignored by English-language writers, thus distorting our understanding of the battle. German-language sources (whether unit reports, personal diaries or published accounts) make it abundantly clear how difficult it was either to resist Plumer's attacks or to make any kind of meaningful dent in the British positions once they had been consolidated. Passchendaele thus revealed how the tactical advantage, which had been so clearly with the defenders since 1914, was now moving over to the attackers.

In contrast to Germany, the controversy over what Lloyd George called 'the campaign of the mud' has never abated in Britain and her former Dominions. Haig died in January 1928. He was accorded a memorial procession through London and a service at Westminster Abbey – witnessed by thousands of mourners – before being laid to rest in Dryburgh Abbey, near his ancestral home of Bemersyde.[11] He was, it seemed, unrepentant to the last, convinced that he had done his best and there had been no other way. When Maurice Hankey gave a small dinner party shortly after the war ended, Haig was invited. During the evening, Hankey repeatedly asked about the fighting in Flanders and whether the decision to attack, and keep on attacking, had been the right one, but Haig never wavered in his responses. Hankey came away from the evening with the certainty that 'Haig's mind was so completely free from anything in the nature of self-reproach'.[12] For Haig, as he wrote in his despatch on the fighting of 1917, notwithstanding the disappointments of the campaign, 'the ultimate destruction of the enemy's field forces has been brought appreciably nearer'.[13] Such a conclusion was strengthened by the publication of Hermann von Kuhl's account in 1929, which suggested that had the British *not* attacked at Ypres, 'the Germans would have seized the initiative and attacked the Allies at their weakest place'. Thus the British 'bridged the crisis in France', drawing in German reserves and allowing time for the French Army to recover from their collapse of morale in the spring.[14]

Haig's justification of Passchendaele as being an ultimately successful attritional battle was, in truth, entirely predictable; after all, he had said the same thing about the Somme a year earlier. The failure to achieve a breakthrough in 1916 – one that Haig had explicitly planned for – was written off as an appropriate and prudent exercise in pre-planning, rather than as a fundamental error in operational thinking. John Terraine, who echoed Haig's comments on Third Ypres as being a key moment in the 'wearing-out struggle', made the same excuse, claiming that the most convincing argument in favour of the offensive was the German reaction to it.[15] The only problem was that such a judgement could only be made in hindsight. Haig did not fight in Flanders to grind down the German Army or to secure important ridges – no matter what he subsequently claimed – but to achieve a breakthrough and liberate the Belgian coast. As for Kuhl's idea that Third Ypres prevented a German attack, this seems unlikely. It is clear that German intelligence knew something was badly wrong in the French Army, but the larger strategic context ruled out any offensive operations against Pétain's forces; they had, after all, just executed a major withdrawal on the Western Front.[16]

Hubert Gough, whose career had been cut short in April 1918, always understood clearly how Haig wanted to fight at Ypres. 'Haig was always dreaming of cavalry pushing through', he wrote to Sir James Edmonds after the war. 'In any battle from Neuve Chapelle in 1915 onwards to the Battle of the Somme he never abandoned this dream.'[17] This grand breakthrough, with cavalry in the vanguard, was not just the stuff of fantasy; after all, Haig himself had raised the tantalizing prospect of using 'cavalry in masses' at the War Cabinet in June. He fought his battle according to his understanding of war that had been drilled into him at the Staff College, which prioritized bold manoeuvres, decisive offensives and culminating attacks. As the historians Robin Prior and Trevor Wilson have noted, 'Haig's overarching determination to exploit the supposed crack in German morale and accomplish a great sweep to the coast distorted the course of action at every stage.'[18] It is true that Haig consented to limited operations under Plumer in September and October, but he never wavered from his belief that, sooner or later, the breakthrough would come. Had Haig wanted the battle to be conducted strictly on attritional or 'step-by-step' methods – as the War Cabinet had instructed – he could easily have done so.

Over the decades, historians have not failed to point out Haig's errors at Third Ypres: his inexplicable optimism in believing that he could clear the Belgian coast; the fatal delay after Messines; his decision to appoint an unsuitable commander in Gough; his failure to thrash out the details of the plan and order Gough to take the Gheluvelt Plateau; and his decision to continue attacking when all hope of a decisive result had gone.[19] Correlli Barnett, who collaborated with John Terraine on the BBC's 1964 television series *The Great War*, found Terraine's analysis of the evolution of the Passchendaele campaign (which was contained in his 1963 work, *Douglas Haig. The Educated Soldier*) to be 'perhaps the least convincing passage in an otherwise excellent biography'. For him, Haig's decision 'to attack the most powerful army in the war with only an Army Group supported by one ally in disintegration and the other paralysed by morale failure' was unnecessary and stupid. It was 'not merely historical hindsight to show how and why Haig's calculations were unsound', he writes, 'for there was, after all, another Commander-in-Chief who at the time read the situation correctly and who adopted the correct policy – Pétain'.[20]

Perhaps the real tragedy of Third Ypres was not that it was fought at all, or that the British did not break through, but that *they did not always fight to their strengths*. By the summer of 1917 the BEF had evolved a battle-winning method of fighting, with artillery-heavy 'bite-and-hold' attacks that could gain (albeit limited amounts of) ground and take a heavy toll on any defenders unfortunate enough to get in their way. Given good weather and enough time, the British were able to inflict at least as many casualties on the enemy as they themselves received.[21] And in General Plumer 'bite and hold' had its greatest architect. Yet the decision to give Gough the lead and allow him to, firstly, mount a high-risk breakthrough attempt on 31 July, and, secondly, get sucked into repeated, small-scale attacks throughout August that wore down divisions and achieved little of note, was a huge mistake that reflects poorly on Haig and his choice of subordinates after three years of war. It was exactly the same mistake that he had made in 1916 on the Somme (albeit involving General Sir Henry Rawlinson, not Gough): going for a hugely ambitious breakthrough, and then, when it failed, letting the battle meander on without sufficient organization and structure. It was only when the operation was on the brink of failure that Haig was forced to intervene and modify his approach.

When Plumer finally got his chance, he took it with both hands. In contrast to Gough's floundering, Plumer's time in the Salient produced three of the most outstanding examples of operational success during the war: Menin Road, Polygon Wood and Broodseinde (on top of his earlier victory at Messines Ridge). Only modest amounts of ground may have been secured in these attacks, but it was of the highest value and regarded as such by the enemy. The effect of these hammer blows was pulverizing: reversing the favourable situation the Germans had enjoyed since the onset of the battle (with their reliance on defence-in-depth and *Eingreif* divisions) and provoking them into repeated, wasteful counter-attacks. Indeed, it has only rarely been appreciated how effective these operations were and how hard they pushed the Kaiser's army. As German commanders ruefully conceded, there was, quite literally, nothing they could do to stop properly executed limited attacks. Moreover, to mastermind a

sequence of such battles in a fortnight was not just very impressive
from a logistical and administrative perspective, but also created – at
least temporarily – a higher operational tempo than the Germans
could cope with. As a solution to the dilemmas of trench warfare, this
was about as good as it was ever going to get.

The system broke down of course. When Plumer was denied the
two vital ingredients for success – time and good weather – it was
almost inevitable that normal service would resume and the British
would come to a halt. And while he must take some criticism for not
remonstrating harder with Haig about the futility of maintaining the
offensive into October and November, Plumer had shown the way.[22]
Had the Second Army commander been in charge from the beginning, had the offensive begun a month earlier, and had 'bite and hold'
been the guiding principle upon which British operations were based,
who knows what could have been achieved? *It is possible that a major
victory could have been won in the late summer and autumn of 1917.* While this
might not have entailed the complete liberation of the Belgian coast, it
is not inconceivable that continued British pressure, heavier German
losses and the effect of regular hammer blows might have convinced
the German High Command that it was best to cut their losses. Had
they decided to retreat to a better defensive position, perhaps giving
up some of the ports and the rail junction at Roulers, it would have
made their hold on western Belgium increasingly precarious and
handed the British a major victory. It would have almost certainly
sparked calls for renewed talks on the status of Belgium and raised the
possibility of a compromise peace.

There is therefore good reason to claim that the Third Battle of
Ypres was a 'lost victory' for the British Army in 1917. Plumer's
battles between 20 September and 4 October have never been given
the recognition they deserve, and the failure to conduct these kinds of
limited attacks earlier in the battle marks a great lost opportunity.
The blame for this must lie with Haig. For him the dramatic breakthrough had to happen, and 'bite and hold', if it was anything, was
just a temporary response to conditions in the field. Thus Haig's popular reputation as a stolid commander, unimaginatively following a
stale doctrine of attrition for four years, masks the truth that he was

a compulsive gambler; with the compulsive gambler's habit of throwing good money after bad, convinced that this time, finally, the cards would fall into place and he would win a big score. The tragedy was that Haig knew how high the stakes were, and how badly the odds were stacked against him.

The true story of Kiggell and the mud – which opened this history – is, in some respects, even worse than the legend would have us believe. Haig and GHQ were *well aware of how bad conditions were*, but still pressed ahead anyway. Both Haig's diary and his despatch on 'The Campaign of 1917' are littered with references to the bad weather and difficult ground conditions.[23] There was no fatal ignorance or wilful blindness, only a stubborn belief that however bad the ground conditions became, they in no way affected the reasons to keep fighting. But this is not to say that Haig was the only one to blame. Indeed, Lloyd George's vitriolic criticism smacks of someone who was only too aware that he bore a heavy responsibility for what happened. While it is true that the War Cabinet did not see all the intelligence that Haig and Robertson possessed (particularly over the state of the German Army), Lloyd George still had the right to intervene and – as had been made perfectly clear to GHQ – stop the offensive at any moment should he deem it unprofitable. Yet the Prime Minister let things slip. He seemed uninterested at times: distracted by his dreams of Italian glory, and only too willing to believe what Robertson told him without subjecting it to proper scrutiny. He would regret it for the rest of his life.

After the war, Lloyd George would profess his innocence: the constraints of the coalition and the iron support the generals received from Bonar Law's Unionists, as well as much of Fleet Street, prevented him from stopping the offensive. 'I had no expert military counsel which I could weigh against theirs', he wrote. 'I was not aware at the time that the French Generals and some of our own Generals thought the attack was a mistake . . . Profound though my own apprehensions of failure were, I was a layman and in matters of military strategy did not possess the knowledge and training that would justify me in overriding soldiers of such standing and experience.'[24]

Whether Lloyd George was right remains a matter of speculation. The historians Robin Prior and Trevor Wilson have dismissed these excuses as little more than special pleading: 'the power to decide on strategy rested with him'. Moreover, they rubbish the idea that had Lloyd George taken on Haig it would have sparked his resignation and ignited a coup against Downing Street (as has sometimes been suggested). 'There can be but one explanation as to why Haig was able to embark on the Third Ypres campaign', they write: 'the civilian rulers of Britain gave their consent.'[25]

This stark conclusion should, however, not be taken too far, and a number of points remain in Lloyd George's favour. Firstly, he maintained (correctly) that he had not seen any detailed plans for the Flanders offensive prior to June 1917, by which time the Battle of Messines, the first element of Haig's 'northern operation', had already taken place. Although Haig had made it clear that should Nivelle fail, he would focus his efforts in Flanders, much was left unsaid. Moreover, Lloyd George's tactical retreat at Paris on 4 May, in which he stated that he would leave the details of any future attacks to the generals, was not a 'blank cheque' that allowed Haig and Robertson to do whatever they liked. Forthcoming operations were always assumed to be based on two premises: firstly, that they would not be major breakthrough attempts, but aimed at wearing down the enemy; and, secondly, that they would depend upon significant French support.[26] The structure of coalition government was another factor. Strategic instructions had to come from the War Cabinet, and, whether he liked it or not, Lloyd George could not simply ride roughshod over the wishes of his closest colleagues – men who had once been some of his fiercest enemies in Parliament. Together, they had to make a decision over the battle and consent to its continuation. Had Lloyd George pressed too hard, it is not inconceivable that there could have been a major breakdown in relations in Whitehall, and, in the end, it was a risk that he was not willing to take.[27]

Battles in the Great War, like enormous planetary bodies, also tended to have huge gravitational pulls. Thousands of tons of shells and supplies; hundreds of miles of extra roads and trenches; and complex billeting arrangements and training schedules – all required many weeks of preparation before an operation could go ahead and made it difficult, if not impossible, to change the location of attacks.[28] While Lloyd George certainly held primary responsibility for the direction of Britain's war effort, his generals exercised a great deal of influence in this matter. As would occur in 1917, the Commander-in-Chief could, effectively, present London with a *fait accompli* by marshalling his forces and, for example, beginning a preliminary bombardment without explicit authorization, thus raising the stakes in any subsequent decision. That Fifth Army's opening bombardment was allowed to begin on 16 July without full Cabinet authorization for the coming battle says much about the influence of Haig and GHQ. As Lloyd George would know all too well, *it was much more difficult to call a halt to an operation when the guns were already firing and the troops moving into position.* This was further exacerbated by the patchy delivery of information from the front and the fact that it was several days, sometimes weeks, after an attack had gone in that sufficient information was available to form an objective judgement on its success or not. But by this time the battle had moved on and the moment for intervention was lost. Unfortunately for Lloyd George, his visit to France in late September, which could have been an opportunity to rein Haig in, occurred at the precise moment of their greatest success so far: the Battle of Menin Road. It is, perhaps, understandable if Lloyd George shied away from taking such a drastic step when things, finally, seemed to be going the way of the British.

This uneasy, blurred situation was not just about personalities, but also reflected the continuing unclear state of Britain's civil and military relations throughout the Great War, where there was no 'fully developed system' for the prosecution of war.[29] At this point, the direction of Britain's strategic policy was shared – whether by design or accident – by both political leaders and military commanders, the balance between them waxing and waning at different times. The problem for Lloyd George was that without a convincing alternative strategic vision for the war, and without enough high-ranking soldiers committed to carrying it out, he was left to try and persuade and haggle as best he could, imprisoned by his own rhetoric of the 'knock out blow'. Indeed, it says much for the paucity of British strategic thinking that, by the fourth year of the war, there was no detailed and considered appreciation of how the war was to be won. In the absence of a thoroughly considered national strategy, Haig was left to get on with things as he saw fit. Tragically, because Lloyd George 'backed the wrong horse' in General Nivelle, he lost a great deal of authority in the spring of 1917, when, arguably, he needed it more than ever.

Few in the British Government emerged well from the swamps of Passchendaele. As the historians Dominick Graham and Shelford Bidwell have noted, Third Ypres remains 'the paradigm of the defects of the British High Command in the First World War: the head of state striving to direct grand strategy without the faintest understanding of its guiding principles, while his commander-in-chief in the field had one simple aim, to continue battering at the German war-machine until it cracked, cost what it may'.[30] Ultimately, the British people and their Dominion allies would pay the price for this fatal disconnect in civil–military relations. Indeed, in the final reckoning, perhaps the only ones who emerged with much credit from the wreck of 1917 were those who had no illusions about what they were up against and who made the best of a poor situation: Philippe Pétain (who looked upon the ruin of the French Army with cold objectivity and did what he could to sustain his men); Sir Herbert Plumer and Tim Harington (who made Second Army the most highly regarded headquarters in the British Army); and Sir Arthur Currie (who commanded one of the most effective forces on the Western Front and did everything he could not to squander it). These commanders, and their men, stared into the face of disaster and did not flinch, but carried on calmly and professionally, trusting in their own expertise to see them through.

At a distance of 100 years it is now possible to see a little more clearly through the fog of war and make a judgement on the Third Battle of Ypres. The story is, as perhaps is to be expected, more complex than the legend of the 'weeping staff officer'; more interesting than the stories of incompetence and ignorance. Arguably, the battle should never have been fought, with the British taking Pétain's lead and conserving their strength for the greater battle to come in 1918 when the

Americans, presumably, would be in France in strength. But if the battle had to be fought, then it was clear – as General Nivelle had discovered to his cost – that the grand, shattering breakthrough was not a viable option. The alternative – 'Pétain tactics' or 'bite and hold' – was the only way of making meaningful advances in the cauldron of the Western Front at this time: *the only game in town*. Haig's failure to grasp the importance of limited advances and firepower – the priceless advantage of being able to attack the enemy on ground and at a time of your own choosing – meant that his army floundered around for two months without really hurting the enemy. The heavy rainfall was unlucky, but the failure to make the most of his force was all Haig's fault. That his men, under the wise direction of General Plumer, almost gave him that decisive victory at Broodseinde on 4 October, was remarkable. Passchendaele, though, would ultimately prove to be a ridge too far.

'At the end of the Battle of Ypres we were as near to being unhinged as it was possible to be', wrote Frank Mellish, who had witnessed much of the battle with his artillery battery. 'We had lost our pals and we had lost much of our zest for life. We had become convinced that it was merely a matter of time before we too would take the count and we didn't seem to care.'[31] Although it would become commonly assumed that their commanders were sublimely indifferent to the conditions in which the rank and file served, a number of senior officers were deeply affected by the battle. Plumer would open the Memorial to the Missing at the Menin Gate in July 1927 with words of comfort for the relatives of those who were never recovered from the battlefield: 'He is not missing; he is here.'[32] As for Tim Harington, he was always haunted by doubts that they were to blame. 'I have knelt in Tyne Cot Cemetery below Passchendaele on that hallowed ground . . .' he wrote in his biography of his old chief. 'I have prayed in that cemetery oppressed with fear lest even one of those gallant comrades should have lost their life owing to any fault of neglect on that part of myself and the Second Army staff . . . All I can truthfully say is that we did our utmost. We could not have done more.'[33]

The cost was enormous. According to Sir James Edmonds, total British 'battle and trench wastage casualties' between 31 July and

12 November 1917 amounted to 244,897 men. Edmonds was at pains to point out that this compared favourably to the 419,654 casualties from the Battle of the Somme the preceding year and that at Ypres thousands of lightly wounded men were included in these figures (of whom up to 64 per cent later returned to front-line duty).[34] German losses were somewhat fewer, although historians have never been able to arrive at a universally accepted figure. According to the Reichsarchiv, Fourth Army – which held the front from the Belgian coast to Armentières – suffered 217,000 casualties for the period of the battle (between 21 July and 31 December 1917), including 55,000 dead and 48,000 missing.[35] The German Medical History recorded a slightly higher figure of 236,241 (consisting of 32,878 dead, 38,083 missing, and 165,280 wounded and evacuated) during a similar time period.[36] Therefore, it seems highly likely that German casualties broadly matched those of their attackers. As an exercise in attrition, it was, in large measure, a bloody draw – but because the BEF was smaller than its opponent, its losses were proportionally greater.[37]

In his great, unfinished work, *On War*, the military theorist Carl von Clausewitz once wrote that to be imbued with 'true military spirit', an army had to have the following defining characteristics:

> An army that maintains its cohesion under the most murderous fire; that cannot be shaken by imaginary fears and resists well-founded ones with all its might; that, proud of its victories, will not lose the strength to obey orders and its respect and trust for its officers even in defeat; whose physical power, like the muscles of an athlete, has been steeled by training in privation and effort; a force that regards such efforts as a means to victory rather than a curse of its cause; that is mindful of all these duties and qualities by virtue of the single powerful idea of the honour of its arms – *such an army is imbued with the true military spirit*.[38]

Such a description would surely belong to the BEF of 1917 as it struggled through one of the most murderous battles in the history of warfare. It was, without doubt, a remarkable army, composed of men from all sections of British life, as well as thousands of volunteers from the overseas Dominions – from Canada, South Africa, Australia and New Zealand – who crossed the seas, 'from the uttermost ends of the earth', to fight and die for King and Empire. That it maintained its morale and kept going through that awful summer and autumn, without sinking into defeatism or flaring up into mutiny, was nothing short of miraculous.

The horror of what happened on that battlefield would never fade. In 1920 the war reporter Philip Gibbs – who had seen Third Ypres at first hand – wrote that 'nothing that has been written is more than the pale image of the abomination of those battlefields, and that no pen or brush has yet achieved the picture of that Armageddon in which so many of our men perished'.[39] Gibbs's remarks remain true to this day. No matter what words are used to describe what happened – 'awful' and 'terrifying'; 'monstrous' or 'appalling' – they all ultimately feel pale and unsatisfactory. Perhaps they will always be, to a certain extent, inadequate in conveying the enormity of the battle with its peculiar sights, sounds and smells: bombardments that ripped men to pieces; gas fumes that choked the lungs and blistered the skin; awe-inspiring air battles that were as lethal as they were spectacular; quicksand-like mud that could suck the unwary traveller down into a bottomless abyss; and, finally, the sight of thousands of white headstones, clustered like small forests, marking the route of the advance. But the stark facts remain. Whatever the flawed reasoning behind the battle, the achievements of the BEF in fighting through the maelstrom of Passchendaele – what a Canadian soldier, Private George Bell, called 'the most awful place in the world' – should never be forgotten.[40]

Acknowledgements

Over the course of the three years that it has taken to research and write this book, I have been assisted by a small army of historians, librarians, archivists and friends. First of all, I would like to thank my agent, Peter Robinson, for his constant advice and support, as well as the great Eleo Gordon at Viking, who has been a wonderful editor. *Passchendaele: The Lost Victory of World War I* is one of the last books that Eleo has been involved with and it has been a privilege, as well as great fun, to work with her on it. Her successor, Daniel Crewe, has ensured that the transition to a new editor has been a seamless process. Mark Handsley also copy-edited the manuscript with commendable thoroughness. In the US, Dan Gerstle has been extremely supportive of the project and his close reading of the text has helped to eliminate a number of inconsistencies, resulting in a better book. The wisdom of a number of fellow historians, researchers and scholars, freely given, has been invaluable throughout and I would like to thank the following: Mrs Delia Bettaney; Dr Jonathan Boff; Dr Tony Cowan; Dr Marcus Faulkner; Dr Robert Foley; Dr Tim Gale; Dr Saul Kelly; Dr William Mitchinson; Philipp Rauh; Professor Andrew Rice; Edwin Ride; and Professor Peter Simkins.

I am fortunate in being able to work at the Joint Services Command and Staff College at the UK Defence Academy in Shrivenham, Wiltshire. To be surrounded by some of the finest military historians in the world, as well as a student body of enormous operational experience and knowledge, is both stimulating and deeply challenging. I am a better historian for it and would like to salute my colleagues, both civilian and military, and my students, past and present, for their input. Shrivenham is also home to one of the great defence libraries in the world and the collection of the JSCSC library is always the starting point for any project. As always, the staff have been extremely helpful, thoroughly professional, and happily willing to overlook my occasional misdemeanours.

During the course of writing *Passchendaele: The Lost Victory of World War I*, I have travelled to a number of libraries and research centres, whose staff have been unfailingly helpful: the Bayerisches Hauptstaatsarchiv, Kriegsarchiv and Bavarian State Library in Munich; the Canadian War Museum, and Library and Archives Canada, Ottawa; the Imperial War Museum, London; the Liddell Hart Centre for Military Archives at King's College London; the Maughan Library, London; and The National Archives of the UK at Kew. Financial support for these trips has been provided by the Defence Studies Department, which has always been incredibly supportive of my scholarship. A special note should go to my colleague at Shrivenham, Dr David Hall, who has been of enormous assistance. I am grateful to him for accompanying me to Munich to conduct archival research on the German Army. He was an excellent companion and freely shared with me his extensive knowledge of German history, culture, football and – perhaps most importantly – *German beer*.

This book is dedicated to my daughters, Eleanor and Isabel, and my wife, Louise, who make everything possible and worth while. This book is for them – in the way of an apology for spending so much of my time hunched over my computer in my office, typing and typing away.

Cheltenham, England
October 2016

References

Introduction

1 'Letters to the Editor', *The Spectator*, 3 January 1958.
2 B. H. Liddell Hart, *The Real War, 1914–1918* (London: Faber & Faber, 1930), p. 367.
3 Ibid., p. 361. The Walcheren Expedition of 1809 was one of the most misconceived military operations of the nineteenth century. A force of 40,000 British troops was assembled at Walcheren, a swampy island at the mouth of the River Scheldt, intending to push on to Antwerp and provide support to Austrian forces fighting against Napoleon Bonaparte. Unfortunately, an armistice between France and Austria was signed shortly before the expedition set sail, and once there the invasion force quickly bogged down. The island was evacuated before the end of the year after the loss of over 4,000 soldiers and thousands more who suffered from so-called 'Walcheren Fever'.
4 Dan Todman sees it as 'almost certainly apocryphal', while Frank Davies and Graham Maddocks call it 'largely a myth'. See D. Todman, *The Great War. Myth and Memory* (London: Hambledon and London, 2005), p. 81, and F. Davies and G. Maddocks, *Bloody Red Tabs. General Officer Casualties of the Great War 1914–1918* (Barnsley: Leo Cooper, 1995), p. 18.
5 D. Cooper, *Haig. The Second Volume* (London: Faber & Faber, 1936), pp. 159–60.
6 LHCMA: Liddell Hart Papers, LH 11/1927/17, 'Talk with General Edmonds – 7/10/27'.
7 See R. D. Heinl, Jr, *Dictionary of Military and Naval Quotations* (Annapolis: United States Naval Institute, 1966), p. 360; M. Dewar, *An Anthology of Military Quotations* (London: Robert Hale, 1990), p. 247; N. Dixon, *On the Psychology of Military Incompetence* (London: Jonathan Cape, 1976), p. 374; R. Pois and P. Langer, *Command Failure in War. Psychology and Leadership* (Bloomington and Indianapolis: Indiana University

Press, 2004), pp. 143–4; Lord Wedderburn, 'Laski's Law behind the Law', in R. Rawlings (ed.), *Law, Society, and Economy. Centenary Essays for the London School of Economics and Political Science 1895–1995* (Oxford: Clarendon Press, 1997), p. 33; and S. Blackburn, *Mirror, Mirror. The Uses and Abuses of Self-Love* (Princeton and Oxford: Princeton University Press, 2014), p. 104.

8 P. Fussell, *The Great War and Modern Memory* (Oxford: Oxford University Press, 2000; first publ. 1975), p. 84.

9 D. Todman, 'Third Ypres: Fact and Fiction', in P. Dennis and J. Grey (eds.), *1917. Tactics, Training and Technology: The 2007 Chief of Army Military History Conference* (Canberra: Australian History Military Publications, 2007), p. 202.

10 A. J. P. Taylor, *The First World War. An Illustrated History* (London: Penguin Books, 1966; first publ. 1963), p. 194.

11 'An Officer's Letter', *The Times*, 31 July 1917. It reported that Sassoon was 'suffering from nervous breakdown'.

12 'Memorial Tablet', in S. Sassoon, *Selected Poems* (London: William Heinemann, 1940; first publ. 1925), p. 58.

13 D. Lloyd George, *War Memoirs of David Lloyd George* (2 vols., London: Odhams Press, 1933–6), II, ch. 63.

14 Cooper, *Haig*, ch. 20.

15 See A. Green, *Writing the Great War. Sir James Edmonds and the Official Histories, 1915–1948* (London: Frank Cass, 2003), ch. 8.

16 Sir J. Edmonds, *Military Operations: France & Belgium 1917* (3 vols., London: HMSO, 1948), II, pp. 366–87.

17 F. Lloyd George, 'Passchendaele', *The Times*, 15 March 1949.

18 Lord Trenchard, 'Lord Haig's Decisions', *The Times*, 29 January 1949.

19 J. H. Davidson, 'Lord Haig's Decisions', *The Times*, 16 February 1949.

20 B. H. Liddell Hart, 'The Basic Truths of Passchendaele', *Journal of the Royal United Services Institution*, Vol. CIV, No. 616 (November 1959), pp. 435–6.

21 For differing views on the value of Edmonds's work on Third Ypres see Green, *Writing the Great War*, p. 194; D. French, '"Official But Not History"? Sir James Edmonds and the Official History of the Great War', *The RUSI Journal*, Vol. 131, No. 1 (1986), pp. 58–63; and T. Travers, *The Killing Ground. The British Army, the Western Front and the Emergence of Modern Warfare 1900–1918* (Barnsley: Pen & Sword, 2003; first publ. 1987), ch. 8.

22 J. A. Terraine, 'Passchendaele and Amiens I', *Journal of the Royal United Services Institution*, Vol. CIV, No. 614 (May 1959), p. 173.

23 J. Terraine, *Douglas Haig. The Educated Soldier* (London: Cassell & Co., 2000; first publ. 1963), p. 373. See also J. A. Terraine, 'Passchendaele and Amiens II', *Journal of the Royal United Services Institution*, Vol. CIV, No. 615 (August 1959), pp. 331–40. See also Terraine's collection of documents on Third Ypres: *The Road to Passchendaele. The Flanders Offensive of 1917: A Study in Inevitability* (London: Leo Cooper, 1977).

24 Terraine and Liddell Hart both worked on the BBC series *The Great War* (1964), but Liddell Hart (who had been appointed Consultant Historian) asked for his name to be removed from the credits for programmes 13 and 17 (dealing with the Somme and Passchendaele) after suggesting amendments, which were ignored. B. H. Liddell Hart, 'The Great War', *The Times*, 19 September 1964, and Todman, *The Great War*, pp. 111–13.

25 L. Wolff, *In Flanders Fields* (London: Longmans, 1960), p. xxiv.

26 See 'Author's Foreword' in L. Macdonald, *They Called It Passchendaele. The Story of the Third Battle of Ypres and of the Men Who Fought in It* (London: Penguin Books, 1993; first publ. 1978), p. xiii.

27 R. Prior and T. Wilson, *Passchendaele: The Untold Story* (New Haven and London: Yale University Press, 2002; first publ. 1996), pp. xviii, 200.

28 Ibid., p. xix. In the third edition of their book, which was published in 2016, Prior and Wilson survey the current literature on the battle and claim that nothing published since 1996 has substantially challenged their findings.

29 For the Australian and New Zealand experiences of Third Ypres see A. Ekins, 'The Australians at Passchendaele', and C. Pugsley, 'The New Zealand Division at Passchendaele', in P. Liddle (ed.), *Passchendaele in Perspective. The Third Battle of Ypres* (London: Leo Cooper, 1997), pp. 227–54, 272–91; G. Harper, *Massacre at Passchendaele. The New Zealand Story* (Brighton: FireStep Books, 2011; first publ. 2000); and A. Macdonald, *Passchendaele. The Anatomy of a Tragedy* (Auckland: Harper-Collins, 2013). Canada's participation has attracted a number of excellent studies, including, for example, D. Oliver, 'The Canadians at Passchendaele', in Liddle (ed.), *Passchendaele in Perspective*, pp. 255–71; T. Cook, *Shock Troops. Canadians Fighting the Great War 1917–1918* (Toronto: Penguin

Canada, 2008); and D. G. Dancocks, *Legacy of Valour. The Canadians at Passchendaele* (Edmonton: Hurtig, 1986).

30 The literature on the German experience of Passchendaele (in English) is extremely limited. See A. Lucas and J. Schmieschek, *Fighting the Kaiser's War. The Saxons in Flanders 1914/1918* (Barnsley: Pen & Sword, 2015); R. McLeod and C. Fox, 'The Battles in Flanders during the Summer and Autumn of 1917 from General von Kuhl's *Der Weltkrieg 1914–18*', *British Army Review*, No. 116 (August 1997), pp. 78–88; G. Werth, 'Flanders 1917 and the German Soldier', in Liddle (ed.), *Passchendaele in Perspective*, pp. 324–32; G. C. Wynne, *If Germany Attacks. The Battle in Depth in the West* (Westport: Greenwood, 1976; first publ. 1940), ch. 12; and '"The Other Side of the Hill". The Fight for Inverness Copse: 22nd–24th of August 1917', *Army Quarterly*, Vol. XXIX, No. 2 (January 1935), pp. 297–303. The most useful account is undoubtedly J. Sheldon, *The German Army at Passchendaele* (Barnsley: Pen & Sword, 2007), which explores the battle through little-known German regimental histories.

Prologue: The Nivelle Offensive

1 Nivelle, cited in R. A. Doughty, *Pyrrhic Victory. French Strategy and Operations in the Great War* (London and Cambridge, Mass.: Harvard University Press, 2005), p. 324.

2 Ibid., pp. 325–6.

3 Ministère de la Guerre, *Les Armées Françaises dans La Grande Guerre*, Tome V, Vol. 2 (Paris: Imprimerie Nationale, 1937), p. 191.

4 General Karl von Einem (GOC Third Army), cited in M. Nebelin, *Ludendorff. Diktator im Ersten Weltkrieg* (Munich: Siedler Verlag, 2010), p. 237. Several other senior officers also expressed discomfort at the 'scorched earth' policy, including Crown Prince Rupprecht, who reluctantly went along with it.

5 H. Hagenlücke, 'The German High Command', in P. Liddle (ed.), *Passchendaele in Perspective. The Third Battle of Ypres* (London: Leo Cooper, 1997), p. 48.

6 C. Falls, *Military Operations: France & Belgium 1917* (3 vols., London: Macmillan & Co., 1940), I, p. 488.

7 J. de Pierrefeu, *L'Offensive du 16 Avril. La Vérité sur l'affaire Nivelle* (Paris: Renaissance du Livre, 1919), pp. 90–91.

8 Ibid., *L'Offensive du 16 Avril*, p. 92.

9 Ibid., *L'Offensive du 16 Avril*, p. 93.

10 E. L. Spears, *Prelude to Victory* (London: Jonathan Cape, 1939), pp. 506–7, 510–11. Original emphasis.

11 C. Barnett, *The Swordbearers. Supreme Command in the First World War* (London: Cassell & Co., 2000; first publ. 1963), p. 193.

12 J. de Pierrefeu, *French Headquarters 1915–1918*, trans. Major C. J. C. Street (London: Geoffrey Bles, 1924), p. 152.

13 Falls, *Military Operations: 1917*, I, pp. 498–9.

14 Ministère de la Guerre, *Les Armées Françaises*, Tome V, Vol. 2, p. 188.

15 Of those divisions that mutinied, forty-six were 'very much affected' and of these thirteen were seriously affected. Ibid., pp. 193–4.

16 Pierrefeu, *French Headquarters*, pp. 179–80.

1. *Manoeuvres of War*

1 E. L. Spears, *Prelude to Victory* (London: Jonathan Cape, 1939), p. 277.

2 'Man of the Moment', *The Times*, 8 December 1916.

3 'Mr Ll. George in Office', *The Times*, 8 December 1916.

4 Lord Hankey, *The Supreme Command 1914–1918* (2 vols., London: George Allen and Unwin, 1961), II, p. 575.

5 Lloyd George's War Cabinet consisted of Andrew Bonar Law (Chancellor of the Exchequer), Lord Curzon (Lord President of the Council), Lord Milner (Minister Without Portfolio) and Arthur Henderson (Minister Without Portfolio). Henderson resigned from the War Cabinet on 11 August 1917. He was replaced by George Barnes (Minister of Pensions).

6 French casualty figures taken from R. A. Doughty, *Pyrrhic Victory. French Strategy and Operations in the Great War* (London and Cambridge, Mass.: Harvard University Press, 2005), p. 309.

7 C. Duffy, *Through German Eyes. The British and the Somme 1916* (London: Orion, 2007; first publ. 2006), p. 324.

8 See for example Lloyd George's speech of 3 November 1916 in which he delivered a typically blunt assessment. 'We are not getting on with the

war . . . At no point had the Allies achieved a definite clear success.' Lloyd George, cited in D. R. Woodward, *Lloyd George and the Generals* (London: Associated University Presses, 1983), p. 118.

9 G. A. Leask, *Sir William Robertson. The Life Story of the Chief of the Imperial General Staff* (London: Cassell & Co., 1917), p. 141.

10 TNA: CAB 24/1/G33, Sir W. Robertson, 'Memorandum on the Conduct of the War', 8 November 1915.

11 D. Lloyd George, *War Memoirs of David Lloyd George* (2 vols., London: Odhams Press, 1933–6), I, pp. 466–9.

12 Woodward, *Lloyd George and the Generals*, pp. 133–4.

13 Hankey, *The Supreme Command*, II, p. 614, and J. Grigg, *Lloyd George. War Leader 1916–1918* (London: Penguin Books, 2003; first publ. 2002), pp. 35–8.

14 Appendix 18, 'Proposed Organization of Unified Command on the Western Front', 26 February 1917, in *Military Operations: France & Belgium 1917: Appendices* (London: Macmillan & Co., 1940), pp. 62–3.

15 Sir W. Robertson, *Soldiers and Statesmen 1914–1918* (2 vols., London: Cassell & Co., 1926), II, p. 206.

16 Appendix 19, 'Agreement Signed at Anglo-French Conference Held at Calais', 26/27 February 1917, in *Military Operations: France & Belgium 1917: Appendices*, pp. 64–5.

17 F. Stevenson, *Lloyd George. A Diary*, ed. A. J. P. Taylor (London: Hutchinson, 1971), p. 157.

18 D. Lieven, *Nicholas II. Emperor of All the Russias* (London: Pimlico, 1994; first publ. 1993), pp. 231–4.

19 D. French, *The Strategy of the Lloyd George Coalition, 1916–1918* (Oxford: Clarendon Press, 1995), pp. 40–41.

20 TNA: CAB 24/11/GT597, J. C. Smuts, 'The General Strategic and Military Situation and Particularly That on the Western Front', 29 April 1917. Lloyd George's notes on the conference can be found in *War Memoirs*, I, pp. 909–27.

21 TNA: CAB 24/11/GT599, Sir W. Robertson, 'Operations on West Front', 30 April 1917.

22 TNA: CAB 23/13, 'War Cabinet 128 a', 1 May 1917.

23 TNA: CAB 24/12/GT657, 'Anglo-French Conference, May 4, and 5, 1917' and 'Statement by General Sir William Robertson'.

24 French, *The Strategy of the Lloyd George Coalition*, pp. 52–3.

25 Haig diary, 4 May 1917, in G. Sheffield and J. Bourne (eds.), *Douglas Haig. War Diaries and Letters 1914–1918* (London: Weidenfeld & Nicolson, 2005), p. 292.

26 P. von Hindenburg, *Out of My Life*, trans. F. A. Holt (London: Cassell & Co., 1920), pp. 204–5. Emphasis added.

27 W. Görlitz (ed.), *The Kaiser and His Court. The Diaries, Note Books and Letters of Admiral Georg Alexander von Müller, Chief of the Naval Cabinet, 1914–1918* (London: Macdonald & Co., 1961; first publ. 1959), p. 222.

28 Crown Prince Wilhelm, *The Memoirs of the Crown Prince of Germany* (London: Thornton Butterworth, 1922), pp. 154, 157.

29 On 24 March 1917, Karl's brother-in-law, Prince Sixtus of Bourbon–Parma, agreed to take a letter to President Poincaré. Prince Sixtus was serving in the Belgian Army and acted as an intermediary between the two powers. Karl promised to support France's claims in Alsace–Lorraine, as well as the liberation of Belgium and Serbia, in exchange for a separate and lasting peace with the Allies. The 'Sixtus Affair' was doomed to failure, however, given the impossibility of reconciling Italy's territorial demands with those requested by Emperor Karl. See A. Watson, *Ring of Steel. Germany and Austria–Hungary at War, 1914–1918* (London: Allen Lane, 2014), pp. 466–7.

30 Reichsarchiv, *Der Weltkrieg 1914 bis 1918*, XII. *Die Kriegführung im Frühjahr 1917* (Berlin: E. S. Mittler & Sohn, 1939), p. 39.

31 Duffy, *Through German Eyes*, p. 324.

32 R. Foley, 'Learning War's Lessons: The German Army on the Somme, 1916', *Journal of Military History*, Vol. 75, No. 2 (April 2011), p. 500.

33 Hindenburg, *Out of My Life*, pp. 245, 246. For the 'Hindenburg Programme' see Watson, *Ring of Steel*, pp. 378–84.

34 Görlitz (ed.), *The Kaiser and His Court*, p. 232.

35 H. Newbolt, *History of the Great War. Naval Operations* (5 vols., London: Longmans, Green & Co., 1928), IV, p. 270. Original emphasis.

36 J. B. Scott (ed.), *Official Statements of War Aims and Peace Proposals. December 1916 to November 1918* (Washington DC: Carnegie Endowment for International Peace, 1921), pp. 1–3.

37 Ibid., p. 7.

38 Ibid., pp. 26–8.

39 Newbolt, *Naval Operations*, IV, p. 370. Original emphasis.

40 Görlitz (ed.), *The Kaiser and His Court*, p. 264.

41 D. Steffen, 'The Holtzendorff Memorandum of 22 December 1916 and Germany's Declaration of Unrestricted U-Boat Warfare', *Journal of Military History*, Vol. 68, No. 1 (January 2004), p. 219.

42 Watson, *Ring of Steel*, pp. 420–21.

43 TNA: CAB 24/20/GT1496, 'War Cabinet. The Submarine Situation', 24 July 1917.

44 Reichsarchiv, *Der Weltkrieg 1914 bis 1918*, XIII. *Die Kriegführung im Sommer und Herbst 1917. Die Ereignisse außerhalb der Westfront bis November 1918* (Berlin: E. S. Mittler & Sohn, 1942), p. 22.

45 Hindenburg, *Out of My Life*, p. 265.

46 E. Ludendorff, *Ludendorff's Own Story. August 1914–November 1918* (2 vols., New York and London: Harper & Brothers, 1919), II, p. 23.

47 How infantry strengths could decrease while the size of the army actually increased was due to the rapid expansion in the artillery, and the growing demand from supporting and technical units. During this period OHL also created fifty-three new divisions.

48 Reichsarchiv, *Der Weltkrieg*, XIII, p. 26.

49 Ibid., p. 27.

50 *Grundsätze für die Führung in der Abwehrschlacht im Stellungskriege vom 1 Dezember 1916* (Berlin: Reichsdruckerei, 1916). It was reprinted in March 1917, before an updated version was published on 1 September 1917.

51 Ibid., pp. 9–10.

52 TNA: WO 157/22, 'German Instructions for a Counter-Attack Organized in Depth' in GHQ Summary of Information, 29 July 1917.

2. Haig and the 'Northern Operation'

1 Haig to Robertson, 13 August 1917, in D. R. Woodward (ed.), *The Military Correspondence of Field-Marshal Sir William Robertson, Chief of the Imperial General Staff, December 1915–February 1918* (London: Bodley Head for the Army Records Society, 1989), p. 215.

2 G. Powell, *Plumer. The Soldiers' General* (London: Leo Cooper, 1990), p. 228.

3 Sir J. Edmonds, *Military Operations: France & Belgium 1917* (3 vols., London: HMSO, 1948), II, p. 8.

4 See Appendix I, 'Project for Combined Naval and Military Operations on the Belgian Coast with a View to Preventing the Enemy Using Ostend as a Submarine Base', 12 November 1916, in Edmonds, *Military Operations: 1917*, II, pp. 396–8.

5 F. Fischer, *Germany's Aims in the First World War* (New York: W. W. Norton & Co., 1967; first publ. 1961), p. 104.

6 P. Barton, *Passchendaele. Unseen Panoramas of the Third Battle of Ypres* (London: Constable & Robinson, 2007), p. 17.

7 IWM: Documents 12332, 'The Journal of John Nettleton of the Rifle Brigade 1914–1919', p. 86.

8 Edmonds, *Military Operations: 1917*, II, pp. 125–6.

9 For Haig and his experiences at Ypres see J. Hussey, 'A Hard Day at First Ypres: The Allied Generals and Their Problems, 31 October 1914', *British Army Review*, No. 107 (August 1994), pp. 75–89; I. F. W. Beckett, *Ypres: The First Battle, 1914* (Harlow: Longman, 2004); D. J. De Groot, *Douglas Haig, 1861–1928* (London: Unwin Hyman, 1988), pp. 165–8; and N. Gardner, *Trial by Fire. Command and the British Expeditionary Force in 1914* (Westport: Praeger, 2003), pp. 219–20. On the afternoon of 31 October 1914, with the BEF coming under sustained attack, Haig rode forward along the Menin Road to rally his troops. While some historians have cast doubt on the wisdom of doing this, what is clear is the lasting legacy that First Ypres had on Haig – a sense of the fragility of the British line and how near it came to collapse.

10 Haig diary, 14 March 1917, in G. Sheffield and J. Bourne (eds.), *Douglas Haig: War Diaries and Letters 1914–1918* (London: Weidenfeld & Nicolson, 2005), pp. 276–7.

11 See P. Simkins, 'Herbert Plumer', in I. F. W. Beckett and S. J. Corvi (eds.), *Haig's Generals* (Barnsley: Pen & Sword, 2006), pp. 141–63.

12 TNA: WO 158/214, 'Army Instructions for Main Offensive on Second Army Front', 12 December 1916.

13 Appendix V, 'GHQ Letter to Second Army', 6 January 1917, in Edmonds, *Military Operations: 1917*, II, pp. 406–7.

14 Appendix VI, 'GHQ Instructions for the Formation of a Special Sub-Section of the Operations Section of the General Staff', 8 January 1917,

in Edmonds, *Military Operations: 1917,* II, pp. 407–9. A memorandum, subsequently produced by the Operations Section, argued for simultaneous assaults at Messines and Pilckem up to the German second line. Two days later a 'body of tanks' would go on to capture Broodseinde. Although Haig seems to have been pleased with this memorandum, it was quietly dropped after objections from the Tank Corps. See Appendix VII, 'Memorandum by Operations Section, General Staff GHQ', 14 February 1917, in Edmonds, *Military Operations: 1917,* II, pp. 410–16, and R. Prior and T. Wilson, *Passchendaele. The Untold Story* (New Haven and London: Yale University Press, 2002; first publ. 1996), pp. 45–8.

15 Edmonds, *Military Operations: 1917,* II, pp. 15–18.

16 See T. Travers, *How the War was Won. Command and Technology in the British Army on the Western Front, 1917–1918* (Barnsley: Pen & Sword, 2005; first publ. 1992), and 'A Particular Style of Command: Haig and GHQ, 1916–18', *Journal of Strategic Studies,* Vol. 10, No. 3 (1987), pp. 363–76.

17 For the influence of the 'structured battle' in 1915 see N. Lloyd, *Loos 1915* (Stroud: Tempus, 2006), pp. 55–7.

18 See R. Prior and T. Wilson, *Command on the Western Front. The Military Career of Sir Henry Rawlinson, 1914–1918* (Oxford: Blackwell, 1992), ch. 15, and H. Sebag-Montefiore, *Somme. Into the Breach* (London: Viking, 2016), ch. 3.

19 Sir J. Davidson, *Haig. Master of the Field* (London: Peter Nevill, 1953), p. 14.

20 Edmonds, *Military Operations: 1917,* II, pp. 37–8.

21 D. Lloyd George, *War Memoirs of David Lloyd George* (2 vols., London: Odhams Press, 1933–6), II, pp. 1249–56.

22 This point is dealt with in J. Terraine, *Douglas Haig. The Educated Soldier* (London: Cassell & Co., 2000; first publ. 1963), pp. 319–21.

23 Haig diary, 18 May 1917, in Sheffield and Bourne (eds.), *Douglas Haig,* p. 294. The attack at Malmaison would actually take place between 23 and 27 October 1917.

24 Davidson, *Haig,* p. 15.

25 See *Statistics of the Military Effort of the British Empire during the Great War. 1914–1920* (London: HMSO, 1922), p. 64 (iii). The strength of the BEF peaked on 1 August 1917 with an estimated complement of 2,044,627 men.

26 P. Simkins, 'The Four Armies 1914–1918', in D. G. Chandler and I. Beckett (eds.), *The Oxford History of the British Army* (Oxford: Oxford University Press, 2003; first publ. 1994), pp. 250–51.

27 C. Falls, *Military Operations. France & Belgium 1917* (3 vols., London: Macmillan & Co., 1940), I, pp. 479–80.

28 See H. Williamson, *The Wet Flanders Plain* (London: Faber & Faber, 2009; first publ. 1929).

29 T. Ashworth, *Trench Warfare 1914–1918: The Live and Let Live System* (London: Macmillan, 1980), p. 21.

30 IWM: Documents 4755, H. S. Taylor, 'Reminiscences of the Great War 1914/1918', p. 9.

31 M. Middlebrook, *The First Day on the Somme* (London: Penguin Books, 1984; first publ. 1971), p. 88.

32 A. P. Palazzo, 'The British Army's Counter-Battery Staff Office and Control of the Enemy in World War I', *Journal of Military History*, Vol. 63, No. 1 (January 1999), p. 63.

33 S. Marble, *British Artillery on the Western Front in the First World War. 'The Infantry Cannot Do with a Gun Less'* (Farnham: Ashgate, 2013), pp. 163–4.

34 J. H. Morrow, Jr, *The Great War in the Air. Military Aviation from 1909 to 1921* (Washington DC: Smithsonian Institute Press, 1993), p. 215.

35 P. Hart, *Bloody April. Slaughter in the Skies over Arras, 1917* (London: Cassell & Co., 2006; first publ. 2005), p. 11.

36 J. T. B. McCudden, *Flying Fury. Five Years in the Royal Flying Corps* (Folkestone: Bailey Brothers & Swinfen, 1973; first publ. 1918), pp. 174–5.

37 Shortly before his death in September 1917, the German ace Werner Voss complained that 'All English single-seaters are superior to the German fighter aircraft in climb, handling, and dive capabilities, and most of them are also superior in speed.' K. Bodenschatz, *Hunting With Richthofen. The Bodenschatz Diaries: Sixteen Months of Battle with JG Freiherr von Richthofen No. 1*, trans. J. Hayzlett (London: Grubb Street, 1996), p. 46.

38 The Mark IV weighed 28 tons and was powered by a Daimler six-cylinder engine. It came in two versions: a male, with two 6-pounder guns and four machine-guns; and a female, with just six machine-guns. Each vehicle had a crew of eight. See D. Crow (ed.), *AFVs of World War One* (Windsor: Profile Publications, 1970), pp. 45–52.

39 The winter of 1916–17 was a watershed in British tactical development. SS 135, *Instructions for the Training of Divisions for Offensive Action*, was published in December 1916. This was followed by SS 143, *Instructions for the Training of Platoons for Offensive Action* (February 1917), and SS 144, *The Organisation*

of an Infantry Battalion and the Normal Formation for the Attack (April 1917). Platoons would now be split into four 'fighting sections': one with grenade-throwers, another with a Lewis gun, a third with riflemen and snipers, and a fourth with rifle grenades. The platoon was thus 'a complete and independent tactical unit'. The historian Paddy Griffith argues that SS 143, in particular, was 'a vital milestone in tactics, marking a changeover from the Victorian era of riflemen in lines to the twentieth-century era of flexible small groups built around a variety of high-firepower weapons'. P. Griffith, *Battle Tactics of the Western Front. The British Army's Art of Attack 1916–1918* (New Haven and London: Yale University Press, 1994), pp. 77–8.

40 See P. Harris and S. Marble, 'The "Step-by-Step" Approach: British Military Thought and Operational Method on the Western Front, 1915–1917', *War in History*, Vol. 15, No. 1 (2008), pp. 17–42.

41 Rawlinson, cited in Harris and Marble, 'The "Step-by-Step" Approach', p. 20.

42 Haig continually prodded Plumer to go deeper into the German lines at Messines. Initially Plumer wanted to advance just 1,500 yards and capture the ridge in two days, but Haig squashed this, telling him to do it all at once. While this was a sensible and appropriate intervention, Haig proved unable to help himself, and in early May urged Plumer to go further, securing not only the villages of Wytschaete and Messines on the ridge, but also marching down the far side of the high ground out to Oosttaverne. This extension would have serious consequences and cause Second Army increased casualties on the afternoon of 7 June. Prior and Wilson, *Passchendaele*, pp. 57–8.

43 I. Passingham, *Pillars of Fire. The Battle of Messines Ridge, June 1917* (Stroud: Sutton, 1998), pp. 29–34.

44 Edmonds, *Military Operations: 1917*, II, pp. 32–49.

45 Haig diary, 22 May 1917, in Sheffield and Bourne (eds.), *Douglas Haig*, p. 295.

46 Sir C. Harington, *Plumer of Messines* (London: John Murray, 1935), p. 84.

3. 'A Great Sea of Flames'

1 W. Beumelburg, *Flandern 1917* (Oldenburg: Gerhard Stalling, 1928), p. 27.

2 Sir C. Harington, *Plumer of Messines* (London: John Murray, 1935), pp. 79, 100, 103.

3 AWM: 2DRL/0260, Account of R. C. Grieve ('Messines'), pp. 8–10. Grieve would win a Victoria Cross for his actions that day. See G. Gliddon, *VCs of the First World War. Arras and Messines 1917* (Stroud: Sutton Publishing, 1998), pp. 185–8.

4 AWM: AWM4 1/32/16 Part 1, II ANZAC Corps War Diary, 7 June 1917.

5 IWM: Documents 11080, A. Johnson to his father, 10 June 1917.

6 Guinness diary, 7 June 1917, in B. Bond and S. Robbins (eds.), *Staff Officer. The Diaries of Walter Guinness (First Lord Moyne) 1914–1918* (London: Leo Cooper, 1987), p. 156.

7 Sir J. Edmonds, *Military Operations. France & Belgium 1917* (3 vols., London: HMSO, 1948), II, p. 71.

8 I. Passingham, *Pillars of Fire. The Battle of Messines Ridge, June 1917* (Stroud: Sutton, 1998), pp. 127–32.

9 TNA: WO 157/115, 'Second Army Summary of Intelligence, 1st to 15th June 1917'.

10 Reitinger in J. Sheldon, *The German Army at Passchendaele* (Barnsley: Pen & Sword, 2007), pp. 7–9.

11 Twenty-five mines had been planted, but two were lost to countermining (at Peckham Farm and Petit Douve). On the southern edge of the battlefield, a cluster of mines were abandoned shortly before the battle began. One of these (at Birdcage III, northeast of Ploegsteert Wood) exploded in 1955 during a heavy thunderstorm. See A. Turner, *Messines 1917. The Zenith of Siege Warfare* (Botley: Osprey, 2010), pp. 44, 55.

12 E. Ludendorff, *Ludendorff's Own Story. August 1914–November 1918* (2 vols., New York and London: Harper & Brothers, 1919), II, p. 31.

13 Rupprecht diary, 9 June 1917, in Crown Prince Rupprecht, *Mein Kriegstagebuch* (3 vols., Berlin: E. S. Mittler & Sohn, 1929), II, p. 191.

14 Edmonds, *Military Operations: 1917*, II, p. 88.

15 Thaer diary, 11 June 1917, in A. von Thaer, *Generalstabsdienst an der Front und in der O.H.L.* (Göttingen: Vandenhoeck & Ruprecht, 1958), pp. 125–6.

16 G. C. Wynne, *If Germany Attacks. The Battle in Depth in the West* (Westport: Greenwood, 1976; first publ. 1940), p. 283.

17 Rupprecht, cited in Edmonds, *Military Operations: 1917*, II, p. 142.

18 BA-MA: MSG 2/13418, J. Schärdel, 'Flandernschlacht 1917', p. 1.

19 DTA: 3502.1, R. Lewald diary, 13 June 1917.

20 Reichsarchiv, *Der Weltkrieg 1914 bis 1918,* XIII. *Die Kriegführung im Sommer und Herbst 1917. Die Ereignisse außerhalb der Westfront bis November 1918* (Berlin: E. S. Mittler & Sohn, 1942), pp. 32–3, 50.

21 Edmonds, *Military Operations: 1917,* II, p. 143.

22 IWM: Documents 12512, G. Brunskill diary, 12 August 1917.

23 Reichsarchiv, *Der Weltkrieg,* XIII, p. 56.

24 Lossberg was known as the 'Lion of the Defensive' and 'directed virtually all the major German defensive battles on the Western Front from the autumn of 1915 to the end of 1917'. See D. T. Zabecki, 'Fritz von Lossberg', in D. T. Zabecki (ed.), *Chief of Staff. The Principal Officers behind History's Great Commanders* (2 vols., Annapolis: Naval Institute Press, 2008), I, pp. 176–86. Evidently some senior officers resented Lossberg's predominance. When Albrecht von Thaer telephoned Ludendorff's Chief of Operations, Georg Wetzell, on 11 June, and told him that Lossberg should be sent to Fourth Army immediately, Wetzell shrugged. 'But that would look like the German General Staff only had one man who could lead a defensive battle. Thankfully this is not the case!' 'Dear Wetzell', Thaer replied, 'if you are so sure of final victory that you can afford to lose the forthcoming battle in Flanders, then just forget about your number one man!' Thaer diary, 11 June 1917, in Thaer, *Generalstabsdienst,* pp. 125–6.

25 Account taken from F. von Lossberg, *Meine Tätigkeit im Weltkrieg 1914–1918* (Berlin: E. S. Mittler & Sohn, 1939), pp. 294–5.

26 Sheldon, *Passchendaele,* pp. 40–41; Edmonds, *Military Operations: 1917,* II, pp. 145–6; Beumelburg, *Flandern,* p. 29.

27 W. Volkart, *Die Gasschlacht in Flandern im Herbst 1917* (Berlin: E. S. Mittler & Sohn, 1957), pp. 20–22. A sixth *Eingreif* division (2nd Guard Reserve) lay on the northern sector of the battlefield as part of Group Dixmude.

28 Lossberg, *Meine Tätigkeit im Weltkrieg,* p. 294.

29 Thaer diary, 14 June 1917, in Thaer, *Generalstabsdienst,* p. 126.

30 P. Maze, *A Frenchman in Khaki* (Kingswood: William Heinemann, 1934), p. 227.

31 H. Gough, *The Fifth Army* (London: Hodder & Stoughton, 1931), p. 193.

32 See A. Farrar-Hockley, *Goughie. The Life of General Sir Hubert Gough* (London: Hart-Davis, MacGibbon, 1975).

33 This view has been echoed widely. Even John Terraine, who was the most eloquent and dogged defender of Sir Douglas Haig, admitted that

'The decision to entrust the main role in the Flanders battle to the Fifth Army under General Gough must be regarded as Haig's gravest and most fatal error.' J. Terraine, *Douglas Haig. The Educated Soldier* (London: Cassell & Co., 2000; first publ. 1963), p. 337.

34 G. Sheffield and H. McCartney, 'Hubert Gough', in I. F. W. Beckett and S. J. Corvi (eds.), *Haig's Generals* (Barnsley: Pen & Sword, 2006), p. 93.

35 C. E. W. Bean, *The Official History of Australia in the War of 1914–1918* (13 vols., Sydney: Angus & Robertson, 1941–2), IV, p. 351.

36 Farrar-Hockley, *Goughie*, p. 218.

37 Gough, *Fifth Army*, p. 192.

38 R. Prior and T. Wilson, *Passchendaele. The Untold Story* (New Haven and London: Yale University Press, 2002; first publ. 1996), pp. 70–77.

39 Appendix XII, 'Memorandum on the Present Situation and Future Plans Written for the War Cabinet by the Commander-in-Chief', in Edmonds, *Military Operations: 1917*, II, pp. 423–7.

40 For Haig's over-optimism in 1915 see N. Lloyd, *Loos 1915* (Stroud: Tempus, 2006), and '"With Faith and Without Fear": Sir Douglas Haig's Command of First Army during 1915', *Journal of Military History*, Vol. 71, No. 4 (October 2007), pp. 1051–76.

41 J. F. C. Fuller, 'Introduction' in L. Wolff, *In Flanders Fields* (London: Longmans, 1960), p. xiv.

42 For a comprehensive examination of Haig and Charteris see J. Beach, *Haig's Intelligence. GHQ and the German Army, 1916–1918* (Cambridge: Cambridge University Press, 2013). Beach concludes that the legend of Charteris as a 'malign intelligence officer', misleading his chief with over-optimistic intelligence, is something of a caricature. More likely, Charteris realized that he was dependent upon Haig's patronage and 'it is not difficult to imagine an almost unconscious process whereby Charteris moulded his assessments to fit with what he believed were Haig's opinions' (p. 322). See also J. M. Bourne, 'Charteris, John (1877–1946)', *Oxford Dictionary of National Biography*, Oxford: Oxford University Press, 2004; online edn, Oct. 2008 [http://www.oxforddnb.com/view/article/57800, accessed 20 Aug 2015].

43 Haig diary, 2 June 1917, in G. Sheffield and J. Bourne (eds.), *Douglas Haig. War Diaries and Letters 1914–1918* (London: Weidenfeld & Nicolson, 2005), p. 297.

44 Appendix XII, 'Note on the Strategic Situation with Special Reference to the Present Condition of German Resources and Probable German Operations', in Edmonds, *Military Operations: 1917*, II, pp. 427–31.

45 D. French, *The Strategy of the Lloyd George Coalition, 1916–1918* (Oxford: Clarendon Press, 1995), p. 86.

46 I. Castle, *London 1917–18. The Bomber Blitz* (Botley: Osprey, 2010), p. 23. On some of the later raids, the Gothas were joined by one or two R.VI 'Giants'. These were enormous four-engined strategic bombers capable of carrying a 1,000kg bomb.

47 J. Grigg, *Lloyd George. War Leader 1916–1918* (London: Penguin Books, 2003; first publ. 2002), pp. 246–8. See TNA: CAB 23/3, 'War Cabinet, 163', 14 June 1917, in which it was agreed to draw upon plans for the further development of aircraft.

48 Robertson to Haig, 13 June 1917, in Grigg, *Lloyd George*, p. 163. Original emphasis.

49 It was one of Haig's most unappealing character traits that he was always something of an intriguer – indeed he had more in common with Lloyd George than either of them would have credited. When Robertson heard of this suggestion he flatly refused to go. Nervous of the ramifications of forcing a move, Lloyd George quickly dropped the matter. J. P. Harris, *Douglas Haig and the First World War* (Cambridge: Cambridge University Press, 2008), pp. 352–4.

50 Lord Hankey, *The Supreme Command 1914–1918* (2 vols., London: George Allen and Unwin, 1961), II, p. 682.

51 D. Lloyd George, *War Memoirs of David Lloyd George* (2 vols., London: Odhams Press, 1933–6), II, pp. 1272–6. Original emphasis.

52 Haig diary, 19 June 1917, in Sheffield and Bourne (eds.), *Douglas Haig*, p. 300. Original emphasis.

53 Lloyd George, *War Memoirs*, II, p. 1277.

54 TNA: CAB 27/6, 'Cabinet Committee on War Policy', 21 June 1917. Lloyd George's objections are also discussed at length in *War Memoirs*, II, pp. 1280–87.

55 Jellicoe's influence on the decision to approve Third Ypres remains contentious. According to Andrew Wiest, Jellicoe was not particularly worried about the number of U-boats based at Ostend and Zeebrugge (about twelve), but rather the dangers that continued German occupation of the

Belgian coast would pose against their crucial line of communication. See A. Wiest, *Passchendaele and the Royal Navy* (New York: Greenwood Press, 1995), pp. 106–11; J. Terraine, *Douglas Haig. The Educated Soldier* (London: Cassell & Co., 2000; first publ. 1963), pp. 333–4; and S. W. Roskill, 'The U-Boat Campaign of 1917 and Third Ypres', *Journal of the Royal United Services Institution*, Vol. CIV, No. 616 (November 1959), pp. 440–42.

56 Milner, cited in French, *The Strategy of the Lloyd George Coalition*, p. 117.

57 TNA: CAB 27/6, 'Cabinet Committee on War Policy', 21 June 1917.

58 TNA: CAB 27/6, 'Cabinet Committee on War Policy', 25 June 1917.

4. 'Have We Time to Accomplish?'

1 Reichsarchiv, *Der Weltkrieg 1914 bis 1918,* XIII. *Die Kriegführung im Sommer und Herbst 1917. Die Ereignisse außerhalb der Westfront bis November 1918* (Berlin: E. S. Mittler & Sohn, 1942), p. 55.

2 J. Charteris, *At G.H.Q.* (London: Cassell & Co., 1931), p. 231.

3 P. Maze, *A Frenchman in Khaki* (Kingswood: William Heinemann, 1934), pp. 228–30.

4 H. Gough, *The Fifth Army* (London: Hodder & Stoughton, 1931), pp. 197–8.

5 Sir J. Edmonds, *Military Operations: France & Belgium 1917* (3 vols., London: HMSO, 1948), II, pp. 126–8.

6 Gough, *The Fifth Army*, p. 198. Contained in this account is a curious recollection in which Gough states that he would have preferred to limit his advance to the Black Line and not go 'all out' for the Green Line. Apparently, both Haig and Plumer disagreed and urged that the Green Line should remain as the main objective. This is highly questionable. At no stage during the planning of the battle had Gough wanted a more limited attack. He remained a firm believer in going as far as they could on the first day. See Edmonds, *Military Operations: 1917*, II, pp. 127–8.

7 Appendix XV, 'Memorandum Dated 26th June, 1917, by Br.-General J. H. Davidson', in Edmonds, *Military Operations: 1917*, II, pp. 436–9.

8 TNA: CAB 45/140, General Sir Hubert Gough, 'Marginal Notes. Chapter VIII'.

9 Appendix XV, 'Memorandum by General Sir Hubert Gough', in Edmonds, *Military Operations: 1917*, II, pp. 440–42.

10 TNA: CAB 45/140, Gough to Edmonds, 2 February 1944. In the letter Gough incorrectly referred to the night attack on the Somme as taking place in *August* 1916 (when it was actually fought on 14 July).

11 Edmonds, *Military Operations: 1917*, II, pp. 129–32.

12 See R. Prior and T. Wilson, *Passchendaele. The Untold Story* (New Haven and London: Yale University Press, 2002; first publ. 1996), chs. 7–8.

13 136 machines would start on the first day. See Edmonds, *Military Operations: 1917*, II, p. 148, and J. P. Harris, *Men, Ideas and Tanks. British Military Thought and Armoured Forces, 1903–1939* (Manchester: Manchester University Press, 1995), p. 102.

14 J. F. C. Fuller, 'Letters to the Editor', *The Spectator*, 10 January 1958. See also J. Terraine, *Douglas Haig. The Educated Soldier* (London: Cassell & Co., 2000; first publ. 1963), p. 342, and C. Campbell, *Band of Brigands. The First Men in Tanks* (London: Harper Perennial, 2008; first publ. 2007), pp. 288–9. According to John Terraine, there is no evidence that Haig ever saw such 'swamp maps'.

15 Sir James Edmonds dealt with this point in the Official History. There was, he wrote, 'no good reason to abandon the strategic advantages of the Flanders sector and relinquish the chance of freeing the Flanders coast in order to provide harder ground for the mass employment of tanks'. Edmonds, *Military Operations: 1917*, II, p. 380. See also N. Steel and P. Hart, *Passchendaele. The Sacrificial Ground* (London: Cassell & Co., 2001; first publ. 2000), p. 88.

16 TNA: WO 95/104, 'Employment of Tanks', 19 July 1917.

17 W. H. L. Watson, *With the Tanks 1916–1918. Memoirs of a British Tank Commander in the Great War* (Barnsley: Pen & Sword, 2014; first publ. 1920), p. 99.

18 Ministère de la Guerre, *Les Armées Françaises dans La Grande Guerre*, Tome V, Vol. 2 (Paris: Imprimerie Nationale, 1937), p. 653.

19 J. P. Harris, *Douglas Haig and the First World War* (Cambridge: Cambridge University Press, 2008), pp. 360–61. See also TNA: WO 95/519, 'Notes on Conference at Lovie Chateau', 16 June 1917.

20 TNA: WO 95/912, 'Corps Commander's Conference with Divisional Commanders', 5 July 1917.

21 Ludendorff, cited in Reichsarchiv, *Der Weltkrieg*, XIII, pp. 1–3. Ludendorff's comment on keeping one's nerve was somewhat ironic. He would suffer a nervous collapse in September 1918. See N. Lloyd, *Hundred Days. The End of the Great War* (London: Viking, 2013), pp. 177–80.

22 E. Ludendorff, *Ludendorff's Own Story. August 1914–November 1918* (2 vols., New York and London: Harper & Brothers, 1919), II, p. 51.

23 Hindenburg to Bethmann Hollweg, 19 June 1917, in E. Ludendorff, *The General Staff and Its Problems. The History of the Relations between the High Command and the German Imperial Government as Revealed by Official Documents*, trans. F. A. Holt (2 vols., New York: E. P. Dutton & Co., 1920), II, pp. 446–9.

24 W. Görlitz (ed.), *The Kaiser and His Court. The Diaries, Note Books and Letters of Admiral Georg Alexander von Müller, Chief of the Naval Cabinet, 1914–1918* (London: Macdonald & Co., 1961; first publ. 1959), p. 276.

25 Bethmann Hollweg to Hindenburg, 25 June 1917, in Ludendorff, *The General Staff*, II, pp. 449–52.

26 Ludendorff to the Kaiser, 12 July 1917, in Ludendorff, *The General Staff*, II, p. 461.

27 F. Fischer, *Germany's Aims in the First World War* (New York: W. W. Norton & Co, 1967; first publ. 1961), pp. 394–6.

28 Reichsarchiv, *Der Weltkrieg*, XIII, p. 11. See Fischer, *Germany's Aims in the First World War*, p. 401. Michaelis did not last long. He was forced to resign on 31 October 1917 and was replaced by Georg von Hertling, a 74-year-old Bavarian politician. Although Hertling seemed a more suitable choice for the left and centre deputies, his age and natural conservatism meant that he was little more than a mouthpiece for OHL. See A. Watson, *Ring of Steel. Germany and Austria–Hungary at War, 1914–1918* (London: Allen Lane, 2014), p. 484.

29 Görlitz (ed.), *The Kaiser and His Court*, p. 285.

30 M. Nebelin, *Ludendorff. Diktator im Ersten Weltkrieg* (Munich: Siedler Verlag, 2010), p. 339.

31 BA-MA: MSG 2/13418, J. Schärdel, 'Flandernschlacht 1917', pp. 3–5.

32 Rupprecht's father, King Ludwig III, was cousin to King Ludwig II, the legendary 'Swan King' of Bavaria, whose love of architecture and long-standing friendship with the composer Richard Wagner attracted both worship and derision. He drowned mysteriously in 1886. His brother, Otto, was declared insane in 1875. See C. McIntosh, *The Swan King. Ludwig II of Bavaria* (London: I. B. Tauris, 2012; first publ. 1982).

33 Reichsarchiv, *Der Weltkrieg,* XIII, pp. 54, 63. German sources seem to have over-exaggerated the strength of British battalions as well as the number of guns.

34 R. Pawly and P. Courcelle, *The Kaiser's Warlords. German Commanders of World War I* (Botley: Osprey, 2003), pp. 27–8. In the German Army, the Chief of Staff was the 'pivotal figure' in the whole chain of command. A kind of 'super-operations officer', a German Chief of Staff could appeal up the chain of command if he disagreed with his commander. He was, simultaneously, a subordinate of his own commander, but also the High Command's liaison officer to that commander. See D. T. Zabecki (ed.), *Chief of Staff. The Principal Officers behind History's Great Commanders* (2 vols., Annapolis: Naval Institute Press, 2008), I, pp. 9–11.

35 Rupprecht diary, 19 June 1917, in Crown Prince Rupprecht, *Mein Kriegstagebuch* (3 vols., Berlin: E. S. Mittler & Sohn, 1929), II, p. 202.

36 Reichsarchiv, *Der Weltkrieg,* XIII, p. 54.

37 F. von Lossberg, *Meine Tätigkeit im Weltkrieg 1914–1918* (Berlin: E. S. Mittler & Sohn, 1939), pp. 295–302. The order is reproduced (in English) in G. C. Wynne, *If Germany Attacks. The Battle in Depth in the West* (Westport: Greenwood, 1976; first publ. 1940), Appendix 1, pp. 332–40.

38 R. McLeod and C. Fox, 'The Battles in Flanders during the Summer and Autumn of 1917 from General von Kuhl's *Der Weltkrieg 1914–18*', *British Army Review,* No. 116 (August 1997), p. 79.

39 Lossberg, *Meine Tätigkeit im Weltkrieg,* p. 304. See also M. D. Karau, 'Wielding the Dagger'. *The MarineKorps Flandern and the German War Effort, 1914–1918* (London and Westport: Praeger, 2003), pp. 150–51.

40 Edmonds, *Military Operations: 1917,* II, pp. 118–22.

5. 'Under Constant Fire'

1 Kuhl, in J. Sheldon, *The German Army at Passchendaele* (Barnsley: Pen & Sword, 2007), p. 52.

2 S. Marble, *British Artillery on the Western Front in the First World War. 'The Infantry Cannot Do with a Gun Less'* (Farnham: Ashgate, 2013), p. 187.

3 C. Falls, *Military Operations: France & Belgium 1917* (3 vols., London: Macmillan & Co., 1940), I, pp. 177–9.

4 Marble, *British Artillery*, p. 173, n. 77. For Haig's 'bold' comment see p. 174.

5 The devastating bombardment prior to the German Spring Offensive on 21 March 1918 could probably lay claim to being the last great preliminary bombardment of the war. However, the crucial difference with Third Ypres was that it was concentrated into a short period of time – just five hours – and aimed at neutralizing enemy defences without sacrificing surprise. See D. T. Zabecki, *Steel Wind. Colonel Georg Bruchmüller and the Birth of Modern Artillery* (London and Westport: Praeger, 1994).

6 Artillery statistics and frontages taken from Sir J. Edmonds, *Military Operations: France & Belgium 1917* (3 vols., London: HMSO, 1948), II, p. 138, n. 2. There seems to be some confusion about the length of front bombarded during the battle. Sanders Marble cites 13,200 yards (7.5 miles), and Robin Prior and Trevor Wilson claim that the frontages of attack at Arras, Messines and Ypres were 'not greatly different'. Both, therefore, seem to underestimate the length of front at Third Ypres. See Marble, *British Artillery*, p. 189, n. 153, and R. Prior and T. Wilson, *Passchendaele. The Untold Story* (New Haven and London: Yale University Press, 2002; first publ. 1996), p. 82.

7 Exact figures for the number of German guns are not available. The German Official History records 389 batteries in Flanders (approximately 1,556 guns), with Edmonds citing a total of 1,040 guns opposite Fifth and Second Armies. A later reference in the German account describes 1,162 guns, so the truth is probably somewhere in between. Confusingly, Prior and Wilson claim that the number of German guns was seriously underestimated by Fifth Army intelligence (by up to 50 per cent). Given that GHQ intelligence had arrived at the reasonably accurate figure of 1,500 guns, this would seem to be incorrect. In his examination of British intelligence, Jim Beach finds that 'the picture of German forces provided before Third Ypres was fairly comprehensive'. See Reichsarchiv, *Der Weltkrieg 1914 bis 1918,* XIII. *Die Kriegführung im Sommer und Herbst 1917. Die Ereignisse außerhalb der Westfront bis November 1918* (Berlin: E. S. Mittler & Sohn, 1942), pp. 54, 63; Edmonds, *Military Operations: 1917,* II, p. 136, n. 2; Prior and Wilson, *Passchendaele,* p. 84; and J. Beach, *Haig's Intelligence. GHQ and the German Army, 1916–1918* (Cambridge: Cambridge University Press, 2013), p. 249.

8 Edmonds, *Military Operations: 1917,* II, p. 137, n. 3.

9 See V. E. Inglefield, *The History of the Twentieth (Light) Division* (London: Nisbet & Co., 1921), p. 145.

10 TNA: WO 95/520, Captain G. W. Monier-Williams to Headquarters, Fifth Army, 14 July 1917.

11 Further gas bombardments followed throughout the month, including on 15 July (when 1,000 rounds were fired on the Ypres–Menin road); 17 and 27 July (when gas targeted British lines of communication and barracks behind Ypres); 20/21 July (battery positions south of Ypres); and 28/29 July (when Armentières and Nieuport were shelled with mustard gas). W. Volkart, *Die Gasschlacht in Flandern im Herbst 1917* (Berlin: E. S. Mittler & Sohn, 1957), pp. 51–2.

12 J. H. Boraston and C. E. O. Bax, *The Eighth Division 1914–1918* (Uckfield: Naval & Military Press, 2001; first publ. 1926), p. 124.

13 IWM: Documents 15758, Account of Colonel F. W. Mellish, pp. 27–8.

14 H. Gordon, *The Unreturning Army. A Field-Gunner in Flanders, 1917–18* (London: J. M. Dent & Sons, 1967), pp. 52–4.

15 IWM: Documents 8214, F. A. Sclater, 'His War', p. 8.

16 P. Maze, *A Frenchman in Khaki* (Kingswood: William Heinemann, 1934), p. 227.

17 I. F. W. Beckett, 'Operational Command: The Plans and Conduct of the Battle', in P. Liddle (ed.), *Passchendaele in Perspective. The Third Battle of Ypres* (London: Leo Cooper, 1997), pp. 110–11.

18 There were 508 British aircraft, plus 200 French, 40 Belgian and another 104 Royal Naval Air Service planes (operating out of Dunkirk). H. A. Jones, *The War in the Air. Being the Story of the Part Played in the Great War by the Royal Air Force* (6 vols., Oxford: Clarendon Press, 1922–37), IV, p. 142.

19 Ibid., pp. 145–6.

20 IWM: Documents 3215, 'Recollections by A. Sambrook', p. 60.

21 K. Bodenschatz, *Hunting With Richthofen. The Bodenschatz Diaries: Sixteen Months of Battle with JG Freiherr von Richthofen No. 1*, trans. J. Hayzlett (London: Grubb Street, 1996), pp. 25–6.

22 E. R. Hooton, *War over the Trenches. Air Power and Western Front Campaigns 1916–1918* (Hersham: Ian Allen, 2010), p. 164.

23 Robertson to Haig, 18 July 1917, in D. R. Woodward (ed.), *The Military Correspondence of Field-Marshal Sir William Robertson, Chief of the Imperial*

General Staff, December 1915–February 1918 (London: Bodley Head for the Army Records Society, 1989), pp. 203–4.

24 Haig to Robertson, 21 July 1917, in Woodward (ed.), *The Military Correspondence of Field-Marshal Sir William Robertson*, pp. 205–6.

25 Similar scenes of operational confusion were not unique to Third Ypres. The Battle of Loos in September and October 1915 was badly hampered by a lack of clarity over whether it was a limited or unlimited attack. See N. Lloyd, *Loos 1915* (Stroud: Tempus, 2006).

26 'The Peace Resolution of the Reichstag of July 19, 1917', in E. Ludendorff, *The General Staff and Its Problems. The History of the Relations between the High Command and the German Imperial Government as Revealed by Official Documents*, trans. F. A. Holt (2 vols., New York: E. P. Dutton & Co., 1920), II, pp. 475–6.

27 J. Charteris, *At G.H.Q.* (London: Cassell & Co., 1931), p. 237.

28 Beach, *Haig's Intelligence*, pp. 246–7.

29 KA: (WK) 1789, Gruppe Ieperen Kriegstagebuch, 17 July 1917.

30 KA: (WK) 1789, Gruppe Ieperen Kriegstagebuch, 25 July 1917. Other divisions received less charitable assessments. 8th, 39th and 55th Divisions were classed as 'average', 25th as 'good average', while 38th Division was only 'mediocre'.

31 F. von Lossberg, *Meine Tätigkeit im Weltkrieg 1914–1918* (Berlin: E. S. Mittler & Sohn, 1939), p. 307.

32 W. Beumelburg, *Flandern 1917* (Oldenburg: Gerhard Stalling, 1928), p. 30.

33 Prior and Wilson, *Passchendaele*, p. 87.

34 Rau in Sheldon, *Passchendaele*, p. 41.

35 *Histories of Two Hundred and Fifty-One Divisions of the German Army Which Participated in the War (1914–1918)* (Washington DC: Government Printing Office, 1920), pp. 725–6.

36 TNA: WO 157/213, Fifth Army Summary of Information, 2 August 1917.

37 Marble, *British Artillery*, p. 189.

38 TNA: WO 95/642, II Corps Summary of Information, 25 July 1917.

39 Reichsarchiv, *Der Weltkrieg*, XIII, p. 61.

40 DTA: 3502.1, R. Lewald diary, 9 August 1917.

41 Edmonds, *Military Operations: 1917*, II, p. 138, n. 1.

42 R. Binding, *A Fatalist at War*, trans. I. F. D. Morrow (London: George Allen and Unwin, 1929), p. 176.

43 BA-MA: MSG 2/13418, J. Schärdel, 'Flandernschlacht 1917', pp. 8–10.

44 Beumelburg, *Flandern*, p. 30.

45 Rupprecht diary, 28 July 1917, in Crown Prince Rupprecht, *Mein Kriegstagebuch* (3 vols., Berlin: E. S. Mittler & Sohn, 1929), II, pp. 230–31.

46 Reichsarchiv, *Der Weltkrieg,* XIII, p. 62.

47 TNA: WO 157/23, Advanced GHQ Summary of Information, 24 August 1917.

48 KA: (WK) 2523, 'Nachrichtenblatt für 29.7.17'.

49 Charteris, *At G.H.Q.*, p. 237.

6. *'A Perfect Bloody Curse'*

1 Thaer diary, 1 August 1917, in A. von Thaer, *Generalstabsdienst an der Front und in der O.H.L.* (Göttingen: Vandenhoeck & Ruprecht, 1958), p. 131.

2 F. von Lossberg, *Meine Tätigkeit im Weltkrieg 1914–1918* (Berlin: E. S. Mittler & Sohn, 1939), p. 307.

3 BA-MA: MSG 2/13418, J. Schärdel, 'Flandernschlacht 1917', pp. 13–14.

4 H. A. Jones, *The War in the Air. Being the Story of the Part Played in the Great War by the Royal Air Force* (6 vols., Oxford: Clarendon Press, 1922–37), IV, pp. 160–62. See also Appendix CII, 'V Brigade R.F.C. Order No. 53 for 31st July 1917', pp. 421–2.

5 IWM: Documents 20504, W. B. St Leger diary, 31 July 1917.

6 See Ministère de la Guerre, *Les Armées Françaises dans La Grande Guerre*, Tome V, Vol. 2 (Paris: Imprimerie Nationale, 1937), pp. 670–75.

7 See C. Headlam, *History of the Guards Division in the Great War 1915–1918* (Uckfield: Naval & Military Press, 2001; first publ. 1924), pp. 243–5.

8 F. W. Bewsher, *The History of the Fifty First (Highland) Division 1914–1918* (Uckfield: Naval & Military Press, 2001; first publ. 1920), p. 205.

9 E. Blunden, *Undertones of War* (London: Penguin Books, 2010; first publ. 1928), pp. 154–5.

10 Sir J. Edmonds, *Military Operations: France & Belgium 1917* (3 vols., London: HMSO, 1948), II, pp. 157–8.

11 TNA: WO 95/2903, '55th (West Lancashire) Division. Report on Operations, Ypres. July 29th to August 4th, 1917'.

12 S. Snelling, *VCs of the First World War. Passchendaele 1917* (Stroud: The History Press, 2012; first publ. 1998), p. 11.

13 TNA: WO 95/104, 'Summary of Tank Operations. 31st July, 1917. 3rd Brigade, Tank Corps'.

14 IWM: Documents 4755, H. S. Taylor, 'Reminiscences of the Great War 1914/1918', p. 13.

15 TNA: WO 95/104, 'Preliminary Report on Tank Operations 31st July, 1917'.

16 TNA: WO 95/101, '2nd Brigade Tank Corps. Report on Tank Operations. 31st July 1917'.

17 J. H. Boraston and C. E. O. Bax, *The Eighth Division 1914–1918* (Uckfield: Naval & Military Press, 2001; first publ. 1926), pp. 128–30.

18 TNA: WO 95/642, 'Narrative of Operations on July 31st, 1917 by II Corps', p. 2.

19 TNA: WO 95/2328, 'Report on Operations between Zero Hour 31st July and 5 a.m. 3rd August 1917. 19th Bn Manchester Regiment'.

20 Edmonds, *Military Operations: 1917*, II, pp. 154–6.

21 BA-MA: MSG 2/13418, J. Schärdel, 'Flandernschlacht 1917', p. 17. The Prussian unit mentioned was 52nd Reserve Division, which moved up that morning to support 6th Bavarian Reserve Division. For the difficulties of this relief see J. Sheldon, *The German Army at Passchendaele* (Barnsley: Pen & Sword, 2007), pp. 51–2.

22 TNA: WO 157/213, Fifth Army, Summary of Information, 4 August 1917.

23 A. Grossmann, *Das K.B. Reserve-Infanterie-Regiment Nr. 17* (Munich: Kriegsarchivs, 1923), pp. 79–80.

24 A. Buttman, *Kriegsgeschichte des Königlich Preußischen 6. Thüringischen Infanterie-Regiments Nr. 95 1914–1918* (Zeulenroda: Verlag Bernhard Sporn, 1935), p. 234.

25 A. Grossmann, *Das K.B. Reserve-Infanterie-Regiment Nr. 17* (Augsburg: D. Eisele & Sohn, 1926), p. 116.

26 KA: (WK) 2523, 'Nachrichtenblatt für 31.7.17'.

27 Sheldon, *Passchendaele*, pp. 57–8.

28 KA: (WK) 8319, 'Gefechtsbericht der am 31. Juli und 1. August 1917 bei der 6. Bayr. Res. Div. eingesetzten Infanterie-Teile der 52. Res. Division'.

29 KA: (WK) 2523, 'Nachrichtenblatt für 31.7.17'.

30 Lossberg, *Meine Tätigkeit im Weltkrieg*, p. 307.

31 These were 2nd Guard Reserve in the north, 50th Reserve and 221st Divisions in the centre, and 207th, 12th and 119th Divisions in support of Group Wytschaete. See Sheldon, *Passchendaele*, pp. 71–2, and Edmonds, *Military Operations: 1917*, II, p. 171, n. 1.

32 KA: (WK) 1789, Gruppe Ieperen. Kriegstagebuch, 31 July 1917.

33 E. Riddell and M. C. Clayton, *The Cambridgeshires 1914 to 1919* (Cambridge: Bowes & Bowes, 1934), p. 107.

34 P. Maze, *A Frenchman in Khaki* (Kingswood: William Heinemann, 1934), p. 245.

35 TNA: WO 95/2903, '55th (West Lancashire) Division. Report on Operations, Ypres. July 29th to August 4th, 1917'.

36 TNA: WO 95/959, XIX Corps War Diary, 31 July 1917.

37 E. R. Hooton, *War over the Trenches. Air Power and Western Front Campaigns 1916–1918* (Hersham: Ian Allen, 2010), p. 182.

38 IWM: Documents 3980, J. S. Walthew to 'my dear Uncle Tom', 2 August 1917.

39 Wohlenberg in Sheldon, *Passchendaele*, pp. 79–80.

40 Riddell and Clayton, *The Cambridgeshires*, p. 118.

41 Boraston and Bax, *The Eighth Division*, p. 134. For Coffin see Snelling, *Passchendaele 1917*, pp. 27–30.

42 Edmonds, *Military Operations: 1917*, II, pp. 171–4, and F. Zechlin, *Das Reserve-Infanterie-Regiment Nr. 60 im Weltkriege* (Oldenburg: Gerhard Stalling, 1926), pp. 129–31.

43 KA: (WK) 1789, Gruppe Ieperen. Kriegstagebuch, 31 July 1917.

44 See for example Zechlin, *Das Reserve-Infanterie-Regiment Nr. 60*, p. 132.

45 A. Farrar-Hockley, *Goughie. The Life of General Sir Hubert Gough* (London: Hart-Davis, MacGibbon, 1975), pp. 221–2.

46 Gough ordered a Court of Inquiry to investigate why 30th Division had been unable to capture the Black Line. It concluded that 'there was neither failure nor neglect' in the handling of the attacking brigades, and that they had suffered from the difficult ground, which caused them to lose their creeping barrage. See TNA: WO 95/2312, 'Proceedings of a Court of Inquiry Assembled at Headquarters 30th Division on the 10th day of August, 1917', and J. Beach, 'Issued by the General Staff:

Doctrine Writing at British GHQ, 1917–1918', *War in History*, Vol. 19, No. 4 (2012), pp. 480–81.

47 H. Gough, *The Fifth Army* (London: Hodder & Stoughton, 1931), p. 201.

48 Edmonds, *Military Operations: 1917*, II, pp. 177–8.

49 Sir J. Edmonds, *Military Operations: France & Belgium, 1916. Sir Douglas Haig's Command to the 1st July: Battle of the Somme* (London: Macmillan & Co., 1932), p. 483.

50 C. Carrington, *Soldier from the Wars Returning* (London: Hutchinson, 1965), p. 189.

51 C. H. Dudley Ward, *History of the Welsh Guards* (London: John Murray, 1920), p. 157.

52 KA: (WK) 1789, 'Kriegstagebuch während der Zeit des Einsatzes als Gruppe Ieperen. 1.7.17–31.7.17'.

53 R. McLeod and C. Fox, 'The Battles in Flanders during the Summer and Autumn of 1917 from General von Kuhl's *Der Weltkrieg 1914–18*', *British Army Review*, No. 116 (August 1997), p. 82.

54 Lossberg, *Meine Tätigkeit im Weltkrieg*, p. 308.

55 Thaer diary, 1 August 1917, in Thaer, *Generalstabsdienst*, p. 131.

56 Reichsarchiv, *Der Weltkrieg 1914 bis 1918, XIII. Die Kriegführung im Sommer und Herbst 1917. Die Ereignisse außerhalb der Westfront bis November 1918* (Berlin: E. S. Mittler & Sohn, 1942), p. 65.

57 W. Volkart, *Die Gasschlacht in Flandern im Herbst 1917* (Berlin: E. S. Mittler & Sohn, 1957), p. 57.

58 Rupprecht diary, 1 August 1917, in Crown Prince Rupprecht, *Mein Kriegstagebuch* (3 vols., Berlin: E. S. Mittler & Sohn, 1929), II, pp. 232–4.

59 Haig diary, 1 August 1917, in G. Sheffield and J. Bourne (eds.), *Douglas Haig. War Diaries and Letters 1914–1918* (London: Weidenfeld & Nicolson, 2005), p. 308.

60 Haig diary, 2 August 1917, in Sheffield and Bourne (eds.), *Douglas Haig*, p. 310.

61 IWM: Documents 7003, A. H. Roberts diary, 3–4 August 1917.

62 TNA: WO 95/14, 'Daily Values of Rainfall', July–August 1917. The accusation that such rainfall could have been foreseen seems to have come from John Charteris. In his biography of Haig, he states that GHQ knew 'that in Flanders the weather broke early each August with the regularity of the Indian monsoon'. See *Field-Marshal Earl Haig* (London: Cassell & Co.,

1929), p. 272. These remarks have led some writers (David Lloyd George, Basil Liddell Hart, Leon Wolff and Gerard De Groot) to criticize Haig for launching an offensive so late in the year when the possibility of wet conditions should have been anticipated. However, there seems little truth in these allegations. The historian John Hussey, who has analysed meteorological data, shows that Third Ypres 'was not a reckless gamble on a rainless autumn'. The weather was extraordinary and unexpected. August and October were abnormally wet. Furthermore, Ernest Gold, who headed the Meteorological Section at GHQ, stated that Charteris's statement was 'so contrary to recorded facts that, to a meteorologist, it seems too ridiculous to need formal refutation'. See J. Hussey, 'The Flanders Battleground and the Weather in 1917', in P. Liddle (ed.), *Passchendaele in Perspective. The Third Battle of Ypres* (London: Leo Cooper, 1997), pp. 140–58.

63 J. Charteris, *At G.H.Q.* (London: Cassell & Co., 1931), p. 241.

7. 'Like the Black Hole of Calcutta'

1 IWM: Documents 12332, 'The Journal of John Nettleton of the Rifle Brigade 1914–1919', p. 100.

2 IWM: Documents 14196, G. Carter diary, 6 August 1917.

3 IWM: Documents 12332, 'The Journal of John Nettleton of the Rifle Brigade 1914–1919', pp. 87–8.

4 TNA: WO 95/520, 'Notes on Conference Held at Lovie Chateau on 7th August'.

5 Sir J. Edmonds, *Military Operations: France & Belgium 1917* (3 vols., London: HMSO, 1948), II, pp. 185–6.

6 IWM: Sound 717, K. Page (interview, 1975).

7 TNA: WO 95/662, 'Daily Progress Report', 4 August 1917.

8 G. H. F. Nichols, *The 18th Division in the Great War* (Edinburgh and London: William Blackwood & Sons, 1922), pp. 216–17. According to the divisional history, to capture Inverness Copse and Glencorse Wood under such conditions would have been a 'military miracle' (p. 218).

9 Guinness diary, 10 August 1917, in B. Bond and S. Robbins (eds.), *Staff Officer. The Diaries of Walter Guinness (First Lord Moyne) 1914–1918* (London: Leo Cooper, 1987), pp. 167–9.

10 Edmonds, *Military Operations: 1917*, II, pp. 189–90, and TNA: WO 95/14, 'Daily Values of Rainfall', August 1917.

11 See Edmonds, *Military Operations: 1917*, II, pp. 190–201.

12 IWM: Documents 12332, 'The Journal of John Nettleton of the Rifle Brigade 1914–1919', pp. 93–7.

13 TNA: WO 95/2947, 'Operations Carried out by 167th Infantry Brigade from 12th to 17th August 1917', p. 2.

14 TNA: WO 95/2947, GA 896, Headquarters, 56th Division, 19 August 1917.

15 Edmonds, *Military Operations: 1917*, II, pp. 194–5.

16 C. Falls, *The History of the 36th (Ulster) Division* (London and Belfast: M'Caw, Stevenson & Orr, 1922), p. 116.

17 N. Steel and P. Hart, *Passchendaele. The Sacrificial Ground* (London: Cassell & Co., 2001; first publ. 2000), p. 154.

18 IWM: Documents 982, R. J. Clarke to his mother, 21 August 1917.

19 Reichsarchiv, *Der Weltkrieg 1914 bis 1918*, XIII. *Die Kriegführung im Sommer und Herbst 1917. Die Ereignisse außerhalb der Westfront bis November 1918* (Berlin: E. S. Mittler & Sohn, 1942), p. 68.

20 According to the official history of the RAF, the weather was misty with cloudy patches. German smoke shells, which spread over the battlefield, also hindered observation. The infantry's reluctance to signal their position through the use of flares may also have contributed to this failure. H. A. Jones, *The War in the Air. Being the Story of the Part Played in the Great War by the Royal Air Force* (6 vols., Oxford: Clarendon Press, 1922–37), IV, pp. 172–3.

21 A. Karl Reber, *Das K.B. 21. Infanterie Regiment. Großherzog Friedrich Franz IV. von Mecklenburg-Schwerin* (Munich: Verlag Max Schick, 1929), pp. 216–17.

22 P. Kilduff, *Richthofen. Beyond the Legend of the Red Baron* (London: Arms & Armour, 1993), p. 146.

23 W. Beumelburg, *Flandern 1917* (Oldenburg: Gerhard Stalling, 1928), p. 90.

24 Rupprecht diary, 16 August 1917, in Crown Prince Rupprecht, *Mein Kriegstagebuch* (3 vols., Berlin: E. S. Mittler & Sohn, 1929), II, p. 246.

25 DTA: 3502.1, R. Lewald diary, 14 August 1917.

26 Ibid., 16 August 1917.

27 KA: (WK) 2523, 'Nachrichtenblatt Nr. 33 (für die Zeit 15.8 mit 16.8.17)'.

28 TNA: CAB 23/3, 'War Cabinet, 204', 3 August 1917.

29 TNA: CAB 24/22/GT1621, 'Report on the Battle of 31st July, 1917, and Its Results', 4 August 1917.

30 Robertson to Haig, 9 August 1917, cited in D. R. Woodward, *Lloyd George and the Generals* (London: Associated University Presses, 1983), p. 193.

31 Haig to Robertson, 13 August 1917, in D. R. Woodward (ed.), *The Military Correspondence of Field-Marshal Sir William Robertson, Chief of the Imperial General Staff, December 1915–February 1918* (London: Bodley Head for the Army Records Society, 1989), pp. 215–16. Original emphasis.

32 G. W. L. Nicholson, *Official History of the Canadian Army in the First World War. Canadian Expeditionary Force 1914–1919* (Ottawa: Queen's Printer, 1962), p. 297.

33 T. Cook, *Shock Troops. Canadians Fighting the Great War 1917–1918* (Toronto: Penguin Canada, 2008), pp. 305–7.

34 TNA: WO 256/21, Haig diary, 19 August 1917. Original emphasis.

35 Haig to Robertson, 13 August 1917, in Woodward (ed.), *The Military Correspondence of Field-Marshal Sir William Robertson*, pp. 215–16.

36 J. Beach, *Haig's Intelligence. GHQ and the German Army, 1916–1918* (Cambridge: Cambridge University Press, 2013), pp. 250–54.

37 J. Charteris, *At G.H.Q.* (London: Cassell & Co., 1931), pp. 245–7. Original emphasis.

38 Lord Hankey, *The Supreme Command 1914–1918* (2 vols., London: George Allen and Unwin, 1961), II, p. 702.

39 D. Lloyd George, *War Memoirs of David Lloyd George* (2 vols., London: Odhams Press, 1933–6), II, pp. 1313–15, for the 'tactics of deception'.

40 TNA: CAB 23/3, 'War Cabinet, 203', 2 August 1917.

41 TNA: CAB 23/3, 'War Cabinet, 217', 17 August 1917.

42 Hankey, *The Supreme Command*, II, p. 693.

43 J. Grigg, *Lloyd George. War Leader 1916–1918* (London: Penguin Books, 2003; first publ. 2002), p. 220. Smuts's report, which recommended the creation of an independent air service, the Royal Air Force, can be found in TNA: CAB 24/22/GT1658, 'War Cabinet Committee on Air Organisation and Home Defence against Air Raids', 17 August 1917.

44 TNA: CAB 24/24/GT1814, 'Report on Operations in Flanders from 4th August to 20th August, 1917', 21 August 1917.

45 See R. Prior and T. Wilson, *Passchendaele. The Untold Story* (New Haven and London: Yale University Press, 2002; first publ. 1996), pp. 104–5.

46 TNA: WO 95/520, 'Notes on Army Commander's Conference Held at Lovie Chateau on 17th August, 1917'. In fairness to Gough, he was also keen to hear from commanders, down to brigade level, about how best to tackle the German defensive system. This sudden urge for agreement and consensus was, however, too little, too late. J. Beach, 'Issued by the General Staff: Doctrine Writing at British GHQ, 1917–1918', *War in History*, Vol. 19, No. 4 (2012), pp. 480–81.

47 H. Gough, *The Fifth Army* (London: Hodder & Stoughton, 1931), p. 205.

48 Steel and Hart, *Passchendaele*, p. 155.

49 For Gough's continuation of small-scale, 'penny-packet' attacks, see Prior and Wilson, *Passchendaele*, pp. 108–10.

50 IWM: Documents 6993, M. W. Littlewood diary, 3–28 August 1917.

51 P. Gibbs, *Now It Can be Told* (New York and London: Harper & Brothers, 1920), p. 476.

52 Falls, *The History of the 36th (Ulster) Division*, p. 122.

53 M. Hardie, cited in A. Watson, *Enduring the Great War. Combat, Morale and Collapse in the German and British Armies, 1914–1918* (Cambridge: Cambridge University Press, 2008), p. 153.

54 Edmonds, *Military Operations: 1917*, II, p. 202, and TNA: WO 95/520, 'Notes on Army Commander's Conference Held at Lovie Chateau on 17th August, 1917'.

8. *'A Question of Concentration'*

1 Lord Hankey, *The Supreme Command 1914–1918* (2 vols., London: George Allen and Unwin, 1961), II, p. 693.

2 W. Görlitz (ed.), *The Kaiser and His Court. The Diaries, Note Books and Letters of Admiral Georg Alexander von Müller, Chief of the Naval Cabinet, 1914–1918* (London: Macdonald & Co., 1961; first publ. 1959), p. 295.

3 Rupprecht diary, 20 August 1917, in Crown Prince Rupprecht, *Mein Kriegstagebuch* (3 vols., Berlin: E. S. Mittler & Sohn, 1929), II, p. 248.

4 R. McLeod and C. Fox, 'The Battles in Flanders during the Summer and Autumn of 1917 from General von Kuhl's *Der Weltkrieg 1914–18*',

British Army Review, No. 116 (August 1997), pp. 82, 87. For German losses see Sir J. Edmonds, *Military Operations: France & Belgium 1917* (3 vols., London: HMSO, 1948), II, p. 230.

5 E. Greenhalgh, *The French Army and the First World War* (Cambridge: Cambridge University Press, 2014), pp. 236–40.

6 Reichsarchiv, *Der Weltkrieg 1914 bis 1918,* XIII. *Die Kriegführung im Sommer und Herbst 1917. Die Ereignisse außerhalb der Westfront bis November 1918* (Berlin: E. S. Mittler & Sohn, 1942), p. 212.

7 Ibid., pp. 218–21. See also J. and E. Wilks, *Rommel and Caporetto* (Barnsley: Leo Cooper, 2001), pp. 8–12, and E. Ludendorff, *Ludendorff's Own Story. August 1914–November 1918* (2 vols., New York and London: Harper & Brothers, 1919), II, pp. 97–100.

8 TNA: WO 95/951, XVIII Corps War Diary, Appendix C, 'Narrative of Operations of 19th August, 1917'. According to J. F. C. Fuller, this 'very memorable feat of arms' produced the 'most remarkable results . . . for instead of 600 casualties the infantry following the tanks only sustained fifteen!' J. F. C. Fuller, *Tanks in the Great War 1914–1918* (London: John Murray, 1920), pp. 122–3.

9 TNA: WO 95/98, '"G" Battalion. Tank Corps. Report on Operations – 19/8/1917'.

10 Elles and Fuller, cited in J. P. Harris, *Men, Ideas and Tanks. British Military Thought and Armoured Forces, 1903–1939* (Manchester: Manchester University Press, 1995), p. 103.

11 TNA: WO 95/104, 'Report on Tank Operations with XIX Corps – 22nd August, 1917'.

12 So determined were the Germans to maintain their hold on this important location that they conducted at least three counter-attacks and even deployed fearsome flamethrower teams to drive the British out of the woods. See G. C. Wynne, '"The Other Side of the Hill". The Fight for Inverness Copse: 22nd–24th of August 1917', *Army Quarterly*, Vol. XXIX, No. 2 (January 1935), pp. 297–303.

13 TNA: WO 95/1871, 'Notes on the Attack by 43rd Light Infantry Brigade. 22nd August 1917'.

14 IWM: Documents 22753, G. N. Rawlence diary, 23–25 August 1917.

15 TNA: WO 95/1871, 43 Brigade, 'Lessons from the Attack', 29 August 1917.

16 KA: (WK) 2523, 'Nachrichtenblatt Nr. 36 (für die Zeit 23.8 mit 24.8.17)'.

17 Rupprecht diary, 23 August 1917, in Rupprecht, *Mein Kriegstagebuch*, II, p. 249.

18 Ibid., 25 August 1917.

19 Thaer diary, 23 August 1917, in A. von Thaer, *Generalstabsdienst an der Front und in der O.H.L.* (Göttingen: Vandenhoeck & Ruprecht, 1958), pp. 133–4.

20 KA: (WK) 2233, 'AOK 4, 26 August 1917. Wichtigste Erfahrungen der Kampf-reserven der Armee aus den Schlachten am 31.7 und 16.8.17'.

21 Lloyd George to Robertson, 26 August 1917, in D. R. Woodward (ed.), *The Military Correspondence of Field-Marshal Sir William Robertson, Chief of the Imperial General Staff, December 1915–February 1918* (London: Bodley Head for the Army Records Society, 1989), pp. 219–20.

22 M. Thompson, *The White War. Life and Death on the Italian Front 1915–1919* (London: Faber & Faber, 2008), p. 243.

23 TNA: CAB 23/3, 'War Cabinet, 224', 27 August 1917.

24 TNA: CAB 23/13, 'War Cabinet, 225 A', 28 August 1917.

25 D. French, *The Strategy of the Lloyd George Coalition, 1916–1918* (Oxford: Clarendon Press, 1995), pp. 137–9; Haig diary, 4 September 1917, in G. Sheffield and J. Bourne (eds.), *Douglas Haig. War Diaries and Letters 1914–1918* (London: Weidenfeld & Nicolson, 2005), pp. 321–2; and TNA: CAB 23/13, 'War Cabinet, 227c', 4 September 1917.

26 TNA: WO 95/951, XVIII Corps, 'Narrative of Operations of 27th August, 1917'.

27 TNA: WO 95/3034, 61st Division War Diary, August 1917.

28 A. G. Lee, *No Parachute. A Fighter Pilot in World War I* (London: Jarrolds, 1968), p. 105.

29 TNA: WO 95/520, 'Summary of Operations of Fifth Army, for Week Ending 6 p.m., 24th Aug., 1917'.

30 TNA: WO 95/520, 'Notes on Conference Held at Lovie Chateau, 25th August, 1917 [issued on 26 August 1917]', and Fifth Army to corps, 28 August 1917.

31 TNA: WO 95/2540, Gough to Fifth Army, 2 September 1917. Every commanding officer received a copy of this letter. Gough was apparently angry with the two Irish divisions, telling Haig that their failure to hold on to their gains was because 'the men are Irish and did not like the shelling'. Haig diary, 17 August 1917, in Sheffield and Bourne (eds.), *Douglas Haig*, p. 317.

32 For an example of Gough's petulance and aggression towards subordinates see his treatment of Major-General E. S. Bulfin (GOC 28th
Division) at the Battle of Loos. Between 27 September and 5 October
1915, Bulfin's division was repeatedly ordered to make a series of hopeless advances across no-man's-land without sufficient artillery support.
See N. Lloyd, *Loos 1915* (Stroud: Tempus, 2006), pp. 192–7.

33 An amphibious landing on the Belgian coast had been considered by
British war planners since at least December 1914 and periodically
resurfaced over the next two and a half years. Haig tasked General
Sir Henry Rawlinson with planning the operation, and envisaged 1st
Division landing along the coast from Westende Bains to Middelkerke,
and then linking up with an attack from the Yser bridgehead, pushing
towards Ostend. The landing seems to have been planned with thoroughness and care. Andrew Wiest argues that it was 'a real and viable
option . . . that could have liberated much of the Belgian coast'. This is
debatable, however. The German historian of the MarineKorps, which
defended the coastal sector, gives it short shrift. 'Given the advanced
state of the Flanders defences, it seems highly unlikely that the British landing would have been anything other than a disaster.' See
Edmonds, *Military Operations: 1917*, II, pp. 116–17; A. Wiest, *Passchendaele
and the Royal Navy* (New York: Greenwood Press, 1995), p. xxiii;
and M. D. Karau, *'Wielding the Dagger'. The MarineKorps Flandern and
the German War Effort, 1914–1918* (London and Westport: Praeger,
2003), p. 161.

34 Haig diary, 25 August 1917, in J. Terraine, *The Road to Passchendaele. The
Flanders Offensive of 1917: A Study in Inevitability* (London: Leo Cooper,
1977), p. 240.

35 TNA: WO 95/520, Kiggell to Gough, 28 August 1917, and R. Prior
and T. Wilson, *Passchendaele. The Untold Story* (New Haven and London: Yale University Press, 2002; first publ. 1996), pp. 108–9.

36 Haig seems to have been influenced by the unpopularity of Gough's
Chief of Staff, Neill Malcolm, who was accused of concealing informa-
tion from his commander. See I. F. W. Beckett, 'Operational Command:
The Plans and Conduct of the Battle', in P. Liddle (ed.), *Passchendaele in
Perspective. The Third Battle of Ypres* (London: Leo Cooper, 1997), p. 110.

37 Edmonds, *Military Operations: 1917*, II, p. 207.

38 TNA: WO 95/275, Plumer to GHQ, 12 August 1917.

39 Appendix XXV, 'Second Army's Notes on Training and Preparation for Offensive Operations', in Edmonds, *Military Operations: 1917*, II, pp. 459–64.

40 Edmonds, *Military Operations: 1917*, II, pp. 236–7.

41 Appendix XXI, 'Second Army Operation Order No. 4 of the 1st September, 1917', in Edmonds, *Military Operations: 1917*, II, pp. 449–50.

42 TNA: WO 95/98, I Brigade Tank Corps, 'Allotment of Tanks to Objectives for Operations on 20th September 1917'.

43 TNA WO 95/275, 'General Principles on Which the Artillery Plan Will be Drawn'.

44 TNA: WO 95/275, 'Statement Showing the Rounds per Gun, Number of Guns and the Number of Rounds Required for a 7 Day Bombardment'. Plumer would also be able to employ significant amounts of the No. 106 Instant Percussion Fuse, which had recently been developed. These fuses offered a much more satisfactory method of wire-cutting by using high-explosive shells, rather than conventional shrapnel. The 106 'detonated the shell immediately it impacted the ground, before it had dug itself into the earth'. This ensured that the blast went outwards, horizontally, rather than upwards, giving better results at breaking down wire entanglements. Moreover, it could do so without cratering the ground. See P. Griffith, *Battle Tactics of the Western Front. The British Army's Art of Attack 1916–1918* (New Haven and London: Yale University Press, 1994), p. 140.

9. *'An Introduction to Hard Work'*

1 TNA: WO 95/275, Plumer to GHQ, 12 August 1917.

2 C. E. W. Bean, *The Official History of Australia in the War of 1914–1918* (13 vols., Sydney: Angus & Robertson, 1941–2), IV, p. 734, n. 149. See also A. Elkins, 'The Australians at Passchendaele', in P. Liddle (ed.), *Passchendaele in Perspective. The Third Battle of Ypres* (London: Leo Cooper, 1997), pp. 231–2.

3 E. P. F. Lynch, *Somme Mud. The Experiences of an Infantryman in France, 1916–1919*, ed. W. Davies (London: Bantam, 2008; first publ. 2006), p. 231.

4 IWM: Documents 3215, 'Recollections by A. Sambrook', p. 56.

5 C. E. W. Bean, *Making the Legend. The War Writings of C. E. W. Bean*, ed. D. Winter (St Lucia, Queensland: University of Queensland Press, 1992), pp. 23–4.

6 Bean, *The Official History of Australia*, IV, p. 734.

7 TNA: WO 95/3535, 'Advance Report on Operations of 5th Australian Division'.

8 AWM: AWM4 1/46/11, 4th Australian Division War Diary, 11–20 September 1917.

9 AWM: 2DRL/0512, B. W. Champion diary, 13 August 1917.

10 Sir J. Edmonds, *Military Operations. France & Belgium 1917* (3 vols., London: HMSO, 1948), II, pp. 243–4. These minor operations were intended to improve the line and secure a number of strongpoints along the front. Both attacks failed.

11 Bean, *The Official History of Australia*, IV, p. 748.

12 C. Carrington, *Soldier from the Wars Returning* (London: Hutchinson, 1965), p. 191.

13 W. H. L. Watson, *With the Tanks 1916–1918. Memoirs of a British Tank Commander in the Great War*, ed. B. Carruthers (Barnsley: Pen & Sword, 2014; first publ. 1920), pp. 126–7.

14 J. T. B. McCudden, *Flying Fury. Five Years in the Royal Flying Corps* (Folkestone: Bailey Brothers & Swinfen, 1973; first publ. 1918), p. 183.

15 Ibid., pp. 186–7.

16 K. Bodenschatz, *Hunting with Richthofen. The Bodenschatz Diaries: Sixteen Months of Battle with JG Freiherr von Richthofen No. 1*, trans. J. Hayzlett (London: Grubb Street, 1996), pp. 37–8.

17 E. R. Hooton, *War over the Trenches. Air Power and Western Front Campaigns 1916–1918* (Hersham: Ian Allen, 2010), pp. 175–8.

18 H. A. Jones, *The War in the Air. Being the Story of the Part Played in the Great War by the Royal Air Force* (6 vols., Oxford: Clarendon Press, 1922–37), IV, pp. 180–81.

19 Ibid., p. 202.

20 Haig diary, 28 August 1917, in G. Sheffield and J. Bourne (eds.), *Douglas Haig. War Diaries and Letters 1914–1918* (London: Weidenfeld & Nicolson, 2005), p. 320.

21 Edmonds, *Military Operations: 1917*, II, pp. 244–7.

22 AWM: AWM4 14/2/2, Chief Engineer I ANZAC Corps, War Diary, 5–18 September 1917.

23 See J. Lee, 'Command and Control in Battle: British Divisions on the Menin Road Ridge, 20 September 1917', in G. Sheffield and D. Todman (eds.), *Command and Control on the Western Front. The British Army's Experience 1914–1918* (Staplehurst: Spellmount, 2004), pp. 119–39, which details the 'blizzard of paperwork' that divisional commanders faced.

24 AWM: 2DRL/0512, B. W. Champion diary, 6 September 1917.

25 Bean, *The Official History of Australia*, IV, pp. 752–3.

26 Appendix XXII, 'Second Army Addendum of 10th September 1917, to Operation Order No. 4 of 1st September 1917', in Edmonds, *Military Operations: 1917*, II, pp. 451–2.

27 Reichsarchiv, *Der Weltkrieg 1914 bis 1918,* XIII. *Die Kriegführung im Sommer und Herbst 1917. Die Ereignisse außerhalb der Westfront bis November 1918* (Berlin: E. S. Mittler & Sohn, 1942), p. 71.

28 Thaer diary, 11 September 1917, in A. von Thaer, *Generalstabsdienst an der Front und in der O.H.L.* (Göttingen: Vandenhoeck & Ruprecht, 1958), pp. 136–7.

29 See C. Duffy, *Through German Eyes. The British and the Somme 1916* (London: Orion, 2007; first publ. 2006), pp. 41–5, for the development of German interrogation techniques.

30 Reichsarchiv, *Der Weltkrieg,* XIII, p. 70. See also R. McLeod and C. Fox, 'The Battles in Flanders during the Summer and Autumn of 1917 from General von Kuhl's *Der Weltkrieg 1914–18*', *British Army Review*, No. 116 (August 1997), pp. 82–3.

31 Thaer diary, 4 and 6 September 1917, in Thaer, *Generalstabsdienst*, pp. 136, 137.

32 Rupprecht diary, 6 and 12 September 1917, in Crown Prince Rupprecht, *Mein Kriegstagebuch* (3 vols., Berlin: E. S. Mittler & Sohn, 1929), II, pp. 258, 260. This was not the case. See Bean, *The Official History of Australia*, IV, p. 758.

33 German unit movements in J. Sheldon, *The German Army at Passchendaele* (Barnsley: Pen & Sword, 2007), pp. 145–7. See also *Histories of Two Hundred and Fifty-One Divisions of the German Army Which Participated in the War (1914–1918)* (Washington DC: Government Printing Office, 1920), p. 372.

34 KA: (WK) 1790, Gruppe Ieperen Kriegstagebuch, 10 September 1917.

35 W. Volkart, *Die Gasschlacht in Flandern im Herbst 1917* (Berlin: E. S. Mittler & Sohn, 1957), pp. 57–8.

36 DTA: 3502.1, R. Lewald diary, 24 August–10 September 1917.

37 Ibid., 13 September 1917.

38 The incident occurred on the evening of 19 August when Ludendorff's train, shunting past the southern end of Brussels, collided with the engine of an ammunition train coming the other way. The carriage was torn apart, throwing Ludendorff and his staff to the ground, but not causing any serious injuries. Apparently, an incorrect switch had placed Ludendorff's train in danger – and with it gave rise to the possibility that the history of the war, and Germany, would have changed dramatically, had Ludendorff being killed or seriously wounded. M. Nebelin, *Ludendorff. Diktator im Ersten Weltkrieg* (Munich: Siedler Verlag, 2010), p. 240.

39 Ibid., p. 225, and E. Ludendorff, *Ludendorff's Own Story. August 1914–November 1918* (2 vols., New York and London: Harper & Brothers, 1919), II, p. 77.

40 Nebelin, *Ludendorff*, p. 240. Pernet was probably shot down by Lieutenant Ralph Curtis and Second Lieutenant H. Munro of 48 Squadron. See J. Guttman, *Bristol F2 Fighter Aces of World War I* (Botley: Osprey, 2007), p. 15.

41 Reichsarchiv, *Der Weltkrieg,* XIII, p. 198.

42 Ludendorff, *Ludendorff's Own Story*, II, pp. 99–100.

43 Ibid., p. 92, and Rupprecht diary, 20 August 1917, in Rupprecht, *Mein Kriegstagebuch*, II, p. 247.

44 TNA: WO 157/24, 'GHQ Summary of Information', 25 September 1917.

45 See J. Förster, 'Ludendorff and Hitler in Perspective: The Battle for the German Soldier's Mind, 1917–1944', *War in History*, Vol. 10, No. 3 (2003), pp. 324–5, and A. Watson, *Ring of Steel. Germany and Austria–Hungary at War, 1914–1918* (London: Allen Lane, 2014), pp. 485–6.

46 R. Binding, *A Fatalist at War*, trans. I. F. D. Morrow (London: George Allen and Unwin, 1929), pp. 182–3.

47 A. Watson, *Enduring the Great War. Combat, Morale and Collapse in the German and British Armies, 1914–1918* (Cambridge: Cambridge University Press, 2008), p. 170. See also *Divisions of the German Army*, p. 363.

48 BA-MA: MSG 2/13418, J. Schärdel, 'Flandernschlacht 1917', p. 7.

49 Schwilden, in Sheldon, *Passchendaele*, pp. 147–8.

50 Reichsarchiv, *Der Weltkrieg,* XIII, p. 73.

51 Edmonds, *Military Operations: 1917,* II, p. 255, n. 1.

10. 'A Stunning Pandemonium'

1 TNA: WO 157/118, Second Army Daily Intelligence Summary, 24 September 1917.

2 G. Powell, *Plumer. The Soldiers' General* (London: Leo Cooper, 1990), p. 216. According to the commander of I ANZAC Corps, Lieutenant-General Sir William Birdwood, 'General Plumer (whose Second Army we had now rejoined) called me up and asked what I thought of postponing the attack for twenty-four hours. I was entirely against this. My 1st and 2nd Divisions were already on the move, quietly making their way to their positions of assembly.' Lord Birdwood, *Khaki and Gown. An Autobiography* (London: Ward, Lock & Co., 1941), p. 314. 5mm of rain fell on the night of 19/20 September. TNA: WO 95/15, 'Daily Values of Rainfall', September 1917.

3 C. E. W. Bean, *The Official History of Australia in the War of 1914–1918* (13 vols., Sydney: Angus & Robertson, 1941–2), IV, pp. 758–9.

4 Ibid., p. 757.

5 IWM: Documents 15177, A. G. MacGregor, 'War Diary 1917–1919', 19/20 September 1917.

6 M. Farndale, *History of the Royal Regiment of Artillery. Western Front 1914–18* (London: Royal Artillery Institution, 1986), p. 205, and Sir J. Edmonds, *Military Operations: France & Belgium 1917* (3 vols., London: HMSO, 1948), II, p. 238.

7 The ground seems to have prevented the tanks from making any effective contribution on 20 September. Of the nineteen machines supporting 58th Division, none were able 'to be of any material assistance to the infantry'. Thirteen ditched and four received direct hits. In 51st Division, one machine helped to capture a German position known as Delta House, but the others were stopped by either receiving direct hits or ditching. In such soft, crater-filled ground, unditching gear proved

useless. TNA: WO 95/98, I Tank Brigade, 'Report on Tank Operations 20.9.17'.

8 TNA: WO 95/1740, '9th (Scottish) Division. Narrative of Events. From September 18th to September 24th 1917', Appendix C, 'Action of Enemy'.

9 TNA: WO 157/118, Second Army Daily Intelligence Summary, 21 September 1917.

10 AWM: 3DRL/1465, A. D. Hollyhoke, 'Battle of Polygon Wood: (Part of "Menin Road Battle")', pp. 1–4.

11 TNA: WO 95/983, I ANZAC Corps, 'Weekly Summary of Operations', 21 September 1917.

12 TNA: WO 95/3256, War Diary, 2nd Australian Division, September 1917, Appendix C: 'Operations of 20th September, 1917'.

13 TNA: WO 95/2566, '39th Division. Report on Operations of 20th September 1917'.

14 TNA: WO 95/2183, 'Operations of 69th Infantry Brigade from 19th September to 25th Sept. 1917'.

15 S. Snelling, *VCs of the First World War. Passchendaele 1917* (Stroud: The History Press, 2012; first publ. 1998), p. 150.

16 Ibid., pp. 151–2.

17 TNA: WO 95/853, 'X Corps Narrative. Zero Hour 20th September, to 6 a.m. 21st September'.

18 H. A. Jones, *The War in the Air. Being the Story of the Part Played in the Great War by the Royal Air Force* (6 vols., Oxford: Clarendon Press, 1922–37), IV, pp. 183, 185.

19 Reichsarchiv, *Der Weltkrieg 1914 bis 1918*, XIII. *Die Kriegführung im Sommer und Herbst 1917. Die Ereignisse außerhalb der Westfront bis November 1918* (Berlin: E. S. Mittler & Sohn, 1942), p. 74. Zone calls had been developed in 1916 in order to engage targets of opportunity. The battlefield was divided into a series of zones (based on the lettered squares of the 1:40,000 map), which were each subdivided into four letters (each covering 3,000 yards square). This gave each zone a two-letter code, which could then be quickly and efficiently sent to ground observers. This 'reduced the necessity for personal liaison between the flying officers and the gunners to a minimum, and so eliminated the confusion which might otherwise arise from difficulty of communication when the armies were moving'. See Jones, *The War in the Air*, II, pp. 175–6.

20 Edmonds, *Military Operations: 1917*, II, pp. 272–7.

21 Reichsarchiv, *Der Weltkrieg*, XIII, p. 74.

22 Kleine in J. Sheldon, *The German Army at Passchendaele* (Barnsley: Pen & Sword, 2007), pp. 161–2. II Battalion had lost over 200 men before it had even got to the front. *Histories of Two Hundred and Fifty-One Divisions of the German Army Which Participated in the War (1914–1918)* (Washington DC: Government Printing Office, 1920), p. 728.

23 KA: (WK) 1246/1, 'Gefechtsbericht des 11 IR Ueber Einsatz des Regts. Als Stossregiment im Abschnitt der bayer. Ers. Div. vom 20.9–22.9.1917'.

24 Haig diary, 20 September 1917, in G. Sheffield and J. Bourne (eds.), *Douglas Haig. War Diaries and Letters 1914–1918* (London: Weidenfeld & Nicolson, 2005), p. 329. Original emphasis.

25 'Menin Road Battle', *The Times*, 21 September 1917.

26 'The British Victory', *The Times*, 22 September 1917.

27 J. Charteris, *At G.H.Q.* (London: Cassell & Co., 1931), pp. 254–5.

28 TNA: WO 157/118, 'Second Army. Comments on Operations, 20th Sept., 1917', 28 September 1917.

29 See G. Sheffield, *Forgotten Victory. The First World War: Myths and Realities* (London: Headline, 2001), p. 176, and *The Chief. Douglas Haig and the British Army* (London: Aurum Press, 2011), pp. 238–9; P. Simkins, 'Herbert Plumer', in I. F. W. Beckett and S. J. Corvi (eds.), *Haig's Generals* (Barnsley: Pen & Sword, 2006), p. 156; N. Steel and P. Hart, *Passchendaele. The Sacrificial Ground* (London: Cassell & Co., 2001; first publ. 2000), p. 233; and A. Ekins, 'The Australians at Passchendaele', in P. Liddle (ed.), *Passchendaele in Perspective. The Third Battle of Ypres* (London: Leo Cooper, 1997), pp. 219–20.

30 R. Prior and T. Wilson, *Passchendaele. The Untold Story* (New Haven and London: Yale University Press, 2002; first publ. 1996), p. 119. Prior and Wilson cite the figure of 27,001 casualties for 31 July 1917, which refers only to those losses within Fifth Army and does not include the 4,849 casualties that Second Army sustained that day. If the combined figure of 31,850 is used, the casualties per square mile rise to 1,769. See Edmonds, *Military Operations: 1917*, II, pp. 177–8, n. 1.

31 A. Farrar-Hockley, *Goughie. The Life of General Sir Hubert Gough* (London: Hart-Davis, MacGibbon, 1975), p. 235.

32 Prior and Wilson, *Passchendaele*, p. 123. These criticisms are largely
    repeated in G. Casey, 'General Sir Herbert Plumer and "Passchendaele":
    A Reassessment', *Firestep*, Vol. 5, No. 2 (November 2004), pp. 40–60.

33 German regimental histories neatly capture this dichotomy. For ex-
    ample, the history of the 239 Reserve Infantry Regiment noted, with
    pride, its performance on 31 July, with the enemy suffering 'terrible
    losses'. See J. Schatz, *Geschichte des Badischen (Rheinischen) Reserve-
    Infanterie-Regiments 239* (Stuttgart: Chr. Belser, 1927), p. 125. Likewise,
    the author of the history of 60 Reserve Infantry Regiment crowed
    about a 'brilliantly executed counter-attack' on 31 July, which contrib-
    uted to the failure of the British to break through on the first day. See F.
    Zechlin, *Das Reserve-Infanterie-Regiment Nr. 60 im Weltkriege* (Olden-
    burg: Gerhard Stalling, 1926), p. 136. For similarly positive views
    ('unsurpassable performance' and 'outstanding bravery') see also
    A. Wiedersich, *Das Reserve-Infanterie Regiment Nr. 229* (Berlin: Verlag
    Tradition Wilhelm Rolf, 1929), p. 93. Contrast this with several histor-
    ies of those regiments that fought on 20 September and the mood is
    much less exuberant. For example, the history of 11 Infantry Regiment
    complains that it suffered 'heavy losses' from the 'overwhelming shell-
    ing', leaving company strengths as low as 25–30 men (as opposed to 100
    men that morning). A. Dunzinger, *Das K.B. 11 Infanterie-Regiment von
    der Tann* (Munich: Bayerische Kriegsarchivs, 1921), p. 55. 459 Infantry
    Regiment also lamented the 'heavy losses' and 'bloody tragedies' of
    20 September. F. von Pirscher, *Das (Rheinisch-Westfälische) Infanterie-
    Regiment Nr. 459* (Oldenburg: Gerhard Stalling, 1926), p. 73. See
    Sheldon, *Passchendaele*, pp. 148–65.

34 Rupprecht diary, 20 September 1917, in Crown Prince Rupprecht, *Mein
    Kriegstagebuch* (3 vols., Berlin: E. S. Mittler & Sohn, 1929), II, p. 263. For
    Fourth Army's report on the battle see Pirscher, *Infanterie-Regiment Nr.
    459*, p. 74.

35 Reichsarchiv, *Der Weltkrieg,* XIII, p. 75.

36 J. Grigg, *Lloyd George. War Leader 1916–1918* (London: Penguin Books,
    2003; first publ. 2002), p. 262.

37 D. Lloyd George, *War Memoirs of David Lloyd George* (2 vols., London:
    Odhams Press, 1933–6), II, pp. 1315–16. Whether this was the case
    remains impossible to verify. Lloyd George admitted that he had 'no

direct evidence' of it, but had been told by an 'unimpeachable' source after the war that someone from GHQ rang up Fifth Army and told them to alter the composition of the prisoner cages prior to the Prime Minister's arrival. For Lloyd George this was 'all in keeping with the effect made to create an impression, that although the Belgian coast was not as yet much nearer, those who stood between us and that objective did not possess the requisite quality to bar the way much longer against our tremendous onslaughts'. At a meeting of the War Cabinet on 27 September, Lloyd George had remarked on the 'poor condition of the German prisoners whom he had seen on the 26th instant'. TNA: CAB 23/4, 'War Cabinet, 240', 27 September 1917.

38 Lord Hankey, *The Supreme Command 1914–1918* (2 vols., London: George Allen and Unwin, 1961), II, pp. 702, 703.

39 TNA: CAB 24/27/GT2143, Decypher Sir A. Hardinge (San Sebastian) to Lord Hardinge, 19 September 1917.

40 TNA: CAB 23/16, 'War Cabinet, 239(a)', 27 September 1917, and 'Cypher Telegram to His Majesty's Representatives, 8 October 1917'.

41 See D. R. Woodward, 'David Lloyd George, a Negotiated Peace with Germany and the Kuhlmann Peace Kite of September, 1917', *Canadian Journal of History*, Vol. 6, No. 1 (1971), pp. 75–93, and D. French, *The Strategy of the Lloyd George Coalition, 1916–1918* (Oxford: Clarendon Press, 1995), pp. 144–7.

42 J. T. B. McCudden, *Flying Fury. Five Years in the Royal Flying Corps* (Folkestone: Bailey Brothers & Swinfen, 1973; first publ. 1918), p. 195.

43 AWM: AWM4 14/2/2, Chief Engineer I ANZAC Corps, War Diary, 19–30 September 1917.

11. 'War with a Big W'

1 IWM: Documents 17248, S. Roberts, 'The Glorious Sixth', p. 151.

2 TNA: WO 256/22, Haig diary, 21 September 1917.

3 Sir J. Edmonds, *Military Operations: France & Belgium 1917* (3 vols., London: HMSO, 1948), II, p. 280.

4 TNA: WO 256/22, Haig diary, 23 September 1917.

5 AWM: 2DRL/0277, S. E. Hunt, 'The Operation at Polygon Wood', pp. 5–6.

6 C. E. W. Bean, *The Official History of Australia in the War of 1914–1918* (13 vols., Sydney: Angus & Robertson, 1941–2), IV, p. 813.

7 AWM: 2DRL/0277, S. E. Hunt, 'The Operation at Polygon Wood', pp. 6–7.

8 AWM: AWM4 23/66/16, 49/Battalion, 'Report on Operation 25–27th September, 1917'.

9 AWM: AWM4 1/48/18 Part 2, 'Report on Operations Carried Out by 4th Aus. Division on 26/9/1917 and Subsequent Days'.

10 Edmonds, *Military Operations: 1917*, II, p. 288.

11 The German attack on 25 September was conducted by two regiments, 229 Reserve and 230 Reserve (of 50th Reserve Division), and was able to make some limited gains between the southern edge of Polygon Wood and the Menin Road. It was supported by twenty heavy and forty-four field batteries, an almost unprecedented amount of artillery for such a modest operation. Tellingly, 33rd Division's history states that they were attacked by 'no less than six Divisions'. See Edmonds, *Military Operations: 1917*, II, p. 283, n. 2, and G. S. Hutchinson, *The Thirty-Third Division in France and Flanders 1915–1919* (Uckfield: Naval & Military Press, 2004; first publ. 1921), pp. 67, 72.

12 S. Snelling, *VCs of the First World War. Passchendaele 1917* (Stroud: The History Press, 2012; first publ. 1998), pp. 166–74.

13 TNA: WO 95/853, '39th Division. Report on Operations of Sept. 26th 1917'.

14 H. A. Jones, *The War in the Air. Being the Story of the Part Played in the Great War by the Royal Air Force* (6 vols., Oxford: Clarendon Press, 1922–37), IV, pp. 191–3.

15 Edmonds, *Military Operations: 1917*, II, p. 292, n. 1.

16 Caspari, in J. Sheldon, *The German Army at Passchendaele* (Barnsley: Pen & Sword, 2007), pp. 169–71.

17 F. von Pirscher, *Das (Rheinisch-Westfälische) Infanterie-Regiment Nr. 459* (Oldenburg: Gerhard Stalling, 1926), pp. 83–4, 89.

18 TNA: WO 95/748, V Corps, 'Report on Attack of 26th September, 1917'.

19 Edmonds, *Military Operations: 1917*, II, p. 293, n. 3.

20 R. Prior and T. Wilson, *Passchendaele. The Untold Story* (New Haven and London: Yale University Press, 2002; first publ. 1996), p. 131. Prior and Wilson (incorrectly) claim that the casualty rate at Polygon Wood was 50 per cent higher than at Menin Road.

21 C. R. Simpson (ed.), *The History of the Lincolnshire Regiment 1914–1918* (London: The Medici Society, 1931), pp. 264–6.

22 IWM: Documents 22718, E. V. Tanner diary, 26 September 1917.

23 Reichsarchiv, *Der Weltkrieg 1914 bis 1918,* XIII. *Die Kriegführung im Sommer und Herbst 1917. Die Ereignisse außerhalb der Westfront bis November 1918* (Berlin: E. S. Mittler & Sohn, 1942), p. 77.

24 A. Wiedersich, *Das Reserve-Infanterie Regiment Nr. 229* (Berlin: Verlag Tradition Wilhelm Rolf, 1929), p. 106.

25 Edmonds, *Military Operations: 1917*, II, p. 292, n. 1.

26 TNA: WO 95/983, I ANZAC Corps War Diary, September 1917, Appendix H, 'Notes on the Situation'. See also *Histories of Two Hundred and Fifty-One Divisions of the German Army Which Participated in the War (1914–1918)* (Washington DC: Government Printing Office, 1920), p. 85, and TNA: WO 157/118, Second Army Daily Intelligence Summary, 24 September 1917.

27 Thaer diary, 28 September 1917, in A. von Thaer, *Generalstabsdienst an der Front und in der O.H.L.* (Göttingen: Vandenhoeck & Ruprecht, 1958), pp. 139–40.

28 Ibid., p. 140.

29 W. Görlitz (ed.), *The Kaiser and His Court. The Diaries, Note Books and Letters of Admiral Georg Alexander von Müller, Chief of the Naval Cabinet, 1914–1918* (London: Macdonald & Co., 1961; first publ. 1959), p. 303.

30 E. Ludendorff, *Ludendorff's Own Story. August 1914–November 1918* (2 vols., New York and London: Harper & Brothers, 1919), II, pp. 102–3.

31 The machine-guns would be grouped in four- and eight-gun batteries. These tactical changes are discussed in G. W. L. Nicholson, *Official History of the Canadian Army in the First World War. Canadian Expeditionary Force 1914–1919* (Ottawa: Queen's Printer, 1962), pp. 316–18.

32 Group Ypres would mount the attack, known as Operation 'Hohensturm' ('Storming Heights'), with four battalions, led by 212 Reserve Infantry Regiment (45th Reserve Division) and supported by 4th Guard Infantry Division, which would hold the sector from where the

attack would take place. By recapturing this ground, particularly a rise known as Tokio Spur, it would provide better observation, allow them to dig in on higher, dryer ground, and strengthen morale. See TNA: WO 95/3256, 2nd Australian Division Intelligence Summary, 6 October 1917, and K. Gabriel, *Die 4 Garde-Infanterie-Division. Der Ruhmesweg einer bewährten Kampftruppe durch den Weltkrieg* (Berlin: Verlag von Klasing & Co., 1920), p. 100.

33 T. T. Lupfer, *The Dynamics of Doctrine. The Changes in German Tactical Doctrine during the First World War* (Fort Leavenworth: U.S. Army Command and General Staff College, 1981), p. 66, n. 116.

34 Fourth Army Operation Order, 30 September 1917, in Sheldon, *Passchendaele*, pp. 184–6.

35 W. Beumelburg, *Flandern 1917* (Oldenburg: Gerhard Stalling, 1928), pp. 120–21.

36 TNA: WO 95/3256, 'Translation of Captured Documents' in I ANZAC Corps Intelligence Summary, 6 October 1917. A number of divisional commanders raised major objections to the massing of troops in this manner, but were overruled. Ludendorff argued subsequently that he only agreed to this because of the opinion of experienced officers at the front, but this seems unlikely. See Beumelburg, *Flandern*, p. 124, and Sheldon, *Passchendaele*, p. 233, n. 2.

37 Edmonds, *Military Operations: 1917*, II, p. 296.

38 TNA: WO 256/22, Haig diary, 28 September 1917.

39 Edmonds, *Military Operations: 1917*, II, p. 297.

40 Haig diary, 2 October 1917, in G. Sheffield and J. Bourne (eds.), *Douglas Haig. War Diaries and Letters 1914–1918* (London: Weidenfeld & Nicolson, 2005), p. 331.

41 Sir C. Harington, *Plumer of Messines* (London: John Murray, 1935), pp. 314–17.

42 AWM: 3DRL/2379, H. A. Goddard, 'Tour of a Company in the Front Line', pp. 1–2.

43 AWM: 3DRL/2316, letter, 1 October 1917, in 'War Letters of General Monash: Volume 2, 4 March 1917–28 December 1918'.

44 C. Edmonds [C. Carrington], *A Subaltern's War* (London: Anthony Mott, 1984; first publ. 1929), pp. 104–6.

45 Edmonds, *Military Operations: 1917*, II, pp. 299–301.

12. 'An Overwhelming Blow'

1 Monash, cited in G. Serle, *John Monash. A Biography* (Carlton: Melbourne University Press, 2002; first publ. 1982), p. 293.

2 The use of jumping-off tapes was because of the lack of 'regular or continuous trenches' from which the attack could be launched. H. Stewart, *The New Zealand Division 1916–1919. A Popular History Based on Official Records* (Auckland: Whitcombe & Tombs, 1921), p. 258.

3 The exact time of the German barrage differs across accounts. In Sir J. Edmonds, *Military Operations: France & Belgium 1917* (3 vols., London: HMSO, 1948), II, p. 303, it is 5.20. Bean has it at 5.27. C. E. W. Bean, *The Official History of Australia in the War of 1914–1918* (13 vols., Sydney: Angus & Robertson, 1941–2), IV, p. 843. The war diaries of the divisions involved put it later (between 5.40 and 5.45 a.m.). See AWM: AWM4 1/42/33, Part 1, 1st Australian Division War Diary, 4 October 1917, and AWM4 1/44/27 Part 2, 2nd Australian Division War Diary, October 1917.

4 AWM: AWM4 1/46/12 Part 2, 42/Battalion Report, 4 October 1917.

5 C. Carrington, *Soldier from the Wars Returning* (London: Hutchinson, 1965), pp. 191–3.

6 AWM: AWM38 3DRL 606/254/1, H. G. Hartnett diary, 4 October 1917.

7 AWM: AWM4 23/1/27, '1st Australian Infantry Brigade. Summary of Intelligence. From 0600, 4th October to 0600, 5th October, 1917'.

8 See O. E. Burton, *The Auckland Regiment* (Auckland: Whitcombe & Tombs, 1922), p. 173.

9 S. Snelling, *VCs of the First World War. Passchendaele 1917* (Stroud: The History Press, 2012; first publ. 1998), p. 184.

10 Peeler, cited in ibid., p. 182. Both men were in action again on 12 October 1917, when McGee was killed.

11 H. A. Jones, *The War in the Air. Being the Story of the Part Played in the Great War by the Royal Air Force* (6 vols., Oxford: Clarendon Press, 1922–37), IV, pp. 184, 203.

12 TNA: WO 95/98, I Tank Brigade, 'Report on Tank Operations 4th, October 1917'.

13 TNA: WO 95/952, 'Operations of 4th Oct. 1917', in XVIII Corps War Diary, October 1917.

14 IWM: Documents 1933, Account of W. A. Rappolt, pp. 94–5.

15 K. Gabriel, *Die 4 Garde-Infanterie-Division. Der Ruhmesweg einer bewährten Kampftruppe durch den Weltkrieg* (Berlin: Verlag von Klasing & Co., 1920), p. 103.

16 Edmonds, *Military Operations: 1917*, II, p. 305, n. 2.

17 TNA: WO 95/276, Second Army Summary of Operations, 27 September–4 October 1917.

18 Edmonds, *Military Operations: 1917*, II, pp. 315–17.

19 See for example 'Broodseinde. Greatest Victory of the War', *Taranaki Daily News*, 25 October 1917.

20 AWM: AWM4 1/44/27 Part 2, 2nd Australian Division War Diary, Appendix XXI, 'Second Army Summary', 6 October 1917.

21 Lord Birdwood, *Khaki and Gown. An Autobiography* (London: Ward, Lock & Co., 1941), pp. 315–16.

22 Lloyd George, cited in Bean, *The Official History of Australia*, IV, p. 877. See also L. Wolff, *In Flanders Fields* (London: Longmans, 1960), p. 195, and R. Prior and T. Wilson, *Passchendaele. The Untold Story* (New Haven and London: Yale University Press, 2002; first publ. 1996), pp. 137–9.

23 Bean, *The Official History of Australia*, IV, pp. 833, 875. See also N. Steel and P. Hart, *Passchendaele. The Sacrificial Ground* (London: Cassell & Co., 2001; first publ. 2000), p. 253, and A. Ekins, 'The Australians at Passchendaele', in P. Liddle (ed.), *Passchendaele in Perspective. The Third Battle of Ypres* (London: Leo Cooper, 1997), pp. 220–21.

24 German Official History in J. Terraine, *The Road to Passchendaele. The Flanders Offensive of 1917: A Study in Inevitability* (London: Leo Cooper, 1977), p. 281.

25 Rupprecht diary, 5 October 1917, in Crown Prince Rupprecht, *Mein Kriegstagebuch* (3 vols., Berlin: E. S. Mittler & Sohn, 1929), II, p. 267.

26 BA-MA: MSG 2/5960, Dieffenbach to Grandfather Balser (letter no. 5), 9 October 1917.

27 See 'Fourth Army Daily Report', 4 October 1917, in J. Sheldon, *The German Army at Passchendaele* (Barnsley: Pen & Sword, 2007), p. 206, which reported the loss of only 'a narrow strip of territory'.

28 TNA: WO 159/119, Second Army Daily Intelligence Summary, 11 October 1917.

29 Gabriel, *Die 4 Garde-Infanterie-Division*, p. 107.

30 A. Macdonald, *Passchendaele. The Anatomy of a Tragedy* (Auckland: HarperCollins, 2013), p. 167.

31 AWM: AWM4 1/44/27 Part 2, 2nd Australian Division War Diary, Appendix XXI, 'Extracts from 2nd Army and 1st ANZAC Intelligence Summaries', 6 October 1917, and W. Beumelburg, *Flandern 1917* (Oldenburg: Gerhard Stalling, 1928), p. 131.

32 AWM: AWM4 1/46/12 Part 2, 37/Battalion Report, 4 October 1917.

33 Beumelburg, *Flandern*, p. 122. Emphasis added.

34 E. Ludendorff, *Ludendorff's Own Story. August 1914–November 1918* (2 vols., New York and London: Harper & Brothers, 1919), II, p. 104.

35 German Official History in Terraine, *The Road to Passchendaele*, pp. 281–2. The line Army Group Rupprecht selected ran from the Yser north of Dixmude, past Merckem, west of Roulers and Menin, and passing the Lys at Deûlémont. See Reichsarchiv, *Der Weltkrieg 1914 bis 1918*, XIII. *Die Kriegführung im Sommer und Herbst 1917. Die Ereignisse außerhalb der Westfront bis November 1918* (Berlin: E. S. Mittler & Sohn, 1942), p. 81.

36 Ludendorff, *Ludendorff's Own Story*, II, p. 104.

37 R. McLeod and C. Fox, 'The Battles in Flanders during the Summer and Autumn of 1917 from General von Kuhl's *Der Weltkrieg 1914–18*', *British Army Review*, No. 116 (August 1997), p. 85.

38 Chief of the General Staff of the Field Army, 9 October 1917, in Sheldon, *Passchendaele*, pp. 226–7. Original emphases. See also Beumelburg, *Flandern*, p. 124.

39 Rupprecht diary, 12 October 1917, in Rupprecht, *Mein Kriegstagebuch*, II, p. 271.

40 Haig diary, 4 October 1917, in G. Sheffield and J. Bourne (eds.), *Douglas Haig. War Diaries and Letters 1914–1918* (London: Weidenfeld & Nicolson, 2005), pp. 332–3.

41 G. S. Duncan, *Douglas Haig as I Knew Him* (London: George Allen and Unwin, 1966), pp. 64–5. Emphasis added.

42 J. Charteris, *At G.H.Q.* (London: Cassell & Co., 1931), pp. 257–8.

43 Steel and Hart, *Passchendaele*, pp. 261–2; G. Harper, *Massacre at Passchendaele. The New Zealand Story* (Brighton: FireStep Books, 2011; first publ. 2000), pp. 52–4; and Prior and Wilson, *Passchendaele*, pp. 138–9 and 160–61. Edmonds (*Military Operations: 1917*, II, p. 325) cites a conference on

7 October in which both Plumer and Gough told Haig that they would prefer it if the campaign were closed down. Prior and Wilson dispute Edmonds's findings and argue that at no point did either general urge a cancellation of future operations.

44 TNA: WO 256/23, Haig diary, 5 October 1917. Apparently, Haig told one senior officer that 'When we get the Ridge, we've won the war.' T. Travers, *How the War was Won. Command and Technology in the British Army on the Western Front, 1917–1918* (Barnsley: Pen & Sword, 2005; first publ. 1992), p. 17.

45 Edmonds, *Military Operations: 1917*, II, pp. 323–5, and TNA: WO 95/276, Second Army G.311, 6 October 1917.

46 Sir C. Harington, *Plumer of Messines* (London: John Murray, 1935), pp. 111–12, and *Tim Harington Looks Back* (London: John Murray, 1940), pp. 63–4.

47 Godley, cited in Macdonald, *Passchendaele*, p. 53.

48 See G. Sheffield, *The Chief. Douglas Haig and the British Army* (London: Aurum Press, 2011), pp. 245–6; T. Cook, *Shock Troops. Canadians Fighting the Great War 1917–1918* (Toronto: Penguin Canada, 2008), p. 317; and N. Cave, *Battleground Europe. Ypres. Passchendaele: The Fight for the Village* (Barnsley: Pen & Sword, 2007; first publ. 1997), pp. 9–10.

49 J. Terraine, *Douglas Haig. The Educated Soldier* (London: Cassell & Co., 2000; first publ. 1963), pp. 367–8.

50 See the report by VIII Corps in M. LoCicero, *A Moonlight Massacre. The Night Operation on the Passchendaele Ridge, 2 December 1917: The Forgotten Last Act of the Third Battle of Ypres* (Solihull: Helion & Company, 2014), pp. 52–7. This refutes the idea that holding on to the Passchendaele Ridge was 'comfortable'. It concludes that there was very little point in holding the ridge unless as a jumping-off point for a spring offensive in 1918. When Sir Henry Rawlinson inspected the positions on 10 November, he readily admitted that Passchendaele was 'untenable' against 'a properly organized attack'. Prior and Wilson, *Passchendaele*, pp. 180–81. I am grateful to Dr K. W. Mitchinson for discussing this question with me and sharing his knowledge of the ground.

51 TNA: CAB 23/4 'Conclusions of an Anglo-French Conference, Held in the Train at Boulogne, on September 25, 1917, at 3.15 p.m.'

52 Haig diary, 3 October 1917, in Sheffield and Bourne (eds.), *Douglas Haig*, p. 331.

53 TNA: CAB 24/28/GT2243, General Headquarters, British Army in the Field to CIGS, 8 October 1917.

54 Robertson to Haig, 9 October 1917, in D. R. Woodward (ed.), *The Military Correspondence of Field-Marshal Sir William Robertson, Chief of the Imperial General Staff, December 1915–February 1918* (London: Bodley Head for the Army Records Society, 1989), p. 234.

55 D. French, *The Strategy of the Lloyd George Coalition, 1916–1918* (Oxford: Clarendon Press, 1995), pp. 154–5. See TNA: CAB 27/6, 'Eighteenth Meeting of the Cabinet Committee on War Policy', 3 October 1917.

56 Lord Hankey, *The Supreme Command 1914–1918* (2 vols., London: George Allen and Unwin, 1961), II, pp. 711–12.

57 Robertson invited Major-General A. A. Lynden-Bell (former Chief of the General Staff, Egyptian Expeditionary Force) to the War Policy Committee on 8 October to discuss the logistical challenges of the Palestine theatre of operations and the difficulty the British would face in reaching the Jaffa–Jerusalem line. TNA: CAB 27/6, 'Cabinet Committee on War Policy', 8 October 1917.

58 Robertson's withering dismissal of the medical analogy can be found in his *Soldiers and Statesmen 1914–1918* (2 vols., London: Cassell & Co., 1926), II, p. 257.

59 Hankey, *The Supreme Command*, II, pp. 712–13.

60 TNA: CAB 27/6, 'Cabinet Committee on War Policy', 11 October 1917.

13. *'The Weakness of Haste'*

1 AWM: PR84/068, A. Birnie to 'Dear Mother and Father', 26 October 1917.

2 TNA: WO 95/15, 'Daily Values of Rainfall', October 1917.

3 TNA: WO 256/23, Haig diary, 8 October 1917. Original emphasis.

4 N. Annabell (ed.), *Official History of the New Zealand Engineers during the Great War 1914–1919* (Wanganui: Evans, Cobb & Sharpe, 1927), pp. 153–4.

5 IWM: Documents 6618, J. A. Whitehead, 'Four Years' Memories', pp. 107–12.

6 IWM: Documents 15758, Account of Colonel F. W. Mellish, p. 29.

7 Sir J. Edmonds, *Military Operations: France & Belgium 1917* (3 vols., London: HMSO, 1948), II, p. 324.

8 For the problems facing the artillery of II ANZAC Corps between 5 and 9 October see A. Macdonald, *Passchendaele. The Anatomy of a Tragedy* (Auckland: HarperCollins, 2013), pp. 178–80.

9 IWM: Documents 17248, S. Roberts, 'The Glorious Sixth', p. 149.

10 Edmonds, *Military Operations: 1917*, II, p. 330.

11 R. Thompson, 'Mud, Blood, and Wood: BEF Operational and Combat Logistico-Engineering during the Battle of Third Ypres, 1917', in P. Doyle and M. R. Bennett (eds.), *Fields of Battle. Terrain in Military History* (London: Kluwer, 2002), pp. 245–6.

12 German pillboxes were also protected with new 'apron wire' that had not been encountered before. See TNA: WO 157/119, Second Army Daily Intelligence Summary, 13 October 1917.

13 C. E. W. Bean, *The Official History of Australia in the War of 1914–1918* (13 vols., Sydney: Angus & Robertson, 1941–2), IV, p. 900, and Edmonds, *Military Operations: 1917*, II, p. 324, n. 1.

14 TNA: WO 157/119, Second Army Daily Intelligence Summary, 14 October 1917.

15 IWM: Documents 15110, Account of N. Hind, pp. 451–2, 474.

16 TNA: WO 95/2768, 49th Division, 'Narrative of Events 8th to 10th October 1917', and Brigadier-General, 148 Infantry Brigade, to Headquarters, 49th Division, 13 October 1917.

17 TNA: WO 95/3120, '66th (East Lancashire) Division. Account of Action East of Ypres 9/10/17'.

18 IWM: Documents 1690, Account of P. R. Hall, pp. 16–17.

19 Edmonds, *Military Operations: 1917*, II, p. 334, n. 1.

20 Second Army intelligence was unimpressed with the 'new policy of defence'. In a report the day after Poelcappelle, it noted that in the case of 195th Division 'there was no material departure from the old principle of the defence in depth' and captured officers apparently denied 'all knowledge of any change in policy'. See TNA: WO 157/119, Second Army Daily Intelligence Summary, 10 October 1917.

21 W. Jürgensen, *Das Füsilier-Regiment 'Königin' Nr. 86 im Weltkriege* (Oldenburg: Gerhard Stalling, 1925), p. 189.

22 H. von Wolff, *Kriegsgeschichte des Jäger-Bataillon von Neumann (1. Schles.) Nr. 5 1914–1918* (Zeulenroda: Verlag Bernhard Sporn, n.d.), pp. 157–8.

23 DTA: 3502.1, R. Lewald diary, 7–10 October 1917.

24 Rupprecht diary, 10 October 1917, in Crown Prince Rupprecht, *Mein Kriegstagebuch* (3 vols., Berlin: E. S. Mittler & Sohn, 1929), II, p. 270.

25 German Official History, cited in J. Terraine, *The Road to Passchendaele. The Flanders Offensive of 1917: A Study in Inevitability* (London: Leo Cooper, 1977), p. 299.

26 W. Beumelburg, *Flandern 1917* (Oldenburg: Gerhard Stalling, 1928), p. 131.

27 *Histories of Two Hundred and Fifty-One Divisions of the German Army Which Participated in the War (1914–1918)* (Washington DC: Government Printing Office, 1920), p. 287.

28 Beumelburg, *Flandern*, p. 131.

29 Menges in J. Sheldon, *The German Army at Passchendaele* (Barnsley: Pen & Sword, 2007), p. 218.

30 Macdonald, *Passchendaele*, p. 185.

31 IWM: Documents 7197, F. J. Rice diary, 10–11 October 1917.

32 This is generally accepted. See for example N. Steel and P. Hart, *Passchendaele. The Sacrificial Ground* (London: Cassell & Co., 2001; first publ. 2000), pp. 273–5, and R. Prior and T. Wilson, *Passchendaele. The Untold Story* (New Haven and London: Yale University Press, 2002; first publ. 1996), p. 169.

33 TNA: WO 256/23, Haig diary, 10 October 1917. See Haig's diary entry for 9 October in which he states that 66th Division took all its objectives and 49th 'gained all except small piece on left'.

34 Macdonald, *Passchendaele*, p. 56.

35 P. A. Pedersen, *Monash as Military Commander* (Carlton: Melbourne University Press, 1985), p. 198.

36 G. Serle, *John Monash. A Biography* (Carlton: Melbourne University Press, 2002; first publ. 1982), p. 294.

37 In Charles Bean's papers he records a talk Harington gave at Second Army HQ prior to Poelcappelle, in which he was strongly in favour of continuing, telling assembled journalists that after one or two more attacks, the cavalry 'would be ready to go through'. Prior and Wilson, *Passchendaele*, pp. 160–61. See also Sir C. Harington, *Tim Harington Looks Back* (London: John Murray, 1940), p. 63.

38 P. Simkins, 'Herbert Plumer', in I. F. W. Beckett and S. J. Corvi (eds.), *Haig's Generals* (Barnsley: Pen & Sword, 2006), pp. 157–8. One of those who saw Plumer at this time was surprised by his optimism and cheerfulness: 'it is the old story: those who live right away from the troops engaged cannot possibly understand the strain and weariness affecting fighting troops at the Front . . .' Jack diary, 8 October 1917, in J. Terraine (ed.), *General Jack's Diary 1914–18. The Trench Diary of Brigadier-General J. L. Jack, D.S.O.* (London: Cassell & Co., 2000; first publ. 1964), p. 280.

39 J. R. Byrne, *New Zealand Artillery in the Field, 1914–18* (Auckland: Whitcombe & Tombs, 1922), p. 192.

40 A. E. Byrne, *Official History of the Otago Regiment, N.Z.E.F. in the Great War 1914–1918* (Dunedin: J. Wilkie & Company, 1921), pp. 211–12.

41 TNA: WO 95/1740, '9th (Scottish) Division. Narrative of Operations, 12.10.17'.

42 AWM: AWM4 23/9/12, 'Ninth Australian Infantry Brigade. Report of Operations Carried out on 12-10-17'.

43 Langford, cited in G. Harper, *Massacre at Passchendaele. The New Zealand Story* (Brighton: FireStep Books, 2011; first publ. 2000), p. 71.

44 Byrne, *Otago Regiment*, pp. 216–18. Cockerell was later awarded a Distinguished Service Order: 'a rare Order for an officer of his rank', notes the battalion history.

45 D. Ferguson, *The History of the Canterbury Regiment, N.Z.E.F. 1914–1919* (Auckland: Whitcombe & Tombs, 1921), p. 198.

46 AWM: AWM4 23/51/12, 34/Battalion War Diary, 12 October 1917.

47 AWM: 2DRL/0185, 'Extracts from the Late Lieut. G. M. Carson'. Original emphasis.

48 Bean, *The Official History of Australia*, IV, pp. 917–18. A small party from 10 Brigade managed to reach Passchendaele church, but, finding it abandoned and with no signs of support, had to withdraw.

49 S. Snelling, *VCs of the First World War. Passchendaele 1917* (Stroud: The History Press, 2012; first publ. 1998), pp. 246–8.

50 AWM: AWM4 23/9/12, 'Ninth Australian Infantry Brigade. Report of Operations Carried out on 12-10-17'. The retreat from the Blue Line would result in a Court of Inquiry held in December 1917. It made a series of recommendations, including better command and control, and the

need for battalion commanders to 'take hold of the situation'. See A. Fox, '"The Word 'Retire' is Never to be Used": The Performance of the 9th Brigade, AIF, at First Passchendaele, 1917', Australian War Memorial, SVSS Paper (2011), pp. 1–28.

51 AWM: PR84/068, A. Birnie to 'Dear Mother and Father', 26 October 1917. Emphasis added.

52 Wolff, *Jäger-Bataillon von Neumann*, pp. 171–2. The reference to the 'English' was probably because German sources often failed to differentiate between different nationalities in the BEF.

53 H. Stewart, *The New Zealand Division 1916–1919. A Popular History Based on Official Records* (Auckland: Whitcombe & Tombs, 1921), p. 291.

54 Russell, cited in C. Pugsley, 'The New Zealand Division at Passchendaele', in P. Liddle (ed.), *Passchendaele in Perspective. The Third Battle of Ypres* (London: Leo Cooper, 1997), pp. 285–6.

55 C. Pugsley, *On the Fringe of Hell. New Zealanders and Military Discipline in the First World War* (Auckland: Hodder & Stoughton, 1991), pp. 249–50.

56 Harper, *Massacre at Passchendaele*, pp. 76–8.

57 AWM: 3DRL/2316, letters, 18 and 21 October 1917, in 'War Letters of General Monash: Volume 2, 4 March 1917–28 December 1918'.

14. 'Not Worth a Drop of Blood'

1 A. H. Atteridge, *History of the 17th (Northern) Division* (Glasgow: Robert Maclehose & Co., 1929), p. 259.

2 IWM: Documents 13966, Account of G. Skelton.

3 IWM: Documents 17248, S. Roberts, 'The Glorious Sixth', p. 153.

4 IWM: Documents 4755, H. S. Taylor, 'Further Reminiscences of World War 1', p. 5.

5 IWM: Document 7613, Account of V. E. Fagence, pp. 6–7.

6 IWM: Documents 7197, F. J. Rice diary, 22 October 1917.

7 AWM: 2DRL/0277, S. E. Hunt, 'The Operation at Polygon Wood', p. 12.

8 IWM: Documents 12332, 'The Journal of John Nettleton of the Rifle Brigade 1914–1919', p. 101.

9 A. Ekins, 'The Australians at Passchendaele', in P. Liddle (ed.), *Passchendaele in Perspective. The Third Battle of Ypres* (London: Leo Cooper, 1997), p. 245. Rates may also have been higher given that the death penalty was not applied to Australian soldiers (owing to a clause in the Australian Defence Act of 1903). See C. Pugsley, *On the Fringe of Hell. New Zealanders and Military Discipline in the First World War* (Auckland: Hodder & Stoughton, 1991). pp. 131–2.

10 A. Macdonald, *Passchendaele. The Anatomy of a Tragedy* (Auckland: HarperCollins, 2013), p. 49.

11 Lord Birdwood, *Khaki and Gown. An Autobiography* (London: Ward, Lock & Co., 1941), pp. 316–17.

12 Haig diary, 13 October 1917, in G. Sheffield and J. Bourne (eds.), *Douglas Haig. War Diaries and Letters 1914–1918* (London: Weidenfeld & Nicolson, 2005), p. 336.

13 TNA: WO 95/15, 'Daily Values of Rainfall', September–October 1917. At Vlamertinge, September produced 25mm of rain less than the average, with October being worse by 32mm.

14 TNA: WO 256/21, Haig to Charteris, 5 March 1927. Original emphasis. See also Sir J. Davidson, *Haig. Master of the Field* (London: Peter Nevill, 1953), p. 59. The offending passages can be found in W. S. Churchill, *The World Crisis 1916–1918. Part II* (London: Thornton Butterworth, 1927), pp. 337–9.

15 Sir J. Edmonds, *Military Operations: France & Belgium 1917* (3 vols., London: HMSO, 1948), II, p. 326.

16 This argument was dismissed as early as 1959. See B. H. Liddell Hart, 'The Basic Truths of Passchendaele', *Journal of the Royal United Services Institution*, Vol. CIV, No. 616 (November 1959), pp. 433–5. For more recent discussions see B. Bond, 'Passchendaele: Verdicts, Past and Present', in Liddle (ed.), *Passchendaele in Perspective*, p. 484, and T. Travers, *How the War was Won. Command and Technology in the British Army on the Western Front, 1917–1918* (Barnsley: Pen & Sword, 2005; first publ. 1992), p. 18.

17 E. Greenhalgh, *The French Army and the First World War* (Cambridge: Cambridge University Press, 2014), p. 234.

18 TNA: WO 256/22, Haig diary, 26, 27 and 29 September 1917.

19 TNA: WO 256/23, Haig diary, 18 October 1917. According to William Philpott, 'Nothing caused more regular and repetitious squabbling

between the allied headquarters than the question of the fair distribution of the defence front between the allied armies.' W. J. Philpott, *Anglo-French Relations and Strategy on the Western Front, 1914–18* (London: Macmillan, 1996), p. 108.

20 TNA: WO 256/23, Haig to Pétain, 19 October 1917. See also 'Note of General Pétain's representations in favour of more line being taken over by the British Armies', in which Haig criticizes Pétain's anxiety and states that the 'prosecution of our offensive' would be 'the wisest military policy' in the event of Russia exiting the war.

21 Macdonogh had suggested that the morale of German troops 'gives no cause for anxiety to the German High Command', which prompted a quite extraordinary entry in Haig's diary for 15 October. 'I cannot think why the War Office Intelligence Department gives such a wrong picture of the situation except that General Macdonogh . . . is a Roman Catholic and is (unconsciously) influenced by information which doubtless reaches him from tainted (ie., Catholic) sources . . .' Haig was referring to a call for peace negotiations that had been made by Pope Benedict XV on 1 August 1917. For many historians this outspoken attack sums up Haig's lack of objective thinking and clarity. Robin Prior and Trevor Wilson conclude that 'self-deception could go no further'. See Haig diary, 15 October 1917, in Sheffield and Bourne (eds.), *Douglas Haig*, pp. 336–7, and R. Prior and T. Wilson, *Passchendaele. The Untold Story* (New Haven and London: Yale University Press, 2002; first publ. 1996), p. 166.

22 Robertson, cited in J. Beach, *Haig's Intelligence. GHQ and the German Army, 1916–1918* (Cambridge: Cambridge University Press, 2013), pp. 258–9.

23 D. G. Dancocks, *Legacy of Valour. The Canadians at Passchendaele* (Edmonton: Hurtig, 1986), pp. 96–7.

24 T. Cook, *Shock Troops. Canadians Fighting the Great War 1917–1918* (Toronto: Penguin Canada, 2008), p. 316.

25 S. B. Schreiber, *Shock Army of the British Empire. The Canadian Corps in the Last 100 Days of the Great War* (Westport: Praeger, 1997), p. 19.

26 Macdonell, cited in Dancocks, *Legacy of Valour*, pp. 97–8. Original emphasis.

27 T. Cook, *The Madman and the Butcher. The Sensational Wars of Sam Hughes and Sir Arthur Currie* (Toronto: Penguin Canada, 2010), ch. 3, pp. 73–4.

28 According to Currie, Haig finally revealed his secret when they met at the Peace Conference at Versailles in 1919. Apparently, Haig wanted to prevent German attacks on the French Army, while also restoring civilian morale with a victory. Interestingly, he made no mention of having to secure ground that would give his troops somewhere to winter. G. W. L. Nicholson, *Official History of the Canadian Army in the First World War. Canadian Expeditionary Force 1914–1919* (Ottawa: Queen's Printer, 1962), p. 328, and Cook, *Shock Troops*, p. 317.

29 *Statistics of the Military Effort of the British Empire during the Great War. 1914–1920* (London: HMSO, 1922), p. 146 (Table X). Totals correct as of 8 October 1917. A fifth division was forming in England, but it never took to the field. Currie had it broken up in February 1918 to furnish much-needed replacement manpower for the corps.

30 Canadian tactical development has attracted considerable attention. See I. M. Brown, 'Not Glamorous, But Effective: The Canadian Corps and the Set-Piece Attack, 1917–1918', *Journal of Military History*, Vol. 58, No. 3 (July 1994), pp. 421–44; T. Cook, *No Place to Run. The Canadian Corps and Gas Warfare in the First World War* (Vancouver: UBC Press, 1999), and *Shock Troops*; C. Pugsley, 'Learning from the Canadian Corps on the Western Front', *Canadian Military History*, Vol. 15, No. 1 (Winter 2006), pp. 5–32; B. Rawling, *Surviving Trench Warfare. Technology and the Canadian Corps, 1914–1918* (Toronto: University of Toronto Press, 1992); and Schreiber, *Shock Army of the British Empire*.

31 Beach, *Haig's Intelligence*, pp. 38–9. Beach states that 'the Canadians were always at least a year ahead of British corps in their intelligence manning'.

32 Rawling, *Surviving Trench Warfare*, p. 111.

33 J. Hansch and F. Weidling, *Das Colbergsche Grenadier-Regiment Graf Gneisenau (2 Pommersches) Nr. 9 im Weltkriege 1914–1918* (Oldenburg: Gerhard Stalling, 1929), p. 417.

34 J. Sheldon, *The German Army at Passchendaele* (Barnsley: Pen & Sword, 2007), pp. 258–9.

35 R. McLeod and C. Fox, 'The Battles in Flanders during the Summer and Autumn of 1917 from General von Kuhl's *Der Weltkrieg 1914–18*', *British Army Review*, No. 116 (August 1997), pp. 85–6.

36 Peistrup, in Sheldon, *Passchendaele*, pp. 245–6.

37 DTA: 3502.1, R. Lewald diary, 19 October 1917.

38 Taken from 'Dreamers', in S. Sassoon, *Selected Poems* (London: William Heinemann, 1940; first publ. 1925), p. 20.

39 Thaer diary, 28 September 1917, in A. von Thaer, *Generalstabsdienst an der Front und in der O.H.L.* (Göttingen: Vandenhoeck & Ruprecht, 1958), p. 140.

40 Sheldon, *Passchendaele*, p. 243.

41 G. Werth, 'Flanders 1917 and the German Soldier', in Liddle (ed.), *Passchendaele in Perspective*, p. 329.

42 Kleysteuber, in Sheldon, *Passchendaele*, p. 215.

43 TNA: WO 157/119, Second Army Daily Intelligence Summary, 12 October 1917.

44 See for example TNA: WO 157/119, Second Army Daily Intelligence Summary, 22 October 1917.

45 Reichsarchiv, *Der Weltkrieg 1914 bis 1918*, XIII. *Die Kriegführung im Sommer und Herbst 1917. Die Ereignisse außerhalb der Westfront bis November 1918* (Berlin: E. S. Mittler & Sohn, 1942), pp. 99–100.

46 W. Jürgensen, *Das Füsilier-Regiment 'Königin' Nr. 86 im Weltkriege* (Oldenburg: Gerhard Stalling, 1925), pp. 187–8.

47 IWM: Documents 1933, Account of W. A. Rappolt, pp. 61–5.

48 Reichskriegsministeriums, *Sanitätsbericht über das Deutsche Heer (Deutsches Feld- und Besatzungsheer) im Weltkriege 1914/1918* (3 vols., Berlin: E. S. Mittler & Sohn, 1934–8), II, p. 708.

49 Reichsarchiv, *Der Weltkrieg*, XIII, p. 86.

50 Rupprecht diary, 5 August 1917, in Crown Prince Rupprecht, *Mein Kriegstagebuch* (3 vols., Berlin: E. S. Mittler & Sohn, 1929), II, pp. 235–6.

51 Sheldon, *Passchendaele*, pp. 314–15. Figures taken from Table 47 in *Sanitätsbericht über das Deutsche Heer*, III, p. 55.

52 Thaer diary, 11 October 1917, in Thaer, *Generalstabsdienst*, p. 143.

53 Rupprecht, in Sheldon, *Passchendaele*, pp. 228–9.

54 Rupprecht diary, 21 October 1917, in Rupprecht, *Mein Kriegstagebuch*, II, pp. 273–4.

55 Ibid., 24 October 1917, II, p. 275.

56 For the creation of Group Staden see Reichsarchiv, *Der Weltkrieg*, XIII, p. 87, and Sheldon, *Passchendaele*, pp. 40–41.

57 DTA: 3244.17, E. Schaarschmidt diary, 20 October 1917.

58 G. C. Wynne, *If Germany Attacks. The Battle in Depth in the West* (Westport: Greenwood, 1976; first publ. 1940), pp. 310, 313.

59 Reichsarchiv, *Der Weltkrieg,* XIII, p. 249.

15. '*Against the Iron Wall*'

1 E. Ludendorff, *Ludendorff's Own Story. August 1914–November 1918* (2 vols., New York and London: Harper & Brothers, 1919), II, p. 106.

2 G. W. L. Nicholson, *Official History of the Canadian Army in the First World War. Canadian Expeditionary Force 1914–1919* (Ottawa: Queen's Printer, 1962), p. 313.

3 D. G. Dancocks, *Legacy of Valour. The Canadians at Passchendaele* (Edmonton: Hurtig, 1986), p. 103.

4 LAC: RG9, III-D-3, Vol. 4957, Reel T-10774, File: 504, Part 2, 'Canadian Corps Artillery Report on Passchendaele Operations Oct. 17th to Nov. 18th 1917', pp. 12, 14.

5 Nicholson, *Canadian Expeditionary Force 1914–1919*, p. 318.

6 CWM: 58A 1 27.11, Memoirs of G. F. McFarland, Vol. II, p. 29.

7 J. Adair, 'The Battle of Passchendaele: The Experiences of Lieutenant Tom Rutherford, 4th Battalion, Canadian Mounted Rifles', *Canadian Military History*, Vol. 13, No. 4 (Autumn 2004), pp. 66–8.

8 LAC: RG9, III-D-3, Vol. 4896, Reel T-10690, File: 289, Part 1, 'Headquarters – 8th Canadian Infantry Brigade War Diary October, 1917. Appendix 22'.

9 S. G. Bennett, *The 4th Canadian Mounted Rifles 1914–1919* (Toronto: Murray Printing Company, 1926), p. 80.

10 CWM: 58A 1 27.11, Memoirs of G. F. McFarland, Vol. II, p. 32.

11 Adair, 'The Battle of Passchendaele', p. 74.

12 They were Private T. W. Holmes (4/CMR); Lieutenant R. Shankland (43/Battalion); Acting Captain C. P. J. O'Kelly (52/Battalion); Private C. J. Kinross (49/Battalion); Lieutenant H. McKenzie (7/Canadian MG Company); Sergeant G. H. Mullin (PPCLI); Major G. R. Pearkes (5/CMR); Private C. F. Barron (3/Battalion); and Private J. P. Robertson (27/Battalion).

13 LAC: RG9, III-D-3, Vol. 4938, Reel T-10744, File: 434, Part 2, 43/Battalion War Diary, 26 September 1917.

14 S. Snelling, *VCs of the First World War. Passchendaele 1917* (Stroud: The History Press, 2012; first publ. 1998), pp. 256–9.

15 J. Hansch and F. Weidling, *Das Colbergsche Grenadier-Regiment Graf Gneisenau (2 Pommersches) Nr. 9 im Weltkriege 1914–1918* (Oldenburg: Gerhard Stalling, 1929), p. 424.

16 C. Stachelbeck, *Militärische Effektivität im Ersten Weltkrieg. Die 11. Bayerische Infanteriedivision 1915 bis 1918* (Paderborn: Ferdinand Schöningh, 2010), pp. 208–9, 215.

17 11th Bavarian Division suffered 1,800 casualties as opposed to over 3,400 in the two attacking Canadian divisions. See C. Stachelbeck, 'Strategy "in a Microcosm": Processes of Tactical Learning in a WW1 German Infantry Division', *Journal of Military & Strategic Studies*, Vol. 13, No. 4 (Summer 2011), p. 18, n. 50.

18 Stachelbeck, *Militärische Effektivität im Ersten Weltkrieg*, p. 222.

19 See TNA: WO 157/119, 'Enemy's New Battery Positions Disclosed Oct. 1st 1917', in Second Army Daily Intelligence Summary, 2 October 1917. A point in the centre of the Canadian Corps area was about 6,000 yards from the front line at Passchendaele, but only 3,000 yards from that to the southeast. LAC: RG9, III-D-3, Vol. 4957, Reel T-10774, File: 504, Part 2, 'Canadian Corps Artillery Report on Passchendaele Operations Oct. 17th to Nov. 18th 1917', p. 32.

20 DTA: 3502.1, R. Lewald diary, 26 October 1917.

21 LAC: RG9, III-D-3, Vol. 4957, Reel T-10774, File: 504, Part 2, 'Canadian Corps Artillery Report on Passchendaele Operations Oct. 17th to Nov. 18th 1917', p. 17.

22 H. A. Jones, *The War in the Air. Being the Story of the Part Played in the Great War by the Royal Air Force* (6 vols., Oxford: Clarendon Press, 1922–37), IV, p. 210.

23 A. Revell, *Brief Glory. The Life of Arthur Rhys Davids, DSO, MC and Bar* (Barnsley: Pen & Sword, 2010), pp. 195, 209. Research indicates that he was shot down by Karl Gallwitz and came down somewhere around the Passchendaele Ridge. His body was never found.

24 Nicholson, *Canadian Expeditionary Force 1914–1919*, pp. 320–21.

25 LAC: RG9, III-D-3, Vol. 4940, Reel T-10747, File: 440, Part 2, 49/Battalion War Diary, November 1917, Appendix A.

26 LAC: RG9, III-D-3, Vol. 4949, Reel T-10760, File: 437, Part 2, '5th CMR Battalion. Summary of Operations, October 30th–31st, 1917'.

27 Snelling, *Passchendaele 1917*, p. 283. The story of Allen Otty, who was surely deserving of a VC, is told in C. Mainville, 'Mentioned in Despatches: Lieutenant Allen Otty and the 5th CMR, at Passchendaele 30 October 1917', *Canadian Military History*, Vol. 23, No. 2 (Spring 2014), pp. 137–63.

28 Currie to Lieutenant-General Sir Richard Turner, 30 October 1917, in A. Currie, *The Selected Papers of Sir Arthur Currie. Diaries, Letters and Report to the Ministry, 1917–1933*, ed. M. O. Humphries (Waterloo, Ont.: Wilfrid Laurier University Press, 2008), pp. 55–6.

29 Sir J. Edmonds, *Military Operations. France & Belgium 1917* (3 vols., London: HMSO, 1948), II, pp. 351–3.

30 TNA: WO 95/3095, 'Report on the Operations of 63rd (Royal Naval) Division East of Ypres 24th October–5th November 1917', p. 10.

31 TNA: WO 95/952, XVIII Corps War Diary, 30 October 1917.

32 J. Grigg, *Lloyd George. War Leader 1916–1918* (London: Penguin Books, 2003; first publ. 2002), p. 271.

33 Robertson to Lloyd George, 27 October 1917, in D. R. Woodward (ed.), *The Military Correspondence of Field-Marshal Sir William Robertson, Chief of the Imperial General Staff, December 1915–February 1918* (London: Bodley Head for the Army Records Society, 1989), pp. 239–40.

34 Lloyd George to Robertson, 27 October 1917, in Woodward (ed.), *The Military Correspondence of Field-Marshal Sir William Robertson*, p. 240.

35 Robertson to Lloyd George, 27 October 1917, in Woodward (ed.), *The Military Correspondence of Field-Marshal Sir William Robertson*, p. 241.

36 TNA: CAB 23/4, 'War Cabinet, 263', 2 November 1917.

37 D. French, *The Strategy of the Lloyd George Coalition, 1916–1918* (Oxford: Clarendon Press, 1995), pp. 161–2.

38 D. Lloyd George, *War Memoirs of David Lloyd George* (2 vols., London: Odhams Press, 1933–6), II, pp. 1439–41.

39 D. R. Woodward, *Lloyd George and the Generals* (London: Associated University Presses, 1983), p. 214.

40 Edmonds, *Military Operations: 1917*, II, p. 355.

41 LAC: RG9, III-D-3, Vol. 4957, Reel T-10774, File: 504, Part 2, 'Canadian Corps Artillery Report on Passchendaele Operations Oct. 17th to Nov. 18th 1917', pp. 22, 23, 25.

42 LAC: RG41, Vol. 21, Testimony of H. L. Sheppard.

43 Nicholson, *Canadian Expeditionary Force 1914–1919*, pp. 323–4.

44 IWM: Documents 7376, M. McIntyre Hood, 'Recording on First World War 1914–1918', p. 12.

45 CWM: 58A 1 221.1, A. R. Coulter diary, 4 November 1917.

46 LAC: RG41, Vol. 8, Testimony of G. Noir.

47 LAC: RG41, Vol. 22, Testimony of W. M. Rae.

48 Currie in Dancocks, *Legacy of Valour*, p. 159.

49 T. Cook, *Shock Troops. Canadians Fighting the Great War 1917–1918* (Toronto: Penguin Canada, 2008), p. 357.

50 LAC: RG9, III-D-3, Vol. 4957, Reel T-10774, File: 504, Part 2, 'Canadian Corps Artillery Report on Passchendaele Operations Oct. 17th to Nov. 18th 1917', p. 8.

51 K. Radley, *We Lead, Others Follow. First Canadian Division 1914–1918* (St Catharines: Vanwell, 2006), p. 166.

52 LAC: RG9, III-D-3, Vol. 4913, Reel T-10704–10705, File: 351, 'Report on Operations Carried Out by [1] Bn. on the 5th, 6th, 7th and 8th November'.

53 LAC: RG41, Vol. 12, Testimony of W. McCombie-Gilbert.

54 LAC: RG9, III-D-3, Vol. 4935, Reel T-10739–10740, File: 425, Part 2, 'Narrative of Operations for the Capture of Passchendaele and the Surrounding Heights. 28th North West Canadian Battalion. November 6th/7th 1917'.

55 LAC: RG41, Vol. 11, Testimony of W. E. Turner.

56 LAC: RG9, III-D-3, Vol. 4935, Reel T-10738–10739, File: 423, Part 2, '27th (City of Winnipeg) Battalion. Narrative of Operations Covering the Attack on Passchendaele'.

57 LAC: RG9, III-D-3, Vol. 4938, Reel T-10744, File: 434, Part 2, Canadian Corps, Summary of Intelligence, 6 November 1917.

58 LAC: RG9, III-D-3, Vol. 4935, Reel T-10738–10739, File: 423, Part 2, '27th (City of Winnipeg) Battalion. Narrative of Operations Covering the Attack on Passchendaele'.

59 H. Nollau, *Geschichte des Königlich Preußischen 4 Niederschlesischen Infanterie-Regiment Nr. 51* (Berlin: Wilhelm Kolk, 1931), pp. 205–6.

60 LAC: RG41, Vol. 11, Testimony of W. E. Turner.

61 IWM: Documents 7376, M. McIntyre Hood, 'Recording on First World War 1914–1918', p. 13.

62 Snelling, *Passchendaele 1917*, pp. 290–91.

63 KA: (WK) 9197, 'Ereignisse bei 4 Armee von 6.11 abends bis 7.11 abends'.

64 Rupprecht diary, 6–7 November 1917, in Crown Prince Rupprecht, *Mein Kriegstagebuch* (3 vols., Berlin: E. S. Mittler & Sohn, 1929), II, pp. 282–3.

65 DTA: 3502.1, R. Lewald diary, 6 November 1917.

66 Haig diary, 6–7 November 1917, in G. Sheffield and J. Bourne (eds.), *Douglas Haig. War Diaries and Letters 1914–1918* (London: Weidenfeld & Nicolson, 2005), p. 339. Original emphasis. Haig seems to have been referring to the number of dead, not total casualties, which were over 2,200. See Nicholson, *Canadian Expeditionary Force 1914–1919*, p. 325.

67 The Canadians were not able to secure all of Hill 52 on 10 November, which led to the sanctioning of an ill-fated night attack on 2 December. This operation is detailed in M. LoCicero, *A Moonlight Massacre. The Night Operation on the Passchendaele Ridge, 2 December 1917: The Forgotten Last Act of the Third Battle of Ypres* (Solihull: Helion & Company, 2014).

68 Sir C. Harington, *Tim Harington Looks Back* (London: John Murray, 1940), p. 65.

69 Currie diary, 9 November 1917, in Currie, *Selected Papers*, p. 57.

70 Lieutenant-Colonel A. Adamson (CO/PPCLI), cited in N. S. Leach, 'Passchendaele – Canada's Other Vimy Ridge', *Canadian Military Journal*, Vol. 9, No. 2 (2008), p. 81.

71 Nicholson, *Canadian Expeditionary Force 1914–1919*, p. 327. The official total was 15,654, although the Canadian Corps Battle Casualties file lists 16,404. See Cook, *Shock Troops*, pp. 365, 686–7, n. 41.

72 Currie to Hearst, 14 November 1917, in Currie, *Selected Papers*, p. 59.

73 T. Cook, *The Madman and the Butcher. The Sensational Wars of Sam Hughes and Sir Arthur Currie* (Toronto: Penguin Canada, 2010), p. 359.

74 See N. Lloyd, *Hundred Days. The End of the Great War* (London: Viking, 2013).

75 Dancocks, *Legacy of Valour*, p. 238.

76 CLIP: K. W. Foster, 'Memoirs of the Great War 1915–1918'.

Epilogue

1 Sir C. Harington, *Plumer of Messines* (London: John Murray, 1935), p. 112.

2 Kuhl, cited in D. Zabecki, *The German 1918 Offensives. A Case Study in the Operational Level of War* (London and New York: Routledge, 2006), p. 94.

3 Sir J. Edmonds, *Military Operations: France & Belgium 1918. The German March Offensive and Its Preliminaries* (London: Macmillan & Co., 1935), p. 254. (German forces on pp. 152–3). Whether the disaster on 21 March 1918 could be directly attributed to the effects of Third Ypres on the BEF remains a matter of debate. Edmonds turned the question around and argued that it is possible 'complete success' only eluded the German Army because of the 'exhaustion, practically the destruction, of their best divisions in Flanders'. Sir J. Edmonds, *Military Operations: France & Belgium 1917* (3 vols., London: HMSO, 1948), II, p. 366. It seems probable that the extent of the retreat in the opening days of the German offensive was, at least in part, because of the hasty expansion of the British front line over the winter, but it is also undeniable that by trying to win a major victory in the summer of 1917, Haig wore down his divisions and left his army in a perilous situation with few reserves left to meet any unforeseen contingencies. Fifth Army would pay the price in March 1918.

4 A. Farrar-Hockley, *Goughie. The Life of General Sir Hubert Gough* (London: Hart-Davis, MacGibbon, 1975), p. 312.

5 Harington, *Plumer*, p. 161.

6 P. Gross (dir.), *Passchendaele* (Montreal: Alliance Films, 2008).

7 Rupprecht in J. Sheldon, *The German Army at Passchendaele* (Barnsley: Pen & Sword, 2007), pp. 312–13.

8 F. von Lossberg, *Meine Tätigkeit im Weltkrieg 1914–1918* (Berlin: E. S. Mittler & Sohn, 1939), p. 309.

9 P. Simkins, 'Foreword' in Sheldon, *Passchendaele*, p. viii.

10 D. Gottberg, *Das Infanterie-Regiment Nr. 465 im Weltkriege* (Osnabrück: Verlag Carl Prelle, n.d.), p. 158.

11 See D. Todman, '"Sans peur et sans reproche": The Retirement, Death, and Mourning of Sir Douglas Haig, 1918–1928', *Journal of Military History*, Vol. 67, No. 4 (October 2003), pp. 1083–1106.

12 Lord Hankey, *The Supreme Command 1914–1918* (2 vols., London: George Allen and Unwin, 1961), II, p. 701.

13 See J. H. Boraston (ed.), *Sir Douglas Haig's Despatches (December 1915–April 1919)* (London: HMSO, 1919), p. 135.

14 See R. McLeod and C. Fox, 'The Battles in Flanders during the Summer and Autumn of 1917 from General von Kuhl's *Der Weltkrieg 1914–18*', *British Army Review*, No. 116 (August 1997), p. 84. Kuhl is quoted approvingly by a number of historians including J. Terraine, *The Road to Passchendaele. The Flanders Offensive of 1917: A Study in Inevitability* (London: Leo Cooper, 1977), p. 342; W. J. Philpott, *Anglo-French Relations and Strategy on the Western Front, 1914–18* (London: Macmillan, 1996), p. 149; and G. Sheffield, *The Chief. Douglas Haig and the British Army* (London: Aurum Press, 2011), pp. 247–8.

15 Terraine, *The Road to Passchendaele*, p. xxi.

16 R. Prior and T. Wilson, *Passchendaele. The Untold Story* (New Haven and London: Yale University Press, 2002; first publ. 1996), p. 33.

17 TNA: CAB 45/140, Gough to Edmonds, 3 May 1944, 'Marginal Notes. Chapter XII'.

18 Prior and Wilson, *Passchendaele*, pp. 199–200.

19 See for example J. P. Harris, *Douglas Haig and the First World War* (Cambridge: Cambridge University Press, 2008), pp. 337–41, 360–61, 378–82; N. Steel and P. Hart, *Passchendaele. The Sacrificial Ground* (London: Cassell & Co., 2001; first publ. 2000), pp. 302–3; T. Travers, *How the War was Won. Command and Technology in the British Army on the Western Front, 1917–1918* (Barnsley: Pen & Sword, 2005; first publ. 1992), p. 11.

20 C. Barnett, *The Swordbearers. Supreme Command in the First World War* (London: Cassell & Co., 2000; first publ. 1963), pp. 236, 237, 239.

21 Prior and Wilson make this point in their conclusion to *Passchendaele* (p. 197), but their earlier dismissal of the effectiveness of Menin Road, Polygon Wood and Broodseinde undermines their case. Because they judge these battles on the amount of ground gained (and not by their effect on the enemy), they fail to realize how successful they were. Ground was *not* the key metric in 'bite-and-hold' operations.

22 Plumer's mastery of 'bite and hold' would provide Bernard Law Montgomery, the future Field Marshal and 'Victor of Alamein', with his

'deepest and most lasting lessons of the war'. As a young staff officer with IX Corps in Second Army, Montgomery was involved in the planning for Menin Road, Polygon Wood and Broodseinde and described them as 'masterpieces'. See N. Hamilton, *Monty. The Making of a General 1887–1942* (London: Coronet, 1984; first publ. 1981), p. 117. Montgomery's comments on Plumer's battles can be found in a letter to his father, 9 October 1917 (p. 120).

23 See for example Haig's diary entries for 1 August ('A terrible day of rain. The ground is like a bog in this low lying country'); 2 August ('this bad weather takes so much out of the men in the trenches that more frequent reliefs are necessary'); 16 August ('the country is very wooded and much broken up by our heavy shell fire'); 17 August (special arrangements were being made to pass freshly cleaned rifles up to the front line 'owing to the mud'); 4 October ('Rain fell heavily this afternoon as I took a walk'); 6 October (the ground 'became very muddy and slippery'); 7 October (discusses the possibility of it being too wet 'to admit of our men going forward'); 9 October ('The ground was so bad that 8 hours were taken in marching to forming up points'); 12 October ('very bad state of ground'); and 13 October (when the ground was so soft that light railway engines had apparently 'sunk halfway up the boilers in the mud'), in G. Sheffield and J. Bourne (eds.), *Douglas Haig. War Diaries and Letters 1914–1918* (London: Weidenfeld & Nicolson, 2005), pp. 309, 310, 316, 317, 333, 334, 335, 336. In Haig's despatch on 'The Campaigns of 1917', frequent references are made to poor weather and muddy conditions. See Boraston (ed.), *Sir Douglas Haig's Despatches (December 1915–April 1919)*, pp. 116, 128, 129, 133.

24 D. Lloyd George, *War Memoirs of David Lloyd George* (2 vols., London: Odhams Press, 1933–6), II, p. 1304.

25 Prior and Wilson, *Passchendaele*, pp. 37–8.

26 Philpott, *Anglo-French Relations*, pp. 138–40.

27 D. R. Woodward, *Lloyd George and the Generals* (London: Associated University Presses, 1983), p. 133.

28 See J. Thompson, *The Lifeblood of War. Logistics in Armed Conflict* (London: Brassey's, 1991), pp. 40–44.

29 H. Strachan, *The Politics of the British Army* (Oxford: Clarendon Press, 1997), p. 142.

30 D. Graham and S. Bidwell, *Coalitions, Politicians and Generals. Some Aspects of Command in Two World Wars* (London: Brassey's, 1993), p. 90.

31 IWM: Documents 15758, Account of F. W. Mellish, p. 30.

32 Harington, *Plumer*, p. 303.

33 Ibid., p. 112.

34 Edmonds, *Military Operations: 1917*, II, pp. 360–61.

35 Reichsarchiv, *Der Weltkrieg 1914 bis 1918*, XIII. *Die Kriegführung im Sommer und Herbst 1917. Die Ereignisse außerhalb der Westfront bis November 1918* (Berlin: E. S. Mittler & Sohn, 1942), p. 96.

36 Reichskriegsministerium, *Sanitätsbericht über das Deutsche Heer (Deutsches Feld- und Besatzungsheer) im Weltkriege 1914/1918* (3 vols., Berlin: E. S. Mittler & Sohn, 1934–8), III, p. 53.

37 The subject of German losses has attracted considerable debate. Sir James Edmonds was convinced that the real figure was significantly greater than the published statistics, perhaps rising to as high as 350,000 or 400,000. Liddell Hart called these estimates 'mythical' and, more recently, Jack Sheldon has accused Edmonds of 'creative accounting' and of showing a 'cavalier handling of the facts' in regard to German casualties. According to Sheldon, it is only possible to reach a total of 400,000 if one takes into consideration all those who were treated for 'minor cuts and wounds' at regimental aid posts (but who were not struck off unit strength). As he notes, 'It is hard to see any merit in insisting that a man remaining with his unit and capable of carrying out his duties, must be regarded as a battle casualty of the same significance as someone evacuated with serious or life-threatening injuries.' See B. H. Liddell Hart, 'The Basic Truths of Passchendaele', *Journal of the Royal United Services Institution*, Vol. CIV, No. 616 (November 1959), pp. 436–7, and Sheldon, *Passchendaele*, pp. 313–15, 319, n. 58.

38 C. von Clausewitz, *On War*, trans. M. Howard and P. Paret (London: David Campbell, 1993; first publ. 1976), p. 220. Emphasis added.

39 P. Gibbs, *Now It Can be Told* (New York and London: Harper & Brothers, 1920), p. 474.

40 LAC: RG41, Vol. 15, Testimony of G. Bell.

Bibliography

Archive Sources

Australian War Memorial, Canberra (AWM)

C. E. W. Bean (AWM38)
A. Birnie (PR84/068)
G. M. Carson (2DRL/0185)
B. W. Champion (2DRL/0512)
H. A. Goddard (3DRL/2379)
R. C. Grieve (2DRL/0260)
A. D. Hollyhoke (3DRL/1465)
S. E. Hunt (2DRL/0277)
J. Monash (3DRL/2316)
Australian Imperial Force Unit War Diaries (AWM4)

Bayerisches Hauptstaatsarchiv, Abteilung IV: Kriegsarchiv, Munich (KA)

Generalkommando III. Armee-Korps (WK) 1789
Generalkommando III. Armee-Korps (WK) 1790
Generalkommando III. Armee-Korps (WK) 2233
Generalkommando III. Armee-Korps (WK) 2523
Infanteriebrigaden (WK) 1246/1 and 1246/2
Infanterie-Division (WK) 8319
Infanterie-Division (WK) 9197

Bundesarchiv-Militärarchiv, Freiburg (BA-MA)

K. Dieffenbach (MSG 2/5960)
J. Schärdel (MSG 2/13418)

Canadian Letters and Images Project (CLIP)

K. W. Foster

Canadian War Museum (CWM)

A. R. Coulter (58A 1 221.1)
G. F. McFarland (58A 1 27.11)

Deutsches Tagebucharchiv, Emmendingen (DTA)

R. Lewald (3502.1)
E. Schaarschmidt (3244.17)

Imperial War Museum, London (IWM)

G. Brunskill (Documents 12512)
G. Carter (Documents 14196)
R. J. Clarke (Documents 982)
V. E. Fagence (Documents 7613)
P. R. Hall (Documents 1690)
N. Hind (Documents 15110)
A. Johnson (Documents 11080)
M. W. Littlewood (Documents 6993)
A. G. MacGregor (Documents 15177)
M. McIntyre Hood (Documents 7376)
F. W. Mellish (Documents 15758)
C. E. Moy (Documents 17166)
J. Nettleton (Documents 12332)
K. Page (Sound 717)
W. A. Rappolt (Documents 1933)
G. N. Rawlence (Documents 22753)
F. J. Rice (Documents 7197)
A. H. Roberts (Documents 7003)
S. Roberts (Documents 17248)
A. Sambrook (Documents 3215)
G. Skelton (Documents 13966)
F. A. Sclater (Documents 8214)
W. B. St Leger (Documents 20504)
E. V. Tanner (Documents 22718)

H. S. Taylor (Documents 4755)
J. S. Walthew (Documents 3980)
J. A. Whitehead (Documents 6618)

Library and Archives Canada, Ottawa (LAC)

Militia and Defence Files (RG9)
Canadian Broadcasting Corporation Fonds (RG41)

Liddell Hart Centre for Military Archives, King's College London (LHCMA)

Liddell Hart papers

The National Archives, London (TNA)

War Office: First World War and Army of Occupation War Diaries (WO 95)
War Office: Intelligence Summaries, First World War (WO 157)
War Office: Field Marshal Sir Douglas Haig: Diaries (WO 256)
War Cabinet and Cabinet: Minutes (CAB 23)
War Cabinet and Cabinet: Memoranda (CAB 24)
War Cabinet and Cabinet: Miscellaneous Committees (CAB 27)
Committee of Imperial Defence, Historical Branch, and Cabinet Office, Historical Section: Official War Histories Correspondence and Paper (CAB 45)

Secondary Sources

Official Histories and Reports

Bean, C. E. W., *The Official History of Australia in the War of 1914–1918* (13 vols., Sydney: Angus & Robertson, 1941–2)
Beumelburg, W., *Flandern 1917* (Oldenburg: Gerhard Stalling, 1928)
Boraston, J. H., (ed.), *Sir Douglas Haig's Despatches (December 1915–April 1919)* (London: Dent & Sons, 1919)
Edmonds, Sir J., *Military Operations: France & Belgium 1917* (3 vols., London: HMSO, 1948), II
Falls, C., *Military Operations: France & Belgium 1917* (3 vols., London: Macmillan & Co., 1940), I

Histories of Two Hundred and Fifty-One Divisions of the German Army Which Participated in the War (1914–1918) (Washington DC: Government Printing Office, 1920)

Jones, H. A., *The War in the Air. Being the Story of the Part Played in the Great War by the Royal Air Force* (6 vols., Oxford: Clarendon Press, 1922–37), IV

Ludendorff, E., *The General Staff and Its Problems. The History of the Relations between the High Command and the German Imperial Government as Revealed by Official Documents*, trans. F. A. Holt (2 vols., New York: E. P. Dutton & Co., 1920)

Macpherson, Sir W. F., *Medical Services General History*, III. *Medical Services during the Operations on the Western Front in 1916, 1917 and 1918; in Italy; and in Egypt and Palestine* (London: HMSO, 1924)

Ministère de la Guerre, *Les Armées Françaises dans La Grande Guerre*, Tome V, Vol. 2 (Paris: Imprimerie Nationale, 1937)

Neumann, P., *The German Air Force in the Great War*, trans. J. E. Gurdon (London: Hodder & Stoughton, 1921)

Newbolt, H., *History of the Great War. Naval Operations* (5 vols., London: Longmans, Green & Co., 1928), IV

Nicholson, G. W. L., *Official History of the Canadian Army in the First World War. Canadian Expeditionary Force 1914–1919* (Ottawa: Queen's Printer, 1962)

Reichsarchiv, *Der Weltkrieg 1914 bis 1918*, XII. *Die Kriegführung im Frühjahr 1917* (Berlin: E. S. Mittler & Sohn, 1939)

Reichsarchiv, *Der Weltkrieg 1914 bis 1918*, XIII. *Die Kriegführung im Sommer und Herbst 1917. Die Ereignisse außerhalb der Westfront bis November 1918* (Berlin: E. S. Mittler & Sohn, 1942)

Reichskriegsministerium, *Sanitätsbericht über das Deutsche Heer (Deutsches Feld- und Besatzungsheer) im Weltkriege 1914/1918* (3 vols., Berlin: E. S. Mittler & Sohn, 1934–8), II

Scott, J. B., (ed.), *Official Statements of War Aims and Peace Proposals. December 1916 to November 1918* (Washington DC: Carnegie Endowment for International Peace, 1921)

Statistics of the Military Effort of the British Empire during the Great War. 1914–1920 (London: HMSO, 1922)

Biographical Sources

Barnett, C., *The Swordbearers. Supreme Command in the First World War* (London: Cassell & Co., 2000; first publ. 1963)

Baynes, J., *Far from a Donkey. The Life of General Sir Ivor Maxse KCB, CVO, DSO* (London: Brassey's, 1995)

Beckett, I. F. W., 'Hubert Gough, Neill Malcolm and Command on the Western Front', in B. Bond et al., *'Look to Your Front'. Studies in the First World War by the British Commission for Military History* (Staplehurst: Spellmount, 1999), pp. 1–12

Bond, B., and N. Cave (eds.), *Haig. A Reappraisal 70 Years On* (Barnsley: Leo Cooper, 1999)

Charteris, J., *Field-Marshal Earl Haig* (London: Cassell & Co., 1929)

Cook, T., *The Madman and the Butcher. The Sensational Wars of Sam Hughes and Sir Arthur Currie* (Toronto: Penguin Canada, 2010)

Cooper, D., *Haig. The Second Volume* (London: Faber & Faber, 1936)

Davidson, Sir J., *Haig. Master of the Field* (London: Peter Nevill, 1953)

Davies, F., and G. Maddocks, *Bloody Red Tabs. General Officer Casualties of the Great War 1914–1918* (Barnsley: Leo Cooper, 1995)

De Groot, D. J., *Douglas Haig, 1861–1928* (London: Unwin Hyman, 1988)

Duncan, G. S., *Douglas Haig as I Knew Him* (London: George Allen and Unwin, 1966)

Farrar-Hockley, A., *Goughie. The Life of General Sir Hubert Gough* (London: Hart-Davis, MacGibbon, 1975)

Goodspeed, D. J., *Ludendorff. Soldier: Dictator: Revolutionary* (London: Rupert Hart-Davis, 1966)

Grigg, J., *Lloyd George. War Leader 1916–1918* (London: Penguin Books, 2003; first publ. 2002)

Harington, Sir C., *Plumer of Messines* (London: John Murray, 1935)

Harris, J. P., *Douglas Haig and the First World War* (Cambridge: Cambridge University Press, 2008)

Kilduff, P., *Richthofen. Beyond the Legend of the Red Baron* (London: Arms & Armour, 1993)

Mead, G., *The Good Soldier. The Biography of Sir Douglas Haig* (London: Atlantic, 2007)

Owen, F., *Tempestuous Journey. Lloyd George: His Life and Times* (London: Hutchinson, 1954)

Pedersen, P. A., *Monash as Military Commander* (Carlton: Melbourne University Press, 1985)

Powell, G., *Plumer. The Soldiers' General* (London: Leo Cooper, 1990)

Prior, R., and T. Wilson, *Command on the Western Front. The Military Career of Sir Henry Rawlinson, 1914–1918* (Oxford: Blackwell, 1992)

Revell, A., *Brief Glory. The Life of Arthur Rhys Davids, DSO, MC and Bar* (Barnsley: Pen & Sword, 2010)

Serle, G., *John Monash. A Biography* (Carlton: Melbourne University Press, 2002; first publ. 1982)

Sheffield, G., *The Chief. Douglas Haig and the British Army* (London: Aurum Press, 2011)

Sheffield, G., and H. McCartney, 'Hubert Gough', in I. F. W. Beckett and S. J. Corvi (eds.), *Haig's Generals* (Barnsley: Pen & Sword, 2006), pp. 75–96

Simkins, P., 'Herbert Plumer', in I. F. W. Beckett and S. J. Corvi (eds.), *Haig's Generals* (Barnsley: Pen & Sword, 2006), pp. 141–63

Terraine, J., *Douglas Haig. The Educated Soldier* (London: Cassell & Co., 2000; first publ. 1963)

Wiest, A., 'Haig, Gough and Passchendaele', in G. D. Sheffield (ed.), *Leadership and Command. The Anglo-American Military Experience since 1861* (London: Brassey's, 1997), pp. 77–92

——, *Haig. The Evolution of a Commander* (Washington DC: Potomac Books, 2005)

Woodward, D. R., *Field-Marshal Sir William Robertson. Chief of the Imperial General Staff in the Great War* (Westport: Praeger, 1998)

Memoirs and Personal Accounts

Bean, C. E. W., *Anzac to Amiens* (Canberra: Australian War Memorial, 1983; first publ. 1948)

Binding, R., *A Fatalist at War*, trans. I. F. D. Morrow (London: George Allen and Unwin, 1929)

Bird, W. R., *Ghosts Have Warm Hands. A Memoir of the Great War 1916–1919* (Nepean: CEF Books, 1997; first publ. 1968)

Birdwood, Lord, *Khaki and Gown. An Autobiography* (London: Ward, Lock & Co., 1941)

Blake, R., (ed.), *The Private Papers of Douglas Haig, 1914–1919* (London: Eyre & Spottiswoode, 1952)

Blunden, E., *Undertones of War* (London: Penguin Books, 2010; first publ. 1928)

Bodenschatz, K., *Hunting With Richthofen. The Bodenschatz Diaries: Sixteen Months of Battle with JG Freiherr von Richthofen No 1.*, trans. J. Hayzlett (London: Grubb Street, 1996)

Bond, B., and S. Robbins (eds.), *Staff Officer. The Diaries of Walter Guinness (First Lord Moyne) 1914–1918* (London: Leo Cooper, 1987)

Carrington, C., *Soldier from the Wars Returning* (London: Hutchinson, 1965)

Charteris, J., *At G.H.Q.* (London: Cassell & Co., 1931)

Churchill, W. S., *The World Crisis, 1911–1918* (London: Thornton Butterworth, 1923–31)

Currie, A., *The Selected Papers of Sir Arthur Currie. Diaries, Letters and Report to the Ministry, 1917–1933*, ed. M. O. Humphries (Waterloo, Ont.: Wilfrid Laurier University Press, 2008)

Dixon, R., and C. Lee (eds.), *The Diaries of Frank Hurley 1912–1941* (London: Anthem Press, 2011)

Edmonds, C. [C. Carrington], *A Subaltern's War* (London: Anthony Mott, 1984; first publ. 1929)

Falkenhayn, E., *General Headquarters 1914–16 and Its Critical Decisions* (London: Hutchinson, 1919)

Feilding, R., *War Letters to a Wife. France and Flanders, 1915–1919*, ed. J. Walker (Staplehurst: Spellmount, 2001)

Gibbs, P., *Now It Can be Told* (New York and London: Harper & Brothers, 1920)

Gladden, E. N., *Ypres 1917. A Personal Account* (London: William Kimber, 1967)

Godley, A., *Life of an Irish Soldier* (London: John Murray, 1939)

Gordon, H., *The Unreturning Army. A Field-Gunner in Flanders, 1917–18* (London: J. M. Dent & Sons, 1967)

Görlitz, W., (ed.), *The Kaiser and His Court. The Diaries, Note Books and Letters of Admiral Georg Alexander von Müller, Chief of the Naval Cabinet, 1914–1918* (London: Macdonald & Co., 1961; first publ. 1959)

Gough, H., *Soldiering On* (London: Arthur Baker, 1954)

Hankey, Lord, *The Supreme Command 1914–1918* (2 vols., London: George Allen and Unwin, 1961), II

Harington, Sir C., *Tim Harington Looks Back* (London: John Murray, 1940)

Hickey, D. E., *Rolling Into Action. Memoirs of a Tank Corps Section Commander* (London: Hutchinson, n.d.)

Hindenburg, P. von, *Out of My Life*, trans. F. A. Holt (London: Cassell & Co., 1920)

Jünger, E., *Storm of Steel*, trans. M. Hoffman (London: Penguin Books, 2003; first publ. 1920)

Lee, A. G., *No Parachute. A Fighter Pilot in World War I* (London: Jarrolds, 1968)

Lloyd George, D., *War Memoirs of David Lloyd George* (2 vols., London: Odhams Press, 1933–6)

Lossberg, F. von, *Meine Tätigkeit im Weltkrieg 1914–1918* (Berlin: E. S. Mittler & Sohn, 1939)

Ludendorff, E., *Ludendorff's Own Story. August 1914–November 1918* (2 vols., New York and London: Harper & Brothers, 1919)

Lynch, E. P. F., *Somme Mud. The Experiences of an Infantryman in France, 1916–1919*, ed. W. Davies (London: Bantam, 2008; first publ. 2006)

Maze, P., *A Frenchman in Khaki* (Kingswood: William Heinemann, 1934)

McCudden, J. T. B., *Flying Fury. Five Years in the Royal Flying Corps* (Folkestone: Bailey Brothers & Swinfen, 1973; first publ. 1918)

Pierrefeu, J. de, *French Headquarters 1915–1918*, trans. Major C. J. C. Street (London: Geoffrey Bles, 1924)

Robertson, Sir W., *Soldiers and Statesmen 1914–1918* (2 vols., London: Cassell & Co., 1926)

Rupprecht, Crown Prince, *Mein Kriegstagebuch* (3 vols., Berlin: E. S. Mittler & Sohn, 1929)

Sheffield, G., and J. Bourne (eds.), *Douglas Haig: War Diaries and Letters 1914–1918* (London: Weidenfeld & Nicolson, 2005)

Spears, E. L., *Prelude to Victory* (London: Jonathan Cape, 1939)

Stevenson, F., *Lloyd George. A Diary*, ed. A. J. P. Taylor (London: Hutchinson, 1971)

Terraine, J., (ed.), *General Jack's Diary 1914–18. The Trench Diary of Brigadier-General J. K. Jack, D.S.O.* (London: Cassell & Co., 2000; first publ. 1964)

Thaer, A. von, *Generalstabsdienst an der Front und in der O.H.L.* (Göttingen: Vandenhoeck & Ruprecht, 1958)

Watson, W. H. L., *With the Tanks 1916–1918. Memoirs of a British Tank Commander in the Great War* (Barnsley: Pen & Sword, 2014; first publ. 1920)

Williamson, H., *The Wet Flanders Plain* (London: Faber & Faber, 2009; first publ. 1929)

Woodward, D. R., (ed.), *The Military Correspondence of Field-Marshal Sir William Robertson, Chief of the Imperial General Staff, December 1915–February 1918* (London: Bodley Head for the Army Records Society, 1989)

Unit Histories

Annabell, N., (ed.), *Official History of the New Zealand Engineers during the Great War 1914–1919* (Wanganui: Evans, Cobb & Sharpe, 1927)

Atteridge, A. H., *History of the 17th (Northern) Division* (Glasgow: Robert Maclehose & Co., 1929)

Bennett, S. G., *The 4th Canadian Mounted Rifles 1914–1919* (Toronto: Murray Printing Company, 1926)

Bewsher, F. W., *The History of the Fifty First (Highland) Division 1914–1918* (Uckfield: Naval & Military Press, 2001; first publ. 1920)

Boraston, J. H., and C. E. O. Bax, *The Eighth Division 1914–1918* (Uckfield: Naval & Military Press, 2001; first publ. 1926)

Buttman, A., *Kriegsgeschichte des Königlich Preußischen 6. Thüringischen Infanterie-Regiments Nr. 95 1914–1918* (Zeulenroda: Verlag Bernhard Sporn, 1935)

Byrne, A. E., *Official History of the Otago Regiment, N.Z.E.F. in the Great War 1914–1918* (Dunedin: J. Wilkie & Company, 1921)

Byrne, J. R., *New Zealand Artillery in the Field, 1914–18* (Auckland: Whitcombe & Tombs, 1922)

Dudley Ward, C. H., *History of the Welsh Guards* (London: John Murray, 1920)

Dunzinger, A., *Das K.B. 11 Infanterie-Regiment von der Tann* (Munich: Bayerische Kriegsarchivs, 1921)

Ellis, A. D., *The Story of the Fifth Australian Division* (London: Hodder & Stoughton, n.d.)

Falls, C., *The History of the 36th (Ulster) Division* (London and Belfast: M'Caw, Stevenson & Orr, 1922)

Farndale, M., *History of the Royal Regiment of Artillery. Western Front 1914–18* (London: Royal Artillery Institution, 1986)

Ferguson, D., *The History of the Canterbury Regiment, N.Z.E.F. 1914–1919* (Auckland: Whitcombe & Tombs, 1921)

Gabriel, K., *Die 4 Garde-Infanterie-Division. Der Ruhmesweg einer bewährten Kampftruppe durch den Weltkrieg* (Berlin: Verlag von Klasing & Co., 1920)

Gottberg, D., *Das Infanterie-Regiment Nr. 465 im Weltkriege* (Osnabrück: Verlag Carl Prelle, n.d)

Gough, H., *The Fifth Army* (London: Hodder & Stoughton, 1931)

Grossmann, A., *Das K.B. Reserve-Infanterie-Regiment Nr. 17* (D. Eisele & Sohn, Augsburg, 1926)

Hansch, J., and F. Weidling, *Das Colbergsche Grenadier-Regiment Graf Gneisenau (2 Pommersches) Nr. 9 im Weltkriege 1914–1918* (Oldenburg: Gerhard Stalling, 1929)

Headlam, C., *History of the Guards Division in the Great War 1915–1918* (Uckfield: Naval & Military Press, 2001; first publ. 1924)

Hutchinson, G. S., *The Thirty-Third Division in France and Flanders 1915–1919* (Uckfield: Naval & Military Press, 2004; first publ. 1921)

Jürgensen, W., *Das Füsilier-Regiment 'Königin' Nr. 86 im Weltkriege* (Oldenburg: Gerhard Stalling, 1925)

Karau, M. D., *'Wielding the Dagger'. The MarineKorps Flandern and the German War Effort, 1914–1918* (London and Westport: Praeger, 2003)

Lucas, A., and J. Schmieschek, *Fighting the Kaiser's War. The Saxons in Flanders 1914/1918* (Barnsley: Pen & Sword, 2015)

Nichols, G. H. F., *The 18th Division in the Great War* (Edinburgh and London: William Blackwood & Sons, 1922)

Nollau, H., *Geschichte des Königlich Preußischen 4 Niederschlesischen Infanterie-Regiment Nr. 51* (Berlin: Wilhelm Kolk, 1931)

Pirscher, F. von, *Das (Rheinisch-Westfälische) Infanterie-Regiment Nr. 459* (Oldenburg: Gerhard Stalling, 1926)

Radley, K., *We Lead, Others Follow. First Canadian Division 1914–1918* (St Catharines: Vanwell, 2006)

Reber, A. K., *Das K.B. 21. Infanterie Regiment. Großherzog Friedrich Franz IV. von Mecklenburg-Schwerin* (Munich: Verlag Max Schick, 1929)

Revell, A., *British Fighter Units. Western Front 1917–18* (London: Osprey, 1978)

Riddell, E., and M. C. Clayton, *The Cambridgeshires 1914 to 1919* (Cambridge: Bowes & Bowes, 1934)

Schatz, J., *Geschichte des Badischen (Rheinischen) Reserve-Infanterie-Regiments 239* (Stuttgart: Chr. Belser, 1927)

Simpson, C. R., (ed.), *The History of the Lincolnshire Regiment 1914–1918* (London: The Medici Society, 1931)

Stachelbeck, C., *Militärische Effektivität im Ersten Weltkrieg. Die 11. Bayerische Infanteriedivision 1915 bis 1918* (Paderborn: Ferdinand Schöningh, 2010)

Stevenson, R. C., *To Win the Battle. The 1st Australian Division in the Great War 1914–18* (Melbourne: Cambridge University Press, 2013)

Stewart, H., *The New Zealand Division 1916–1919. A Popular History Based on Official Records* (Auckland: Whitcombe & Tombs, 1921)

Wiedersich, A., *Das Reserve-Infanterie Regiment Nr. 229* (Berlin: Verlag Tradition Wilhelm Rolf, 1929)

Wolff, H. von, *Kriegsgeschichte des Jäger-Bataillon von Neumann (1. Schles.) Nr. 5 1914–1918* (Zeulenroda: Verlag Bernhard Sporn, n.d.)

Zechlin, F., *Das Reserve-Infanterie-Regiment Nr. 60 im Weltkriege* (Oldenburg: Gerhard Stalling, 1926)

General Works

Adams, R. J. Q., *Arms and the Wizard. Lloyd George and the Ministry of Munitions* (London: Cassell & Co., 1978)

Asprey, R. B., *The German High Command at War. Hindenburg and Ludendorff and the First World War* (London: Warner Books, 1994; first publ. 1991)

Barton, P., *Passchendaele. Unseen Panoramas of the Third Battle of Ypres* (London: Constable & Robinson, 2007)

Beach, J., *Haig's Intelligence. GHQ and the German Army, 1916–1918* (Cambridge: Cambridge University Press, 2013)

Bidwell, S., and D. Graham, *Firepower. British Army Weapons and Theories of War, 1904–1945* (Boston: Allen & Unwin, 1982)

Bond, B., *The Unquiet Western Front* (Cambridge: Cambridge University Press, 2002)

Brown, I. M., *British Logistics on the Western Front, 1914–1919* (Westport: Praeger, 1998)

Campbell, C., *Band of Brigands. The First Men in Tanks* (London: Harper Perennial, 2008; first publ. 2007)

Cave, N., *Battleground Europe. Ypres: Sanctuary Wood and Hooge* (London: Leo Cooper, 1993)

——, *Battleground Europe. Ypres. Passchendaele: The Fight for the Village* (Barnsley: Pen & Sword, 2007; first publ. 1997)

——, *Battleground Europe. Polygon Wood* (Barnsley: Pen & Sword, 1999)

Cecil, H., and P. H. Liddle (eds.), *Facing Armageddon. The First World War Experienced* (Barnsley: Leo Cooper, 1996)

Chasseaud, P., *Artillery's Astrologers. A History of British Survey and Mapping on the Western Front 1914–1918* (Lewes: Mapbooks, 1999)

Chickering, R., *Imperial Germany and the Great War, 1914–1918* (Cambridge: Cambridge University Press, 1998)

Cook, T., *No Place to Run. The Canadian Corps and Gas Warfare in the First World War* (Vancouver: UBC Press, 1999)

——, *Shock Troops. Canadians Fighting the Great War 1917–1918* (Toronto: Penguin Canada, 2008)

Dancocks, D. G., *Legacy of Valour. The Canadians at Passchendaele* (Edmonton: Hurtig, 1986)

Dennis, P., and J. Grey (eds.), *1917. Tactics, Training and Technology: The 2007 Chief of Army Military History Conference* (Canberra: Australian History Military Publications, 2007)

Doughty, R. A., *Pyrrhic Victory. French Strategy and Operations in the Great War* (London and Cambridge, Mass.: Harvard University Press, 2005)

Duffy, C., *Through German Eyes. The British and the Somme 1916* (London: Orion, 2007; first publ. 2006)

Falls, C., *The First World War* (London: Longmans, 1960)

Ferguson, N., *The Pity of War* (London: Allen Lane, 1998)

Fischer, F., *Germany's Aims in the First World War* (New York: W. W. Norton & Co., 1967; first publ. 1961)

Foley, R., *German Strategy and the Path to Verdun. Erich von Falkenhayn and the Development of Attrition* (Cambridge: Cambridge University Press, 2005)

French, D., 'Who Knew What and When? The French Army Mutinies and the British Decision to Launch the Third Battle of Ypres', in L. Freedman, P. Hayes and R. O'Neill (eds.), *War, Strategy, and International Politics. Essays in Honour of Sir Michael Howard* (Oxford: Clarendon Press, 1992), pp. 133–53

——, *The Strategy of the Lloyd George Coalition, 1916–1918* (Oxford: Clarendon Press, 1995)

Fuller, J. F. C., *Tanks in the Great War 1914–1918* (London: John Murray, 1920)

Fussell, P., *The Great War and Modern Memory* (Oxford: Oxford University Press, 2000; first publ. 1975)

Giles, J., *The Ypres Salient* (London: Leo Cooper, 1970)

Graham, D., and S. Bidwell, *Coalitions, Politicians and Generals. Some Aspects of Command in Two World Wars* (London: Brassey's, 1993)

Green, A., *Writing the Great War. Sir James Edmonds and the Official Histories, 1915–1948* (London: Frank Cass, 2003)

Greenhalgh, E., *Victory Through Coalition. Britain and France during the First World War* (Cambridge: Cambridge University Press, 2005)

——, *The French Army and the First World War* (Cambridge: Cambridge University Press, 2014)

Grieves, K., *The Politics of Manpower, 1914–18* (Manchester: Manchester University Press, 1988)

Griffith, P., *Battle Tactics of the Western Front. The British Army's Art of Attack 1916–1918* (New Haven and London: Yale University Press, 1994)

—— (ed.), *British Fighting Methods of the Great War* (London: Frank Cass, 1996)

Harper, G., *Massacre at Passchendaele. The New Zealand Story* (Brighton: FireStep Books, 2011; first publ. 2000)

Harris, J. P., *Men, Ideas and Tanks. British Military Thought and Armoured Forces, 1903–1939* (Manchester: Manchester University Press, 1995)

Hart, P., *Bloody April. Slaughter in the Skies over Arras, 1917* (London: Cassell & Co., 2006; first publ. 2005)

Herwig, H., *The First World War. Germany and Austria–Hungary 1914–1918* (London: Arnold, 1997)

Hooton, E. R., *War over the Trenches. Air Power and Western Front Campaigns 1916–1918* (Hersham: Ian Allen, 2010)

Leach, N., *Passchendaele. Canada's Triumph and Tragedy on the Fields of Flanders: An Illustrated History* (Regina: Coteau Books, 2008)

Lee, J., 'Command and Control in Battle: British Divisions on the Menin Road Ridge, 20 September 1917', in G. Sheffield and D. Todman (eds.), *Command and Control on the Western Front. The British Army's Experience 1914–1918* (Staplehurst: Spellmount, 2004), pp. 119–39

Liddell Hart, B. H., *The Real War, 1914–1918* (London: Faber & Faber, 1930)

Liddle, P., (ed.), *Passchendaele in Perspective. The Third Battle of Ypres* (London: Leo Cooper, 1997)

Lloyd, N., *Loos 1915* (Stroud: Tempus, 2006)

——, *The Amritsar Massacre. The Untold Story of One Fateful Day* (London: I. B. Tauris, 2011)

——, *Hundred Days. The End of the Great War* (London: Viking, 2013)

LoCicero, M., *A Moonlight Massacre. The Night Operation on the Passchendaele Ridge, 2 December 1917: The Forgotten Last Act of the Third Battle of Ypres* (Solihull: Helion & Company, 2014)

Lupfer, T. T., *The Dynamics of Doctrine. The Changes in German Tactical Doctrine during the First World War* (Fort Leavenworth: U.S. Army Command and General Staff College, 1981)

Macdonald, A., *Passchendaele. The Anatomy of a Tragedy* (Auckland: HarperCollins, 2013)

Macdonald, L., *They Called It Passchendaele. The Story of the Third Battle of Ypres and of the Men Who Fought in It* (London: Penguin Books, 1993; first publ. 1978)

Marble, S., *British Artillery on the Western Front in the First World War. 'The infantry cannot do with a gun less'* (Farnham: Ashgate, 2013)

McCarthy, C., *Passchendaele. The Day-by-Day Account* (London: Cassell & Co., 1995)

McGreal, S., *Battleground Europe. Boesinghe* (London: Leo Cooper, 2010)

Millman, B., *Pessimism and British War Policy 1916–1918* (London: Frank Cass, 2001)

Morrow, Jr, J. H., *The Great War in the Air. Military Aviation from 1909 to 1921* (Washington DC: Smithsonian Institute Press, 1993)

——, *The Great War. An Imperial History* (London and New York: Routledge, 2004)

Nicholls, J., *Cheerful Sacrifice. The Battle of Arras 1917* (London: Leo Cooper, 1990)

Palazzo, A., *Seeking Victory on the Western Front. The British Army and Chemical Warfare in World War I* (Lincoln, Nebr., and London: University of Nebraska Press, 2000)

Paschall, R., *The Defeat of Imperial Germany 1917–1918* (Chapel Hill: Algonquin Books, 1989)

Passingham, I., *Pillars of Fire. The Battle of Messines Ridge, June 1917* (Stroud: Sutton, 1998)

Pedersen, P., *Anzacs on the Western Front. The Australian War Memorial Battlefield Guide* (Milton: John Wiley & Sons Australia, 2012)

Philpott, W. J., *Anglo-French Relations and Strategy on the Western Front, 1914–18* (London: Macmillan, 1996)

——, *Attrition. Fighting the First World War* (London: Little, Brown, 2014)

Pierrefeu, J. de, *L'Offensive du 16 Avril. La Vérité sur l'affaire Nivelle* (Paris: Renaissance du Livre, 1919)

Prior, R., and T. Wilson, *Passchendaele: The Untold Story* (New Haven and London: Yale University Press, 2002; first publ. 1996)

Pugsley, C., *On the Fringe of Hell. New Zealanders and Military Discipline in the First World War* (Auckland: Hodder & Stoughton, 1991)

Rawling, B., *Surviving Trench Warfare. Technology and the Canadian Corps, 1914–1918* (Toronto: University of Toronto Press, 1992)

Reynolds, D., *The Long Shadow. The Great War and the Twentieth Century* (London: Simon & Schuster, 2013)

Samuels, M., *Command or Control? Command, Training and Tactics in the British and German Armies, 1888–1918* (London: Frank Cass, 1995)

Sheffield, G., *Forgotten Victory. The First World War: Myths and Realities* (London: Headline, 2001)

Sheldon, J., *The German Army at Passchendaele* (Barnsley: Pen & Sword, 2007)

Showalter, D., and W. J. Astore, 'Passchendaele', in D. Showalter (ed.), *History in Dispute*, Vol. 8, *World War I: First Series* (Farmington Hills: St James Press, 2002), pp. 218–24

Simkins, P., *Kitchener's Army. The Raising of the New Armies, 1914–16* (Manchester: Manchester University Press, 1988)

Simpson, A., *Directing Operations. British Corps Command on the Western Front 1914–18* (Stroud: Spellmount, 2006)

Snelling, S., *VCs of the First World War. Passchendaele 1917* (Stroud: The History Press, 2012; first publ. 1998)

Spagnoly, T., *The Anatomy of a Raid. Australia at Celtic Wood 9th October 1917* (London: Multidream Publications, 1991)

Steel, N., and P. Hart, *Passchendaele. The Sacrificial Ground* (London: Cassell & Co., 2001; first publ. 2000)

Terraine, J., *The Western Front* (London: Hutchinson, 1964)

——, *The Road to Passchendaele. The Flanders Offensive of 1917: A Study in Inevitability* (London: Leo Cooper, 1977)

——, *The Smoke and the Fire. Myths and Anti-Myths of War 1861–1945* (London: Sidgwick & Jackson, 1980)

Thompson, M., *The White War. Life and Death on the Italian Front 1915–1919* (London: Faber & Faber, 2008)

Thompson, R., 'Mud, Blood, and Wood: BEF Operational and Combat Logistico-Engineering during the Battle of Third Ypres, 1917', in P. Doyle and M. R. Bennett (eds.), *Fields of Battle. Terrain in Military History* (London: Kluwer, 2002), pp. 237–55

Todman, D., *The Great War. Myth and Memory* (London: Hambledon and London, 2005)

Travers, T., *The Killing Ground. The British Army, the Western Front and the Emergence of Modern Warfare 1900–1918* (Barnsley: Pen & Sword, 2003; first publ. 1987)

——, *How the War was Won. Command and Technology in the British Army on the Western Front, 1917–1918* (Barnsley: Pen & Sword, 2005; first publ. 1992)

Volkart, W., *Die Gasschlacht in Flandern im Herbst 1917* (Berlin: E. S. Mittler & Sohn, 1957)

Watson, A., *Enduring the Great War. Combat, Morale and Collapse in the German and British Armies, 1914–1918* (Cambridge: Cambridge University Press, 2008)

——, *Ring of Steel. Germany and Austria–Hungary at War, 1914–1918* (London: Allen Lane, 2014)

Wiest, A., *Passchendaele and the Royal Navy* (New York: Greenwood Press, 1995)

Wolff, L., *In Flanders Fields* (London: Longmans, 1960)

Woodward, D. R., *Lloyd George and the Generals* (London: Associated University Presses, 1983)

Wynne, G. C., *If Germany Attacks. The Battle in Depth in the West* (Westport: Greenwood, 1976; first publ. 1940)

Articles

Adair, J., 'The Battle of Passchendaele: The Experiences of Lieutenant Tom Rutherford, 4th Battalion, Canadian Mounted Rifles', *Canadian Military History*, Vol. 13, No. 4 (Autumn 2004), pp. 62–80

Brown, I. M., 'Not Glamorous, But Effective: The Canadian Corps and the Set-Piece Attack, 1917–1918', *Journal of Military History*, Vol. 58, No. 3 (July 1994), pp. 421–44

Foley, R., 'Learning War's Lessons: The German Army and the Battle of the Somme 1916', *Journal of Military History*, Vol. 75, No. 2 (April 2011), pp. 471–504

Fox, A., '"The word 'retire' is never to be used": The Performance of the 9th Brigade, AIF, at First Passchendaele, 1917', Australian War Memorial, SVSS Paper (2011), pp. 1–28

French, D., '"Official but not history"? Sir James Edmonds and the Official History of the Great War', *The RUSI Journal*, Vol. 131, No. 1 (1986), pp. 58–63

——, 'Watching the Allies: British Intelligence and the French Mutinies of 1917', *Intelligence and National Security*, Vol. 6, No. 3 (1991), pp. 573–92

Harris, P., and S. Marble, 'The "Step-by-Step" Approach: British Military Thought and Operational Method on the Western Front, 1915–1917', *War in History*, Vol. 15, No. 1 (2008), pp. 17–42

Leach, N. S., 'Passchendaele – Canada's Other Vimy Ridge', *Canadian Military Journal*, Vol. 9, No. 2 (2008), pp. 73–82

Liddell Hart, B. H., 'The Basic Truths of Passchendaele', *Journal of the Royal United Services Institution*, Vol. CIV, No. 616 (November 1959), pp. 433–9

Lloyd, N., '"With Faith and Without Fear": Sir Douglas Haig's Command of First Army during 1915', *Journal of Military History*, Vol. 71, No. 4 (October 2007), pp. 1051–76

Mainville, C., 'Mentioned in Despatches: Lieutenant Allen Otty and the 5th CMR at Passchendaele, 30 October 1917', *Canadian Military History*, Vol. 23, No. 2 (Spring 2014), pp. 137–63

McLeod, R., and C. Fox, 'The Battles in Flanders during the Summer and Autumn of 1917 from General von Kuhl's *Der Weltkrieg 1914–18*', *British Army Review*, No. 116 (August 1997), pp. 78–88

Palazzo, A. P., 'The British Army's Counter-Battery Staff Office and Control of the Enemy in World War I', *Journal of Military History*, Vol. 63, No. 1 (January 1999), pp. 55–74

Pugsley, C., 'Learning from the Canadian Corps on the Western Front', *Canadian Military History*, Vol. 15, No. 1 (Winter 2006), pp. 5–32

Roskill, S. W., 'The U-Boat Campaign of 1917 and Third Ypres', *Journal of the Royal United Services Institution*, Vol. CIV, No. 616 (November 1959), pp. 440–42

Stachelbeck, C., 'Strategy "in a Microcosm": Processes of Tactical Learning in a WWI German Infantry Division', *Journal of Military & Strategic Studies*, Vol. 13, No. 4 (Summer 2011), pp. 1–20

Terraine, J. A., 'Passchendaele and Amiens I', *Journal of the Royal United Services Institution*, Vol. CIV, No. 614 (May 1959), pp. 173–83

——, 'Passchendaele and Amiens II', *Journal of the Royal United Services Institution*, Vol. CIV, No. 615 (August 1959), pp. 331–40

Travers, T., 'A Particular Style of Command: Haig and GHQ, 1916–18', *Journal of Strategic Studies*, Vol. 10, No. 3 (1987), pp. 363–76

Williams, M. J., 'Thirty per Cent: A Study in Casualty Statistics', *Journal of the Royal United Services Institution*, Vol. CIX, No. 633 (February 1964), pp. 51–5

Woodward, D. R., 'David Lloyd George, a Negotiated Peace with Germany and the Kuhlmann Peace Kite of September, 1917', *Canadian Journal of History*, Vol. 6, No. 1 (1971), pp. 75–93

Wynne, G. C., '"The Other Side of the Hill": The Fight for Inverness Copse, 22nd–24th of August 1917', *Army Quarterly*, Vol. XXIX, No. 2 (January 1935), pp. 297–303

——, 'The Development of the German Defensive Battle in 1917, and Its Influence on British Defence Tactics: Part I', *Army Quarterly*, Vol. XXXIV (April 1937), pp. 15–32

——, 'The Development of the German Defensive Battle in 1917, and Its Influence on British Defence Tactics: Part II', *Army Quarterly*, Vol. XXXIV (April 1937), pp. 249–66

Index

Nick Lloyd is an English historian and writer.
He is Reader in Military & Imperial History
at King's College London, based at the Joint
Services Command & Staff College in Shrivenham, Wiltshire, UK. He is the author of four
books including *Hundred Days: The Campaign
that Ended World War I* (Basic Books, 2014). He
lives with his family in Cheltenham, England.